T0339844

# NATIONAL INTEGRATION AND

# CONTESTED AUTONOMY

# NATIONAL INTEGRATION AND CONTESTED AUTONOMY

## The Caribbean Coast of Nicaragua

EDITED BY
LUCIANO BARACCO

Algora Publishing
New York

Library of Congress Cataloging-in-Publication Data —

National integration and contested autonomy : the Caribbean coast of Nicaragua /
edited by Luciano Baracco.
     p. cm.
   Includes bibliographical references and index.
     ISBN 978-0-87586-822-6 (soft: alk. paper) — ISBN 978-0-87586-823-3 (hard: alk.
paper) — ISBN 978-0-87586-824-0 (ebook) 1. Mosquitia (Nicaragua and Honduras)—
Politics and government. 2. Atlantic Coast (Nicaragua)—History—Autonomy and
independence movements. 3. Miskito Indians—Nicaragua—Government relations. 4.
Miskito Indians—Politics and government. I. Baracco, Luciano.
     F1529.M9N36 2011
     972.85—dc22
                         2010050439

   Front cover: Nicaragua - Miskito indigenous people on a small boat on the Coco River.
Climate change has caused damage to the Nicaraguan rainforest also damaging rivers, its
only route for communication.
   IMAGE: © David de la Paz/EFE/Corbis

# The Caribbean Coast of Nicaragua

# CONTRIBUTORS

Luciano Baracco: Assistant Professor of Political Science and International Relations, Faculty of Political Science and International Relations, Middle East Technical University, Northern Cyprus Campus, Turkish Republic of Northern Cyprus

David C. Brooks: US State Department

Jane Freeland: Research Fellow, Centre for Transnational Studies, University of Southampton, UK

Mary Finley-Brook: Assistant Professor of Geography, Department of Geography and the Environment, University of Richmond, US

Wolfgang Gabbert: Professor of Development Sociology and Cultural Anthropology, Institute for Sociology, Leibniz University. Hanover, Germany

Miguel González: Assistant Professor of International Development Studies, York University, Canada

Ken Henriksen: Associate Professor of Latin American Studies, Department of Language, Literature and Culture, University of Aarhus, Denmark

Laura Hobson Herlihy: Lecturer in Latin American Studies, Centre for Latin American Studies, University of Kansas, US

Mark Jamieson: Lecturer in Anthropology, School of Humanities and Social Sciences, University of East London, UK

Christopher Kindbald: Associate Professor, School of Social and Health Sciences, University of Halmstad, Sweden

Baron Pineda: Associate Professor of Anthropology, Department of Anthropology, Oberlin College, US

Michael J. Schroeder: Assistant Professor of History, Department of History and Political Science, Lebanon Valley College, US

# TABLE OF CONTENTS

# PREFACE

Nicaragua is a small country with two historically, geographically, economically, demographically and socially different regions. In 1984, after many struggles, the indigenous and ethnic communities of the Caribbean Coast of Nicaragua succeeded in persuading the central government to undertake the first steps to address their demands for greater self determination by forming the National Autonomy Commission. A series of judicial, political, economic and cultural transformations followed from this decision that established the conditions for socio-economic development and respect for the rights of the indigenous, Afro-descendant and mestizo populations of the Caribbean Coast of Nicaragua.

A law entitled the *Autonomy Statute for the Regions of the Atlantic Coast of Nicaragua* was approved in 1987; it created two regional councils. Three years later the first regional councils were elected, paving the road towards the increasing participation of Costeño peoples in the decisions that affect their conditions of life and re-establishing a right that had been denied to them since 1894 when the region was incorporated into Nicaragua.

The regional councils, the highest governmental organs in the autonomous regions, are multiethnic institutions that reflect the legitimate recognition that the region is inhabited by diverse indigenous and ethnic communities with their own identities and are a concrete expression of the Nicaraguan government's promise to guarantee the exercise of the collective and individual rights of the peoples of Caribbean Nicaragua.

Regional autonomy represents for the country in general, and the Caribbean Coast in particular, an opportunity to establish dignity and respect between Nicaragua's diverse populations, reducing economic and social inequalities between the two regions and strengthening national unity. It is an opportunity to construct an inclusive, multiethnic and intercultural nation.

A series of difficult negotiations have achieved multiple advances in diverse aspects of life for Costeños. It has created laws and institutions that established their own autochthonous model of public administration. Today communal, territorial and regional governments exist which together have come to constitute regional autonomy. There have been advances in areas of vital importance for the inhabitants of the Caribbean Coast, such as the demarcation and titling of the lands of the indigenous and Afro-descendant populations, the recognition and respect of the identity and cultures of each group and ethnic community from a pluricultural vision, and the participation of leaders from all the Costeño peoples in the decisions that affect them. Nevertheless, the vicissitudes of the journey and the many obstacles that have been overcome serve to demonstrate that a number of challenges remain, especially the exercise of Costeños' rights in daily life.

There are many positive aspects to the process of establishing Nicaragua's regional autonomy, yet its deficiencies and limitations are clearly visible. The analysis of this experience serves to identify models of public administration that guarantee the fulfillment of the rights of indigenous peoples and ethnic communities living in multiethnic territories. This book presents a number of studies by academics who have conducted extensive research on Nicaragua's model of regional autonomy. Their writings provide us with an opportunity to learn part of the story, the context, and the advances of this model of autonomy, and so this volume constitutes a further contribution to the current debates on the subject.

Gustavo Adolfo Castro Jo
Bluefields Indian and Caribbean University
Bluefields

# INTRODUCTION

The Caribbean Coast of Nicaragua represents one of the first cases of regional autonomy in Latin and Central America.[1] The region has a history of cultural and ethnic distinctiveness from the rest of Nicaragua that stretches back into the colonial era and has experienced constant demographic flux and high degrees of miscegenation that today has created a heterogeneous, pluricultural population referred to collectively as Costeños. The Miskitu, Rama and Sumu-Mayangna Indian populations of the Coast have all shared a close relationship with Afro-descendant black English-speaking Creoles whose presence in the region began with the arrival of slave-owning British colonizers. There is also a small population of Garífunas[2] living around the Pearl Lagoon area as well as a large number of Spanish-speaking mestizos who today constitute the majority of the Coast's population.

Unlike the rest of what was to become Nicaragua, the Caribbean Coast was colonized by the British, an encounter which is commonly cited as the foundation for Costeños' contemporary distinctiveness from Pacific Nicaraguans. Under Spanish rule, Pacific Nicaragua shared a common experience with Spain's other American colonies: the appropriation of land by Spanish

---

1  During the early stages of writing this book, the contributors discussed whether to use the term Caribbean Coast or the more traditional Atlantic Coast. Despite our agreement to use the term Caribbean Coast as a name for the region, most of us slipped back into using what is for many people the more familiar term of the Atlantic Coast. Thus the two terms are used interchangeably throughout the book.
2  Descendents of indigenous Caribbean people who intermarried with Africans.

colonizers and the violent subjugation and replacement of the indigenous inhabitants by a mixed Spanish and indigenous mestizo population through a process referred to as *mestizaje*. British colonialism followed a very different path in its exploitation of the Caribbean Coast and its inhabitants that involved a strategic alliance with the Miskitu Indians. In return for valuable mahogany, gold, rubber and turtle, the British provided the Miskitu with diplomatic and military protection from other imperial powers present in the region. The region had become the centre of intense imperial rivalry owing to its geographical features that offered a possible site for an interoceanic canal, starting on the delta of the San Juan River, at San Juan del Norte (Greytown). Under these circumstances, the British saw their relations with the Miskitu as an important lever in Britain's competition with Spain to dominate any future interoceanic canal route.

The Anglo–Miskitu alliance was formalized in 1687 with the creation of the Kingdom of Mosquitia and the crowning of the first Miskitu king by the governor of Jamaica. The lack of coercion involved in Anglo–Miskitu relations was accompanied by a strong embrace of what Charles Hale (1994) describes as Anglo-cultural affinities, which was further reinforced by the spread of Protestant Christianity with the arrival of Moravian missionaries in 1847. Although the British withdrew and legally ceded the region to Spain in the Treaty of Versailles (1783), Spanish attempts to consolidate their rule over the region were successfully frustrated by the Miskitu king. With the collapse of the Spanish empire in 1821 and the internecine civil war that characterized the early years of Central America's independence, the British returned to the region in 1844 and established a protectorate. By the end of the nineteenth century power had shifted to a new imperial actor in the form of US companies which established a number of economic enclaves involved in extractive enterprises that tapped the rich resources of the Coast. This was not without consequences for the Miskitu, for with the arrival of the US companies, the Miskitu lost their privileged status in the racial hierarchy of the region in favor of English-speaking Creoles.

When the Coast was forcibly "reincorporated" into the rest of Nicaragua by president José Santos Zelaya in 1894, the legacy of British colonialism and US neocolonialism was all too apparent, and it remains so today. Whatever miscegenation had taken place between and amongst Indians, Creoles and Anglo-American colonizers, the region remained pluricultural, with strong indigenous and ethnic characteristics. Rather than initiating an homogenizing process similar to that of mestizaje that had occurred in Pacific Nicaragua, the distinctive nature of Anglo-American colonialism had encouraged the genesis of a heterogeneous population. Today, Nicaragua's Caribbean Coast offers a rich, pluricultural environment that has at times occupied an ambiguous position within the predominantly mestizo Nicaraguan nation. The Caribbean Coast's status as an integral part of Nicaragua became the subject of an intense confrontation in the turbulent years of the Sandinista revolution (1979–90). During this period, elements within the CIA-backed counter-revolutionary forces, or Contras, attempted to ferment a separatist movement that aimed to transform the Coast into an independent country as a means of undermining the revolution. While support for such a project amongst Costeños was far from universal, CIA efforts combined with major policy errors committed by the Sandinistas provided the seedbed for a protracted and violent insurgency against the national government that began to be resolved gradually by the initiation of the autonomy negotiations in 1984. Since the passing of the autonomy statute in 1987, autonomy on Nicaragua's Caribbean Coast has proved to be a highly contested process that has been challenged by national institutions as well as by the competing interests of different indigenous and racial groups on the Coast itself. However, whatever its shortcomings, and despite the frustrations expressed by many Costeños with the outcome of autonomy, the process has endured and become a feature of life and politics on Nicaragua's Caribbean Coast that has delivered important if limited victories for Costeños.

This book is intended to provide a broad understanding of Nicaragua's Caribbean Coast and the autonomy process through a multidisciplinary approach that draws on contemporary perspectives in anthropology, sociology, political science, history, gender studies, linguistics and geography. The opening chapter by Wolfgang Gabbert maps the history of the Coast's relations with imperial powers such as Britain, Spain and the United States as well as the Nicaraguan national state. The chapter also explains the nature and origins of coastal institutions, particularly the Kingdom of Mosquitia and the subsequent Mosquito Reserve, as well as their demise with the *Reincorporación* of 1894. Through a detailed analysis of these institutions and the people who occupied leading positions within them, questions are raised concerning the degree to which the Miskitu actually exercised control over them and indeed how far these institutions served the interests of the local inhabitants. Despite the symbolic importance of the Kingdom of Mosquitia and the Mosquito Reserve for contemporary supporters of the autonomy process, some of the conclusions drawn from the analysis suggest that the commonly assumed relationship between these historical institutions and the contemporary autonomy process is mistaken.

Chapter 2 addresses the activities on the Coast of Nicaragua's national hero Augusto César Sandino during his anti-imperialist and nationalist rebellion against the presence of US marines in Nicaragua between 1927 and 1933. Through a detailed analysis of archival evidence, including US Marine Corps intelligence reports, David C. Brooks and Michael J. Schroeder suggest that the Costeños generally exhibited a degree of reluctance to become involved in the rebellion, either by supporting Sandinista columns in the Coast or by collaborating with the US Marines who patrolled the Coast in their search for Sandinista "bandits." With the epicenter of support for the Sandino rebellion being identified as the north central highland department of Las Segovias and its poverty-stricken mestizo peasant population, the chapter depicts the Sandino rebellion on the Coast as a rebellion imposed from "without." Despite attempts by Sandino and a number of his generals to garner support for their anti-imperialist rebellion, the evidence surveyed by the authors strongly suggests that these efforts failed to develop an organic link between the anti-imperialist nationalist cause of Sandino and the Costeños.

In chapter 3, Baron Pineda continues the analysis of Sandino on the Coast. What becomes clear from Pineda's account is Sandino's simultaneous expression of both progressive and orientalist views on the Costeños. While Sandino sought to empower marginalized and exploited groups within Nicaraguan society, often through a language of class war that was novel to Nicaraguan politics at the time, the chapter clearly demonstrates how Sandino also drew upon racialized and gendered metaphors that subordinated Costeños to the well-established civilizing strategy of mestizoization, metaphors held by most mestizo Nicaraguan political actors. While Sandino became the bearer of a new politics of class liberation, he is also depicted as simultaneously reinforcing existing subordinating sentiments amongst mestizos about the uncivilized, feminized and racially inferior identity of the Costeños.

Chapter 4, by Luciano Baracco, looks at the impact that the Sandinista revolution (1979–90) had on the Coast, and particularly the Coast's Miskitu population. The chapter has a focus on the transformations of Miskitu political consciousness consequent on Sandinista modernization and cultural policies that unexpectedly galvanized a distinctive Miskitu identity and formed the basis of an emergent Miskitu nationalism that competed directly with the anti-imperialist brand of Nicaraguan nationalism borne by mestizo Sandinistas. The findings of the chapter suggest that modernization policies designed to integrate Costeños into the Nicaraguan nation actually acted as a catalyst for the formation of Miskitu nationalism, generating conflict between Costeños and the national government that provided the context for the adoption of autonomy as a viable and acceptable conflict resolution mechanism by the mid 1980s.

In chapter 5, Miguel González surveys the complex pattern of party and electoral politics that has emerged under the autonomy regime. The chapter shows how a mosaic of coastal and national political parties have vied for power in the regional autonomous assemblies of the North Atlantic Autonomous Region (RAAN) and the South Atlantic Autonomous Region (RAAS) established by the autonomy statute. Within this fractious political environment, González describes the legal and political strategies of national parties and governments that have largely adopted co-optive political alliances with coastal parties; a factor that has substantially undermined the autonomous nature of politics in both the RAAS and the RAAN. The author also provides a detailed account of the electoral and organizational fortunes of YATAMA,[1] the former Miskitu armed organization which fought against the Sandinista government that successfully transformed itself into a constitutional political party after 1990.

In chapter 6, Ken Henriksen and Christopher Kindbald assess the impact of the neo-liberal policies pursued by Nicaragua's post-revolutionary governments throughout the 1990s. They note that the increasing pressure for the marketization and commodification of communal property highlighted in their case study of Tasbapauni produced a transformation in economic and social practices. Yet they observe that the response to post-revolutionary neo-liberal policies was not an enthusiastic embrace of the market but a renewed emphasis on a community spirit that the authors identify as the outcome of a deep-seated and pervasive Moravian ethic within the life of the community. Thus, despite the social changes emerging from ten years of war and the neo-liberal programs of successive post-revolutionary

---

1 Yapti Tasba Masraka Nanih Aslatakanka (The Sons of Mother Earth).

governments, the authors suggest that Tasbapauni developed a more self-conscious community spirit that actively resisted the legal and illegal commodification of communal property.

Chapter 7 discusses the concept of indigenous feminism in relation to women's participation in autonomous higher education institutions, regional NGOs and political parties and elections in the RAAN. Through extended reference to interview material, Laura Hobson-Herlihy reveals the leading role played by women in many autonomous institutions, yet also notes their exclusion from elected positions of political leadership. She explains this as the outcome of the administrative practices of most political parties active in the RAAN, particularly national parties that have their headquarters in the Nicaraguan capital, Managua, which have a discriminatory impact on women's participation in political leadership. She also identifies this exclusion as a result of highly gendered local attitudes on the participation of women in political leadership roles that perceive elected political positions as a largely, though not exclusively, male arena. She then analyses attempts to overcome such exclusionary practices and attitudes by indigenous women's organizations which have drawn on the experience of the political exclusion of indigenous women from the rest of Latin and Central America.

Jane Freeland's analysis of intercultural and multilingual education in chapter 8 provides a detailed account of the history and struggles surrounding educational provision in the Caribbean Coast since the Literacy Project in Language (1981). The chapter raises complex and fundamental questions arising from the planning and implementation of educational programs in the pluricultural, multilingual context of the Caribbean Coast. The chapter discusses the language ideologies that informed the early programs of bilingual education implemented during the early years of the Sandinista revolution on the Coast and the factors behind the complex evolution of education policies away from bilingualism towards a multilingual, intercultural approach that has radically changed the role languages play in the maintenance of diverse identities between and amongst different coastal groups.

Chapter 9, by Mark Jamieson, considers problems with the process brought into being by the Nicaraguan government in 2003 through legislation commonly known as Law 445: *The Communal Property Regime of the Indigenous Peoples and Ethnic Communities of the Autonomous Regions of the Atlantic Coast of Nicaragua and the Bocay, Coco, Indio and Maiz Rivers*. This law is concerned with the demarcation of territories claimed by indigenous and Afro-descendent peoples and represents an attempt to fortify rights guaranteed to these peoples by the autonomy statute in 1987. Although welcome in terms of its objectives of protecting their rights to lands and sea territories which they have traditionally inhabited and worked, the chapter demonstrates how the process initiated by Law 445 has thrown up a number of unforeseen consequences that the intended beneficiaries are currently attempting to work out. Jamieson analyses the nature of these unintended consequences, as well as Law 445 itself, through the experience of the predominantly Miskitu community of Kakabila in the Pearl Lagoon area and discusses some of the dilemmas faced by this community as a consequence of this well intentioned, yet highly contested, legislation.

In chapter 10, Mary Finely-Brook analyses a number of foreign-sponsored community forestry projects in the Prinzapolka watershed. These projects also involved local NGOs and communal and autonomous institutions, which acted as intermediaries between overseas donors and the local inhabitants who participated in the projects. While the chapter shows how important transformations in policy have taken place over the past decade that have increased local decision-making power, an examination of recent events also highlights the limiting impact that the funding requirements imposed by foreign donors can have on the administrative capacity of autonomous institutions in their role as intermediaries in these projects. The chapter also discusses the consequences of political fragmentation within regional institutions that is identified as an additional factor that undermines the capacity of these institutions to play a more influential role in relation to foreign-sponsored projects in the RAAN.

The many issues raised by the authors in this book underscore the highly contested and at times contradictory nature of the contemporary autonomy process on Nicaragua's Caribbean Coast. Such contestation has been a feature of the process from its inception in the 1980s. The original autonomy statute of 1987 emerged out of a bitter and protracted armed struggle which forced a suspicious national Nicaraguan state to concede to Costeño demands for autonomy. The resulting statute was vague enough to leave many of its clauses wide open to interpretation, and the evolution of the process since that time has tended to add to the confusion about the nature and limits of autonomy. Yet Costeños have shown an enduring commitment to define and give shape to the process through practical attempts to implement their interpretation of what autonomy should be. It is these many attempts to realize the promise of autonomy, and the historical sentiments of difference that have inspired such attempts, that the authors have focused upon in their respective chapters.

Finally, I think it only right to acknowledge the major contribution that many Costeños have made in the completion of this book. This book could never have been possible without the friendly and enthusiastic help that the authors received from numerous Costeños who proved so generous with their time and memories. We hope that in return for their invaluable co-operation we have produced a work that will inform people about their long and continuing struggle for autonomy which offers an example, however imperfect, to peoples across Latin America and the rest of the world.

Luciano Baracco
Middle East Technical University
Northern Cyprus Campus

# CHAPTER 1. THE KINGDOM OF MOSQUITIA AND THE MOSQUITO RESERVATION: PRECURSORS OF INDIAN AUTONOMY?

*Wolfgang Gabbert*

Nationalism — like any ethnic world view — is a political ideology that frequently evokes intense feelings among its adherents. It draws its emotional force from addressing one of the most fundamental challenges of our existence: the fact that individual life is finite. By assuming bonds to supposedly contemporary co-natural people and constructing a common past and future, nationalism transcends the limits of individual existence. This partly explains why historical arguments are the backbone of most discussions about national integration or autonomy. Thus, the Nicaraguan government has based its claims to sovereignty over the Atlantic Coast (Mosquitia) on the rights established by the Spanish conquest. The Spanish conquerors, however, did not succeed in subduing the indigenous inhabitants of the Kingdom of Mosquitia during the colonial era. The region lost some of its independence in 1860 when the Treaty of Managua established the Mosquito Reservation and granted it certain rights. Up to this time, the local population had been able to secure its political autonomy to a large degree by establishing friendly relations with Great Britain, the second colonial power in the region.

Regardless of their real historical significance, the Kingdom of Mosquitia and the Mosquito Reservation have become symbols of past glory and the political independence of the coastal population. In the early twentieth century a Moravian missionary introduced an annual festival involving the re-enactment of the Miskitu king's return to the Atlantic Coast. The concept of kingship was also kept alive by the reading of Old Testament passages about the greatness of the Israelite kings, such as David or Solomon, who conquered many of their neighbors.[1] In the early 1960s, Helms reported that "a few informants claimed that the king would someday be restored to his position and that the Miskito again be an independent 'nation'" (Helms 1969: 83).[2] Memories of "king times" include the notion of an inversion of the ethnic hierarchy, restoring the Miskitu to a prominent position (Hale 1994: 64). Thus, the Mosquito Kingdom and the Reservation still have political significance in debates on regional autonomy.

In the following I will discuss certain features of the political organization on the Atlantic Coast in the nineteenth century. Far from judging the veracity of Indian memories of past autonomy and glory, the aim is to achieve a greater understanding of key aspects of the painful struggle for autonomy in the twentieth century and its ambivalent results. Addressing the political and social structure of the Mosquito Reservation in particular, I will analyze the internal contradictions that made possible its formal integration into the Nicaraguan state, the so-called Reincorporación (Reincorporation) of 1894.

Historical Background

The establishment of Spanish colonial rule in Latin America was a difficult and protracted process. Although the indigenous state societies in Middle America and the Andes were overthrown in a relatively short period of time, Spanish attempts to conquer decentralized indigenous groups in the lowlands met with fierce resistance. Large tracts of the continent, seen as part of the Iberian empire by the conquerors, effectively remained outside Spanish domination until the end of the colonial period or beyond independence in the early nineteenth century. This was also the case with most of the Atlantic coast of Central America, including areas known as the

---

1 See Dennis (1982: 395); Bourgois (1986: 5-6); Hale (1994: 63-67); Hawley (1996: 324-327, 332-333).
2 See also Hawley (1996: 333).

Mosquitia, where the Spanish presence was generally opposed and brief. However, the Atlantic coast of what is today Nicaragua and Honduras did not remain outside European influence, providing as it did convenient hideouts for pirates and, with its rich stands of logwood and mahogany, an attractive belt for woodcutters. In addition, the prospect of contraband with Spanish towns further inland drew traders to these places. From the 1630s, the different groups, mostly of British origin, established numerous small colonies between the Bay of Honduras in the north and Panama in the south, including Belize, Black River, Cape Gracias a Dios and Bluefields. These settlements, whose political and legal status was long disputed, were repeatedly subjected to both diplomatic and military attacks by the Spanish, who claimed sovereignty. Spain, however, was unable to establish permanent political control over most of the area (Floyd 1967; Sandner 1985: 67-120; Offen 1999: 97-140). The British settlements emerged as private ventures independent of official colonial policy and for a long period Britain made no formal territorial claims. It was only after the *War of Jenkin's Ear* (1739–48) that the British Crown installed a superintendent in the Mosquitia and in 1749 officially made the territory a protectorate. In the Treaty of Paris (1763), Spain underlined its claim to sovereignty but granted British residents at least the right to cut logwood in the Bay of Honduras and elsewhere along the Caribbean coast. Thus, British settlements were consolidated in the course of the seventeenth and eighteenth centuries, with settlers bringing along African slaves to work for them (Floyd 1967: 55-70, 103-118; Potthast 1988: 120-155, 225-240; Offen 1999: 260-289).

After the war of independence of the North American colonies, which Spain had joined as an ally of the Americans, the Peace of Versailles (1783) and the Anglo–Spanish Convention of London (1786) led to the evacuation in 1787 of the few British troops and 2,650 settlers and slaves from the Mosquitia. Most of them found a new home in Belize, which had consolidated following the concession to cut logwood and the confirmation of the British presence by the peace treaty of 1783 (Floyd 1967: 153-166; Potthast 1988: 272-303; Bolland 1977: 31). When the British had to leave the Mosquitia, many of their slaves and a significant number of free coloreds remained. Numerous slaves managed to flee in the general turmoil, while others were left behind for various reasons (Bolland 1977: 40f; Potthast 1988: 240f; Brown 1990: 56f). Although the Convention of London guaranteed all Catholics who swore allegiance to the Spanish the right to remain, a few British residents also decided to remain. One was Robert Hodgson, the wealthy son of the first superintendent in the Mosquitia, who remained in Bluefields under Spanish rule. These British men were also allowed to continue using their slaves on the plantations and woodcutting camps (Dawson 1986: 43; Potthast 1988: 321). However, after Hodgson and his family had been ousted from Bluefields by Miskitu Indians in 1790 and Black River had been destroyed in 1800, no slave owner of any prominence remained in the Mosquitia, and slavery lost much of its significance as a structuring element of regional society. It was only offshore, on Corn Island, that slavery continued to play a major role until it was finally abolished in 1841 (Roberts 1827: 108; Dunham 1850: 76).

With the white planter class almost completely gone, other representatives of the British colonial system absent, and Spain (as well as the newly independent Central American republics after 1821) unable to bring the Mosquitia effectively under political control, a new local elite, mostly people with some Afro-American ancestors, were able to rise to a level of economic and political importance unknown in other parts of the Caribbean. These people, who later became known as Creoles, were engaged in trade and mahogany cutting, and for the most part controlled local politics.[1] They managed to consolidate their position when Britain's interest in the region revived in the 1830s as a result of the international trade in mahogany.

At first, Britain was content to defend its leading position in the trade with the independent republics of Central America and backing land claims by individual venturers and merchants seemed unwise. British policies began to change, however, when in 1836, lumber operations reached the area around the Román River in the northern part of Mosquitia. In addition, the Mosquitias' southern limits had become an issue when the San Juan River was gradually adjudged to be the point of entry for a canal that would link the Atlantic and Pacific oceans. As a result, Britain renewed its protectorate over the region in April 1844. Claims by woodcutters, traders and businessmen speculating in land grants as well as by the British govern-

---

1   See GBFO (1862: 676-678, 689-692); Roberts (1827: 108f, 132); Dunham (1850: 70, 89); Naylor (1967: 56). Up to the nineteenth century, the term Creole referred to those who did not belong to the Indian population but were natives of the Caribbean. While the term became a designation for the descendants of Spaniards in Spanish America, it has been used since the 1840s to categorize English-speaking Afro-Americans in the Caribbean (Gabbert 1992: 9, 78f). For the ethnogenesis and history of the Creoles, see Gabbert (1992; 1995a; 1995b, 2007), Gordon (1998), and Goett (2006).

ment were legitimized with reference to a sovereign Kingdom of Mosquitia. In the British interpretation, the latter was the embodiment of the rights of the native Amerindian population.[1]

The long and intense quarrels between Great Britain, defending its protectorate, and the Central American republics (supported by the United States) seeking to establish hegemony in the region, were temporarily settled in 1860. The Treaty of Managua recognized Nicaraguan sovereignty over the Atlantic region and brought the Kingdom of Mosquitia to an end. On the other hand, it also granted the Mosquito Indians the right to self-government in the newly created Mosquito Reservation.[2]

## Of Kings and Contexts

Up to this day, Nicaraguan claims to the Atlantic Coast have been generally contested by the region's inhabitants, alluding to Mosquitia traditions of self-rule and its historical and cultural peculiarity.[3] Hence, the character of the region's political institutions has been hotly debated between Nicaraguan governments and representatives of the local population, or Costeños, and their respective international allies, the United States and England. It was above all disputed in the nineteenth century when Spanish colonialism had come to an end, Central American nation states were attempting to consolidate themselves, and Britain and the United States vied for hegemony in a region that had gained in significance as a possible location for the construction of a new communication route linking the Atlantic and Pacific oceans.

The British and the Creole elite made efforts to uphold the image of a legitimate and sovereign Mosquito monarchy, at least in their diplomatic statements. They provided the Mosquito king with regalia such as a crown and a scepter. Coronations took place in Belize and were organized in a formal manner with considerable pomp including services, parades, salutes

---

1  See Marcoleta to Marcy, (May 4, 1854), Manning (1932-35), IV: 404-409; Fellechner, Müller and Hesse (1845: 228); Naylor (1960: 365, 375-378 and 1967: 59-61).

2  The treaty was published in NMHD (1990: 315-317). See also Gabbert (1992: 99-102).

3  See, for example, The Chief of the Mosquito Indians to the Earl of Rosebery, (March 8, 1894), PRO, FO, Confidential Print 6547: 87-104; Exposición de los Costeños (August 20, 1925), Ruiz (1927: 135f); Consejo de Ancianos ... n.d.; Jarquín (2004).

and, at least in two instances, the anointing of the king.[1] Nicaragua and the US, on the other hand, depicted Miskitu kings as mere puppets of British interests and frequently castigated them as drunkards:

> The King, George W. A. Hendy, who is also called Chief and President, seems to be a mere figurehead, and takes no active part in the government excepting to appear at the Council and sign whatever documents are presented to him by his advisers. He is kept well supplied with drink and spends most of his time with his harem at Lagoona [Pearl Lagoon].[2]

The historical polemic about the character of Miskitu kingship is reflected in more recent scholarly debates among anthropologists, historians and geographers. Some authors accept or confirm the Nicaraguan position that sees Miskitu kings as pawns in the hands of foreign businessmen and British diplomats (e.g., Conzemius 1932: 101; Parsons 1954: 11). Others regard them mainly as middlemen between Indians and Europeans (Helms 1969: 76-79) and interpret Miskitu leaders — including the king — as rivaling big men competing for power and influence (Helms 1986).[3] Michael Olien, Philip Dennis and others, in contrast, recognize a native tradition of supreme overlordship (*wita tara*, king, chief) that reaches back to the early seventeenth century at least. A Miskitu king (later chief) had supposedly ruled an independent polity these authors characterize as a chiefdom (the Mosquito Kingdom), where the king ruled over a hierarchy of political offices (general, governor and admiral).[4] Olien suggests the existence of an unbroken line of succession from 1655 to 1894 and concludes: "In spite of greater or lesser English influence, the structure of the Miskitu Kingdom remained remarkably stable for about 240 years" (Olien 1983: 199).

Although this debate has brought to light much valuable information on the history of Miskitu leadership patterns, I have stressed the need to

---

1 See Walker to Aberdeen, Belize (May 10, 1845), LAL, MIC 757; Roberts (1827: 147f); Thompson (2000). A proper Christian coronation would have been difficult in the Mosquitia since at that time there was no church or resident priest.

2 US Consulate to James Porter, Ass. Secretary of State, Belize (May 17, 1886), LAL, MIC 736. See also Abbott Lawrence to John Clayton, London (April 19, 1850), Manning (1932-35), VII: 364.

3 A "big man" is an informal political leader whose power and authority depend on his personal qualities and deeds (for example, magic powers, gardening prowess, eloquence or bravery in feuds and war). He does not hold an office but has considerable standing in interpersonal relations. See Sahlins (1963).

4 See Olien (1983: 199); Dennis and Olien (1984: 730); Olien (1998). See also Offen (1999: 191-210, 396-434); Goett (2006: 111).

contextualize and periodize more rigidly the data on the degree of power, authority and influence that Miskitu leaders possessed at different times (Gabbert 1990, 2002).[1] Some of the conclusions will be summarized here: as far as we know, the necessary economic foundations for the development of political centralization were lacking in the pre-Columbian indigenous societies on the Atlantic coast of Nicaragua.[2] As mentioned earlier, these groups were confronted with competing colonial powers (Spain and England) that had tried to gain hegemony in the region since the sixteenth century. The development of indigenous societies was decisively shaped by these encounters. Although the matter of Miskitu origins is still disputed, Mary Helms (1969) hinted at a salient point when she designated the Miskitu a "colonial tribe," highlighting the importance of colonialism for their history.[3] How-

---

1 Power can be defined in the Weberian tradition as the exercise of constraint and compulsion against the will of an individual or group. Authority refers to the acknowledged right to exercise power. Influence, in contrast, is the capacity to cause someone to act, behave or think in a particular way by example, persuasion or advice.

2 Political centralization can develop only in a society with the potential to produce an economic surplus and where access to key resources (e.g. water for the irrigation of fields) can be restricted (Earle 1997: 67-104).

3 Bernard Nietschmann argued that "[t]he Miskito's distinctiveness as a group with a well-defined adaptation to a littoral environment was quite evident at the time of contact with Europeans" (1973: 25). Mary Helms, in contrast, suggests that the Miskitus' existence "as an identifiable ethnic group with a distinctive way of life is a direct result of trade with the West" (1971: 228). According to Conzemius (1932: 16f) and Helms (1971: 18f), the Miskitu may originally have been a small group of Bawihka speakers living near Cape Gracias, who gained political suzerainty over their neighbors with the help of European guns. More recently, Offen has also argued that "a Miskitu ethnic identity came together in the 18th century" (1999: 17). However, at the time of the Helms-Nietschmann debate in the early 1970s, culture and ethnicity were still considered synonymous in much of anthropology. In fact, the debate was more about culture than ethnicity as this term is currently understood. In contrast to earlier interpretations, I have argued elsewhere that the Miskitu only became a subjectively self-conscious ethnic community in the late nineteenth or early twentieth century due to fundamental social and economic change and the effects of missionary activity (Gabbert 1992: 228f and in press). Originally, the term "Mosquitos" was the name European sailors gave to a group of small islands off the eastern coast of Nicaragua. It was extended to refer to the inhabitants of the coast in the seventeenth century (Potthast 1988: 66). See also Offen (2002: 333). Up until the end of the nineteenth century, however, "Mosquito Indians" not only referred to the speakers of several related dialects but, in a more general sense, to the indigenous inhabitants of the entire Atlantic region of Nicaragua. See, for example, Fellechner, Müller and Hesse (1845: 19). Thus, the Mosquito Convention that established the integration of the Atlantic region into the Nicaraguan state in 1894 was also signed by delegates of Rama-speaking settlements. The term "Mosquito Indians" or later "Miskito" was primarily a category

ever, the amount of influence Europeans and North Americans exerted on the Miskitu varied considerably between the seventeenth and nineteenth centuries. Therefore, generalizations about the character of leadership and the political structure over extended periods of time are problematic. Since the position of Miskitu leaders mainly depended on their access to foreign resources (trade goods, firearms) and not on local production, Miskitu political processes cannot be fully understood without reference to change in a more encompassing political economy.[1]

Prior to contact with Europeans, Miskitu society was essentially egalitarian and acephalous. Later trade in imported goods allowed some men polygamous marriages, thereby increasing the agricultural production of such households. Surpluses were used to arrange vast feasts. This, and the growing importance of warfare stimulated by conflicts between Britain and Spain and the slave trade with Jamaica, opened up new opportunities to certain individuals to gain prestige. They became regional big men with substantial zones of influence, frequently misunderstood as dominions. The importance of regional leaders began to decline, however, when the British evacuated the Mosquitia in 1787. Not only did Miskitu big men lose much of their ground as middlemen in the contraband trade with the Spanish, but they also lost their position as Britain's military allies after the war between the colonial powers came to an end. With the exception of the king, none of the prestigious titles Indian leaders had adopted since the seventeenth century, such as general, governor or admiral, developed into the designation of an office, i.e., a position of authority over permanent groups.[2] Their influence depended on individual qualities and personal loyalties or obligations and faded away when circumstances became unfavorable for regional big men, due, among other things, to the end of raiding, a decline in Miskitu

---

defined by outsiders (the Spanish, the British, the Nicaraguans, and German missionaries). It was based on linguistic similarities and did not pay attention to the actual social organization of the indigenous groups based on locality and (fictive) kinship. This began to change when the Moravian mission that fostered linguistic unification made Miskitu a written language, providing a means of communication and organizational structures that linked the Miskitu residence groups.

1  This was also the case during conflicts with the Sandinista government after the overthrow of the Somoza dictatorship in 1979.

2  This is also indicated by the fact that the use of even the most distinguished titles (general, admiral), with the possible exception of king, had evidently not been monopolized by individuals (Porta Costas 1908: 265, 272f); Roberts (1827: 113, 124, 131); Young (1842: 32, 80); Macgregor (1847: 31); Dunham (1850: 52, 55, 64, 75, 105); MB (1848: 228) and (1859: 142, 256, 259f); GBFO (1862: 682, 687, 689, 693).

importance as commercial middlemen after the Spanish trade monopoly fell in 1821, the attack on polygamy by Moravian missionaries after 1849, and the development of an extractive and plantation economy based on rubber, wood and bananas since the 1850s.[1]

But what about kingship? During the eighteenth century the British did not take Miskitu kingship too seriously beyond employing it as a diplomatic argument to legitimize their activities in the region. The king was neither consulted when they installed a superintendent and declared the Mosquito Shore a protectorate nor when they withdrew in 1787 (Oertzen 1985: 6f). Robert Hodgson, the aforementioned son of a British superintendent of the same name, referred to the term [Miskitu] "king" as a "nickname" (Hodgson 1766: 32). Kingship, on the other hand, developed into an office in the course of the nineteenth century. However, as will be shown in the following, at that moment in time the king was not the head of a Miskitu government but the symbolic representative of non-Indian political institutions. Both the chiefdom and the big-men model are insufficient to characterize the political role of the Miskitu kings for this period. Whatever prestige and power the latter possessed was neither a reflection of their personal qualities nor of their standing in Miskitu society but hinged almost completely on outside forces. In contrast to the situation of any of their predecessors, their position depended more or less directly and almost entirely on the backing of Europeans, especially British officials, traders, and entrepreneurs active in mahogany cutting and members of the Creole elite.

## The Kingdom of Mosquitia

With the renewal of British interest in the Mosquitia in the 1830s, the creation of more formalized institutions of government became a diplomatic and practical necessity for the London government to secure British influence, regularize land claims and create favorable conditions for trade and the exploitation of mahogany. As early as 1832, several laws were passed in the name of the Miskitu king regulating, among other things, taxation for the free male population (GBFO 1862: 688f; Macgregor 1847: 59). However, institutions to enforce such decisions were rare even in Bluefields, which was the largest Afro-American settlement after Pearl Lagoon. When the

---

1  See Gabbert (1990, 1992: 93-98 and 2002) for the full argument.

British diplomat Patrick Walker reached the town in 1844, he described the inhabitants as follows:

> Not the least arduous part of my task has been in endeavouring to inculcate a spirit of order and improvement among the Creole part of the population, who hitherto unawed by any control, uninfluenced by the presence of any minister of Religion and distinguished by a more than common share of tropical inactivity have been living like a community of Buccaneers, heedless of a respectable appearance either in their houses or in their persons. Accustomed to count upon six months turtle fishing as adequate to supply their wants for the remaining six, [the] greater part of their time has been passed in idleness and dissipation.[1]

As the sources show, a situation of arbitrariness and insecurity prevailed. Some traders, for example, were so powerful that they did not hesitate to "flog an Indian because he could not, at the stipulated time, pay a small debt" (Roberts 1827: 132).[2] Loggers complained about Indians in remote exploitation areas who did not show up for work in spite of having accepted advance payments. Others lamented theft, threats or depredation of their property (Dozier 1985: 66; Olien 1987: 261).

Until the dispatch of Patrick Walker as British consul general, a small group of local merchants, entrepreneurs from Belize and (following his appointment in 1837) the British superintendent in Belize, Alexander McDonald, had dominated politics in the Mosquitia. Political institutions in Bluefields consisted of a commander, the Briton James Bell, and a magistracy comprised of local Creoles.[3] With their relatively large and sedentary population, Bluefields and Pearl Lagoon seemed to be the only settlements where a kind of capital could be installed. Beyond this, Bluefields was relatively close to the strategically vital endpoint of the trans-isthmian route in San Juan del Norte (Greytown).

The distance between the life-worlds of Indians and Creoles was further increased after the Protestant Moravian Church took up systematic mission work in 1849. In addition to establishing a congregation, the missionaries supplied secular schooling for the local population, first and foremost in the

---

1  Walker to Aberdeen (December 31, 1844), LAL, MIC 757.
2  See also Fellechner, Müller and Hesse (1845: 187); Potthast (1988: 202, 217f, 265).
3  See Bell to Geddes (March 29, 1854), PRO, FO 53, 34; Fellechner, Müller and Hesse (1845: 48f); Naylor (1960: 377); Oertzen (1990: 28-32). It is not clear when the magistracy was formed. However, it probably came into existence in the late 1820s or early 1830s, since neither Roberts (1827) nor Dunham (1850) mentions such an institution in their accounts.

Creole communities. Considering their sedentary life-style, their greater involvement in the money economy and their cultural closeness to the British, it comes as no surprise that Creoles held leading positions in the new political institutions of the kingdom. Beyond this, they controlled skilled occupations and some became comparatively wealthy in the rubber or alcohol trade or by participating in the emerging banana industry.[1] In 1853, the chief magistrate of San Juan del Norte, the Briton Henry Grant Foote, reported to the Foreign Office: "The Mosquito Indians, my lord, are totally unfit to manage their own affairs; the creoles and negroes on the coast enslave them and treat them like beasts of burden" (Foote to FO, June 2, 1853, BL, OPC, Confidential Print 308: 420).

However, it should be kept in mind that Afro-Americans on the Coast were by no means a homogeneous group. Firstly, many of them did not perceive themselves as blacks but as Creoles or British subjects, in an attempt to downplay or deny their African ancestry. Secondly, Afro-Americans cannot be treated as a community during this period, since the prerequisite for community is the existence of a consciousness of kind, which in my view did not exist at that time. Even when slaves were emancipated in 1841, the newly freed Afro-Americans remained part of the lowest stratum of the social hierarchy. They were held in disdain and often harassed by wealthy coloreds and the few whites residing on the Coast (see, e.g., J.S. Bell to Fancourt, October 21, 1843, PRO, FO 53, 1). For decades, the vast majority of Afro-Americans in the region, whose number was augmented by immigrants from San Andrés, Curaçao and Jamaica, lived a simple life sustained by turtle fishing, subsistence agriculture (cassava, yams, maize, rice, bread, fruit, plantains, sugar cane, oranges), and hunting (tapir, monkey, deer, warree, iguana).[2]

The political predominance of a small circle of Creoles and the non-Indian character of the new institutions are clearly demonstrated by the composition of the Council of State formed on September 10, 1846. Its members were James Green, a British doctor, a Scottish secretary and five Cre-

---

1  See MB (1861: 135); (1867: 103, 107); (1869: 143f); (1874: 243); (1884: 177); (1887: 79), Jahresbericht: 16; (1895: 99); (1900: 282); PA I, 28: 314; 34: 383f; II, 1: 446; Girsewald (1896: 73f); *New York Times* (August 8, 1894: 8); Vice-Consul Harrison to the Earl of Kimberley (February 26, 1895), NMHD: 405.

2  See Roberts (1827: 109); Dunham (1850: 80); Bell (1899: 17, 27, 36f, 40f); Martin (1899: 9f); Walker to Aberdeen (October 1, 1844), and Walker to Aberdeen (December 31, 1844), both in LAL, MIC 757. See Gabbert (1992: 219-227; 1995b; 2007: 55-61) for fuller treatments of the Creoles' social and cultural heterogeneity.

oles from Bluefields (in addition to James Bell). With the exception of the Miskitu king Robert Charles Frederic, no Indian was present.[1] Moreover, one month later the king decreed the abolition of "Indian law and customs" and proclaimed the Law of England as the foundation for the administration of justice with the following argument:

> Whereas the Laws of England were proclaimed from time to time by the late King Robert to be the laws by which justice was to be administered in this kingdom, yet notwithstanding said proclamations the practice of awarding punishments for crimes and settling disputes according to the old Indian system has been continued in many places, whereby immorality has been encouraged and the innocent made to suffer for the guilty.[2]

The Mosquito Indians were by definition the subjects of the kingdom's sovereignty. However, they were neither fit nor willing to occupy positions in the new government institutions. Leadership among the Indians was still largely informal, their settlement patterns dispersed and semi-nomadic.[3] Although the struggles between local settlers, British diplomats, the Nicaraguan government and the US hinged on the rights of the Mosquito Indians at the discursive level, in reality they were about land claims, commercial interests and the inter-oceanic connection. Since these matters mostly affected regions outside the Miskitu settlement area (the rich mahogany stands around the Román River in the north and the environs of San Juan del Norte, or Greytown, in the south), Indians were no longer needed as military allies and — their numbers significantly reduced by epidemics — became for the most part politically irrelevant.[4] While intrusions into In-

---

1   "Senior member" George Hodgson was a planter, born around 1794 on Corn Island, possibly still as a slave. He was the grandson of Robert Hodgson and the son of the "colored" William Hodgson and a "black" woman. Alexander Hodgson, son and ex-slave of Robert Hodgson, was a trader and had already been part of Bluefields' magistracy in 1844. John Dixon, "another man very slightly removed from the African," was from Bluefields and participated in the mahogany trade. The carpenter William Halstead Ingram and James Porter were probably coloreds who had emigrated from Jamaica. See Constitution of the Council of State and Christie to Palmerston (September 5, 1848), both in NMHD: 108, 121; GBFO (1862: 689); Declaration of George Hodgson (January 1, 1848), enclosed in Salinas to Savage (January 24, 1848), Manning 1965, III: 269; Olien (1988a: 10, 12-14). Bell did not participate in the first meetings of the council and was not sworn in, First Meeting of the Council of State, NMHD: 109f.

2   Abolition of Indian Law and Customs (October 12, 1846), NMHD: 116.

3   See, for example, MB (1857: 104; 1859: 118, 220, 247; 1860: 209; 1864: 42; 1887: 208; 1890: 17; 1897: 206f) Schneider (1899: 85f).

4   For population losses due to epidemics, see MB (1870, Anhang: 37); (1878: 86f); Young (1842: 24, 73); Fellechner, Müller and Hesse (1845: 21, 58, 70); Schneider

---

dian community life by the Mosquitian and Nicaraguan governments had been rare for decades, Indians had almost no bearing on the diplomatic and political struggles that would determine their destiny.

After 1800, the Miskitu kings gradually came under the sway of British or Creole entrepreneurs, merchants and diplomats. In accordance with changing political and economic conditions the kings' residence moved southward. George Frederic had his principal abode in Cape Gracias a Dios and maintained other dwellings in Sandy Bay and on the Rio Coco (Roberts 1827: 53, 128, 148; Dunham 1850: 119). His successor, Robert Charles Frederic, kept a dwelling place on the Rio Coco but moved his main residence to Pearl Lagoon (GBFO 1862: 687f; Young 1842: 25; Olien 1983: 222). The Miskitu around Cape Gracias a Dios lost contact with the political center of the Coast almost entirely when the king's residence was transferred to Bluefields in 1844 on the initiative of Consul Walker.[1] The separation of the kings from their fellow Miskitu was not merely geographical distancing but also cultural estrangement. Beginning with George Frederic, who was sent to Jamaica in 1800 to be educated and was crowned in Belize in 1816, the Miskitu kings were more or less alienated from indigenous culture (Roberts 1827: 133f, 148). This tendency was even more pronounced in the case of his successors. A contemporary observer described George Augustus Frederic, also educated in Jamaica and crowned in Belize in 1845 as a thirteen-year-old boy, as follows: "[H]e is thoroughly English in his habits, thoughts, and dress, and having received a first-rate education at Jamaica ..., he considers English his proper language; ... the impression he makes is that of a thorough English gentleman. His costume is that of a yachting man in the season..." (Pim 1863: 93).[2]

When William Henry Clarence assumed office on September 22, 1874, having completed his education in Jamaica, he was barely able to speak Miskitu. On the occasion of his return, he held his speech in English, which was then translated into Miskitu by missionary Martin (MB 1875: 18).

---

(1899: 8, 105f); Potthast (1988: 103, 161, 266); Bell (1899: 83). See Gabbert (1992: 82-90) for an extensive discussion of the changes in the region's ethnic hierarchy.

1  See also Vilas (1992: 70).

2  For the cultural alienation of the kings, see also US Consulate to James Porter, Ass. Secretary of State, Belize (May 17, 1886), LAL, MIC 736; Young (1842: 30, 159); Fellechner, Müller and Hesse (1845: 48); Pim and Seemann (1869: 269); Schneider (1899: 17-19, 26).

Thus the existence of the Kingdom of Mosquitia cannot be interpreted as evidence for Miskitu political influence. Kingship had become an institution of symbolic importance in the international diplomatic struggle for regional hegemony. However, kings did not wield real power. Although formally the head of Mosquitia's government, in actual fact they had little say. Apart from this, the kings were never able to establish a position of authority in Miskitu communities beyond their own following, the backing of the British notwithstanding. George Frederic, for example, was not in a position to oblige leading Indian men to show up at his feasts, and the description given by Roberts suggests that the king was treated with little formality (Roberts 1827: 132-139).[1] The kings had also lost much of their effectiveness as middlemen to the Indian part of the population. During the nineteenth century the Miskitu kings received presents on a regular basis. These came first from the settlers of Belize. In 1838, expenses were covered by the British government.[2] Without opportunities to gain renown as a great warrior, the king's prestige primarily depended on the distribution of presents obtained from the British (Roberts 1827: 149; Dunham 1850: 96). However, the king was unable to monopolize commercial relations with Belizean or Jamaican traders (Roberts 1827: 113f, 166; Dunham 1850: 52, 89, 133).

The political marginalization of the Miskitu and other indigenous groups in the region increased in the decades that followed. Great Britain lost ground rapidly in the emerging conflict with the US for hegemony in Central America. Beyond this, the canal issue, and thus territorial control of the Mosquitia and Greytown, became less important and was gradually displaced by commercial considerations for Great Britain:

> The British government had become convinced that the region, exploited by American enterprise, protected by a stable Anglo-Saxon government, would contribute much more to British commercial wealth than would be possible in a state of political independence attended by confusion and unrest which paralyzed all industrial development.... England began to hope as well as to expect that the

---

1  See also MB (1851: 28).

2  For gifts to the Miskitu kings, see, for example, Col. Cockburn to FO (February 4, 1830) and Alexander MacDonald to CO (November 17, 1838), both in PRO, CO 714, 79; Walker to Col. McDonald (November 12, 1838) and Foreign Office to Treasury (December 7, 1848), both in PRO, FO 53, 15; MB (1855: 203); Oertzen (1990: 28-30).

Central American states would eventually become a part of the American Union (Williams 1965: 268).[1]

From the Kingdom of Mosquitia to the Mosquito Reservation

The Treaty of Managua from January 28, 1860 marks a decisive step in the political retreat of Great Britain. As already mentioned, therein the British government renounced the continuation of its protectorate and for the first time recognized Nicaraguan sovereignty over the Mosquitia. The treaty did, however, create a district, the Mosquito Reservation (Reserva Mosquita), between Río Rama in the south, Río Hueso in the north, the Atlantic Coast to the east and 84°15' degrees longitude to the west. Here, the Mosquito Indians were to: "...enjoy the right of governing, according to their own customs, and according to any regulations which may from time to time be adopted by them, not inconsistent with the sovereign rights of the Republic of Nicaragua, themselves, and all persons residing within such district" (Treaty of Managua, NMHD: 316).

In combination with another agreement, which recognized Honduran rights to the northern part of Mosquitia in 1859, the treaty had vital consequences for the political future of the region, further weakening the position of the Miskitu. Firstly, it laid the foundation for the separation of the Miskitu-speaking population in Nicaragua and Honduras. Secondly, the majority of the Nicaraguan Miskitu lived outside the Reservation's boundaries, and were officially under the direct administration of the Nicaraguan government. It is estimated that in 1861 more than half of the Miskitu population lived north of the Río Coco in the now Honduran part of the Mosquitia (Pim 1863: 82). Of the Reservation's 12,000 inhabitants in 1874, around fifty percent were Miskitu, forty percent Sumu and Rama, and less than ten percent Creoles (Wünderich 1990: 63).[2] However, Creoles made up almost the entire population in the towns of the southern Reservation, while the Miskitu predominated in the northern parts. In 1855, a sixth of the 600–700

1 See also Olien (1987: 280f).
2 Sources vary considerably in the data on population size and composition. In addition, they frequently correspond to overlapping but not identical areas that include or exclude, for example, the Nicaraguan and Honduran parts of the Mosquitia. Several sources estimate the population of the entire Mosquitia in the middle of the nineteenth century at between 15,000 and 30,000 inhabitants (Bell 1862: 250; Pim 1863: 75; Sonnenstern 1971: 16). The number of Creoles can be estimated at 900 to 1,200 at that time (MB 1855: 204, 208f; 1859: 123; PA I, 22: 411).

inhabitants of Bluefields were Indians, "mostly Mosquitos," most of whom soon abandoned the town as a result of the discrimination and cheating they experienced at the hands of Afro-American and white residents. Thus, only a handful of Indians lived in Bluefields around 1860, apart from the Miskitu king and his family (MB 1855: 204; 1857: 65, 104; PA I, 22: 349, 412; Schneider 1899: 56f, 63f).

Political institutions in the former British protectorate had to be reorganized as a consequence of the Treaty of Managua. The title of King of Mosquitia was changed to that of Hereditary Chief. On September 12, 1861, the British consul in Bluefields proclaimed the *Municipal Constitution for the Government of the Mosquito Reservation*. On the same day, the forty-three members of the first parliamentary chamber, the legislative General Council, were designated by the chief on the recommendation of the "Public Convention of the Headmen of the Mosquito Indians and of the mixed population." The seventeen members of the second chamber, the Executive Council, were named by the General Council on the following day. The British consul, missionary Feurig, who was a member of the Moravian Church, and several other individuals acted as advisory members. Feurig was also designated treasurer, an office held by Moravian missionaries until the end of the Reservation in 1894.[1] The influence of the missionaries must have been enormous. They accomplished administrative functions in various communities, collecting taxes and administering the law (MB 1858: 98 and 1890: 207; Martin 1899: 49, 79, 144). The extent of their political importance is evident from a mission source that stresses the influence of Feurig's predecessor, Pfeiffer, who formally held the office of magistrate in the Kingdom of Mosquitia but "the virtual authority of a prime minister, which was informally his" (PA I, 32: 280).

The Reservation's constitution and laws led to the exclusion of most Indians as well as the Afro-American lower classes from political participation. To be eligible for the General Council, candidates had to be resident in the Reservation for at least three years preceding the appointment and own personal property worth not less than US$ 250. In the case of the Executive Council, they had to be a "native of Mosquito" or recommended by the chief, have resided in the reserve five years prior to the election, own per-

---

1  See MB (1862: 19f; 1890: 109; 1895: 26; PA II, 1: 447); Schneider (1899: 43). The text of the Municipal Constitution can be found in Government of the Mosquito Reservation (1884: 3-15) and, more accessible, in NMHD: 323-326.

sonal property amounting to US$500, and be literate.[1] As in the Kingdom of Mosquitia, the laws of England were adopted, yet further evidence that the constitution and the institutions it brought forth were more suited to the life-world of the few urban settlements and their overwhelming Creole population (*Municipal Constitution*, NMHD: 323f).[2] According to the captain of a British warship:

> The Indians, for whom the Treaty was made, really care for very little, provided they are left alone; and, therefore, the authority has been gradually acquired by a few educated Jamaica coloured gentlemen, who have ruled the country as Mosquito Indians, with the Chief at their head as a show-piece and puppet.[3]

Another contemporary observer noted:

> The Indian ... seems to have less political genius. The machinery of government impresses him as a mysterious something which he cannot comprehend, and which he hates because he feels the pressure of its iron heel when he disobeys its regulations. Instead of seeking to control it himself by constitutional means, he speculates as to methods for outwitting it, or for crushing it. The negroes, on the contrary, respond with enthusiasm to the call for conventions, participate in debate, which is only confusion and more mystery to the Indian, and so, when the sense of the meeting is taken, it is found to be wholly African.... As a result the Mosquito men are almost entirely excluded from power, and the government falls easily into the hands of the mixed population ... consisting chiefly of Jamaicans who still claim to be British subjects (Kalb 1893: 275).[4]

Vice-president and secretary were the most important offices in the Reservation. Afro-Americans assumed the roles of counselor to the chief and the General Council when the seat of the British consul was transferred to Greytown in 1849. The same men held these positions over extended periods of time. Thus, Henry Patterson, a Creole from Pearl Lagoon, was vice-president from 1860 until his death in 1874. His son Charles succeeded him

---

1 Kalb (1893: 272) suggests that the Mosquito Indians were exempt from the restrictions mentioned. However, there is no hint of such an exemption in the text of the constitution.

2 Some adjustments of British law to local conditions were codified in the Form of Criminal and Civil Procedure three years later (Government of the Mosquito Reservation, 1884: 34-71; Wünderich 1990: 65).

3 Captain Curzon-Howe to Vice-Admiral Sir J. Hopkins (Bluefields, March 18, 1894), in Confidential Print 6547, NMHD: 374.

4 This evaluation is confirmed by Girsewald, who wrote: "All offices, from the secretaries to the police-men, are occupied by coloreds ..." (1896: 96, transl. W.G.).

in this office, which he held until the Reservation was dissolved in 1894.[1] James W. Cuthbert, who had emigrated from Jamaica in 1853 or 1854, also lived in Pearl Lagoon and acted as attorney general and secretary of the chief from 1862 to 1894. In the final years of the Reservation the position of sec-retary was filled by his son, James W. Cuthbert Jr.[2] Hence, a small group of Afro-Americans (in addition to those mentioned above, John Herbert Hooker, John Oliver Thomas and several others) held most of the leading positions in the Reservation and survived the coming and going of five dif-ferent Chiefs. Indeed, their offices were well on their way to becoming he-reditary" (Wünderich 1990: 65).[3] Their political influence was particularly pronounced since the formal head of state, the chief, was frequently a minor living in the custody of the British consuls, Creoles and missionaries or being educated abroad. William Henry Clarence, for example, was elected chief in 1866 at the age of ten. He was under the tutelage of the Reserva-tion's vice-president, Henry Patterson, until his coming of age in 1874.[4] In his comment on Jonathan Charles Frederic, a successor to William Henry Clarence, the Moravian Bishop Romig left no doubt that the role of the chief in Reservation politics was negligible: "It was of little use to speak with him on affairs connected with our mission work, as he is only the nominal head of the Government, and knows little of its affairs" (PA II, 1: 442).

Further evidence of the power relations in the Reservation can be gained by analyzing the ethnic origins of the members of the General and Executive Councils. At the public convention of 1861, only eleven of the fifty-one del-egates can be identified as Miskitu[5] and four as Rama. Four of the remain-

---

1 See MB (1874: 239); (1875: 20); (1891: 31); (1895: 99f); Taylor (1891: 3); Consul Bingham to F.O. (February 4, 1890), PRO, FO, Confidential Print 6198; Vice-Con-sul Harrison to the Marquis of Salisbury (Bluefields, October 16, 1895), PRO, FO, Confidential Print 6757: 40.

2 See MB (1869: 144); (1874: 243); (1889: 72); (1894: 174); (1895: 99f); Commander Stuart to Admiralty (September 12, 1894), PRO, FO, Confidential Print 6585: 166.

3 See, for example, Vice-Consul Harrison to the Marquis of Salisbury, Bluefields (December 23, 1895), PRO, FO, Confidential Print 6885: 14-21; US Consulate to James Porter, Ass. Secretary of State, Belize (May 17, 1886), LAL, MIC 736.

4 See MB (1866: 235, 276f); (1872: 192); (1875: 16-18). For his predecessor George Augustus Frederic, see Green to FO, (July 20, 1850), PRO, FO 53, 23B; Walker to Chatfield (December 12, 1844), PRO, FO 252, 28; McDonald to FO (September 14, 1845), PRO, FO 53, 4; Grey to Earl Grey, CO (November 22, 1847), PRO, FO 53, 14; MB (1849: 120, 188); (1850: 159); (1855: 203); Pim and Seemann (1869: 265, 267, 270-272). For Robert Henry Clarence, see Consul Bingham to FO (February 4, 1890), PRO, FO, Confidential Print 6198.

5 Seven of them came from communities outside the Reservation.

ing thirty-six delegates were whites,[1] the missionaries Feurig, Jürgensen, Lundberg and Grunewald, and the rest, in all likelihood, Creoles, since they came from Bluefields, Pearl Lagoon and Corn Island (Municipal Constitution, NMHD: 319f; Wünderich 1990: 63). With the exception of eight of the eleven Miskitu, all of the delegates were selected as members of the General Council. The Executive Council was composed of three Miskitu, three Rama and twelve others, probably Creoles (*First Legislation of the General Council*, September 13, 1861, NMHD: 329). Indian participation seems to have increased later on, at least formally, to meet Nicaraguan challenges to the legitimacy of the Reservation government. Thus, thirty Indians and thirteen non-Indians belonged to the General Council in the 1880s (Martin 1899: 182).

A similar trend can be observed with respect to the bodies that elected the new chiefs. Only twelve of the thirty-three people "present at the election" of Chief William Henry Clarence in 1866 were classed as Indians (Names of Persons present at the election of the chief, Bluefields, May 23, 1866, NMHD: 335f).[2] The conventions that elected the new chiefs after the death of the incumbents in 1889 and 1891, in contrast, were composed en-

---

1  Olien (1988a: 18) mentions four other "Whites," an American and three British, but provides neither the names nor the source of this information.

2  Seven others were classed as Half-Indian. However, among them were people such as Henry Patterson from Pearl Lagoon and Michael Quin from Corn Island, who were normally considered Creoles. The ascription of ethnic or "racial" identities by contemporaries was frequently inconsistent. While some observers stressed phenotype or descent, others regarded cultural features, such as language or urban life-style, as more important. The term Creole could therefore refer to blacks and coloreds but also to the offspring of unions between whites and Indians, provided they spoke English and lived outside the Indian communities (e.g., PA I, 22:349). This was the case with the Creole Charles Patterson, for example, who was also classed as "quadroon" (a person with one-fourth African and three-fourths Caucasian ancestry), Indian and Half-Indian (NMHD: 377; MB 1875: 20; 1895: 99; Martin 1899: 149; PA I, 275). His father, Henry, was the son of a Scottish trader and a Miskitu mother. He spoke English and Miskitu and was born and lived in Pearl Lagoon, which was considered a Creole community (MB 1874: 243). Diverging ascriptions of ethnic or racial status not only reflected a political strategy — such as to legitimize or delegitimize the Reservation's government — but also expressed preferences for matrilineal or patrilineal descent reckoning (see also Wünderich 1990: 67f). While the male line was more important in ascribing ancestry in Nicaraguan custom, Miskitu practice frequently preferred the female line (Helms 1971: 72, 98f). Thus, the Nicaraguan government declared that "on no account is the word Mosquito to be considered as including the children of the foreigners born in the Mosquito territory, although they may have been begotten of Indian women of that tribe" (Cortez, R. to Vaughan, W. June 26, 1866, BL, OPL, Confidential Paper 4013).

tirely of Indians.[1] Apparently, however, this did not affect Afro-American political dominance. In 1894, for example, the ethnic composition of the Executive Council was as follows: Chief Robert Henry Clarence, Charles Patterson, twelve other Creoles, three Rama and a white North American (Olien 1988a: 20).

The evidence presented here demonstrates that the representation and political participation of the Mosquito Indians in the Reservation was minimal at best, although the Treaty of Managua had made them subjects of the Reservation's autonomy rights. To uphold the appearance of indigenous self-government in the Reservation it was essential that at least the chief be a "genuine" Indian, since according to the constitution the holder of the office was at the same time the president of the General Council and the chairman of the Executive Council (*Municipal Constitution*, NMHD: 324). Thus, the chief's ancestry attracted the growing attention of the interested parties, especially the governments of the United States, Great Britain, Nicaragua and the Reservation (cf., for example, Kahle and Potthast 1983: LXXV, 155f, 184).

Nicaragua's secretary of state was still referring to the Mosquito Indians' lack of civilization in 1847, when he denied territorial claims on behalf of the Kingdom of Mosquitia:

> Such Mosquito kingdom could not have existed at any time, nor does it now exist. As a matter of fact, Sir, the whole thing is reduced to certain savages who roam the desert and the forests of the coast of Honduras and Nicaragua, living by hunting and fishing, without buildings, without a known language, illiterate, without arts, without commerce, without laws, and without religion, which in accordance with recognized principles would give them the appearance before the civilized world, as constituting regular society, and, what is much more, an empire.... [A] few British subjects ... were able to come to the said coasts and become acquainted with that tribe ... were seized with the desire to appropriate it, deciding as a means to this end to teach improperly their English language and part of their customs to some of the said Mosquitos, to take with them the son of some favourite family among them, to educate him in their fashion,

---

1 Bingham to the Marquis of Salisbury, November 5, 1889, (NMHD: 353f; Taylor 1891: 3f). Kalb mentions that the "headmen" participating in the conventions were "delegated by local conventions, which are seldom conducted with much formality" (1893: 274). However, we have no details of the selection process which might have given an idea of the delegates' degree of representation.

and thus prepare that instrument which could serve their designs with the title of King.[1]

E.G. Squier, US chargé d'affaires in Central America from 1849 to 1850, supported the position of Honduras and Nicaragua, denying Mosquitia's sovereignty in numerous writings in the 1850s (published anonymously as well as under his own name or the alias Samual Bard). He also characterized the Miskitu and the kings as savages, drunkards and British puppets in order to delegitimize any claim to autonomy. In addition, he argued that they were predominantly Africans rather than genuine Indians and thus "intruders" with no right to Nicaraguan territory. Interestingly enough, he did not mention the Creoles since this would have complicated his endeavor.[2] Without having met him, he describes king George Augustus Frederic personally as follows: "He is nothing more or less than a negro, with hardly a perceptible trace of Indian blood, and would pass at the South for a likely young fellow, worth twelve hundred dollars as a body-servant!" (Bard 1855: 63f). This argument became a core element of the US and Nicaraguan polemic against the sovereignty of the Mosquito Kingdom initially and later, the Mosquito Reservation.

In accordance with their interests, many British authors depicted the "royal family" as cultured and, of course, of pure indigenous descent:

> His Majesty then is a Mosquito Indian of pure blood, in direct descent from a long line of regal ancestors. He is ... much fairer than the generality of his countrymen... His Majesty's residence is a large American lumber house, most tastefully built in the villa style with a capital verandah, and well fitted up. His sanctum contains a very good collection of books by some of our best authors.... (Pim 1863: 93, 95).[3]

To bolster the Reservation's diplomatic position, the leading groups (the British consul, the missionaries and the Creole elite) ensured that only individuals of pure indigenous descent could become Hereditary Chief. When George Augustus Frederic died on November 27, 1865, his children were considered ill-suited as candidates for succession because they were the product of a relationship with a Creole woman. Consequently, Wil-

---

1  Salinas to Chatfield, October 14, 1847, Manning (1932-35, III: 251f). See also Crowe (1850: 208-211); Squier (1854: 54).

2  Cf. Bard (1855: 58f); Squier [1855] (1969: 364f); Olien (1985: 119f; 1988b: 33, 43).

3  See also Pim and Seemann (1869: 268f, 294); MB (1874: 239). Pim and Seemann (1869: 267, 270f). What they saw was, in fact, the house of the British Consul, Green.

liam Henry Clarence, a nephew of the deceased, became the new chief (MB 1866: 57, 235; Lundberg to Paton, July 25, 1866, BL, OPC, Confidential Paper 4013).

## The Character of the Reservation Government

The Reservation government was an administration typical of notables. Its members were natives or at least long-term residents of the Mosquitia and their main businesses were located within its confines. They were concerned with the economic, social and cultural development of the area and shared an attitude of benevolent paternalism towards the Afro-American lower classes and the Indians, all of whom needed "civilizing" with the help of the government. This included integrating the population into the market economy and spreading education and Christianity. On December 18, 1861, for example, a head tax was imposed on all males between the ages of eighteen and sixty, while compulsory education was introduced by law on October 1, 1875 (Government of the Mosquito Reservation 1884: 20f, 34). Polygamy was outlawed in 1862 (MB 1863: 89f; Schneider 1899: 95). In an attempt to suppress widespread "obeah" among the lower classes, the government of the Reservation passed a "law against sorcery" in 1889, which laid down severe punishment in the case of violation (Documentos 1946: 48).

The constitution of the Reservation established a complex legal system that included an extraordinary court of impeachment, a supreme court (with jurisdiction over all serious cases involving heavy penalties or large sums of money), the local magistrates' courts (to handle minor civil and criminal cases) and courts of arbitration as an accessory of the magistrates' court:

> In any civil case the plaintiff and defendant may, instead of carrying the matter into an ordinary court, each appoint an arbiter, and the two thus chosen are to appoint an umpire. This tribunal, being duly sworn before the magistrate, is constituted a court of arbitration, with full powers of a court of justice (Kalb 1893:273f).[1]

The creation of the Courts of Arbitration was an attempt to adjust the new legal institutions formed after the British model to the reality of everyday life in the rural areas and customary forms of dispute management. Beyond this, the position of magistrate was introduced to represent the government at local level. Theoretically, at least, the magistrate enjoyed ample

---

1 See also Thomas to Baker (Bluefields, April 28, 1894), NMHD: 377.

"opportunities for petty tyranny" (Kalb 1893: 273) due to the fact that he combined police and juridical functions. Among other things, magistrates possessed "summary powers of arrest, trial, conviction, and punishment" over "disorderly persons," "vagrants" and "juvenile offenders for petty crimes and misdemeanors" (Government of the Mosquito Reservation 1884: 58).

The Reservation government tried to spread what they considered civilization among the territory's population. On the one hand, they repressed important aspects of Indian and Afro-American "folk culture" and exerted pressure on the population to submit to government control. On the other hand, they pursued paternalistic policies in an effort to defend the local population from overexploitation and mistreatment. Thus, in 1863 for example, imprisonment for debt (unless fraudulently contracted) was abolished. Personal belongings of debtors were protected from execution and sale up to a monetary value of US$250 (Government of the Mosquito Reservation 1884: 34). It seems that at least some of the chiefs considered themselves advocates of the Indians. Hence, William Henry Clarence declared on assuming office:

> I have to call your attention to the oppressions under which the poor Indians suffer from those who trade among them. I am of their blood, and feel it my duty in every way to vindicate the wrongs committed amongst them. Regulations should therefore be made to free them at once from the slavery under which they labour (Bluefields, October 5, 1874, NMHD: 167).

Although Indians were exposed to pressure and exploitation since the 1860s, particularly in the rubber trade, communities remained primarily autonomous, with the new political and legal order implemented only in the larger Creole settlements, such as Bluefields and Pearl Lagoon.[1] However, in settlements where a mission station had been established, missionaries were active in persuading the local population to obey the government. Thus, they endeavored to collect taxes (mostly in the form of rubber) and to enforce school attendance, which was made compulsory in 1875 (Martin 1899: 92; MB 1876: 125). They also made efforts to suppress the indigenous custom of blood revenge and to deliver the culprits to the relevant authorities (MB 1877: 98 and 1884: 108f; Schneider 1890: 53). Their endeavor, however, met with little success, not least in the more remote indigenous

---

1  See MB (1858: 54f; 1859: 123; 1862: 88); Exposición de los Costeños, Bluefields, August 20, 1925, Ruiz (1927: 134); Keely (1894: 166); Oertzen (1990: 38); Wünderich (1990: 63); Gabbert (1996: 91-93).

settlements (MB 1875: 142; 1876: 242; Martin 1899: 79, 134). One missionary complained as late as the mid-1890s: "Many Indians ... cared neither for the laws nor for the punishment or fines prescribed in case of their infringement. They knew the Wita [headman, W.G.] could not compel obedience" (PA II, 2: 612).

## The End of the Reservation

The end of the Mosquito Reservation came in 1894, when Nicaraguan troops occupied Bluefields and deposed the Reservation government. This was justified with reference to the armed confrontation between Nicaraguan and Honduran troops in the vicinity of Cabo Gracias a Dios. The chief's protest at the military presence of Nicaraguan troops in the Reservation was considered high treason in a state of war. Moreover, the Nicaraguan government argued that the Treaty of Managua had been violated, since "Jamaican negroes, i.e., aliens, had usurped the Reservation government.[1] As a rule, such allegations did not distinguish between Afro-Americans born on the Coast and those who had emigrated to the region more recently.[2]

That the events of 1894 have been termed Reincorporación by mestizo Nicaraguans and Overthrow (*uovatruo*) by Afro-American Creoles is a clear indication of the contested perspectives each group adopted on national history.[3] Although the Reservation's integration into the Nicaraguan state occurred by force and apparently against the will of the majority of its inhabitants, little violence was actually used.[4] Nicaraguans were driven out of Bluefields by an uprising on the 5th of July backed mainly by parts of the Afro-American population.[5] However, casualties were small in number and

1  See Madriz to Guzmán (April 1, 1894) and Informe del comisionado del gobierno al ministro de la gobernación, Managua (May 30, 1894), both in Pérez-Valle (1978: 177, 205f); Lacayo to Bingham, Bluefields (March 3, 1894), Cuadra Chamorro (1964: 190f); Barrios to the Earl of Kimberley, London (September 22, 1894) and From the Military Prosecutor, Bluefields, (August 16, 1894), both in Confidential Print 6585: 133, 279f.
2  One exception is Madriz to Ministro de Gobernación (Bluefields, March 30, 1894), Pérez-Valle (1978: 169).
3  For detailed discussions of the Reincorporation, see Cuadra Chamorro (1964); Laird (1972); Rossbach and Wünderich (1985); Gabbert (1992: 138-167).
4  A petition to the British Queen Victoria "not to allow a forcible incorporation" was signed by 1,800 people, including around fifty Miskitu headmen. The overwhelming majority was Creole. See The Chief of the Mosquito Indians to the Earl of Rosebery, Bluefields (March 8, 1894), PRO, FO, Confidential Print 6547: 87-104.
5  See Gabbert (1992: 149-158) for a detailed analysis of this event.

the attempt to reinstate the Reservation government was frustrated within days due, for the most part, to Britain's refusal to back this endeavor.

Besides this lack of external support, the political order of the Reservation no longer matched the local power balance. While the Afro-American population had grown considerably, the position of the Creole-dominated Reservation government had already begun to erode in the 1880s.[1] At that time primarily US firms began to invest in banana plantations, woodcutting and mining in the region (Gabbert 1992: 93-98). US entrepreneurs eventually became the most powerful economic group in the region, but lacked political representation in the government of the Reservation. The US colony had grown to five hundred people, one-fifth of whom resided in Bluefields alone (Morrow 1930: 3). They rejected the Reservation government not only for its policies, but also because it was composed of Creoles, whom they despised as "Jamaica niggers" (MB 1894: 307; Rossbach and Wünderich 1985: 71; Bravo to Gosling, September 13, 1892, Alvarez Lejarza, Vega Bolaños and Aleman Bolaños 1966: 29). Afro-Americans were not allowed to appear at meetings of US businessmen: "The members of the Club hold the coloured population in such contempt that they never admitted one amongst their members, not even the most prominent of the Jamaican oligarchy" (*Remarks*, n.d., PRO, FO, Confidential Print 6585: 315).

However, essential conflicts of interest lay at the bottom of white contempt for the Reservation government. While foreign entrepreneurs considered the Reservation a tax haven and a place to make short-term profits, the missionaries and the Reservation government had the long-term prosperity of the region on their agenda and tried to protect small holders and middle-range entrepreneurs.[2] A British captain concluded:

1 Kalb (1893: 263f) estimates the Reservation population at 7,500 inhabitants (4,000 Indians and 3,500 Afro-Americans and whites) in 1893. However, this estimate is probably too low. The Nicaraguan engineer José Vitta (1946) provides the most detailed population information for 1894. A calculation based on his data comes to a total population of 31,000 inhabitants in the Departamento Zelaya, as the Nicaraguan part of Mosquitia was called after the Reincorporation. I estimate the Reservation's population in 1894 at 23,000–25,000 inhabitants (including 1,500 on the Corn Islands, which the Nicaraguans had occupied in 1890). Among them were probably 8,500 to 9,500 Afro-Americans. Their share in the Reservation's population would thus have risen from less than ten percent to between thirty-seven and forty-one percent. They were concentrated in a few settlements. 4,500 Afro-Americans lived in Bluefields and Pearl Lagoon alone (Vitta 1946: 26, 32).

2 See MB (1893: 244); Kalb (1893: 282); Schneider (1899: 100f, 128); Gabbert (1992: 141); Wünderich (1990: 76); Vilas (1992: 85f).

The whole arrangement was admirably suited when the Treaty and Constitution were originally formed for the wants and happiness of the Indians, and the country has been most prosperous and happy. But the increased trade and development of business with the United States has caused an invasion of exploiters (some of doubtful character), and with whom this mild and patriarchal kind of Government was quite unable to cope or keep in order.[1]

Another crucial weakness of the Reservation lay in the marked bipolarity of the Nicaraguan Mosquitia between a rural northern area, mostly inhabited by Miskitu and Sumu, and the south where Afro-Americans prevailed and the only major towns were situated. The Reincorporation affected the Miskitu in the north much less than the Afro-Americans in the southern urban centers. As mentioned earlier, part of the Miskitu population had been under Nicaraguan rule since 1860, at least formally, and even those who lived within Reservation territory were politically marginalized, as were other indigenous groups. The leading groups in the Reservation, the Creole elite and the Moravians, never tried to mobilize the active support of the Indians. During the Reincorporation the missionaries and the deposed Reservation government did everything possible to prevent them from engaging in acts of resistance to the Nicaraguans, directing their hopes entirely towards protection by the British government (MB 1894: 155; PA II, 2: 322; Danneberger 1951: 333).

For the Miskitu and other indigenous groups in the region, the Reincorporation went hand in hand with growing integration into the enclave economy in a subaltern position, mostly as small producers of cash crops, rubber gatherers or unskilled laborers (Gabbert 1992: 170f). In general, however, this did not lead to complete proletarianization, since most Indians retained access to basic means of production, such as arable land, boats and fishing equipment. Integration into the Nicaraguan state remained nominal and the government had little or no presence in the villages up to the 1970s (Helms 1971: 158-159, 166, 174-179; Nietschmann 1973: 59-60).

The growing presence of foreign capital since the 1880s prevented the Creole elite from becoming a regional bourgeoisie. The Afro-American population lost most of its control over the means of production. Although banana plantations had contributed to the economic prosperity of many Creoles, they were now almost completely dominated by North Ameri-

---

1  Captain Curzon-Howe to Vice-Admiral Sir J. Hopkins, Bluefields (March 18, 1894), PRO, FO, Confidential Print 6547, NMHD: 374.

can companies (Gabbert 1992: 97f, 168-178). Thus, the year 1894 not only marked the triumph of Nicaraguan nationalism but also, and possibly even more so, the victory of foreign companies. Although many Afro-Americans were able to fill middle-level positions in these large enterprises, in the commercial sector and in professions that required a high standard of education, they were barred from access to leading posts in the regional economy of the US-owned enclaves in banana production, mining and lumbering. Up to the 1930s, when foreign investment declined, these positions were filled for the most part by North Americans (Gabbert 1992: 204-206).

The Mosquito Convention, which sanctioned the Reincorporation, marked the end of the region's political autonomy. It granted a number of privileges to the Mosquito Indians, such as tax and military service exemption, and it is important to note that this document had the character of a treaty. Hence the local population was recognized as a contractual partner and not treated merely as subjects of government dispositions (Rossbach and Wünderich 1985). The Creoles, however, were not even mentioned in the document. In fact, both Creoles and Indians were excluded from leading positions in local political and administrative institutions established by the Nicaraguan government after 1894, most of which were held by mestizos from the Pacific areas of the country (cf., e.g., Ruiz y Ruiz 1927: 72f, 100, 126).

Conclusion

As the material presented here has shown, the Miskitu were largely excluded from political participation in the government of the Mosquitia from the 1830s. The Mosquito kingdom and the Mosquito Reservation were dominated by foreign interests, such as Belizean traders, the British, German missionaries, and a small circle of Creoles. However, penetration of the Indian communities by government structures remained minimal, allowing the villages to preserve a high degree of autonomy. Although the Miskitu constituted the largest population group, their political role was almost nil. This reflected their geographical dispersion and segmentary political structure, as well as their division between three political entities after 1860: Honduras, Nicaragua and the Mosquito Reservation.

Miskitu political fragmentation and the cleavages between the north, with a Miskitu majority, and the south, where Creoles account for a significant portion of the population, have influenced the development of the Nicaraguan Mosquitia to the present day. They form the origins, for example, of two autonomous regions created in 1987 as a result of a great divergence in the interests of each group.[1]

## References

BL, OPL — British Library, London, Official Publications Collection, Confidential Paper 4013 Confidential Print 308.

GBFO — Great Britain, Foreign Office, British and Foreign State Papers, 1849-1850. Vol. 38 (1862). London.

LAL — Latin American Library, Tulane University, New Orleans. MIC 736: US Dept. of State, Dispatches from US Consuls in Belize, January 2, 1869 - Sept. 28, 1875, reel 4. MIC 757, Great Britain, Foreign Office, Mosquito, consular reports, 1844-45, reel 1.

MB —Missionsblatt der Brüdergemeine, Herrnhut. Vols. 1848-1900.

NMHD — *The Nicaraguan Mosquitia in Historical Documents, 1844-1927.* Oertzen, Eleonore von; Lioba Rossbach and Volker Wünderich (Eds) (1990) (Berlin: Reimer).

PA — *Periodical Accounts relating to the Foreign Missions of the Church of the United Brethren.* London. I. Series, Vols. 19-22 (1847-1858); II. Series, Vols. 1-2 (1890-1895).

PRO, FO — Public Record Office, Foreign Office, London Confidential Prints 6198, 6547, 6585, 6757, 6885.

### Books and Articles

Alvarez Lejarza, E.; Vega Bolaños, A. and Bolaños Gustavo, A. (1966) 'Como reincorporó Nicaragua su costa oriental' in *Revista Conservadora* Vol. 14, No. 6, pp. 1-35.

Bard, S. A. (1855) *Waikna, or, Adventures on the Mosquito Shore* (New York, Harper & Brothers).

Bell, C. N. (1862) 'Remarks on the Mosquito Territory, its Climate, People, Productions' in *Journal of the Royal Geographical Society* Vol. 32, pp. 242-268.

Bell, C. N. (1899) *Tangweera. Life and Adventures among Gentle Savages* (London, E. Arnold).

Bolland, N. O. (1977) *The Formation of a Colonial Society. Belize, from Conquest to Crown Colony* (Baltimore, The John Hopkins University Press).

Bourgois, P. (1986) 'The Miskitu of Nicaragua. Politicized Ethnicity' in *Anthropology Today* Vol. 2, No. 2, pp. 4-9.

Brown, W. (1990) 'The Mosquito Shore and the Bay of Honduras during the Era of the American Revolution' in *Belizean Studies* Vol. 18, No. 2/3, pp. 43-64.

---

1 See Gabbert (1992: 331-334 and 2006: 94-96) for a discussion on the contradictions between the Miskitu and Creoles in the autonomy process and the disparate character of each ethnic community, on which these contradictions were based.

Consejo de Ancianos de la Nación Moskitia (n.d. [1994?]) 'Que es el Consejo de Ancianos de la Nación Moskitia?' http://www.puebloindio.org/moskitia/consejo. htm [consulted 2/18/2010].

Conzemius, E. (1932) *Ethnographical Survey of the Miskitu and Sumu Indians of Honduras and Nicaragua* (Washington, D.C., Smithsonian Institution).

Crowe, F. (1850) *The Gospel in Central America* (London, Charles Gilpin Publishers).

Cuadra Chamorro, P. J. (1964) *La réincorporación de la Mosquitia* (León, Ed. Hospicio).

Danneberger, A. (1951) 'The Atlantic Coast of Nicaragua, Central America: Its Political, Economic and Religious Conditions' in *Transactions of the Moravian Historical Society* Vol. 14, pp. 325-340.

Dawson, F. G. (1986) 'Robert Kaye y el doctor Robert Sproat: Dos británicos expatriados en la costa de los mosquitos, 1787-1800' in *Yaxkin* Vol. 9, No. 1, pp. 43-63.

Dennis, P. A. (1982) 'Coronation on the Miskitu Coast' in *The Geographical Magazine* Vol. 54, No. 7, pp. 392-395.

Dennis, P. A. and Olien, M. D. (1984) 'Kingship among the Miskitu' in *American Ethnologist* Vol. 11, No. 4, pp. 718-737.

Documentos (1946) 'Documentos en los cuales se refieren los sucesos ocurridos en Bluefields, república de Nicaragua en el año de 1894' in *Revista de la Academia de Geografía e Historia de Nicaragua* Vol. 8, No. 2, pp. 49-68.

Dozier, C. L. (1985) *Nicaragua's Mosquito Shore. The Years of British and American Presence* (Alabama, University of Alabama Press).

Dunham, J. (1850) *Journal of Voyages* (New York, The Author).

Earle, T. (1997) *How Chiefs Come to Power. The Political Economy in Prehistory* (Stanford, Stanford University Press).

Fellechner, A. M.; Müller, D. and Hesse, C. L. C. (1845) *Bericht über die im höchsten Auftrage seiner Königlichen Hoheit des Prinzen Carl von Preussen und Sr. Durchlaucht des Herrn Fürsten v. Schoenburg-Waldenburg bewirkte Untersuchung einiger Theile des Mosquitolandes, erstattet von der dazu ernannten Commission* (Berlin, A. Duncker).

Floyd, T. S. (1967) *The Anglo-Spanish Struggle for Mosquitia* (Albuquerque, University of New Mexico Press).

Gabbert, W. (1990) 'Das 'Königreich Mosquitia' - eine ethnohistorische Untersuchung zur politischen Organisation der Miskitu, 1670-1821' in *Wiener Ethnohistorische Blätter Heft* Vol. 35, pp. 45-70.

Gabbert, W. (1992) *Creoles - Afroamerikaner im karibischen Tiefland von Nicaragua* (Münster, Lit).

Gabbert, W. 'Ethnogenesis in Caribbean Nicaragua: The Creoles' in Bugge, H. and Rubiés, J. P. (Eds) (1995a) *Shifting Cultures. Interaction and Discourse in the Expansion of Europe* [Periplus Parerga Vol. 4] (Münster, Lit), pp. 203-217.

Gabbert, W. 'Two Cultures or One? Social Stratification and Cultural Diversity among Afro-Americans on Nicaragua's Mosquito Coast' in Hoogbergen, Wim et al. (Eds) (1995b) *Born out of Resistance* (Utrecht, ISOR Press), pp. 263-273.

Gabbert, W. (1996) 'Gesellschaftlicher Umbruch und relative Deprivation - eine religiöse Heilsbewegung in der Atlantikregion Nicaraguas 1881/82' in *Sociologus* Vol. 46, No. 1, pp. 78-106.

Gabbert, W. (2002) 'Miskitu Political Organization, 17th to 19th Centuries' 101 meeting of the American Anthropological Association, New Orleans, November 20-24.

Gabbert, W. (2006) 'Concepts of Ethnicity' in *Latin American and Caribbean Ethnic Studies* Vol. 1, No. 1, pp. 85-103.

Gabbert, W. (2007) 'In the Shadow of the Empire - The Emergence of Afro-Creole Societies in Belize and Nicaragua' in *Indiana* Vol. 24, pp. 39-66.

Gabbert, W. 'Ethnicity and Social Change - Miskitu Ethnogenesis in Eastern Nicaragua' in Raab, J. (Ed) (in press) *New World Colors: Ethnicity, Conflict, and Belonging in the Americas* (Hamburg, Lit).

Girsewald, K. V. (1896) *Sechs Monate in Nicaragua* (Braunschweig, Rauert & Rocco Nachf.).

Goett, J. A. (2006) *Diasporic Identities, Autochthonous Rights: Race, Gender, and the Cultural Politics of Creole Land Rights in Nicaragua* (The University of Texas at Austin, Ph.D. dissertation).

Gordon, E. T. (1998) *Disparate Diasporas. Identity and Politics in an African-Nicaraguan Community* (Austin, University of Texas Press).

Hale, C. R. (1994) *Resistance and Contradiction. Miskitu Indians and the Nicaraguan State, 1894-1987* (Stanford, CA, Stanford University Press).

Government of the Mosquito Reservation (1884) *Formation of the Municipal Authority for the Government of the Mosquito Reservation. Its Constitution, Laws, and Regulations and Code and Form of Civil and Criminal Procedure* (New York, Burr Publishing House).

Hawley, S. 'Does God Speak Miskitu? The Bible and Ethnic Identity among the Miskitu of Nicaragua' in Brett, M. G. (Ed) (1996) *Ethnicity and the Bible* (Leiden, New York and London, E. Brill), pp. 315-342.

Helms, M. W. (1969) 'The Cultural Ecology of a Colonial Tribe' in *Ethnology* Vol. 8, No. 1, pp. 76-84.

Helms, M. W. (1971) *Asang. Adaptations to Culture Contact in a Miskitu Community* (Gainesville, University of Florida Press).

Helms, M. W. (1986) 'Of Kings and Contexts: Ethnohistorical Interpretations of Miskitu Political Structure and Function' in *American Ethnologist* Vol. 13, No. 3, pp. 506-523.

Hodgson, R. (1766): 'Some Account of that Part of the Continent of America, called the Mosquito Shore, as at Present actually both possessed and used by the Subjects of G. Britain' Public Record Office, Foreign Office Correspondence 53, Vol. 10 (London).

Jarquín M, H. (2004) 'Proclama independentista inquieta en la RAAN' in La Prensa June 6, *http://www.laprensa.com.ni/archivo/2004/junio/06/regionales/* [access 1/4/2009].

Kahle, G. and Potthast-Jutkeit, B. (1983) *Der Wiener Schiedsspruch von 1881: Eine Dokumentation zur Schlichtung des Konfliktes zwischen Grossbritannien und Nicaragua um Mosquitia* (Köln, Böhlau).

Kalb, C. d. (1893) 'Nicaragua: Studies on the Mosquito Shore in 1892' in *Journal of the American Geographical Society of New York*, Vol. 25, pp. 236-288.

Keely, R. N. (1894) 'Nicaragua and the Mosquito Shore' in *Popular Science Monthly* Vol. 45, pp. 160-174.

Laird, L. K. (1972) 'Origenes de la reincorporación nicaragüense de la Costa Atlántica' in *Revista Conservadora* Vol. 28, No. 149, pp. 1-57.

Macgregor, J. (1847) 'Commercial Tariffs and Regulations of the Several States of Europe and America', Parts 17, 18, and 19: *The Spanish American Republics* (London).

Manning, W. R. (ed.) *(1932-35): Diplomatic Correspondence of the United States. Inter-American Affairs 1831-1860* (Washington D.C.: Carnegie Endowment for International Peace).

Martin, C. A. 'Dreißig Jahre praktischer Missionsarbeit in Moskito von 1859-1890' in Schneider, H. G. (Ed) (1899) *Moskito. Zur Erinnerung an die Feier des fünfzigjährigen Bestehens der Mission der Brüdergemeine in Mittel-Amerika* (Herrnhut, Missionsbuchhandlung), Teil 2.

Morrow, R. L. (1930) 'A Conflict between the Commercial Interests of the United States and its Foreign Policy' in *Hispanic American Historical Review* Vol. 1, pp. 2-13.

Naylor, R. A. (1960) 'The British Role in Central America prior to the Clayton-Bulwer Treaty of 1850' in *Hispanic American Historical Review* Vol. 40, No. 3, pp. 360-382.

Naylor, R. A. (1967) 'The Mahogany Trade as a Factor in the British Return to the Mosquito Shore in the Second Quarter of the Nineteenth Century' in *Jamaican Historical Review* Vol. 7, pp. 40-67.

Nietschmann, B. (1973) *Between Land and Water; the Subsistence Ecology of the Miskitu Indians, Eastern Nicaragua* (New York, Seminar Press).

Oertzen, E. v. (1985) 'El colonialismo británico y el reino Misquito en los siglos XVII y XVIII' in *Encuentro* Vol. 24/25, pp. 5-28.

Oertzen, E. v. 'The British Protectorate up to 1860' in Oertzen, E. v.; Rossbach, L. and Wünderich, V. (Eds) (1990) *The Nicaraguan Mosquitia in Historical Documents, 1844-1927. The Dynamics of Ethnic and Regional History* (Berlin, Reimer), pp. 18-40.

Offen, K. H. (1999) *The Miskitu Kingdom. Landscape and the Emergence of a Miskitu Ethnic Identity, Northeastern Nicaragua and Honduras, 1600-1800* (PhD dissertation, University of Texas at Austin).

Offen, K. H. (2002) 'The Sambo and Tawira Miskitu: The Colonial Origins and Geography of Intra-Miskitu Differentiation in Eastern Nicaragua and Honduras' in *Ethnohistory* Vol. 49, No. 2, pp. 319-372.

Olien, M. D. (1983) 'The Miskitu Kings and the Line of Succession' in *Journal of Anthropological Research* Vol. 39, No. 2, pp. 198-241.

Olien, M.D. (1985) 'E. G. Squier and the Miskitu: Anthropological Scholarship and Political Propaganda' in *Ethnohistory* Vol. 32, No. 2, pp. 111-133.

Olien, M. D. (1987) 'Micro/Macro-Level Linkages: Regional Political Structures on the Mosquito Coast, 1845-1864' in *Ethnohistory* Vol. 34, No. 3, pp. 256-297.

Olien, M. D. (1988a) 'Imperialism, Ethnogenesis and Marginality: Ethnicity and Politics on the Mosquito Coast, 1845-1864' in *Journal of Ethnic Studies* Vol. 16, No. 1, pp. 1-29.

Olien, M. D. (1988b) 'Were the Miskitu Indians Black? Ethnicity, Politics, and Plagiarism in the mid-nineteenth Century' in *Nieuwe West-Indische Gids* Vol. 62, No. 1/2, pp. 27-50.

Olien, M. D. (1998) 'General, Governor, and Admiral: Three Miskitu Lines of Succession' in *Ethnohistory* Vol. 45, No. 2, pp. 277-318.

Parsons, J. J. (1954) 'English-speaking Settlement of the Western Caribbean' in *Yearbook of the Association of Pacific Coast Geographers* Vol. 16, pp. 2-16.

Pérez-Valle, E. (Ed) (1978) *Expediente de campos azules: Historia de Bluefields en sus documentos* (Managua).

Pim, B. (1863) *The Gate to the Pacific* (London, Lovell Reeve & Co.).

Pim, B. and Seemann, B. (1869) *Dottings on the Roadside in Panama, Nicaragua, and Mosquito* (London, Chapman and Hall).

Porta Costas, A. 'Relación del Reconocimiento Geométrico y Político de la Costa de Mosquitos' [1790] in Suárez, V. (1908) *Relaciones históricas y geográficas de América Central. Colección de libros y documentos referentes a la historia de América* (Madrid), Vol. 8, pp. 257-286.

Potthast, B. (1988) *Die Mosquitoküste im Spannungsfeld britischer und spanischer Politik 1502-1821* (Köln/Wien, Böhlau).

Roberts, O. W. (1827) *Narrative of Voyages and Excursions on the East Coast and in the Interior of Central America; Describing a Journey up the River San Juan, and Passage across the Lake of Nicaragua to the City of León: Pointing out the Advantages of a Direct Commercial Intercourse with the Natives* (Edinburgh, Printed for Constable & Co.).

Rossbach, L. and Wünderich, V. (1985) 'Indianische Vertragsrechte und nicaraguanischer Nationalstaat: Die Miskito-Konvention von 1894' in *Peripherie* Vol. 20, pp. 65-92.

Ruiz y Ruiz, F. (1927) *La Costa Atlántica de Nicaragua* (Managua, Tipografía Alemana).

Sahlins, M. D. (1963) 'Poor Man, Rich Man, Big-Man, Chief: Political Types in Melanesia and Polynesia' in *Comparative Studies in Society and History* 5, pp. 285-303.

Sandner, G. (1985) *Zentralamerika und der ferne Karibische Westen: Konjunkturen, Krisen und Konflikte, 1503-1984* (Stuttgart, Steiner).

Schneider, H. G. 'Kurzer Abriß einer Geschichte der Brüdermission in Moskito von 1849-1898' in Schneider, H. G. (Ed) (1899) *Moskito. Zur Erinnerung an die Feier des fünfzigjährigen Bestehens der Mission der Brüdergemeine in Mittel-Amerika* (Herrnhut, Missionsbuchhandlung), Teil 1.

Sonnenstern, M. v. (1971) 'Geografía de Nicaragua para el uso de las escuelas primarias de la república' [Original 1875] in *Revista Conservadora* Vol. 27, No. 131, pp. 1-28.

Squier, E. G. (1854) 'San Juan de Nicaragua' in *Harper's New Monthly Magazine* Vol. 10, pp. 50-61.

Squier, E. G. (1969 [1855]) *Notes on Central America; particularly the States of Honduras and San Salvador* (New York, Harper and Brothers).

Sujo Wilson, H. (1991) 'Historia oral de Bluefields' in *Wani* Vol. 9, pp. 25-39.

Taylor, M. A. (Ed.) (1891) *Election and Inauguration of the Hereditary Chief of the Mosquito Reservation* (Bluefields, Office of the *Bluefields Messenger*).

Thompson, D. A. (2000) 'Masters of Ceremony: The British Monarchic Project in Mosquitia, 1800-1860' in *South Eastern Latin Americanist* Vol. 43, No. 3, pp. 1-20.

Vilas, C. M. (1992) *Estado, clase y etnicidad: La costa atlántica de Nicaragua* (México, D.F., Fondo de Cultura Económica).

Vitta, J. (1946) 'La Costa Atlántica' [Original 1894] in *Revista de la Academia de Geografía e Historia de Nicaragua* Vol. 8, No. 2, pp. 1-46.

Williams, M. W. (1965) *Anglo-American Isthmian Diplomacy, 1815-1915* (New York, Russell & Russell).

Wünderich, V. 'The Mosquito Reserve and the Aftermath of British Presence' in Oertzen, E. v.; Rossbach, L. and Wünderich, V. (Eds) (1990) *The Nicaraguan Mosquitia in Historical Documents, 1844-1927. The Dynamics of Ethnic and Regional History* (Berlin, Reimer), pp. 60-87.

Young, T. (1842) *Narrative of a residence on the Mosquito Shore, During the Years 1839, 1840, & 1841; with an Account of Truxillo, and the adjacent Islands of Bonacca and Roatan* (London, Smith, Elder and Co.).

# CHAPTER 2. REBELLION FROM WITHOUT: FOREIGN CAPITAL, MISSIONARIES, SANDINISTAS, MARINES & GUARDIA, AND COSTEÑOS IN THE TIME OF THE SANDINO REBELLION, 1927–1934

*Michael J. Schroeder and David C. Brooks[1]*

On 7 January 1929 Stephen Boudier, the "head of the community Mosquito Tungla" on Nicaragua's Atlantic Coast penned a semi-literate English-language petition to the "Commander in Chief of the U.S.M.C." (United States Marine Corps) in the area:

> We of this Canton Tungla beg to inform you of our state and situation about this place, It seems our Government has throwed us away here, I think or we think that since there is business movements around these places, it should be no more than whrite [right] that there should be some kind of Protection, should be sent here for fear of Rebels and out lawed people, as there is a lot of Liquor sold around here, or even a Commission of the Government part should pass here every once in a while. We rites to you as we know that the U.S.M.C. or [are] here to keep peace and order in the country. So we waits that you will try and do something for us, or please inform the one that can do something for us here. Also we rites you as our first station, that should look at us if we have to look further for this please inform us. And still we hope to get good informations

---

1 The authors would like to point out that the views expressed in this chapter do not represent the views of the US State Department.

from you. Remaining yours and Obedient, Head of the Community of Mosquitos Tungla, /s/ Stephen Boudier.[1]

This rustic and all-but-forgotten petition, which prompted a two-man Marine patrol to journey up the Prinzapolka River to investigate conditions in Tungla, represents but one of thousands of untapped archival documents that offer a new window on the dynamics of war, rebellion, community struggle, collective identity, collective action, state formation, and Coast autonomy during a critical period in Nicaraguan and Atlantic Coast history: from the civil war of 1926–27 to the emergence of Sandino's armed nationalist challenge to US military intervention and the US-supported government in Managua (May 1927–February 1933), to the final withdrawal of the US Marines in January 1933 and Sandino's assassination by the Guardia Nacional in February 1934. The Tungla petition, for instance, echoes the language of the period of the British protectorate of Mosquitia (what the British called the Mosquito Reserve) before the Reincorporation of 1894, when the Miskitu governed themselves under British aegis. Appealing to the "first station" of the US Marines for "protection" from "rebels" and "to keep peace and order" — the "second station," presumably the king or his equivalent — the Tungla Miskitu community used an old political tactic in a new and dangerous political and military milieu. Over the next few years, as the Sandino rebellion simmered and the Great Depression threw thousands out of work, other Miskitu communities on the east coast did the same thing, petitioning both the US and British governments for protection from the "tyrannical" rule of Nicaragua — the "Spaniards," based in Managua, who governed a land that they had never fully incorporated into the national polity.

In this chapter we delve into several largely ignored but exceptionally illuminating collections of documents to offer a fresh interpretation of the dynamics of warfare, social revolution, and community struggle in Nicaragua's Atlantic Coast region in the time of the Sandino rebellion. The most important collection, to which we devote the bulk of our attention here, are the records of the US Marines and Nicaraguan Guardia Nacional (Record Group 127), housed in the US National Archives in Washington D.C. The records include not only military reports of stunning variety but also petitions from communities like the one cited above; letters from citizens; cap-

---

1 Stephen Bouldier, Tungla, to Commanding Officer USMC, Puerto Cabezas, RG127/204/1.

tured rebel correspondence; official investigations and legal proceedings; newspaper clippings; photographs; and others.

Supplementing this sprawling collection of documents are a variety of other, largely untapped archival sources, including those housed in the UK's Public Record Office, the US State Department, the personal papers collections in the US Library of Congress, the Marine Corps Research Center in Quantico VA, the archives of the Moravian Church in Bethlehem PA, as well as newspapers and published and unpublished Sandinista correspondence. In this effort we challenge scholars interested in the question of *Sandino en la costa* (the title of Volker Wünderich's 1989 book) to cast a broader net to encompass these and other sources in order to construct a more robust and compelling interpretation of an exceptionally complex subject. To help serve this end, we are publishing many of these documents online as a documentary annex to the present chapter.[1]

Overall, the scholarly literature on the Sandino rebellion on Nicaragua's Atlantic Coast can be described as interpretation-rich and evidence-poor. We divide this literature into two broad schools of thought: those who see a fundamental confluence of interest between Costeños and Sandino and widespread popular support for the rebel movement, especially among Miskitu Indians, and those who see a fundamental conflict of interest between Sandino and Coast folk and little Miskitu sympathy or support for Sandino or the Sandinistas.

In the first camp are scholars such as Jorge Jenkins Molieri (1986), Volker Wünderich (1989), Charles R. Hale (1994), and Jorge Eduardo Arellano (2008). The Nicaraguan Sandinista anthropologist Jorge Jenkins Molieri examines Miskitu political–cultural history and struggles for autonomy in the context of what he analyzes as foreign and imperialist domination — first by Great Britain and the Moravian Church, then by US-dominated extractive enclave companies and the US Marines, then through the complex combination of finance capital acting in concert with the US national security state. Molieri argues that Sandino and the Sandinistas garnered widespread support among non-Christianized Miskitu Indians and black West Indian laborers and their descendants, and that Sandino's project of national sovereignty was in fundamental concert with Costeño popular aspirations and interests. Molieri also discerns a major divide between Moravian-influenced indigenous communities — who tended to see Sandino as

---

1  See http://www.sandinorebellion.com/HomePages/eastcoast.html.

a "bandit" — and those indigenous communities not under the influence of the Anglophile Moravian missionaries (Molieri 1986: 117–172).

Volker Wünderich, in his carefully wrought 1989 study, argues that "it has been impossible to reconstruct the perspective of the indigenous peoples of the Atlantic Coast" because most extant sources consist of "texts produced by missionaries, anthropologists, and journalists." Framing his conclusions as "very preliminary," he argues that "in general one can observe that in all the places where the indigenous were not under the direct influence of the missionaries [Moravians] . . . emerged the spontaneous cooperation of Miskitus and Sumus with Sandino's Defending Army of Nicaraguan National Sovereignty [abbreviated EDSN]" (Wünderich 1989: 15). In other words, in general the "pagan Indians" aided Sandino while the "Christian Indians" opposed him — though Wünderich also rightly acknowledges that "the possibilities for cooperation depended on many other factors. We are not able to construct a general position of indigenous peoples" (Wünderich 1989: 78-79). Yet despite this explicit caution in framing the analysis, the overall thrust of the study imputes a significant degree of "spontaneous cooperation of Miskitus and Sumus" with the EDSN and an organic confluence of interest and identity between the two groups.

Building on Wünderich, Charles R. Hale argues that in the 1920s and 1930s the Sandinistas enjoyed "extensive Miskitu support" (Hale 1994: 54). But while Hale's Miskitu on the whole sympathized and cooperated with Sandino and the Sandinista rebels, over time, Hale maintains, the indigenes' "Anglo affinity" and "contradictory consciousness" transformed and distorted individual and collective memories, such that by the 1970s and 1980s, most Miskitus remembered not cooperation but conflict between themselves and Sandino's Sandinistas (Hale 1994: 15, 36). Hale's is a daring, creative, and ultimately unconvincing argument. In addition to the published literature, Hale's evidence consists mainly of fine-grained (and often arguable) interpretations of oral interviews he conducted during his fieldwork in the 1980s. In his most recent book, Jorge Eduardo Arellano, the undisputed dean of Nicaraguan letters, essentially reprises to the Molieri thesis. In broad strokes, Arellano asserts that, with respect to the question of "popular support" for Sandino, "this support did not exclude the Zambos — a good portion of them fought with Sandino — and Sumu and Miskitu Indians in the zone between the Coco and Grande de Matagalpa rivers, who also lent their immensely valuable services, such as serving as officials and boatmen" (Arellano 2008: 74).

Offering a very different interpretation of the Costeños' reception of Sandino and the Sandinistas are scholars such as Mary W. Helms (1971), Philip Dennis and Baron L. Pineda (2006). In addition, Jeffrey L. Gould (1998), who does not specifically address the question of popular support for Sandino on the east coast but instead focuses on the struggles of indigenous communities in Western Nicaragua, offers an insightful analysis of the potential inherent conflicts between Sandino's ideology and nationalist program and the historical experiences and aspirations of the Atlantic Coast's indigenous peoples. Helms, an American anthropologist who conducted a community study of the Miskitu village of Asang in the mid-1960s, observed that community members remembered Sandino and the Sandinistas as "bandits" and the period of the Sandino rebellion as the "bandit" period (Helms 1971: 113). Anthropologist Philip Dennis found similar recollections of the period under examination here in the Atlantic Coast village of Awastara. In the memory stream he encountered, Miskitu villages recalled Sandinista brutality directed against Americans in highly negative terms. As he recounted, the Miskitu

> . . . personally knew American plantation managers and other foreigners, whom they generally admired, who were killed by the [Sandinista] guerrillas. Sandinista attacks devastated the Standard Fruit Company installations in April 1931, which directly hurt the Miskito small holders who sold bananas to the company. Far from feeling exploited by Standard Fruit, the Miskito were delighted to have a market for their products and a chance to buy consumer goods in the company commissary at Puerto Cabo Gracias a Dios [sic]. Drawn into the wage economy during the last 100 years, the Miskito strongly identified with the companies and with their foreign managers (Dennis 1981: 28384).

Hale and Molieri dismiss Helms's informants' memories as distorted and inaccurate and do not engage with Dennis's account.[1] Historian Jeffrey L. Gould argues that Sandino's "Indohispanic" nationalism embraced the paternalistic, mestizo-centric ideology and perspective that Spanish-speaking Western Nicaraguans had conventionally imposed on the indigenous

---

1 Molieri 1986, chapter 3, Sandino y los mískitos," does not cite Helms or engage with her evidence, though he cites her in chapter 2, p. 83; the only secondary works cited in chapter 3 are the writings of Sandino, Carlos Fonseca, and a variety of other pro-Sandino texts; Hale explicitly dismisses Helms' argument; Hale (1994: 56-58).

peoples across the country, including the Atlantic Coast region. Anthropologist Baron Pineda characterizes Sandino's attitude toward indigenous Costeños as "patriarchal and condescending," asserting that "Sandino was generally unpopular among Costeños. . . . During my fieldwork in Puerto Cabezas, I spoke to a number of Costeños who were Sandino's contemporaries and who claim that Sandino was known in the Atlantic Coast as a "bandit" in the 1930s. In the present, Costeños generally continue to refer to Sandino as a bandit" (Pineda, 2006: 101-02).[1]

In sum, the existing literature on "Sandino en la costa" evinces a significant bifurcation, with some scholars positing a high degree of popular support for Sandino's rebels among Costeños, particularly Miskitu Indian communities, while others see little collaboration but ample conflict, tension, and indigenous opposition to the Sandinistas' nationalist, anti-interventionist, anti-imperialist movement. In our view, none of the extant literature offers a sufficiently compelling interpretation of the social and cultural dynamics set in motion on the Coast by the complex interplay of US military intervention, the formation of the Guardia Nacional (a Nicaraguan constabulary officered by U.S. Marines during the time of the intervention), the sporadic military incursions of the Sandinistas, the growth of the mostly US-owned mining, lumbering, and fruit companies and enclaves, the steady expansion of the influence of the Moravian Church in the 1920s and 1930s, and the spread of labor unrest and popular organizing, especially from the onset of the Great Depression in early 1930.

In what follows we map out an alternative interpretation of "Sandino en la costa" based on our reading of the thousands of documents referenced above — particularly the voluminous records of the US Marines and Nicaraguan Guardia Nacional. The story told by these documents is very different and considerably more nuanced than the scholarly interpretations surveyed above. That story shows, for instance, that individual Miskitu and Creole men did indeed fight in Sandino's ranks — and in the ranks of the Guardia Nacional — but mainly that the Miskitu and Creole men, women, and communities in the Atlantic Coast region worked to keep themselves at arm's length from the struggle. It shows that the Creole population of Bluefields, Puerto Cabezas, and elsewhere did not see either national redemption or liberation in Sandino's nationalist program. While many avoided actively helping the Marines and Guardia Nacional, others quite possibly

---

1  See also chapter 3 of this volume.

a sizable majority, hoped that US forces might stay and that Washington might adopt the Coast as a protectorate in the fashion of the British. Importantly, it shows the extraordinarily variegated nature of the Costeño physical and human landscape, and points up the need for a more nuanced social-geographic and cultural-geographic understanding of the region as a whole as well as its numerous sub-regions. What it mainly shows is that the principal concern of the great majority of ordinary Costeños was in maintaining their community autonomy, human dignity, and customary rights in the face of multiple internal and foreign threats and opportunities — from rebels and outlaws, from Nicaraguan and US military forces, and from the ever-present specters of poverty, hunger, and violence. Despite Sandinista and some scholarly interpretations to the contrary, for most Coast folk, Sandino and Sandinismo represented yet another imposition from Spanish-speaking Western Nicaragua, an imposition they worked diligently to blunt and avoid. We begin with the premise that understanding "Sandino en la costa" and the Marines and Guardia on the Coast requires a *Costeño-centric* approach, which is what we try to sketch in the following pages using the bodies of evidence outlined above. These records, largely ignored by scholars, comprise an immensely rich and valuable source that can go a long way toward addressing the apparent deficit of evidence for this critical period of Coast history. Some might find problematic our extensive reliance on these records, arguing that the Marines and Guardia Nacional likely under-reported Sandinista activity due to their one-sided view of the rebels, whom they dismissed as mere "bandits". We disagree, and we explain why more fully below.

In order to impose some order on the documents from which we take representative soundings here, we divide the following discussion into three sections, each focusing on a key set of social relationships. We begin with relations between Costeños and two key foreign actors on the Coast: the mostly US-owned export enterprises (mining, lumbering, and banana companies) and the Moravian Church. We then turn to what is probably the most controversial of these relationships: those between various groups of Costeños and members of Sandino's EDSN. Finally we turn to relations between Costeños and the US Marines and Nicaraguan Guardia Nacional. In so doing, we cannot pretend to offer more than a rough sketch of an exceptionally complex set of social relationships that did not remain static but changed in response to key events — such as the onset of the Great

Depression from early 1930, or the Sandinistas' murder of the Moravian missionary Karl Bregenzer by EDSN general Pedro Blandón in March 1931. Following Wünderich, our treatment here is "very preliminary" while at the same time, we hope, highly suggestive of further avenues of research.

Costeños, Foreign Capital, and Moravian Missionaries, 1920s–1930s

Scholars since the 1970s have shown the variety of ways that Nicaragua's Atlantic Coast region became firmly integrated into the global capitalist economy by the second half of the nineteenth century, with the rubber boom of the 1860s and 1870s, the growth of mahogany lumbering and banana production from the 1880s, and the expansion of gold and silver mines from the 1890s (Helms 1971: 27-30; Hale 1994: 39-40). By the first decades of the twentieth century, these export-oriented economic activities had created a highly complex and variegated regional political economy. The two major social groups on the Coast — Miskitu Indians and Africa-descended Creoles — had come to depend on these foreign enterprises for their livelihoods, fostering among both a generalized cultural sensibility that Hale (1994) and others describe as "Anglo affinity."

For the Miskitu in particular, periodic labor in the mostly US-owned export enclaves and trade and barter relations with agents of foreign capital built on a long tradition of mutually friendly relations with Great Britain and English merchants and traders, an era of British suzerainty that officially ended with the Nicaraguan government's "Reincorporation" of the Atlantic Coast region in 1894. Miskitu men would typically work for several days or weeks in the export enclaves to earn enough money to purchase useful items such as metalware (machetes, guns, kettles, tools), clothing, and other manufactured goods — or sell locally-produced goods to local traders — to earn the cash needed to purchase these and other items. Despite their growing integration into the global economic system, in short, the Miskitu did not relinquish their traditional reliance on hunting, fishing, craftwork, agriculture, and horticulture. Instead they formed what Helms called a "purchase society," in which these new forms of goods procurement were synthesized with more traditional Miskitu ways of making a living (Helms 1971: 6).

For Creoles, dependence on foreign capitalist enterprises was on the whole far more pronounced. A small but significant proportion became city-based small business owners, particularly in Bluefields, wholly reliant upon markets, credit, and buyers, while most worked as laborers in the mostly US-owned fruit, lumbering, and mining enclaves in the interior, wholly reliant upon wage labor (Pineda 2006: 21-66). For coastal folk in general, and as the Great Depression clearly demonstrated for West Indian laborers (who out-migrated by the thousands from mid-1930), prosperity and living standards hinged on continued foreign investment from the United States and Great Britain.

The records of the US Marines and Guardia Nacional de Nicaragua offer an important window on these economic and cultural patterns as they persisted into the period of the US military occupation of the Coast (1927-33). Here we work to read these US military records "against the grain" (Guha 1988). Many reports include information about coastal people's economic and political activities that is incidental to the main points being conveyed — bits of data, often from the margins and interstices, that offer tantalizing glimpses of specific events. Comparing, contrasting, and analyzing those accumulated nuggets of information with respect to time-period, location, and theme can offer an exceptionally nuanced portrayal of events and trends.

A typical example is a report by Guardia Nacional Second Lieutenant Francisco Gaitan on the subject, "Information of attack to Cuartel of Kisalaya on 21 April 1932 by bandits." It begins with a brief background to the attack that references Miskitu activities in the zone:

> On the 20th of the present month, about 8:00 a.m., several pitpans with Mosquito Indians went down the River [Río Coco] from Saulala, Santo Domingo, Laguna Tara, Pranza and Urapany who the day before had gone to bring bananas from their properties and to sell the bananas to the contractor of the company B. L. C. of Puerto Cabezas, Señor Eduardo Araña, who travels by Urapany on the Coco River about 30 miles from this Headquarters [Kisalaya]. On further questioning they stated that they had seen the bandits who had gone after them and that two Indians who had gone along with them had disappeared and that possible had been made prisoners or killed by the bandits.

The next day "an old woman, Silvia Martinez, mosquito Indian who was made prisoner by the bandits a couple of days ago at Urapany returned to our camp; while she was with her husband picking bananas bandits appeared, her husband ran away but she could not do it and was apprehended by the bandits."[1] From this report, and many others like it, we catch glimpses of the Miskitu "purchase society" described by Helms (1971), among other things. In a rich portrayal of one aspect of the local political economy, Lt. Gaitan describes Miskitu Indians from five proximate villages along the Río Coco harvesting bananas from their individual properties and acting in concert, perhaps to fetch a higher price or as part of a regular trading schedule, transporting the produce to a private contractor. Araña and other such contractors, we can reasonably infer, made regular trips up and down the Coco River purchasing such commodities from local Indian communities. Gaitan had no reason to lie or embellish his report with respect to the economic activities of these Miskitu Indians. If the official Guardia discourse that the Sandinistas were "bandits and outlaws" provides the overarching structure of his narrative, there is little reason to doubt the information about Miskitu economic activities. What might be doubted here is the depiction of these Miskitu being made prisoner. Perhaps Silvia Martinez voluntarily joined the rebels for a day to share information and camaraderie before returning to her community? Without more evidence it is impossible to determine in this case. With more evidence — with an accumulated body of such nuggets over time and space — an accurate answer becomes more probable. By our reading, this accumulated body of evidence strongly suggests that Silvia Martinez and the other "two Indians" were indeed temporarily seized as prisoners by the EDSN, probably to serve as food preparers and camp laborers.

Another glimpse into Miskitu economic and cultural practices comes from the published account of two Marine pilots "forced down in the jungles" of the coastal interior by enemy fire in July 1931. For days the two aviators slogged through mosquito-infested swamps and jungles toward Puerto Cabezas. "At times we waded up to our necks in muck, mire and rushes. To our great relief we met a friendly Indian from Sandy Bay, a trading post of the United Fruit Company. He was hunting alligators . . . the Indian helped us into his pipante [canoe] . . . and we finally arrived in Sandy Bay about dusk. Here we were the guest of other Indians, some of whom spoke spiggoty English. They gave us hot coffee, tortillas, and six eggs each" (Heritage 1932: 14–15). There is no reason to doubt this brief narrative, consistent with everything else we know about the period and suggestive of broader patterns in Miskitu society and culture. If one chanced to encounter any given

---

1 F. Gaitain, Kisalaya, 22 April 1932, RG127/202/1.

Miskitu man during this period, the odds were not small that he would be hunting alligators or turtle or other game, or that he worked sporadically for foreign export companies, or that if he were to come across two lost and bewildered US Marines he would spontaneously render his assistance and his community extend its hospitality. The story offers a glimpse of key aspects of Miskitu economy and culture during this period.

Cutting logs to float downstream to sell to American and other lumber companies was another way that Miskitu Indians earned cash to purchase useful items, as illustrated in a *Report of conditions on Wangks River* (Coco River) by department commander H. D. Linscott. Remarking on a report that "Honduranean soldiers are occupying Waspook" and other points along the river, Linscott noted that "it is further reported that they have prohibited the Indians from cutting logs."[1] In other words, absent the reported interference by Honduran soldiers, the Indians in question would have been "cutting logs" and floating them downstream to sell to buyers — another way the Miskitu earned cash to buy useful items.

In these and other ways, Marine-Guardia reports provide valuable information on local political economies and everyday economic practices of ordinary Coast dwellers during this period. Such data can help us to construct a richer understanding of the extraordinarily variegated nature of the social relations of labor, production, trade, and consumption in the Atlantic Coast, and a more nuanced understanding of its economic and social geography and how it changed over time. In particular, weekly intelligence reports from late 1927 to late 1932 from Bluefields and Puerto Cabezas offer a fine-grained portrait of local economic conditions and trends, while reports from the region's various outposts permit a richer understanding of economic conditions and demographic patterns in the interior. To cite one typical report, Bluefields commanding officer, D. J. Kendall, reported in November 1927 the following under the heading ECONOMIC CONDITIONS:

> Economic conditions on this coast are now extremely serious due to the fact that the Mahogany companies have given but very few contracts and are expected to almost completely retire from business on this coast. If this occurs it is not believed that the banana companies and the Bragman Bluff Lumber Company with its yellow pine lumber business and railroad construction can possibly absorb the extra labor. If such occurs Indians formerly working in the logging crews will go back into the hills and continue their existence without difficulty but only a small number of the Spaniards from

---

1 Linscott, Report, 3 Sept. 1929, RG127/204/1.

the cutting crews can be absorbed in the banana plantings and prac-
tically all the negros who have been occupied in operating power
boats in the mahogany business and stevedoring the mahogany
ships will be without a means of livelihood. Some of the younger
ones can return to their homes in the Gran Caymans Islands or Jamaica but the majority of them are older men who have spent their
lives here and own small properties in the towns and their situation
will be very severe.[1]

From this single paragraph one can glean considerable information
about local economic conditions, the region's racial demography, and related topics. Kendall's analysis of the likely differential impact of economic
changes on distinct Coast ethnic groups is both sound and penetrating. Especially notable is his portrayal of the strong dependence of non-Indian east
coast working people, i.e., Creoles and Spaniards, on foreign-owned fruit
and lumber companies.

In considering the key role played by foreign capital and the Moravian
Church in shaping social identities in the Atlantic Coast, it is important to
reflect on the synthetic nature of Coast culture and the Costeños' creative
and historically-rooted establishment of synergies with external forces as a
way of defining themselves and their culture and bolstering their autonomy
from Spanish-speaking Nicaragua. From the seventeenth century, Coast
folk had used foreign alliances with English buccaneers and appropriated
foreign symbols such as the Miskitu king to counteract the power of the
Spanish and reinforce their own culture. Far from purely "outside" influences, Costeños borrowed from the British to bolster their autonomy and
independence. In this way, the persistent identity of the Miskitu should
not be seen as the endurance of some unchanging primordial indigenous
culture. In key respects the Miskitu survived their encounters with modernity by selectively adopting foreign customs, symbols, and resources that
fit their needs.

We can see this dynamic operating during the period under study here.
Miskitu Indians related to enterprises like Standard Fruit company at
Bragmans Bluff and the Moravian Church in a similarly "part time" fashion.
Bragmans' managers persistently complained of the inconstancy of Miskitu
workers, who would work in the fields long enough to buy a desired tool
or article, like an ax or a shotgun, and then return to their villages. With
regard to both Moravian missionaries and foreign companies, the Miskitus'

---

1  Kendall, Intelligence Report, 9 Nov. 1927, RG127/43A/9.

material position and the limited resources and goals of the outsiders afforded them this autonomy. Companies like Bragmans Bluff were not the first wave of a white settler movement destined to push the indigenes off their land, and the Moravians were a pacifist, purely missionary church, unaccompanied by any military arm (unlike, for example, the Spanish Catholic Church's spread across Latin America). Thus, to a degree highly modulated by the indigenes' own customs, both foreign companies and the Protestant faith became integrated into Coast culture as sources of intermittent income and spiritual solace. By the time under study here, work for the lumber and fruit companies and membership in the Moravian Church, though neither universal nor constant, had become incorporated as parts of Atlantic Coast social structure and culture. These were both elements that would play a strategic role in the conflict to come.

In terms of demography, the 1920 census enumerated 638,119 people in Nicaragua and 42,806 on the Atlantic Coast, comprised of the Department of Bluefields and the Comarca of Cabo Gracias a Dios. Of the latter, 16,710 spoke Miskitu and 19,975 were "Protestants."[1] Data in the 1920 census may well understate the influence of religion as a major distinguishing element of Coast (vs. Hispanic Nicaraguan) culture. In fact, the Moravian Church had converted many Coast inhabitants to Protestantism after that institution's missionaries first reached the region in 1847. The Miskitu Indians had never converted to Catholicism, and so the Moravians real competition came not from Catholic Christians, but from the indigenes own traditional shaman, the *sukias*. In a way that resembled their on-again, off-again relationship with the large fruit companies, Miskitu Indians converted to Moravian Protestantism in a highly selective and partial way. Despite mass conversions during the so-called "Great Awakening" of the 1880s, Moravian Church missionary records also contain consistent complaints of backsliding among the faithful, particularly in the areas of alcohol consumption and fornication. The Indians undoubtedly benefited from the missionaries' presence, especially in regard to health, education and sanitation. By the time of the Sandino rebellion, conversion was nearly universal along the coast and became less pronounced as one moved inland.[2] For these reasons, daring Moravian missionaries like Karl Bregenzer moved deep inland — in Bregen-

---

1  *Censo general de 1920.*
2  MCA, Periodical Accounts, v. 5, 19021904, p. 263.

zer's case into the Sumu Indian village of Musawas — precisely to bring the Bible to the unconverted Indians of the interior.

## Coastal Folk and Sandinistas

Bregenzer, in fact, remains a Moravian martyr, remembered by Coast folk to this day. On March 31, 1931, he was killed by Sandinista troops led by Sandinista general Pedro Blandón, who ordered one of his men to split Bregenzer's head with a machete. Blandón had accused Bregenzer of operating as a "miserable spy" for the Guardia Nacional and the Marines.[1] Bregenzer's murder would prove a severe setback for the Sandinistas, a stain on their reputation that would affect Costeño attitudes decades later. His death was not an isolated incident, but instead represented one episode on a larger struggle among the Sandinistas themselves as to how to treat the culturally distinct inhabitants of the Atlantic Coast. Sandino himself, in an apparent debate with his trusted Coast interlocutor, Abraham Rivera, talked about the need eventually to deal with "the priests who are on the Río Coco," a clear reference to the region's Moravian pastors:

> Perhaps, when we have the opportunity to take civil, military and religious control of our Republic. . . . In those happy days for our people, there will take place among us an analysis of all that blocks our human progress, and these elements will be swept away with brooms of bayonets. In this, I refer to the priests who are on the Río Coco.[2]

Though Sandino apparently planned to eliminate the missionaries, the Moravians themselves recognized that his movement did attract some followers from among their flocks in the interior. Moravian records portray a population suddenly stressed and divided by the presence of the Sandinistas, with the threat of death for collaboration with the Marines–Guardia operating as a key to the calculus of survival for the indigenes. As Moravian Brother Dannenberger wrote to his ecclesiastical superior in June 1932:

> Apart from those who have fled down the river there seem to be three groups. One group has made common cause with lawlessness and violence. Another set of men are trying hard to have nothing to do with wickedness, but do not leave the district partly because

---

1   Bregenzer had in fact had contact with Marine-Guardia patrols that had passed through the area, but he was in no sense a "spy"; on the killing see MCA, E. Bregenzer to S. H. Gapp, 22 April 1931, SPG Corr. 1931, S.H. Gapp Files; see also Borhek, 1949: 3541.

2   Sandino to Rivera, 22 Feb. 1931, in Ramírez 1984, v. 2: 163; our translation.

they are afraid that if they go they may lose their land, and partly because they have been threatened with death if they have anything to do with the Guardia. They have suffered greatly and are often in hiding. Such are Reuben Wilson of San Carlos, Jesus of Asang, and with them Petrona Spicer of Sang Sang whose husband — a bad character — is dead. In between these two groups is another which does not wish to commit any crime, but which co-operates [*sic*] with the insurgents in the honest belief that they are the real rulers of the land. They have been told that the Lower Wangks and Bilwi are the only parts that still hold out; and that soon as these are captured the Indians who took refuge there will be severely punished.[1]

In fact, as seen below, the Sandinistas established a strong if intermittent presence upriver in Bocay, a launching base for operations that apparently imposed significant burdens on local populations. In 1934, after the conflict between Sandino and the Marines–Guardia had ended, Moravian missionary Guido Grossman toured this area and recorded three significant vectors of difficulty that the indigenes had experienced in their contacts with Sandinista fighters: material losses, the exploitation of Miskitu women, and attacks on Moravian churches. As noted, the Miskitu prized items they were able to purchase through intermittent wage labor with the fruit and lumber companies along the Coast. These same articles were evidently coveted by at least some of the Sandinista fighters who ventured into the interior. Grossman reported numerous instances of theft perpetrated against the locals; for example:

> The rebels stole everything from the people - whatever they had on their bodies: shoes, hats and other pieces of clothing. Some who did not want to hand their property over were killed. . . . One lady told me that "We thank God that he gave us tunu [a local bark traditionally used by the Indians as clothing] because otherwise we would have had to walk around naked."[2]

Implicit gender-based behaviors appear to have characterized the sometimes tense relations between Sandinista fighters and Moravian Miskitu. Grossman, for example, noted that Miskitu men had been forced to row for the Sandinistas. Particular burdens fell upon Miskitu women, who were frequently obligated to cook and clean for the Sandinista fighters. According to the missionary, some Sandinistas also "forced innocent maidens

1 MCA/SPG Corr., Jan.July 1932, S.H. Gapp Files, letter from G.R. Heath to Bro. Danneberger, 8 June 1932.

2 *Missionsblatt der brudergemeine*, MaiJun 1934, pp. 7782, MCA; trans. by Bruce Gudmundsson, Institute for Tactical Education, Quantico VA, and Matthew Boyse, US Dept. of State; hereafter "Grossman Visit".

into immorality." Such actions were reportedly resisted by the Indians. As Grossman related, one mother refused to let her daughters be taken by the Sandinistas, who then "mishandled her" and "threatened to kill her." The Miskitu woman responded by crying and praying. At that moment a higher Sandinista official (possibly Abraham Rivera) arrived and ordered both the mother and her daughters released. Despite his criticisms of the Sandinistas, Grossman drew a generous conclusion from this: "And out of this . . . I saw again that the higher [Sandinista] officials didn't approve of what was blamed on General Sandino, all the bad things that the lower ones and the bandits did."[1]

Sandinista fighters also directly threatened Moravian churches in the villages of Asang and San Carlos. In both cases, Grossman attributed the survival of the houses of worship to divine intervention. In fact, in each case, a Sandinista leader had restrained his men, preventing them from destroying the structures. As Grossman described the incident in San Carlos, the Sandinista fighters operated in a way reminiscent of the fierce anti-clericalism that had affected other revolutionary and rebel movements in Latin America, openly mocking the Moravians' spiritual authority:

> [The] bandits called all the people from the town together at the church and said mockingly, "All right, pray and see if your God will save the church from fire." Before the bandits could light the fire to the leaf roof, two large boats came from the upper river and when a higher leader landed and he saw what his people were about to do, he forbade it and said let the church stand. It can serve as a dance hall or school house.[2]

In the final analysis, the Sandinistas appear to have alienated a key Coast institution in their actions against the Moravian Church. Sandino's Indo-Hispanic nationalism was ill-equipped to help him understand the complexity and density of the Coast inhabitants' relationship to the Moravians. As with the fruit and lumber companies, Coast folk adopted and adapted Moravian religious beliefs in ways that reinforced their identity. In taking a sometimes harsh line toward the Moravians, the Sandinistas created self-inflicted wounds that persist in Coast memories to this day. The divisions among Sandinista leaders on the question of how to treat the Moravians testify powerfully to this dynamic.

---

1 Grossman Visit.
2 Grossman Visit.

Let us cast a broader net to consider the Coast population as a whole. Recalling the range of colonists' attitudes toward the American Revolution and the war of independence against Great Britain (1776–1783), the American patriot John Adams famously observed that approximately one-third of the populace were patriot; one-third were loyalist; and one-third were indifferent to the struggle. Subsequent generations of historians have largely affirmed Adams's proportions. Analyzing Coast folks' attitudes toward the Sandinistas and the Marines–Guardia, we discern a quite different set of proportions. Overall we suggest that only a tiny percentage actively aligned themselves with either side. In general and overall, support for the Sandinistas appears to have been strongest among Spanish-speaking Western Nicaraguans and weakest among Creoles and Miskitus, while opposition to the Sandinistas and support for the Marines–Guardia appears to have been strongest among Creoles and Miskitus and weakest among Spanish-speaking Western Nicaraguans. This lack of popular support for the Sandinistas and lack of opposition to the Marine intervention is expressed in the documentary record in multitudinous ways, but mainly through silence: i.e., in the systematic absence of positive evidence that the Marines–Guardia detected among the great majority of Coast dwellers any significant degree of popular support for the rebels or popular opposition to themselves. This stood in stark contrast to the situation in Las Segovias, where the Marines and Guardia continually (and as the war intensified in 1931–32 increasingly) detected widespread popular support for the rebel movement. In the "Eastern Area" (the Marine–Guardia designation for the Atlantic Coast region), their reports consistently failed to mention any such dynamic, and frequently positively identified its opposite.

One characteristic of the local reaction which remains to be more closely examined is the apparent fundamental pacifism of the Miskitu and the Creoles, who generally appeared very reluctant to bear arms for either side. Simultaneously, we have also discovered a very strong — yet also essentially pacifist — hope that the U.S. forces would stay permanently on the Coast and essentially adopt the region as a kind of U.S. version of British Honduras (later Belize), effectively reproducing the pre-1895 international connections that had guaranteed Coast autonomy from Nicaragua. The petitions themselves vary in quality, with some far better written than others, suggesting that they originated with both Miskitu and Creoles (Coast Creoles tended to be better educated). The historical importance of this strong preference for the United States should not be underestimated. Part of the problem in interpreting Coast history, we maintain, is the tendency of outsiders — whether Nicaraguan, Sandinista (then and today) North American, or European scholars — to try to shoehorn concepts of Coast identity into preconceived nationalistic categories. If the Miskitu and Creole preference for the United States over the Sandinistas was not expressed in violent ways, it was expressed strongly and persistently (as a later generation of Sandinistas would find out in the 1980s when they brought their own version of militant nationalism to the Coast). For Sandino, this political preference, what Hale has aptly called "Anglo affinity," constituted a serious cultural barrier he was unable to overcome. This same Anglo affinity also presented complications for Washington, which had no intention of re-creating or assuming the burdens of maintaining a permanent Coast presence. Further research into this phenomenon could fruitfully inquire into the origins of Coast folks' strong pacifism. Was it purely a pragmatic response to the intrusion of armed foreigners from Western Nicaragua (the EDSN) and the United States (the Marines)? How did Moravian teachings reinforce these pacifist tendencies? And finally, how does the Miskitu and Creole's political strategy compare to the efforts of other ethnic minority groups to maintain their autonomy via emphasis on long-distance historical connections (e.g., Quebecois, Hong Kong Chinese, English-speaking inhabitants of the Malvinas/Falklands, and the Nepalese Gurkhas)? In this way, the Miskitu could become subjects for fruitful comparative study on how indigenous peoples have tried to use international alliances to reinforce local autonomy.

While it was rare for Marine reports from the Coast to express concern about pro-Sandino sentiments of the populace, occasionally they did, as in the following April 1928 report that followed on the heels of the first major Sandinista incursion into the Bonanza and Pis Pis mining districts. Evident here is what Brooks has called the "ethnic differential" in the political preferences of Coast folk regarding US intervention and the Sandinista rebellion:

> GENERAL STATE OF THE TERRITORY OCCUPIED. Unsettled. The recent movements of a group of bandits in the vicinity of Tunky and the Pis Pis mines has created considerable unrest. The foreigners here and in the vicinity with capital invested on this coast feel that more protection should be afforded them than is available at present. There is an undercurrent of feeling here sympathetic to

the Sandinista forces. No outward sign of this feeling is in evidence but nevertheless it exists. The Creoles are not disposed toward Sandino, they are for the continuance of present conditions and realize that any break down of business activities in this area means money out of their pockets. As far as the Mosquitos are concerned they are more or less indifferent to events, if a band appears and forces them to join they will follow along without argument and if not bothered they will go about their regular routine of eating and sleeping with enough labor at times to obtain certain necessities.[1]

The pro-Sandinista sentiments detected by Sage were not apparent among Creoles, Miskitu Indians, or propertied foreigners. The only other sizeable demographic group on the Atlantic Coast consisted of transplanted Western Nicaraguans and other Spanish-speaking Latin Americans working in the mostly US-owned export enclaves. It was this group, we argue, to which Sage was referring when he noted an "undercurrent of feeling sympathetic to the Sandinista forces."

In a more compelling demonstration of the generalized absence of popular support for Sandino's nationalist rebellion in the Atlantic Coast, for most of the five years from early 1928 to late 1932, Marine–Guardia intelligence reports consistently described military and political conditions in the Eastern Area as "quiet." The only exceptions were during and immediately following major Sandinista incursions into the region (see Table 1, below). This contrasts sharply with the situation in Las Segovias, where Marine–Guardia reports show that armed rebel bands were common and "organized banditry" endemic. By November 1929, the Marine contingent in the Eastern Area consisted of a mere 102 Leathernecks (eight officers and 94 enlisted) and 201 native Guardia (16 officers and 185 enlisted), for a total of 303 Marines and Guardia charged with "maintaining law and order" in the entire Eastern Area.[2] From January 1930 until the end of the war, the number of active Guardia stationed in the Eastern Area hovered between 250 and 310 — roughly ten percent of the overall Guardia size of between 2,400 and 3,000 during this period. In the Eastern Area, the number of armed "civi-

---

1  A. H. Sage, Intelligence Report, Bluefields, 28 April 1928, NA127/197/1.

2  The Eastern Area extended from the Costa Rican border in the south to Cape Gracias in the north, and inland approximately 100 miles to include the Bonanza and La Luz mining districts; Major C. H. Metcalf, "An Estimate of the Situation in the Eastern Area of Nicaragua," 21 Nov. 1929, RG127/43A/24.

cos" organized in militias in various posts and outposts roughly equaled the number of men in the Guardia.[1]

How do Marine–Guardia reports portray Miskitu Indians and the relations between Miskitus and the Sandinistas? A March 1930 "Estimate of the Situation in the Eastern Area of Nicaragua" described the Miskitu Indian villages along the lower Río Coco as follows:

> Coco River from Cape Gracias to limit of navigation. A large number of Indian villages are scattered along this entire stretch of river. They are harmless peaceful people and will cause no difficulty to the government. Local government is practically non-existent but the Indian tribal government seems to be functioning to a sufficient extent to control the situation. The people are very poor, no work is available except on their own little ranches.[2]

In fact, for the entirety of the war, the Marines and Guardia were simply not concerned about Miskitu Indians allying with Sandino. By mid-1930 they were seriously considering a complete withdrawal from the whole of the Eastern Area, given its relative quiescence and the costs of maintaining an armed occupation. The only "critical points in the Area" were seen as "Puerto Cabezas and railway extension to the northwest . . . Foreign developments in the vicinity of Bluefields . . . [and the] La Luz Mining Area." None were considered under any type of serious threat.[3] As Marine Lt. W. W. Benson wrote in a personal letter to fellow Leatherneck Lt. W. C. Hall in July 1930, following Sandinista general Pedrón's brief raid on Bonanza Mine in mid-May, "Things are all quiet now . . . As far as the rest of the East Coast is concerned, things are pretty dull."[4] The *Record of Events* for July 1930 similarly reported, "No contacts with enemy forces during this period. . . . General state of the territory occupied: QUIET. . . . No known enemy in this area at the present time."[5]

This was during the same period that Las Segovias in Western Nicaragua seethed with popular resentment against the Marines and Guardia and teemed with rebel bands. During the same month of July 1930, in a rebel surge that followed Sandino's return from Mexico, Marine–Guardia

---

1 Annual Report of the Guardia Nacional de Nicaragua for the Period Commencing October 1, 1930 and Ending September 30, 1931, RG127/43A/30; on "civicos" see Weekly Intelligence Reports for Bluefields and Puerto Cabezas, *op cit.*
2 Major C. H. Metcalf, 11 March 1930, RG127/204/1.
3 Ibid.
4 Benson to Hall, 7 July 1930, LOC/Edson/19.
5 J. Marston, Record of Events for July 1930, Eastern Area, 31 July 1930, RG127/202/2.

intelligence reports for the Northern and Central Areas (encompassing the departments of Nueva Segovia, Estelí, northern Chinandega, and Jinotega) reported eleven active rebel *jefes* (chieftains) and fourteen military contacts with the rebel forces — an average of one armed encounter every 2.2 days.[1] Las Segovias, in short, was the heartland of the rebel movement and the east coast on the far periphery.

Notably, the Marines in the Eastern Area frequently grew concerned about labor unrest among banana and lumber company workers. Given Sandino's frequent appeals to Nicaraguan workers, an alliance between his forces and the Coast's agro-export working class would appear to have been a natural one. Indeed, conditions appear to have been ripe for striking just such a deal during much of the period. Yet in fact the Marines evinced very little concern about possible connections between the banana workers' organizing efforts and the Sandinista rebel movement. In his monthly report of November 1930, for instance, Bluefields-based U.S. Marine Captain John Marston observed:

> I have noticed on my inspections the ragged and tattered and ill-nourished appearance of hundreds of river dwellers who have lost their employment as workers with banana or mahogany companies. Under these conditions robbery and thievery and allied misdemeanors are certain to increase. Already two commissaries of the United Fruit Company subsidiary, the Cukra Development Company, have been robbed. . . . No serious disorders have yet occurred, but there is sufficient evidence to indicate a restlessness on the part of the laboring element, which may break out in violence at any time. There is growing resentment against the Government because of the high duties placed on food stuffs and other essentials of existence on the East Coast.[2]

Despite growing social stresses due to deteriorating economic conditions, Capt. Marston and others saw no evidence indicating Sandinista participation or involvement in these events. The Marines–Guardia kept scrupulous track of such trends, following up on rumors and reports on Sandino's influence among wage laborers. None proved substantive. For instance, in February 1929 the Periodic Intelligence Report in Puerto Cabezas, covering the previous week, noted in its closing paragraph: "MISCELLANEOUS: A report received of Sandino recruiting among laborers of farms on RIO GRANDE RIVER was investigated and it appears that most of farm

---

1  E. E. Larson, B-2 Report, Managua, 1 Aug. 1930, RG127/43A/4.
2  Marston, Record of Events for Nov. 1930, 3 Dec. 1930, RG127/202/2.

laborers lost within last month have gone to PANAMA looking for more lucrative work."[1]

Had Sandino's appeals resonated among East Coast wage laborers, more evidence of it would appear in the written records. Those records make clear, for instance, that some individual black Creoles and Caribbean laborers joined with Sandino's forces. But there is no evidence in Marine–Guardia records that Sandino's efforts to win over the support of Creoles and West Indian laborers generated any kind of institutional links with the east coast's emergent labor unions, mutual aid societies, or disgruntled working people in city or countryside. The reasons for this disconnect are complex, but at bottom the labor organizing efforts of wage laborers on the docks and in the banana plantations developed on an entirely separate economic, ideological, and cultural plane than Sandino's Segovias-based campesino-based nationalist rebellion. The origins, characteristics, and aspirations of the two groups were at core very different. In the economic sphere, Sandino stood squarely opposed to American intervention and American companies, while Creoles and West Indians depended upon those same companies to survive. The latter sought bargaining power with the foreign export companies — seeking higher wages, more secure employment, and the like through union organizing. Most working people on the Atlantic Coast did not want to destroy American capitalism in Nicaragua, as Sandino did. At a more cultural level, many Coast dwellers may have also viewed the "Spaniards" of Western Nicaragua as excessively violent and recoiled at the gruesome killings and mutilations that the Sandinistas so often inflicted on their enemies (Brooks 1997). In these and other ways, the core economic interests and basic cultural orientations of the Segovias-based Sandinista movement and the West Indian wage laborers of the Atlantic Coast were fundamentally at odds.

Some unemployed workers expressed their frustration and outrage at mounting unemployment and hunger by assaulting and robbing company stores and Guardia outposts, as in the case of the attack on the Guardia garrison in Rama on July 19, 1931, but overall their relations to the Sandinista movement remained tenuous. As area commander major C. A. Wynn described the origins of the assault on Rama:

> There were some hundred and thirty five laborers employed on the Rama-Managua Road just outside of Rama. These men gave no

---

1  H. Utley, 12 Feb. 1929, RG127/204/1.

trouble so long as they received pay for their work. When the Government took over this project recently there was immediately apparent a feeling of discontent. This feeling burst into mutiny Sunday night, July 19th when it became known that the Government had ordered work on the road to cease, and discharged the laborers without pay. The attack on the Guardia post at Rama resulted.[1]

The monthly record of events for Southern Bluefields also described the attack: "On July 19 at 20.00 a group of about 25 disgruntled employees of the Rama-Tipitapa carretera attacked the cuartel of the Guardia at Rama at the instigation, it is reported, of [Sandinista general] Pedron Altamirano." Later reports made no mention Pedrón's involvement, who was nearly 100 miles west of Rama at the time, sacking and looting the Javali mine near Santo Domingo in Chontales Department. The same monthly record of events for July 1931 described the "General Police Conditions" in the Eastern Area: "There have been a considerable number of robberies in Bluefields. This is due directly to unemployment and the consequent hunger suffered by the inhabitants.[2] The attack on Rama, like the great majority of such robberies and assaults on the east coast during this period, resulted from local conditions, expressed local grievances, and was neither planned nor carried out by the Sandinistas.

Indeed, considering the entire six years of the rebellion, Sandinista activities in the Eastern Area can best be described as a sporadic series of military incursions intended to garner material supplies for the war effort in the West, to gain recruits, and to score propaganda victories by striking at the symbols of US imperialism (mainly by looting and destroying US-owned mines and commissaries). Altogether there were eight major Sandinista military incursions into the Eastern Area. None lasted more than a few weeks, and all were conceived and carried out by the rebels as "expeditions" from their home bases in Las Segovias and adjacent zones in Jinotega and the Bocay River Valley. These rebel incursions are summarized in the following table.

---

1  C. A. Wynn, Conditions on the East Coast, 22 July 1931, RG127/202/1; see also F. Riewe, Report of Contact at Rama, 21 July 1931, RG127/200/1.
2  C. A. Davis, Monthly Record of Events for the Department of Southern Bluefields for July 1931, 11 Aug. 1931, RG127/202/2.

Table 2.1. Sandinista Military Incursions into the Eastern Area, 1927–1934[1]

| Dates | Description | Estimated No. of Rebels | Duration |
|---|---|---|---|
| 1928: April 12– May 8 | Gen. Gen. Girón Ruano, others, raids on La Luz and Bonanza Mines | 200 | 3 weeks |
| 1930: May 9–21 | Gen. Pedrón Altamirano, others, raids on La Luz & Bonanza Mines | 100 | 2 weeks |
| 1931: April 1–15 | Gen. Pedro Blandón, Timoteo Altamirano, Abraham Rivera, others raid on Logtown, Cabo Gracias & other points (Blandón killed) | 150 | 2 weeks |
| 1931: July 2–19 | Gen. Pedrón w/ 300 into Chontales; Gen. Carlos Salgado, Col. Abraham Rivera, others w/ 150 to Siuna Mines, Bocay & Lower Coco | 450 | 2.5 weeks |
| 1931: October 24–27 | Gen. Carlos Salgado, Lt. Col. Perfecto Chavarría to Lower Coco, raid on Louisiana Farm near Puerto Cabezas | 150 | 1 week |
| 1931: December 7–24 | Gens. Pedrón, Irías, Salgado, Cols. Rivera, Chavarría, others raid on Siuna Mine (Dec. 14), Neptune Mine (Dec. 18), Prinzapolka incl. Tungla (Dec. 20-25) | 400 | 2 weeks |
| 1932: May 15–25 | Gen. Pedrón raid on Bonanza Mine, Gen. Morales, Col. Rivera near Puerto Cabezas | 400 | 1.5 weeks |
| 1932: Nov. 1–5 | Unknown jefes near Cabo Gracias, Neptune Mine | 100 | 1 week |

It appears that none of these incursions gained the numbers of hoped-for recruits among Coast dwellers — though, it must be said, not for want of effort. In this previously unpublished manifesto of June 20, 1931, Sandino appealed for the support of the "oppressed men of our Atlantic Littoral."

MANIFESTO TO THE OPPRESSED MEN OF OUR ATLANTIC LITTORAL. Dear Brothers: You all understand that this continent in which we live was discovered on the 12th of October of 1492 by the Spanish. From the seas surged this continent when Atlantis sank, eighty-seven centuries ago. The Atlantic existed in the place that

---

1 Summary of information in Marine-Guardia intelligence reports, RG127.

today we call the Mediterranean Sea. Americo Vespucio [*sic*] was the name of the man who first mapped this continent, and for this reason this continent is called America. You have all probably also heard of the prophets, who were descended from the People of Israel, who, through Abraham, the SPIRIT of "LIGHT AND TRUTH," promised the people of Israel a Land that in those times was not known on the other continents. Spain was the country designated to discover the Land in question. Santiago, the brother of Jesus and also the son of Joseph and Maria, lived in Galicia. In this Promised Land discovered by the Spaniards there were founded all the races [of people] of the Earth. Jesus and all the Prophets have been Communists. For this reason, we will be, on this Promised Land, the principle sprouts of the followers of THE UNIVERSAL COMMUNITY. The dominant ones [*los suprematicos*] made a business of bringing from Africa Negros and selling them as slaves. Those who did this the most were the English. England, Germany, France and other European countries dedicated themselves to piracy after the discovery of America and in this way the Europeans set up colonies in the Americas. For a time, our very Nicaraguan Atlantic Coast was under the domination of England. Central America became independent from Spain on the 15th of September 1821, but, because of our natural resources, we in Nicaragua have become the special target of imperialist Ambitions. The Yankee bankers have set up a school for traitors of the Homeland in Nicaragua, but here in this same Nicaragua has surged up our Army of Liberation, which will show to the men of the Earth that this is not the hour of injustices. *Our Army is composed to Negroes, Indians, whites, etc. etc. and, without either racial or class bias, is dedicated to implanting the principles of human fraternity in Nicaragua.* And to do this, this Supreme Command asks for the ineffable moral and material support of all of the Nicaraguan People. Our Army understands that our people have been betrayed by their caudillo leaders and that, for this reason, they have remained indifferent before the calls to action that previous Manifestos like this one have made. Our Army is not a caudillo army. From its most humble soldier to its Supreme Chief, all its members are workers and peasants without prejudices in regard to [social] class, technocrat-intellectual [*cientificos*] or religion. Headquarters of the Defending Army of the National Sovereignty of Nicaragua, June 20, 1931. Homeland and Liberty, /s/ A. C. Sandino.[1]

In many ways it is a bizarre document, a fantastical epic narrative woven of Hispano-centric and Anglophobic images and tropes. On the one hand, Sandino reached out to the working people of the Atlantic Coast by emphasizing the universal and multi-ethnic nature of his army. On the other, he did so through a petition written in Spanish (a language not likely to be understood by many Miskitu and Creoles) expressing an almost magical-realist concept of history, a narrative that might have resonated among

---

1 Original document with seal, RG127/38/30; our translation and emphasis.

some Spanish speakers but that would likely have fallen on deaf ears when presented to Costeños. Sandino also condemned the imperialist domination of England and the *yanquis*. In these various ways, his narrative thus ran directly counter to the Coast's long history of Anglo affinity and creative responses to foreign connections, and for these and other reasons was highly unlikely to be well received by Miskitu Indians and Creoles.

The imported, external nature of the Sandinista movement in the Atlantic Coast region was expressed in many ways. Sandino called his forces operating outside Las Segovias "expeditionary columns" (*columnas expedicionarios*) led by "expeditionary chiefs" (*jefes expedicionarios*). The historian Neill Macaulay describes these incursions into the Coast as "raids," while even Charles Hale, who argues unconvincingly for "extensive Miskitu support" in the region, calls them "incursions" (Macaulay 1985: 186-213; Hale 1994: 53). Whether we label these "expeditions," "raids," or "incursions" — in our view all three terms are apt — the point is that these military actions by the EDSN were conceived and carried out as efforts to export Sandino's rebellion to zones outside of its core base of social support in Las Segovias and western Nicaragua. The revolution on the Coast, in short, was imposed from without, and despite their best efforts, the EDSN on the whole failed to create an organic and sustainable base of popular support among the Miskitu, Creoles, or other coastal folk.

Despite the cultural disjunctures and difficulties described above, the Sandinistas did succeed in garnering the support of indigenous communities further west, among the mostly Sumu Indians of the Río Bocay region. This vast, isolated, and sparsely settled zone (extending from the frontier of the eastern Segovias to the western frontier of the Bonanza-La Luz mining district, east of El Chipote, south to the upper reaches of the Pantasma Valley and Peña Blanca Mountain, and north up to the mouth of the Bocay and the town of the same name). This is the area where Sandino established his celebrated headquarters "El Chipotón," and where Sandinista general Pedrón Altamirano and his lieutenants regularly retreated after their periodic raiding expeditions into the Jinotega-Matagalpa coffee districts, Chontales, and the Eastern Area. It is also the same region that the anthropologist Mary Helms and others have identified as the heartland of the Sumu Indians (Helms 1971: 16-19; see also Brooks 1997: 215-19).

Much evidence indicates that the Sandinistas succeeded in winning over the majority of the Indians of the Río Bocay region and in gaining effective dominion over the entire zone. In his intelligence report of 20 February 1931, for instance, Northern Bluefields Department commander, colonial H. Stent, described Marine–Guardia knowledge of the situation:

> Reports from spies and Indians returning from up river state that. . . the bandit group at Bocay has become greatly increased in members during the past six (6) months. The main camp is some distance up the Bocay River. . . . A deliberate effort has been made [by the Sandinistas] to gain favor with the Bocay Indians with a view to having their support, and has met with considerable success. The Indians in this region professing themselves ready to take part in any attack on Guardia or expedition to Puerto Cabezas or Cabo Gracias. What means, exactly, has been used to gain the confidence of the Bocay Indians is not known, but their feelings and sympathies have been cleverly brought over to the side of the bandits [Sandinistas].[1]

Much other evidence supports Stent's observations on the Sandinista sympathies of the Río Bocay Indians. For instance, in his "Intelligence report on bandit activities" in the Siuna mining district, Capt. O. A. Inman reported that of the 300 "bandits" who raided the mines in December 1931, "75% of the band were Indians from Segovia and the Upper Coco, not to be used as machete men but as actual fighting men."[2]

Were these Río Bocay Indians "Costeños"? We argue that including them in Coast culture is problematic and inaccurate. The fuzzy frontier separating Western or Hispanic Nicaragua from the Atlantic Coast during this period represented a highly complex transitional zone in which mining enclaves had attracted significant numbers of Spanish-speaking immigrants to the region. Indeed, Sandino got his revolutionary start organizing Spanish-speaking workers at the San Albino mine in the eastern Segovias. Geographical factors also underscore the need for a careful definition of this transitional region, between Western Nicaragua and the Atlantic Coast. Over 100 miles of jungle and savannah separated Bocay Indians from the Atlantic littoral, where many of the key elements of Coast culture (Moravian influence and integration into the larger Caribbean economy) were present. The case of the Río Bocay Indians underscores the need for a more nuanced social-geographic understanding of what exactly constitutes Nicaragua's "Atlantic Coast" region. We argue that the Bonanza and La Luz/Siuna mining districts were also outside the Atlantic Coast region properly defined, despite their inclusion in the Marine–Guardia's "Eastern Area" designation.

---

1  Stent, Intelligence, 20 Feb. 1931, RG127/43A/1.
2  O. A. Inman, Intelligence Report, Puerto Cabezas, 1 Jan. 1932, RG127/206/1.

In our view, the western frontier of the Atlantic Coast region was located east of these much-mentioned (and frequently looted) mining zones.

Much more might be said on the mines — Bonanza Mine and the adjacent town of Neptune; the La Luz/Siuna/Wuani mining zones; and others. Because these were mostly US-owned properties, and sites of repeated Sandinista raids and relentless Marine–Guardia counter-insurgency operations, there exists considerable documentation about them. Scholars generally include these mining zones in their discussions of "Sandino en la Costa." We do not, except by way of these few words of explanation. In our view these mining zones were located outside of the Atlantic Coast region properly defined, and were not populated in their majority by coastal folk. Instead ownership, operations, and management were mostly American (with some elite east coast and European involvement) and the mine workers predominantly Spanish-speaking Western Nicaraguans, with Indians and Creoles in the minority.[1]

A highly revealing Marine–Guardia map produced during the war provides additional support for the foregoing arguments about Bocay Indians, the mining zones, and the absence of Sandinista sympathies and lack of opposition to the Marine intervention among most Costeños (see Map 1). Indeed, the map is suggestive of new ways of conceptualizing the political, social, and cultural geography of Nicaragua and the Atlantic Coast region during this period. The map identifies three zones: "Unoccupied Zone," "Disputed Zone," and "Pacified Zone." The "Pacified Zone" includes the entire east coast region (as well as the Pacific Coast region). The "Unoccupied Zone" embraces much of the north-central part of the country east of eastern Segovias, from a line extending north from the Jinotega highlands through Quilalí up to the Honduran border, including the entire Rio Bocay Valley — a vast and isolated zone that the Marines and Guardia only sporadically penetrated and never occupied. The "Disputed Zone" extends from Las Segovias to the coffee districts of Jinotega-Matagalpa, further south into Chontales, and north in a slender ribbon of territory up to the Río Coco, including the Bonanza and La Luz mining districts. In other words, the Marines–Guardia understood the entire east coast region to be a "Pacified Zone," despite having only a few hundred troops stationed there

---

1 C. F. Cresswell, Report of Neptune Mine, 12 Sept. 1929, RG127/204/1; see also the collection of documents at http://www.sandinorebellion.com/Top100pgs/Top100-p9a.html.

in a series of widely scattered outposts supported by only two main garrisons (Puerto Cabezas and Bluefields).

Map 1: US Marine Corps Map of Nicaragua, showing Unoccupied, Disputed, and Pacified Zones, and Rebel Routes of Supply & Communication, Jan. 1929. Source: RG127/43A/14.

This cartographic representation of the regional distribution of Sandinista support finds ample confirmation in Marine–Guardia intelligence reports. It might be argued that the Marines–Guardia systematically underreported the prevalence of rebel activity and popular sympathy for the rebels in the Eastern Area. The documentary record does not support this argument. In fact the Guardia Nacional proved increasingly adept at uncovering evidence of rebel activity and civilian rebel support in specific zones and locales, as the documentary record on Las Segovias makes plain. If a zone or district appeared "bandit infested," i.e., marked by generalized popular sympathy for the rebels, Guardia reports repeatedly hammered the point home. That was their mission: to "protect American lives and property."[1] What remained was to eradicate "organized banditry" (the EDSN) from the national territory. This was the Guardia's central mission until Sandino's assassination in February 1934, and they used most every tool at their disposal to achieve that end. It also bears emphasizing that by 1931 and 1932, Marine–Guardia spy networks and other sources of actionable intelligence became considerably denser and more sophisticated. For nearly six years the Marines and Guardia expended every effort to generate an accurate understanding of the size, strength, numbers, weapons, and locations of enemy forces across the country — a task they got considerably better at as time went on. For the Marines and Guardia, the accuracy and integrity of their internal reports was literally a matter of life and death.

This context established, let us examine what might be considered the "master" intelligence report — the GN-2 Report — from its inception in September 1930 until December 1932, after which the Marines departed.[2] The GN-2 represented a significant streamlining and centralization of the Guardia's military intelligence apparatus. Before the GN-2s appeared, each area, regiment, and battalion produced its own serial intelligence report (B-2s, R-2s, and Bn-2s, respectively). There was no single intelligence report covering the whole country. The GN-2s did just that, making it possible for scholars to compare the amount of space and attention devoted to different regions.

These 27 GN-2 Reports, totaling 567 pages and each covering a one-month period (an average of 21 pages per month), devoted a total 48 pages to events on the east coast — 8.5 percent of the total. Notably, this period (Sept. 1930-Dec. 1932) also includes six of the eight major Sandinista incursions into the Atlantic Coast region. In other words, more than 90 percent of the intelligence that the Marines and Guardia deemed worth disseminating, in their most comprehensive and sophisticated reporting mechanism,

---

1 This was the case until April 1931, when in response to Pedro Blandón's raid on Logtown and the evident impossibility and prohibitive cost of achieving that aim, the Hoover administration dropped it from its overall mission in Nicaragua; see e.g. Macaulay (1985: 198-99).

2 One GN-2 Report, for April 1932, has not been located; the complete list of serial intelligence reports, including the GN-2s, can be found at http://www.sandinorebellion.com/HomePages/IR-Docs.html.

dealt with the problem of "organized banditry" in Las Segovias and adjacent areas in the Pacific Coast region, and only a small fraction (8.5 percent)
dealt with the Atlantic Coast.

A similar proportion of military "contacts" took place on the east coast
(a "contact" was defined by the Marines–Guardia as a military encounter
between ground forces in which both sides discharged firearms). According to Schroeder's calculations, of a total of 735 military contacts from July
1927 to December 1932, thirty took place on the east coast.[1] In other words,
of 735 total ground combats and skirmishes between EDSN bands and the
Marines–Guardia, fewer than 4.1 percent took place in the Atlantic Coast
region — a number consistent with the 8.5 percent of the text of the GN-2
Reports devoted to events in the Atlantic Coast. These two independent
measures of Marine–Guardia documentation relative to the war between
themselves and the Sandinistas offer compelling evidence that the east
coast of Nicaragua was not of military concern for the Marines–Guardia.

In our view, the sources cited above make a strong case that the vast
majority of Coast folk did not join Sandino's movement. This is not to
argue that the Sandinistas garnered no support among Costeños. On the
contrary, there is ample evidence that some Miskitu and Creole men (and
perhaps women) joined the rebel ranks as combatants, soldiers, spies, boat-
paddlers, and in other capacities, particularly after the effects of the worldwide economic depression began to sink in from around mid-1930. Most
served close to their homes and communities, while some carried the fight
far into the Pacific Coast region. For example, during the Sandinista raids
on Chinandega and León departments in late 1932, Lt. W. Elmore reported
that "there are ten East Coast negroes" serving under "bandit" general Juan
Pablo Umanzor, while Lt. L. A. Kalman, describing the "bandit" group led
by "[Juan Gregorio] Colindres and [Carlos] Salgado, and possibly [Ismael]
Peralta" in the same EDSN offensive, included "about two hundred men,
some of them mosquito Indians, the latter I personally seeing, about five of
them escorting the Lewis Gun."[2] What exactly motivated these and other
Miskitus and Creoles to join with Sandino is not known. It is plausible that
Sandino's nationalist, anti-imperialist ideology attracted some, and that the
prospect of loot and adventure motivated others. Whatever the case, it is

---

1  Defined generously in this case to include the Bonanza and La Luz mining districts; Schroeder (1993: 321-40).
2  Guardia Newsletter No. 130, 3-16 Dec. 1932, RG127/43A/24.

clear that some Costeños journeyed far from their homes to fight for the Nicaraguan rebel leader.

A substantial percentage of the Miskitu Indians who cooperated with the rebels participated as the loyal clients of two key Sandinista actors on the east coast: Abraham Rivera and Adolfo Cockburn. Abraham and his cousin Guadalupe Rivera, members of a prominent Liberal family in Jinotega, ran a lumber concession in Santa Cruz at the confluence of the Pantasma and Coco Rivers in the eastern Segovias. A sizeable operation, their farm employed scores of Miskitu Indians and Spanish-speaking Nicaraguans cutting and floating logs down the Río Coco to Cape Gracias a Dios or Puerto Cabezas. Commissioned as a colonel in Sandino's army in May 1928, Rivera became one of Sandino's must trusted and important cultural intermediaries with the Miskitu. Rivera spoke Miskitu fluently and led columns up and down the Río Coco in various attacks (we also suspect that Rivera was the Sandinista commander who prevented the burning of the Moravian church in Asang). He also appears to have argued with Sandino over tactics to be used on the Atlantic Coast, maintaining that a softer approach was necessary (Brooks 1997).

Adolfo Cockburn, whose family hailed from the Grand Cayman Islands, was half-Miskitu, the son of an English man and Miskitu woman. Owner of a farm called Pitkira at Sacklin on the Río Coco and dubbed the "King of the Miskitu" by locals, Cockburn was not only physically imposing (at over 240 pounds) but fluent in Spanish, English, and Miskitu. He was also a Deputy in the National Assembly and one of the most important Sandinista leaders in the entire east coast until his death at the hands of the Guardia in 1931.[1] Like Rivera, Cockburn created a rare pole of support for Sandino in the region. But despite the best efforts of able lieutenants like Rivera and Cockburn, the fact remains that the Sandinistas were not able to garner the support of any other prominent cultural intermediaries capable of bridging the vast cultural divide between the "Spaniards" of Las Segovias and the predominantly Anglophile Creole, Miskitu, or "bamboo white" (a Marine term for propertied European-descended) Costeños. In a like vein, we have not uncovered a single Marine–Guardia report that identifies a specific Creole or Miskitu village or community on the east coast that was firmly allied

---

[1] Stent to Marston, 7 Feb. 1931, and Marston to Jefe Director, 4 May 1931, RG127/206/1.

with the EDSN. Nor is any such evidence reported in any of the published scholarly literature.

On the contrary, there is ample evidence of conflict and tension between the EDSN and east coast indigenous communities. As Captain M. A. Edson reported by telegram in early 1929 regarding conditions on the Upper Coco River, "this vicinity said to have been stripped [of] . . . beans, rice, beef, and fowls . . . last spring . . . by bandits".[1] Reports of Sandinista rebels looting Indian villages are peppered throughout the documentary record, accounts that find significant corroboration in the Moravian records. Operating without an enthusiastic social base, Sandinista columns depended on material aid requisitioned from a generally wary and ideologically distant local population. For instance, a highly credible intelligence report of February 1931 that corresponds in many specifics to everything else known about the period was framed as "information elicited from natives for the most part reliable":

> That the raid of the bandits in January last [1931], under Abram Rivera as Jefe was a mere scouting expedition, made to secure information, procure boats, and supplies, get recruits, and test out the Guardia strength. Arms were also taken from the Indians upon every possible occasion, but it was not the policy of Rivera to offer violence to the Indians or other natives along their route, unless they were known to be Marine or Guardia sympathizers. At least two persons were killed, one negro and one Mosquito Indian, although most reports state four persons killed, all of whom were either negros or Mosquito Indians. These killings were perpetrated by Timoteo Altamirano who was sub-jefe of group under Abram Rivera. It was partly on account of those killings that Rivera and Altamirano disagreed. This disagreement resulted in a fight between Rivera and Altamirano, and the latter with four of his friends were kicked out of the group at Waspuk on the way up the river. Rivera, with the remainder of the group, about 30 men, returned to Bocay. . . . The bandit group at Bocay has become greatly increased in numbers during the past six (6) months.[2]

Everything in this report corresponds to what we know of the Sandinistas during these years — including information gleaned from a handwritten captured Sandinista *Guard Book* from the EDSN's Atlantic Coast expedition of April 1931. The commanding officer's entry for 29-30 April explicitly prohibited EDSN soldiers from sacking the houses of the Zambos

---

1  Edson to Utley, 3 Jan. 1929, MCRC/Utley/2.
2  Stent, Puerto Cabezas, Intelligence, 20 Feb. 1931, GN-2 Report, 1 March 1931, RG127/43A/29.

and sternly reminded them that "the Miskitu are poor and it is unjust to take their things for personal use":

> General Orders of the Chief of Operations given in Aguas Vila, 29–30 April 1931. . . . Chiefs, Officers and Soldiers: Dear Brothers: It is strictly forbidden to plunder the houses of the villages of our brothers the Zambos who are contributing their services for our re-turn journey and putting us in contact with other operational fronts where the other expeditionary chiefs are operating. One must bear in mind that the Miskitus are poor and providing their immediate cooperation, it is unjust to take their things for personal use, it is better that we are obliged to give them whatever urgent necessities they need . . . Homeland and Liberty, / s / Z. Padilla R., Interim Ex-peditionary Chief.[1]

It is clear that the prohibitions against sacking the houses and villages of the Zambos and taking things from the Miskitu were deemed necessary because of numerous cases of rebel soldiers doing precisely that.[2]

In a brief but tantalizing letter to Major Metcalf, longtime east coast businessman and stalwart Marine Corps ally Albert "Frenchie" Webster of-fered a glimpse of how the most effective Sandinista leaders allowed Miski-tu communities a large degree of autonomy in their production and trade pursuits. "I got up to Sang Sang 8 days after leaving Bragman Bluff," wrote Webster. "Sambos came from Bocay, and I found that what we heard of Pedrón being in Bocay were all l—s [lies] . . . he had sent a few men out to the main river, to tell the natives to go ahead with their work (plantations) that he did not expect to bother any more, certainly, this is hear-say from mosquito Indians."[3]

In other words, in Webster's portrayal, EDSN general Pedrón Altami-rano, one of the most powerful and shrewdest of the Sandinista chieftains, changed his position with respect to Miskitu communities, adopting a hands-off policy in lieu of a more interventionist approach that had failed to achieve its aims. As depicted here, Pedrón would no longer interfere with the Miskitus' work in their fields and plantations and not "bother" them any more (probably a translation of *molestar*, which is stronger than "bother" and connotes physical intimidation and violence). In short, it seems that by late 1929 Pedrón had decided to leave the Miskitu alone. At the same time,

---

1  Original captured EDSN Guard Book, MCRC/Personal Papers Collection/San-dino; our translation.
2  See also Grossman Visit, *op. cit.*
3  A. Webster, Cape Gracias, to Major Metcalf, Puerto Cabezas, 23 Oct. 1929, RG127/204/1.

as abundant evidence makes clear, Pedrón was utterly ruthless in dealing with the despised *machos* (Marines), the "dogs" (*perros*) of the Guardia Nacional, US citizens (whom he generally butchered when they fell into his hands) and their allies (Macaulay 1985; Schroeder 1996). The Miskitu, it seems, required a much lighter touch to keep them from gravitating to the other side.

In sum, we argue that over the course of the rebellion the EDSN undertook a series of military-political incursions into the east coast region, but despite their best efforts, this Segovias-based rebel movement was never able to create a base of social support on the east coast. For a host of reasons rooted in the region's distinct history and culture and Costeños long tradition of Anglo affinity, Sandino's stridently anti-imperialist, "Indo-Hispanic," anti-American, anti-Anglo-Saxon rhetoric simply did not resonate with the political predilections and personal aspirations of the huge majority. In short, for Nicaragua's Atlantic Coast region as a whole, the Sandino rebellion remained, from beginning to end, a revolution from without.

Costeños and the US Marines and Guardia Nacional de Nicaragua

Many of the same patterns that one detects in Costeño-Sandinista relations can also be seen in coastal folks' relations with the Marines and Guardia Nacional. For instance, just as the Sandinistas came to depend on individual Miskitu to serve as scouts, spies, porters, boatmen, messengers, and in other capacities, so too did the Marines and Guardia. Examples abound, from the Marines' first forays up the Río Coco in mid-1928 until the final Marine withdrawal in January 1933. Captain Merritt Edson, for instance, hired Miskitu Indian boatmen to guide his patrol up the Río Coco, the first in a long string of Marine commanders who did much the same thing. One sees repeated references in Marine–Guardia reports to Indian spies, scouts, guides, porters, and boatmen who lent or sold their services to Marine–Guardia patrols.

In a typical example, in late 1931 Ramón Rodríguez, described as a Miskitu Indian from the village of Wasla, was "sent by the Guardia Nacional on a mission of espionage and in a search for Company animals taken by bandits from Louisiana Farm." As Capt. O. A. Inman described it, "[The] above mentioned man (mosquito Indian) . . . was sent up the river over a month ago and made his escape from the Bandits about the 24th of December [1931].

. . . Air reconnaissance, made by the undersigned on the 31st of December, leads me to believe that a great part of Rodriguez's statement is true."[1] Soon after, in February 1932, Lt. E. J. Surprenant led a patrol of "eleven Guardia and twenty Indians (Indians who had been driven from their homes above Kisalaya by bandits) in pitpans for Laimus, where a small group of bandits was reported stealing cattle." The patrol discovered a considerable cache of loot in a hidden Sandinista camp, most of which "was identified as their property by the Indians with me." The twenty Miskitu Indians employed by Surprenant proved to be crucial to the overall success of the patrol.[2]

In another typical case, in October 1929 Area Intelligence Officer W. C. Hall reported that Lt. Benson, commander of the La Luz and Neptune outposts "has employed two native agents to make more or less regular trips to the north, west and south to personally ascertain conditions and report them. . . . One of these agents is a native traveling doctor, the other a native peddler and merchant trader. They were selected for their reliability, their friendship for the Marine forces, their knowledge of the territory and because their normal occupations permit them to make extended tours without exciting suspicion." Notably, "No special agents are maintained in the southern part of this area . . . the southern half of the Eastern Area is in a more stable state than the northern and western parts" — in other words, by this time the Marines and Guardia considered the southern Eastern Area, including the port city of Bluefields "pacified," a designation that did not change for the remainder of the Marine occupation.[3]

From early on the Marines sought to recruit and train Miskitu and other east coast folk for service in the Guardia Nacional and local police departments. For instance, "The first thing Col. Marston did, upon his arrival [in Bluefields in 1929], was to gather some 70 Indians from all the villages along the Coast, and he has been drilling them for policemen , he has been remarkably patient with them, and has given strict orders to his under-officers that the Indians are not to be abused in any way, and he evidently means what he says, for a drill-master struck an Indian and he was told that if he did it again he would be reduced to the ranks."[4] In September 1929, Department of Northern Bluefields commander H. D. Linscott reported on the "enlistment

---

1  O. A. Inman, Intelligence Report, 4 Jan. 1932, RG127/206/1.
2  E. J. Surprenant, Patrol Report, 29 Feb. 1932, RG127/43A/16.
3  W. C. Hall, Special intelligence agents, 24 Oct. 1929, RG127/204/1.
4  S. London to Mr. Craigie, 5 July 1929, PRO 140717, FO 371/13471.

school" intended to instill literacy in Guardia recruits. "The progress of this school has been very gratifying to me," he noted approvingly.

> Most of the men, especially the Mosquito boys (most of whom en-listed largely for the educational advantages of service in the Guar-dia) take a great interest in their school work and are making good progress. As a matter of fact I was surprised to find that the Mos-quito illiterates made better progress than the Spanish illiterates, due I think to their ambition. . . . I can conceive of no more valuable soldier than a properly trained and disciplined Mosquito boy with his knowledge of woodcraft and tracking and at the same time an ability to read a simple map and perhaps make a simple sketch.[1]

As it turned out, few of the "Mosquito boys" completed their courses of study, and most were rejected for service in the Guardia for their perceived lack of discipline and persistent reluctance to take to the field arms in hand in pursuit of the "bandits."

Indeed, the Marines had a very difficult time recruiting suitable Guardia officers and enlisted men on the east coast, largely because the wages paid by export firms equaled or exceeded the salary paid to Guardia troops. "I know from experience that the proximity of Bragmans Bluff Lumber Com-pany (and fruit industry), with work easily accessible to laborers, has pre-vented the best elements of the population from enlisting in the Guardia at Puerto Cabezas," reported Major Linscott in January 1930. "The bulk of the men in the department are Indians and it is uphill and sometimes discourag-ing work to produce desired results with them."[2]

How did ordinary Miskitu respond to spontaneous solicitations from Marine–Guardia patrols for information on the locations and activities of rebel bands? Predictably, and in keeping with the general disposition of *campesinos* (rural folk) in Las Segovias, most Indian communities in the east coast generally opted for a strategy of reticence and discretion. A typical example appears in a patrol report of the same Capt. Inman, whose heav-ily armed 24-man patrol reconnoitered the lower Río Coco by motorboat in July 1931. "The Indians at the various villages on the lower river would give no information but appeared very restless. At Saklin the people over did themselves in assuring us that there was no sign of bandits on the river above us which immediately aroused my suspicion." Captain Inman's sus-picion proved well-founded, as soon after his patrol was ambushed by a rebel band concealed in the brush along the riverbank. At the conclusion

---

1 Linscott, Enlisted school, progress of, 6 Sept. 1929, Puerto Cabezas, RG127/202/1.
2 Linscott, Remarks, 15 Jan. 1930, RG127/202/1.

of his report he expressed his "firm belief that Adolfo Cockburn and one Slate (Comandante at Saklin) are in league with the bandits. According to information from an Indian messenger of the bandits who was intercepted, Adolfo Cockburn and Slate received a message from the bandits delivered by this man the morning of the day our patrol arrived in Saklin and when questioned both claimed there was no sign of Bandits on the River" [sic].[1] As we have seen, Captain Inman"s suspicions regarding Cockburn were also accurate.

How do we interpret the lies and deceptions of the Miskitu Indian communities encountered by Inman's patrol? By this time, much of the lower Coco River was indeed under the dominion of local strongman Ad-olfo Cockburn, commissioned as a general by Sandino, and no doubt his influence with the locals in this zone played a role in overriding the Coast's generalized "Anglo affinity." But does this mean that the Miskitu Indians encountered by the patrol were "in league with the bandits" and opposed to the Marine intervention? It is impossible to know with certainty, but it is reasonable to infer that their reticence, lies, and deceptions were part of a larger defensive strategy whose principal objective was to protect their communities from Sandinista reprisals. As an abundance of evidence makes clear, the Sandinistas often treated Marine–Guardia collaborators with a very heavy hand, killing and often mutilating the corpses of persons known to have collaborated with the enemy. Thus, the Sacklin Indians' evasions in this case can be interpreted as part of a larger effort to maintain favor with Cockburn and to keep a critical distance from both sides in this conflict, with the overarching goal of maintaining their community autonomy in the face of an unforgiving war between two groups of foreigners — "Spaniards" from the west and Americans from the north.

As illustrated in the petition from the Miskitu community of Tungla asking the Marines for "protection" from "bandits" that opens this chap-ter, some indigenous communities sought the patronage and protection of the Marines and Guardia from the "tyranny" of the Nicaraguan government based in Managua. Only weeks after the Tungla petition, Major H. H. Utley, commanding officer in Puerto Cabezas, "was visited by a delegation of In-dian chiefs from this sector, seeking my advice and assistance on behalf of their people." In their petition to the Moncada government, which Utley advised them not to send to Managua, the Indians expressed their deep dis-

---

1 Inman, Patrol Report, 21 July 1931, RG127/202/11.

gruntlement that the Miskitu Convention of 1895 had been "entirely disregarded, ignored, and cast aside by the Nicaraguan Government."[1]

The Miskitu petitions continued to flow in, particularly after the big Sandinista offensive on the Coast in April 1931. On 15 May 1931, the Miskitu Indian community in Bilwi (adjacent to Puerto Cabezas) sent a petition to area commander Colonial Wynn proclaiming that "We Miskitu Indians are clamoring for the Americans to sever us from our bonds, from this Nicaraguan yoke, give us as before our reservation, and hold the sole rights of protectorate, given by us." In closing, the petitioners addressed Colonial Wynn as "your highness," a clear echo of the era of the British protectorate.[2] Three days later, on 18 May 1931, "petitioners in behalf of the Mosquito Indians and Creoles of Bluefields" petitioned the British government to assist in "separation from Nicaragua":

> Your humble petitioners beg most respectfully to state on behalf of the Indians and Creoles of the Atlantic Coast, that unless a separation be made to the Atlantic Coast from Nicaragua there will forever be no peace. Many Indians are being killed for no cause whatsoever. . . . The Nicaraguans are a tyranical nation . . . Now the Indians and Creoles of the Atlantic Coast demands a recognise flag to rule, not America if possible the Union Jack, or the Canadians and if not to be under the Jamaican Government. The recent trouble in the vicinity at Bragman shows that the Nicaraguans are a tyranical nation [*sic*].[3]

The petitions continued for the rest of the war and even up until the 1950s, demonstrating the persistence of the spirit of autonomy that had long sustained Coast culture. In the end, neither the United States nor Great Britain was interested in adopting the Coast as a permanent protectorate.

At the other end of the social spectrum, the great majority of elite propertied Costeños strongly supported the Marine intervention, as did most newspapers. While some elites and newspaper stories denounced what they perceived as specific instances of Marine excess and heavy-handedness, overall the Marines–Guardia were able to establish friendly relations with the propertied elite and press of the east coast. In addition, just like the Sandinistas, the Marines were able to garner the support of key individuals

---

1 Utley to London, 18 Feb. 1929, MCRC/Utley/3; for the petition, see PRO 140717, FO 371/13471, encl. no. 6 in S. London's no. 56 of June 21, 1929.
2 Godfrey Williams et al., Bilwi, to Col. Wynn, Bluefields, 15 May 1931, RG127/206/1; in this case as in others, the Marine response was "to listen but say nothing"; Salzman to Wynn, 20 June 1931, RG127/200/1.
3 Edward Wilson, Creole, and Alfred Gordon, Indian, Bluefields, to the Under-Secretary of State Foreign Affairs, London, 18 May 1931, PRO FO 571/15073.

who served as cultural intermediaries between themselves and the Miskitu and Creole populations. Benny Muller was one such cultural intermediary, as was American businessman and longtime Coast resident Albert Fagot. "At Cape Gracias Mr. Albert Fagot, an American, is acting regularly as agent and making periodic reports regarding conditions on the Coco River. Mr. Fagot . . . owns property at Waspuc and maintains close business relations with many natives living and working along the river; through these people Mr. Fagot is able to render excellent reports regarding general conditions along the Coco River from Cape Gracias a Dios to Bocay."[1]

In sum, by our reading, most Coast folk passively accepted or even tacitly welcomed the Marine intervention. For many, as the numerous petitions suggest, a return to the benign neglect of the pre-Reincorporation period likely would have been a hoped-for ideal. The vast majority did not want to fight or die in a war that was not their own, or see their jobs vanish, properties destroyed, or families killed in a brutal conflict between two groups of outsiders. Overall, the caches of documents examined here indicate that most coastal folk harbored a strong passive preference for the British, the Americans, the US Marines, the fruit and lumber companies, and, among the Miskitu, the Moravians.

Conclusion

In this chapter we have sought to shed new light on an old set of questions regarding the Sandino rebellion in Nicaragua's Atlantic Coast. We have focused in particular on hitherto largely neglected bodies of evidence to offer a more robust and compelling interpretation of the responses of various groups of coastal peoples to Sandino's nationalist challenge. We argue that overall this evidence makes clear that, in stark contrast to the situation in Las Segovias, the Sandinistas were never able to establish an organic base of social support in the east coast region, where from beginning to end the Sandino rebellion remained a "revolution from without."

While our treatment cannot be considered the final word, the bodies of evidence cited above offer a salutary reminder of the exceptionally complex geographical, cultural and political terrains that the Sandinistas, and the Marines and Guardia, had to negotiate when they entered the expansive

---

1  Hall, Puerto Cabezas, Special intelligence agents, 24 Oct. 1929, RG127/204/1; on key intelligence on the EDSN received from his son J. A. Fagot see GN-2 Report, 1 June 1931, pp. 9-10, RG127/43A/29.

yet inherently amorphous cultural area of Nicaragua known as the Atlantic Coast. The conflict possessed a particular underlying structure, with the Sandinista guerrillas enjoying strong poles of support in transitional areas between Western Nicaragua and the Atlantic Coast, like the mining zones and the Bocay valley, as well as at least one particular pole of sympathy downriver on the Río Coco at Sacklin, due to the efforts of Sandinista general Adolfo Cockburn. Nonetheless, overall it appears that support for the Sandinistas among Costeños was the exception rather than the rule, a reality shaped by Sandinista approaches to the region — straining the guerillas' capacity to develop more subtle approaches to a geographically distant, culturally distinct, and politically wary population, at times opening up fissures among Sandinista leaders, and in the end foreclosing the possibility for developing a locally based and sustained insurgency. In this way, it could be said social and cultural realities on the Coast shaped and limited the Sandinistas in ways similar to the ways in which they had influenced Costeño relations with foreign companies, the market economy, and the Moravian Church.

By our reading, the predominant response among Coast folk to Sandino's nationalist challenge and the US intervention was to try to avoid participation in the military conflict altogether — and particularly to avoid the Sandinistas and their frequent recourse to beheadings, mutilations, and other forms of spectacular violence and retribution against Americans and their native collaborators. At the same time, Coast folk used a range of more peaceful strategies to try to shape post-rebellion, post-intervention conditions in a way that would reinforce the pre-1895 autonomy that they had enjoyed by convincing the US to take the area under its wing, in the fashion of the British. In the end, Sandino had little to offer most Coast dwellers — far less than the US-owned fruit and lumbering enclaves did. As a result, the great majority of Costeños did not gravitate toward Sandino and did not oppose US export firms, the intervention of the Marines, or the formation of the Guardia.

These conclusions differ from one school of thought on this era in Coast history and add depth and critical detail to another. For too long, scholars have thought that documentary evidence on "Sandino en la costa" was too thin to be of much use. We hope we have demonstrated that this is not the case, and we invite others to delve into the sources cited above, much of which we have published online, to decide for themselves whether these conclusions represent an accurate interpretation of events. Approaching the question from the perspective of Sandino's public discourse, the next chapter by Baron Pineda makes clear that Sandino's nationalist, anti-imperialist, "Indo-Hispanic" ideology represented yet another paternalistic "Spanish" imposition as perceived by the peoples and cultures of the Atlantic Coast.

# References

### Archives and Citation Abbreviations

Library of Congress. Personal Papers Collection, Papers of Merritt A. Edson (LOC/ Edson).

Marine Corps Research Center, Quantico VA. Personal Papers of Harold H. Utley (MCRC/Utley).

Moravian Church Archives, Bethlehem PA (MCA).

Public Record Office, National Archives, United Kingdom (PRO).

United States National Archives and Records Administration:

Records of the United States Marines and Guardia Nacional de Nicaragua, 1927-1932, Record Group 127 (RG127/[Entry no.]/[Box no.]).

Records of the United States Department of State Relating to Internal Affairs of Nicaragua, 1910-1929 and 1930-1945 (USDS).

### Published Materials

Arellano, J. E. (2008) *Guerrillero de Nuestra América: Augusto C. Sandino (1895-1934).* (Managua, HISPAMER).

Borhek, M. V. (1949) *Watchman on the Walls* (Bethlehem, PA: Society for Propagating the Gospel).

Brooks, D. C. (1989) 'Marines, Miskitus, and the Hunt for Sandino: The Río Coco Patrol in 1928.' in *Journal of Latin American Studies* Vol. 21, No. 1-2, pp. 311-342.

Brooks, David C. (1997) 'Revolution from Without: Culture and Politics along Nicaragua's Atlantic Coast in the Time of the Sandino Revolt.' (Unpublished Ph.D. dissertation, University of Connecticut at Storrs).

República de Nicaragua, Oficina Central del Censo (1920) *Censo general de 1920* (Managua: Tip. Nacional).

Gould, J. L. (1998) *To Die In This Way: Nicaraguan Indians and the Myth of Mestizaje, 1880-1965* (Durham, NC: Duke University Press).

Guha, R. 'The Prose of Counterinsurgency' in Ranajit, G. and Spivak, G. C. (Eds) (1988) *Selected Subaltern Studies* (Oxford: Oxford University Press), pp. 45-86.

Hale, C. R. (1994) *Resistance and Contradiction: Miskitu Indians and the Nicaraguan State, 1894-1987* (Stanford: Stanford University Press).

Helms, M. W. (1971) *Asang: Adaptations to Culture in a Miskito Community.* Gainesville: University of Florida Press).

Heritage, G. W. 'Forced Down in the Jungles of Nicaragua' *The Leatherneck*, May 1932, pp. 13-17.

Macaulay, N. (1985) *The Sandino Affair* (Durham, NC: Duke University Press).

Molieri, J. J. (1986) *El desafío indígena en Nicararagua: el caso de los mískitos.* (Managua: Editorial Vanguardia).

Pineda, B. L. (2006) *Shipwrecked Identities: Navigating Race on Nicaragua's Mosquito Coast* (New Brunswick: Rutgers University Press).

Ramírez, S. (Ed) *El pensamiento vivo: Augusto C. Sandino* 2 vols (Managua, Nueva Nicaragua).

Schroeder, M. J. (1993) ' "To Defend Our Nation's Honor": Toward a Social and Cultural History of the Sandino Rebellion in Nicaragua, 1927-1934.' (Unpublished Ph.D. dissertation, University of Michigan).

Schroeder, M. J. (1996) 'Horse Thieves to Rebels to Dogs: Political Gang Violence and the State in the Western Segovias, Nicaragua, in the Time of Sandino, 1927-1934.' in *Journal of Latin American Studies* Vol. 28, No. 2, pp. 383-434.

Wünderich, V. (1989) *Sandino en la costa: de las Segovias al litoral atlántico* (Managua: Editorial Nueva Nicaragua).

# CHAPTER 3. A "STRANGE POTPOURRI": REVISITING SANDINO'S LEGACY IN THE ATLANTIC COAST OF NICARAGUA

*Baron Pineda*

In 1933, as the six year episode of civil war and US marine occupation was winding down, a Spanish Basque journalist with "a name so long that... there's no way to pronounce it" (Conrad 1990: 459), Ramón de Belausteguigoitia, spent two weeks with Augusto César Sandino in the Segovian town of San Rafael del Norte. The visit resulted in a heroic portrayal of the Nicaraguan rebel entitled *Con Sandino en Nicaragua, la hora de la paz* (Belausteguigoitia 1981 [1934]). With the marines having withdrawn from the country, Sandino could now begin to put into practice his ambitious plans for a civilian future for himself and his movement. Sandino aspired to create a new province that would be called *Luz y Verdad* in which he could put into practice his dreams of socialism and a Pan-American model for economic development that would break the cycle of dependence on North American capital and its "Wall Street bankers."[1] Sandino, in his most grandiose moments, hoped that the 36,000 square kilometer territory of *Luz y Verdad* would host the Federal District of a united Central America (Wunderich 1989: 147).

Although this plan was not granted in the peace treaty that Sandino eventually signed, *Luz y Verdad* would have extended well past the Segov-

---

1 See "Protocol for Peace" in Conrad (1990: 432).

ian highlands which were the Sandinista stronghold. It was to extend all the way to the Caribbean Sea to "Sandibe," Sandy Bay as it is known to Costeños, and all the way up into Honduras at the outlet of the Patuca River (Conrad 1990:432). The territory that Sandino coveted was to encompass the entire southern section of the Coco River or Wangki watershed from its mountainous Segovian headwaters to about 100 kilometers to the north and south of its outlet into the Caribbean; an area that represents the heart of Miskitu and Mayangna population in Nicaragua and Honduras. In conversation with Nicaraguan journalist José Román, Sandino estimated that about 100,000 "Indians" occupied the Atlantic Coast (Román 1983: 103). He told Román:

> It is evident that our work here will be very difficult but we will have made a great triumph even if we just instill in them hope and plans for the future and the most elemental notions of morality and hygiene. Between Zumos, Zambos, Miskitos and Caribs there are thousands and thousands of Indians in Nicaragua's Atlantic Coast of Nicaragua and the shores of its rivers (my translation, Román 1983:103).

In his conversations with Román and Belausteguigoitia, as well as many other interviews and comunicados, Sandino described these lands as uncultivated empty lands, *tierras baldías*, with great mineral (particularly gold) and agricultural potential. He believed that its strategic geographic position made it suitable for another interoceanic canal, could provide the core of a rejuvenated economy led by the "Indo-Hispanic" republics.

Clearly, Sandino's arrogance in unilaterally claiming this territory was an unmistakable example of a long-standing tradition of colonialism in the Americas, and beyond, in which the most basic rights of native and poor people were disregarded by conquering Euro-Americans. On the other hand, Sandino explicitly cast his nationalist project in racial terms claiming that his ultimate goal was to uplift what he explicitly called "the Indo-Hispanic race." He was admired by Latin American leftists of his day as a "mestizo rebelado" who dared to defy Uncle Sam (Salvatierra 1934: 69). In his words and his actions, Sandino attempted to embody an alternative to a Eurocentric Creole nationalism that viewed the Indian presence as a deficiency (Hooker 2005b: 26). In his conversations with Belausteguigoitia he described himself, and Nicaraguans more generally, as "Indian Spaniards of America" and he laid out a program for economic development that he believed would most benefit the downtrodden Nicaraguan masses that he routinely described as Indian. How, then, are we to reconcile Sandino's stated identification with Nicaragua's Indians and, in the words of Belausteguigoitia, "his project to colonize the Coco River region"; the Miskitu and Mayangna homeland? (Belausteguigoitia 1981: 184).

There is a passage in *Con Sandino en Nicaragua* that for me is particularly revelatory in beginning to sort the apparent contradictions in Sandino's approach towards race in Nicaragua, as well as the relationship of the land and people of the Atlantic Coast with those of the Pacific Coast. Belausteguigoitia reconstructs a conversation that he has with the general in which Sandino expresses pride in his light-skinned wife, Blanca Arauz, and two "Zambo Indians of the Atlantic Coast" that were members of his militia. At one point, Belausteguigoitia asks Sandino whether his wife was, "an obstacle or a stimulus in carrying on the struggle." Sandino replies that she was a stimulus, but he lamented the five years of separation from her. For the most part, she stayed in San Rafael del Norte while Sandino moved from camp to camp in the Segovias and traveled abroad. Later she was briefly able to join him in the mountains. Sandino then calls her into the room and Belausteguigoitia describes the scene thusly: "The caudillo's wife appeared. She is a very young lady with good features, a sweet manner, and a very white skin. I greeted her and she left quickly after a few brief words" (Conrad 1990: 459). The following conversation ensues:[1]

> Sandino: "My wife is from this place and is ninety-five percent Spanish. Here the Spaniards mixed very little with the Indians."

> I [Belausteguigoitia]: "Generally the Spaniard has mixed with the Indians outside the places where they were very warlike. In Mexico, for example, they have mixed very little in Sonora and Sinaloa. In the rest of the country, almost completely."

> Sandino: "Well, here very little. The Indian fled to the mountains. But there's some of it here. So much so, that there is a refrain that says: 'God will speak for the Indian of the Segovias.' And he has certainly spoken! They are the ones who have done a great part of all

---

1 In *Con Sandino en Nicaragua*, Belausteguigoitia reconstructs long dialogues with Sandino, either from memory or notes. Although there is no reason to doubt the veracity of this account it should be kept in mind that these transcripts do not necessarily represent accurate reconstructions of Sandino's words. The most reliable accounts of Sandino's opinions and positions on these matters are found in his various self-authored comunicados that have been reprinted widely (See Somoza 1941; Ramírez 1988 and Conrad 1990). In this essay I use Conrad's English translations when available. When not available I present my own translations.

this. An Indian is timid, but cordial, sentimental, intelligent. You will see it now with your own eyes."

Then the general ordered a soldier to be called in and asked him to speak with his leader, who was sitting in the guardhouse and belonged to the same race as the Zambo Indians of the Atlantic coast.

The two spoke, and a mishmash of words of several languages, from English and French to Spanish, could be made out in the dialect.

"Now speak to him in English," he said to me. I spoke for a while and noted that the two conversed perfectly together.

"And now Spanish," he added.

Indeed they spoke it perfectly.

Sandino: "Well, now you see that they are intelligent. But they have been entirely abandoned. There are some hundred thousand of them without communications, without schools, without anything of government. This is what I want to do with the colony, to lift them up and make true men of them." (Conrad 1990: 459-60).

In this chapter I am going to use an analysis of this passage as a point of departure from which to explore the role of the Atlantic Coast in the political formation of Sandino. I will draw on a brief critical look of the biography of Sandino as a way of exploring the racialized "gaze" of Pacific Nicaraguans towards the Atlantic Coast; one that has changed a great deal since the times of Sandino, but which continues to hamper the development of a just relationship between Atlantic and Pacific Nicaragua.

There are many interesting issues pertaining to constructions of gender and whiteness that arise in this passage. Clearly, as a *caudillo* Sandino displays his ability to make his subordinates, his wife and his Costeño troops, appear, disappear and perform on command for him. Sandino self-consciously cast himself as a patriarchal figure to his followers (Grossman 2006: 152). Within this patriarchal framework this passage can be viewed as Sandino performing his status and masculinity on his subordinates; women and Indians. Historian Richard Grossman claims that Sandino's self-fashioning as a patriarch was the "internal face" of the Sandinista movement that most resonated with his Segovian followers who recalled a benevolent Sandino who "dominated, like a father to the family" (Grossman 2006: 158). While this passage leaves one to wonder whether his Costeño soldiers would have viewed being required to perform this charade for the visiting Spanish journalist as consistent with Sandino's benevolence, Sandino manifests a paternalistic pride in the abilities of his "Zambo Indian" compatriots. Yet, in this and many other moments he talked about Indians as child-like beings who needed guidance and supervision. So, for example, he tells Belausteguigoitia that: "What our Indians need is instruction and culture so they can know themselves, respect themselves, and love themselves" (Conrad 1990: 452). The passage reveals a contradiction between the gendered and raced paternalism of Sandino vis-à-vis Indians that stands in contrast to his expression of admiration for the linguistic abilities of Costeños.

The passage also provides a hint of the "colorism" that anthropologist Roger Lancaster fruitfully theorized in his ethnography of Managua entitled *Life is Hard* (Lancaster 1991, 1992). Lancaster is one of the few social scientists who have tried to understand constructions of race in Nicaragua within a framework that takes into account Pacific Nicaraguan perceptions of the "blackness" of the Atlantic Coast. Lancaster writes:

> Though significant, prejudice against the Atlantic Coast minorities is scarcely the most pervasive form of racism in Nicaragua. Indeed, whatever racism exists toward the Atlantic Coast minorities is but an extension of a much deeper-seated pattern internal to mestizo culture, not external to it. A more apposite term in this case might be "colorism" rather than racism. People put color into discourse in a variety of ways. The ambiguity of Nicaraguan speech about color is perhaps its crucial feature. "Negro" refers to Atlantic Coast natives of African heritage, but it may also refer to dark-skinned Indians like the Miskitos. It can also refer to dark-skinned mestizos — the majority of Nicaragua's population (Lancaster 1991: 342).

It is precisely the ambiguity of Sandino's speech about race, symptomatic of the larger Nicaraguan problem of "Atlanticity" (Lancaster 1992: 213), that I want to identify in this essay. As a Pacific Nicaraguan son of a landowning *patron*, Sandino manifests an approach to race typical amongst his contemporaries. Indian is an adjective that was typically used to identify subservience, poverty and lack of sophistication. But by this time in Pacific Nicaragua, with the myth of Nicaragua mestizaje well in place in the 1930s, Indian was not a term that was typically used to identify a self-recognizing communal grouping of people (Gould 1993). Yet, in this passage, Sandino shifts casually from one usage to another when he calls on his "Sambo Indian" compatriots. As a result of his years of experience in the Atlantic Coast of Nicaragua, Sandino, unlike many of his fellow Nicaraguans who had little or no knowledge of the inaccessible Atlantic Coast, was well aware that terms such as Miskitu Indian, Sambo Indian, Sumu Indian, Creole, *Negro* and others were an important part of how Mosquito Coast society was organized communally.

Today Pacific Nicaraguans often use terms like *Negro, Indio* and *Miskitu* interchangeably. The issue of whether Miskitu Indians are "really" *Negros* or *Indios* is very much unresolved if not consciously debated. Part of this ambiguity has to do with the use of *Negro* and *Blanco* as relational color terms in one moment and as ethnic terms, used to identify perceived communal groupings, in other moments (Lancaster 1991: 341). Pacific Nicaraguans, when operating in a color context, use *Negro* as a descriptive term for dark-skinned people in the Pacific and Atlantic, but some also use the term to refer to all Costeños as a communal group even those who prefer to self-identify as Miskitu Indians. In his conversations with poor Managuans Lancaster heard many quite appalling expressions of anti-Costeño and anti-black sentiment. Lancaster recalled a conversation in which Jaime, one of his informants, told him: "Never, ever, call a negro negro," Jaime warned me, "at least not to his face." "Why not," I wondered? Virgil laughed. "Do you want to die?"

Apart from this mental association of blackness with violence, one that contrasts with the archetype of the "timid" Indian, this quotation exemplifies this double usage of *Negro* as a color term and as an ethnic term. Once more, even when used as an ethnic term many Pacific Nicaraguans commonly label Miskitu Indians as both *Indios* and *Negro* in a way that is not intended to draw attention to racial mixing. Paradoxically, all Costeños are *Negro* and, in a similar way, all Nicaraguans including Sandino's "Sambo Indian" soldiers are *Indio*.

In light of this well-documented prejudice of many Pacific Nicaraguans for Costeños, it is noteworthy that in this passage Sandino's intention was to put on display the "intelligence" and, in other words, the valuable cultural capital that Costeños brought to the table. Sandino has his Costeño soldiers perform their cosmopolitan attributes; notably their multilingualism. Sandino had just finished fighting a war against English-speaking "Anglo-Saxons" in which he hoped to rally the people and governments of the twenty-one "Indo-Hispanic" republics, which he described as being united by Spain's "gift" of "her language, her civilization, and her blood" (Conrad 1990: 462). One might presume that the Sambo Indians performance of speaking Spanish "perfectly" would have potentially qualified them for citizenship in the New Nicaragua. Indeed, his praise of their perfect English seems to contradict his claim that they have been "abandoned...without communications, without schools." In today's Nicaragua it is worthy of note that the same young professionals who lament that their career opportunities in Nicaragua are limited without fluency in English do not consider the possibility of English-language study in the Atlantic Coast, where Mosquito Coast Creole English is one of the oldest varieties of English spoken outside of Great Britain (Holm 1978), as a viable national opportunity for English-language study. Unfortunately, *el inglés de la costa* is often viewed as a bastardized form of English which does not possess value in the global market. It is often overlooked or undervalued as part of the cultural and linguistic patrimony of the Nicaraguan nation. In light of this ongoing problem within Nicaragua of failing to value Costeño contributions to the nation, Sandino's expression of pride in their linguistic abilities stands out as progressive.

The soldiers spoke a third language which we can presume was Miskitu. Tellingly, Belausteguigoitia referred to this language as a "dialect" comprised of a "mishmash of words of several languages, from English and French to Spanish." Here Belausteguigoitia's descriptions illustrate two persistent prejudicial views towards Miskitu. First, Miskitu continues to be denigrated in popular speech as a dialect that is inferior to European languages, such as English and Spanish. Within this unabashedly Eurocentric formulation, native languages are by definition "dialects" and therefore inferior to European languages. Second, in seeming contradiction to this first view, it is commonly believed in Nicaragua that Miskitu is not an indigenous language at all in the sense that it is not believed to be related to languages that were spoken in the pre-Columbian period.[1] Rather it is viewed as a degraded mix of European languages that happens to be spoken by *Negros* and/or *Indios* of the Atlantic Coast. This view of the nature of the Miskitu reinforces the ambivalence in Pacific Nicaragua as to the "true" racial identity of the Costeños and allows the Costeños to often be viewed as a degenerate mix of peoples and cultures that by virtue of its mixedness lacks value.[2] In his journalistic adventures in Nicaragua, Belausteguigoitia picked up on this ambivalence and tried to capture it poetically when he wrote:

---

1 As anthropologist Philip Dennis notes that the interpenetration of English and Miskitu is considerable, but not nearly as deep as is commonly presumed. He cites linguistic research that maintains that only "5–10% of the vocabulary of Miskitu" is borrowed from English (Dennis 2004: 38).

2 See Pineda (2006) for a more thorough discussion of these dynamics.

> Nicaragua in the midst of its small size is a complicated place. There is an imaginative and Andalucian Nicaragua in the Pacific. But there is another Nicaragua that is predominantly Indian, peppered with immigration from the north of Spain, mostly from Galicia, that is more active and deep. And there is an Atlantic zone, primitive and abandoned, where an Indian population has mixed a good deal with a Black one and even with residual Europeans forming a strange mix and blend, as picturesque as its dialect where Indian words camp out with Spanish and English and French ones forming this strange potpourri of the coasts of the Americas (my translation, Belausteguigoitia 1981: 36).

The Coast is simultaneously the most "abandoned" and the most worldly part of Nicaragua. It is the most Indian, the most black and the most European. Yet somehow the sum of these parts are not recognized as being greater than the whole. In other words, the "mix" of the Atlantic Coast is often cast in a negative light in Nicaragua. Belausteguigoitia's quotation reveals an enduring paradox embedded in the ongoing formulation of Nicaraguan nationalism in which the eclectic origin of the Atlantic Coast is often not viewed as having been uplifting. It is ironic that the mixed origins of the Coast would be the subject of scorn given the fact that mestizo nationalism is an ideology that at some level tries to reconcile the mixed American and European elements of Nicaraguan culture and history.

Political scientist Juliet Hooker reminds us of the importance of including gender and race in the analysis of these processes in the national formation of Nicaragua (Hooker 2009).[1] Hooker lays out three distinct phases in the twentieth and twenty-first century development of official mestizo nationalism in Nicaragua; vanguardismo, Sandinismo and mestizo multiculturalism (Hooker 2005a: 15). She notes that, although progress has been made towards a more just and equitable inclusion of Costeños in national life as a result of measures like the autonomy statute of 1987 and the Land Demarcation Law of 2003, Afro-Nicaraguans and Afro-Latin Americans more broadly have been at a disadvantage with respect to mestizos and indigenous peoples (Hooker 2005b: 286). Part of this marginalization has to do with the ways which mestizo nationalism evolved in the twentieth century starting with the Nicaraguan vanguardistas who supplanted an unequivocal glorification of the Spanish legacy in Nicaragua with their own approach that looked to Nicaragua's indigenous past as a source of inspira-

---

1   See also Mollett (2006) for an analysis of racial dynamics in the Honduran Mosquitia.

tion, but ignored the place of "Costeños (and blacks in particular)' in their vision of the past and present of the nation (Hooker 2005a: 21). Also, *vanguardismo* recapitulated a vision of a submissive and feminized Indian historical subject. She writes:

> For Cuadra, however (like his father), the process of mestizaje is gendered such that Spanish contributions are dominant because they are masculine. Nicaraguan culture, he claims: "is made up of two components. For historical and cultural reasons, one of these components was the passive, feminine, terrestrial sign: the Indian component. The other — the Spanish — was the active sign, fertile, masculine, oceanic." The use of gender/familial tropes to portray mestizaje as harmonious fusion in vanguardismo ultimately served to justify mestizo political power. As Anne McClintock has noted, the use of familial metaphors to describe nations (as "fatherlands" and "motherlands," for example), is used to naturalize hierarchical relations within what is supposed to be a community of equals (Hooker 2005a: 23-4).

Understanding the role of these gendered dynamics that Sandino in part inherited from the *vanguardistas* helps to contextualize the role of Costeños and the Atlantic Coast in the original Sandinista movement.

Although many of the *vanguardistas* supported Sandino's cause, Sandino himself and later the next generation of Sandinistas in the 1960s, developed a new "revolutionary" brand of nationalism that they hoped would "awaken" the Atlantic Coast *"gigante que despierta."* The new generation of Sandinistas, such as Carlos Fonseca and Jaime Wheelock, studied Sandino's campaigns and pronouncements regarding Nicaraguan nationalism and fashioned a set of perspectives that diverged significantly from what went before in the sense that they "emphasized the violent nature of the Spanish colonial enterprise, and the importance of indigenous ancestry to contemporary mestizo national identity...Sandinismo thus contested the myths of harmonious mestizaje, indigenous passivity, and colonial peace that were central elements of *vanguardismo*." (Hooker 2005a: 26). Hooker argues that despite their efforts to distance themselves from *vanguardismo*, their formulation continued to downplay the role of Costeños and blacks in Nicaraguan history as well as constructing a mestizo revolutionary subject in a manner that provided little room for an ethnically marked one (Hooker 1995a: 31).[1] Beyond forming a modest cooperative at Wiwilí that was destroyed by the

---

1   There has been a similar reticence on the part of Sandinista administrations to specifically confront issues related to other marginalized groups, such as women and "sexual minorities" (Howe 2007: 238).

National Guard after his assassination, Sandino was never able to carry out on a large scale his plans for the colonization of the Atlantic Coast. Yet the Sandinista government that came to power in 1979 did attempt to increase the integration of the Atlantic Coast within the national sphere, but this effort failed miserably as the government received widespread international condemnation for its handling of the escalating tensions with Costeños in the course of the counter-revolutionary, or Contra, War.[1]

With the demise of most of the traditional Marxist national liberation movements after the Cold War, Latin America has increasingly witnessed a turn to "multicultural" policies on the part of national governments, many of which have officially recognized their "multiethnic and pluricultural" nature. The autonomy statute of 1987 was part of this larger wave of cultural and legal recognition of the rights of ethnic minorities (Brysk 2000).[2] There remains suspicion about whether these changes in the legal status of minorities represent more than cosmetic changes — ones which fail to address underlying structural inequalities (Hale 2002).

In the case of today's Nicaragua much has changed since the time of Sandino. New Indian and black universities like BICU (Bluefields Indian and Caribbean University) and URACCAN (University of the Autonomous Regions of the Caribbean Coast of Nicaragua), with installations in the major cities of Bluefields and Bilwi as well as smaller towns, have started to operate in the last twenty years with the help of international cooperation. The main URACCAN campus is actually located in Kamla, just outside of Bilwi, on the grounds of a former Sandinista People's Army (EPS) military base. In the RAAN, Miskitu politicians have had unprecedented success in holding leadership positions in national parties. YATAMA, the main Miskitu political party, has made a relatively successful transition to a civilian role and has won major positions in the region, such as when Elizabeth Henriquez was elected the mayor of Bilwi in 2004.[3] Whereas in the past the government in Managua routinely made decisions that affected the Atlantic Coast without consultation, Costeños have had some success in using official and unofficial means to exercise a de facto veto power on large scale development in the region. They have been particularly successful in getting the

---

1 See chapter 4 of this volume for a further elaboration of this point.
2 See also Frühling, González and Buvollen (2007) for a comprehensive new long-term assessment of the autonomy process.
3 See chapter 5 of this volume for a detailed description of the political fortunes of YATAMA.

attention of international agencies to the extent that within development circles the complaint is heard that international aid is disproportionately oriented towards the Atlantic Coast.

However, by far the greatest test to the re-positioning of the Atlantic Coast within the Nicaraguan national context has to do with the land titling process that after decades of inaction was finally put into law in 2003. Land pressure is a critical issue in the Atlantic Coast as the so-called "agricultural frontier" has steadily pushed to the East over the last fifty years, threatening communally held lands of Miskitu and Mayangna communities and shifting the demographics in favor of mestizo majorities in the RAAN and RAAS (Horton 1998). The issue of "communal lands" has been alive in Costeño communities since soon after the Reincorporation of the Mosquito Coast in 1894 (Finley-Brook and Offen 2009: 349). During the autonomy process that issue was revived and since then Costeños along with their international collaborators have been actively mapping lands in order to legally lay claim to them (Hale 2006, Finley-Brook and Offen 2009). In the Awas Tingni case (2001) the Inter-American Court of Human Rights ruled in favor of the Mayangna Indians requiring the Nicaraguan government to demarcate and title Awas Tingni's traditional lands in accordance with its customary land and resource tenure patterns. This was a historic decision that represented "the first legally binding decision by an international tribunal to uphold the collective land and resource rights of indigenous peoples in the face of a state's failure to do so" (Anaya and Grossman 2002: 2). The Bosawas Biosphere Reserve was created in 1991 and after years of contentious wrangling between international agencies, national governments, regional governments, Mayangna, mestizo colonists and Miskitu communities a ceremony was held in 2005 that celebrated a "reserve" arrangement, including tentative land titling for indigenous communities, that encompassed 7450 square kilometers on the upper half of the Coco River (Finley-Brook and Offen 2009: 353). In an ironic twist of fate, this reserve includes Wiwilí, the former site of Sandino's short-lived cooperative and planned capital of Central America, and represents a reasonable facsimile of what Sandino seventy-five years before had imagined for his utopian province of *Luz y Verdad*.

Sandino on the Coast

Although Sandino was born and raised in Niquihohomo, a small town in the densely populated lowland strip bordered by the Pacific Ocean and Nicaragua's two great lakes, Lake Nicaragua and Lake Managua, he spent many of the politically formative years of his life in Caribbean port cities in Mexico and Central America. In 1920, after shooting and injuring a man during a Catholic mass, Sandino made recourse to a strategy that he would continue to use later in life as a rebel leader and revolutionary; he took refuge in the Atlantic Coast: "To avoid a trial and other undesirable results...I left at once for the Atlantic coast, using another name, and from there I left for La Ceiba, Honduras, where I worked at the Montecristo sugar plantation" (Conrad 1990: 31).

Sandino worked as a mechanic and warehouseman in La Ceiba, the largest port of Honduras's Caribbean coast and also the Central American stronghold of the Vacarro Brother's Company of New Orleans (Macaulay 1967: 50; Kepner 1935: 102). At this time the Vacarro Brother's Company, which later was reorganized as the Standard Fruit Company, had already started to expand its operations into Nicaragua. It was this same company which in the six-year period from 1921 to 1927 transformed the village of Bilwi into a major port and export zone.[1] Sandino and his troops would by the end of the decade repeatedly attack the Nicaraguan installations of the Standard Fruit Company; the same company for which he had labored in Honduras.

In 1923 Sandino moved from Honduras to Guatemala where he continued to work for other US agro-export companies (Macaulay 1967: 51). In Quiriguá, Guatemala, Sandino worked as a laborer for the largest and most well renowned US banana enterprise in the Caribbean, the United Fruit Company (Ramírez 1988: xxii). In that same year Sandino traveled to Mexico's Caribbean port of Tampico, working first for the South Pennsylvania Oil Company, and then for the Huasteca Petroleum Company, which was affiliated with Standard Oil of Indiana. Tampico in this period was a Mexican center for US business interests, particularly the oil industry. US companies employed thousands of Mexican workers and the US presence lent the city a bustling, international atmosphere. Tampico and Vera Cruz consequently possessed a well-developed and militant labor movement

---

1 See Pineda (2006) for a detailed history of Bilwi/Puerto Cabezas.

(Bendaña 1994: 27-37). Sandino witnessed a great deal of labor upheaval including many strikes. Not surprisingly, given the nature of the relationship between the United States and Latin America, Sandino also witnessed the US military and US companies intervene in Mexican internal affairs, supporting the Obregón government against the rebel forces of General Adolfo de la Huerta (Macaulay 1967: 52). In this post-revolutionary environment of extreme US military and economic domination, Sandino embraced the political philosophies that would later mobilize his six-year war against the United States in Nicaragua, between 1927 and 1933.

While in Mexico Sandino assimilated, to different degrees, at least four philosophical currents; Anarchism/Communism, Freemasonry/Spiritualism, Anti-Yankeeism (*anti-yanquismo*)/Anti-Imperialism and Indo-Hispanism/Pan-Latin Americanism (Hodges 1986). The Mexican revolution, which freed some sectors of society to express their contempt for United States domination, inspired Sandino and instilled him with an overwhelming sense of indignation towards the US. He soon became aware of the contempt with which Nicaragua was held by anti-imperialist Latin Americans for allowing such extremes of subordination to the United States (Hodges 1986: 9). He explained:

> [...] This same intervention has been the reason why the other peoples of Central America and Mexico detest us Nicaraguans. And that hatred was confirmed for me during my travels in those countries.
>
> I felt most deeply wounded when they said to me, "Sell-out of your own country, shameless, a traitor" (Conrad 1990: 43).

In his early writings, and later in his actions, Sandino reacted to US imperialism in Nicaragua and Latin America as an intensely personal affront which he depicted in gendered terms. In other words, Sandino conceived of US domination over Latin American countries through a personal idiom; in terms of the domination of one person over another, particularly one man over another man.

Sandino interpreted US intervention in Latin America as a violation of the honor of the Latin American man and his country. Gendered ideologies of chivalry and male honor infused the fervent anti-yankeeism that he would violently unleash in Nicaragua. Sandino recalled:

> Back in the year 1925 I wanted to believe that everything in Nicaragua had become ignominious and that honor had disappeared entirely from the people of that land. At that time [in Mexico]...I succeeded in surrounding myself with a group of spiritualist friends,

with whom day after day I discussed the submission of our Latin American peoples before the hypocritical or forceful advance of the murderous Yankee empire (Conrad 1990: 41).

It appears that although Sandino was involved with anti-imperialist and anti-capitalist groups in Mexico, he did not participate actively in political or labor agitation. In fact, his North American bosses highly praised him as "a most satisfactory employee" (Macaulay 1967: 53).

Sandino was influenced by the *indigenista* movements in Latin America that attempted to include Indian and mestizo symbolism within Latin American national self-definition. These movements, rather than exclusively looking towards the Spanish cultural and racial patrimony as the basis for Latin American singularity, incorporated (in theory if not in practice) indigenous American traits as the source of a unique Indo-Hispanic mestizo identity (Hooker 2005: 29). Nicaraguan historian Alejandro Bendaña described the indo-hispanism that flourished in Latin America in the 1920s in the following manner:

> Indohispanism responded to the necessity of counteracting the negative and demoralizing influence of racism against oppressed people by awakening in them a new pride and feeling of dignity which are indispensable to fight and nullify the prejudices between mestizos and indigenous people and also to unify politically and culturally dominated peoples - making sources of inspiration, patriotism and unity out of indigenous traditions and origins in order to serve the fight against foreign and domestic oppressors (Bendaña 1994: 93; my translation).

The writings of indigenist (not to be confused with indigenous) Latin American revolutionaries, such as Mexican author José Vasconcelos and Peruvians Victor Raul Haya de la Torre and José Carlos Mariátegui, helped shape Sandino's formulation of revolutionary Nicaraguan nationalism (Bendaña 1994: 91). It is important to note that this revolutionary indigenist current was not radically different from the Creole nationalism of the nineteenth-century independence movements which officially valorized indigenous symbolism while simultaneously manifesting paternalistic and condescending attitudes toward the mestizo and Indian. In both of these nationalist formulations the Indian was perceived as an obstacle to national progress. Sandino, who labeled himself *"hijo de Bolívar,"* came to view the war that he soon initiated against the United States as a first step in the fulfillment of "the supreme dream of Bolívar" (Ramírez 1988: 157, 218).

Gregorio Sandino, Sandino's father, was the grandson of "a certain *Señor* Sandino arrived in Nicaragua from Spain" whose son married a "pure Indian girl named Agustina Múñoz" (Conrad 1990: 27). Sandino was the bastard child of Don Gregorio Sandino, who himself was the son of a Spanish immigrant and an "India de origin nahuatl" (Torres Espinosa 1983: 14). Sandino's mother, Margarita Calderón, was a *campesina* who worked on one of his father's farms. He was traumatized by the twist of fate that deprived him "the warmth of a home." Only after being accepted into his father's home at age eleven did Sandino adopt his father's last name: Sandino replaced Calderón, his mother's last name. From this point forward he enjoyed the social advantages of the Spanish descended Sandino family "which occupies one of the most prominent places...in Niquinohomo." But he never forgot the misery, rejection and "lack of power" of being raised a poor bastard child (Conrad 1990: 27). This painful contradiction generated in Sandino a profound ambivalence with regard to his origin. For example, although glorifying the social prominence of his paternal line, Sandino described his father in the following manner: "My father is short and strong. In him predominates the blood of his mother, because he is markedly of the Indo-Hispanic type and a man of good manners and sober behavior" (Conrad 1990: 27).

In this statement, Sandino attributed his father's positive traits to his maternal "Indian" heritage rather than to the Spanish heritage to which the Sandino family owed its social prominence. This valorization of Indian heritage was not a trivial stance in a country in which Spanish and European "blood" and "culture" were commonly perceived as providing a civilizing influence on a savage and backwards Indian past; an attitude which continues to a lesser extent in the present across the Americas.

Sandino became a mildly successful trader as a young man and clearly "whitened" himself in the process. In Latin America, wealth is a means for social whitening but, as Mary Weismantel reminds us in her chilling exposition of the myth of the Andean "Pishtaco's" sexual predation, whiteness is also demonstrated through sexual predation of whites on Indians (Weismantel 2000). In the case of his appeal to his father for recognition, Sandino clearly did not reject the raced and gendered patriarchy of his time, but later as a militia leader he explicitly forbade the most gruesome examples of the sexualized violence of war that had been practiced in the Segovias, such as ritualized gang rape of civilian women (Schroeder 1996). Yet later in life, after years of waging war in and around the Atlantic Coast, Sandino's state-

ments revealed a disturbing racism towards the corporeal presence of Atlantic Coast Indian communities as opposed to the more symbolic presence
of Pacific Indianness. Take for example this statement delivered to Román:

> I want to be frank with you when it comes to women. Of course I
> like them! But I don't find these Zambas and even less these prosti-
> tutes to be appetizing. That is why I brought Teresa [his Salvadoran
> mistress]. Here my soldiers can try to romance anyone they want,
> they can be Zambas or others but it has to be consensual. Because
> one of the fixed laws of our army is that whoever rapes or abuses a
> woman will be shot without questions. And because there are so
> many Indians and peasants there are no problems. There haven't
> been any cases of homosexuality during the war. Those acts of urban
> degeneracy are taboo here (my translation, Román 1983: 86).

Here we see the intersection of ideologies of sex and gender with racial
and regional ideologies as well as the problematic conflation of highly di-
vergent definitions of Indianness that I am arguing is symptomatic of larger
ongoing problems in Atlantic–Pacific relations in Nicaragua.

The Indo-Hispanic formulations that flourished in post-revolutionary
Mexico appealed to a young Sandino who was haunted by ambivalence
with regard to his racial and social position:

> Sandino found in Tampico a Mexican nationalism that glorified
> in Mexico's Indian heritage. Although not a pure Indian, he could
> exult that more Indian blood than any other type coursed his veins.
> He began to identify himself with a broad nationality embracing all
> Americans of Iberian and Indian descent (Macaulay 1967: 53).

Soon after returning from Mexico Sandino wrote in a "Manifesto" addressed to "the Nicaraguans, to the Central Americans, to the Indo-Hispanic Race":

> I am a Nicaraguan and I am proud because in my veins flows above
> all the blood of the Indian race, which by some atavism encompasses
> the mystery of being patriotic, loyal and sincere....The oligarchs...will
> say that I am a plebeian, but it doesn't matter. My greatest honor is
> that I come from the lap of the oppressed, the soul and spirit of our
> race, those who have lived ignored and forgotten (Conrad 1990: 74).

By the time Sandino returned from Mexico he had synthesized an indigenist glorification of the indigenous race with a class-based critique of
Nicaraguan society and its complicity with US imperialism. In Mexico Sandino anxiously followed the political developments in Nicaragua where in
1926, one year after the withdrawal of the US troops which had occupied
Nicaragua since 1910, a Liberal revolution erupted against the US-backed

Conservative government. In May of 1926, after receiving a letter from his father bidding him to return, Sandino, who in Mexico had boasted that: "if in Nicaragua there were a hundred men who loved their country as much as I do, our nation would restore its absolute sovereignty, threatened by that same Yankee empire," resigned his position in the Huasteca Petroleum Company and returned to Nicaragua (Conrad 1990: 41).

Sandino, who shared his father's Liberal Party sympathies, considered that Nicaragua had never completely recovered its sovereignty from the events of 1909 in which the Liberal government of José Santos Zelaya was overthrown by a US backed Conservative rebellion. Zelaya had fallen out of favor with the United States because of his refusal to grant the United States the exclusive right to build a trans-isthmian canal. It was rumored that he was negotiating such an arrangement with Japan or Germany in blatant disregard of the US Monroe Doctrine. Zelaya also irritated the United States by cultivating more active financial relationships with European powers, negotiating a large loan from Britain. Zelaya's policy of canceling or threatening to cancel US land and mining concessions, primarily in the Atlantic Coast, also contributed significantly to his demise (Hodges 1990: 7). Not surprisingly, these actions attracted the ire of the US State Department led by Secretary of State, Philander C. Knox, who not coincidentally was a major stockholder and consultant to one of the affected companies, the La Luz and Los Angeles Mining Company.

It seems at first ironic that the Conservative revolution and the subsequent invasion of Nicaraguan territory by US troops "to protect American lives and property" started in Bluefields — a port city that only 17 years before had been officially incorporated into the Nicaraguan state. English, as opposed to Miskitu in the north, was the dominant language of the Bluefields region. US companies had created a typical enclave economy in the area in which they occupied a quasi-governmental role. However, it was precisely this isolation from Managua and concentrated presence of US business interests which favored this area as a staging ground for a US backed rebellion. The revolt, led by Conservative Party general Emiliano Chamorro, began on October 8 in Bluefields with the help of Juan Estrada, the turncoat Liberal governor of the Department. Adolfo Diaz, a clerical employee of the aforementioned La Luz and Los Angeles Mining Company, loaned US$600,000 to the rebels, a sum which could not have come from his US$1,000 yearly salary, and clearly represented the meddling of "the Wall

Street bankers" — Sandino's favorite shorthand term for US imperialism (Hodges 1986: 5, 221). The initial enthusiasm of the US consul in Bluefields, who within the first five days of the rebellion wired Washington with the good news that a reduction in taxes and favorable land and mining conces-sion terms under the rebel government was assured, proved premature as the civil war dragged on for another year. By May of 1910 Liberal forces, ap-pearing to be on the verge of victory, demanded the surrender of the Conser-vatives in Bluefields. This victory, however, was prevented by the landing of the US warship Paducah which declared Bluefields a neutral zone and reconstructed the Conservative army which captured Managua on August 27, 1910 (Hodges 1986: 6). The events of the 1920s and 1930s in and around Puerto Cabezas followed a very similar pattern to the previous events in Bluefields. The geographic isolation of the Atlantic Coast made it a staging ground for the kinds of national indignities, as they were perceived by San-dino and many, that Nicaragua suffered at the hands of the United States.

The United States occupied Nicaragua militarily from 1910 to 1924, propping up unpopular Conservative governments, which of course were friendly to US interests. In 1912 the occupation increased in scale as thou-sands of US troops invaded to support president Díaz, the former La Luz Mining Company cleric, against a Liberal uprising led by general Benjamín Zeledón. The Nicaraguan government granted the US exclusive rights to the construction of a Nicaraguan trans-isthmian canal "free from all taxa-tion or other public charge" and it also leased to the US extensions of Nica-raguan territory for US naval bases, which were to be "subject exclusively to the laws and sovereign authority of the United States" (Hodges 1986: 9–10). The Corn Islands, located off the Nicaraguan Atlantic Coast, were thus unceremoniously handed over to the United States. During this period US army officers routinely commanded Nicaraguan police departments and controlled Nicaraguan customs offices.

The Conservatives stayed in power until the 1924 election in which a mixed ticket with Conservative Carlos Solórzano as president and Liberal Juan Bautista Sacasa as vice-president was victorious. Eight months after this coalition took the reins of government, the last of the marines withdrew from Nicaragua. Two weeks later the same Conservative general who had overthrown Zelaya in 1910, Emiliano Chamorro, organized a coup d'etat. However, this time the United States did not recognize the illegitimate Conservative government. In May of 1926, the US enclaves in the Atlantic

Coast were once again drawn into the center stage of Nicaraguan national politics as a Liberal force, calling themselves Constitutionalists, captured Bluefields. US forces, which had been absent for less than a year, once again occupied Nicaraguan territory, declaring Bluefields a neutral zone again. The Conservatives stayed in power and, in order to achieve US recognition, appointed Adolfo Díaz to the presidency. Immediately the Coolidge administration recognized the Díaz presidency. The exiled Sacasa, however, who had been legitimately elected vice-president in the election of 1924, continued to have pretensions of recovering his office, if not the presidency. His Liberal supporters both inside and outside the country prepared themselves for the overthrow of the Díaz government.

The Nicaraguan Liberals at this point adopted an anti-imperialist rhetoric that focused on the right of self-determination and sovereignty of Latin American governments. This Liberal sentiment, although far milder than the extreme anti-Yankeeism of Sandino, coincided with the political philosophies Sandino had developed in Mexico. After the establishment of a neutral zone by the invading US army, a Liberal official wrote the following impassioned appeal to Secretary of State Stimson:

> Since similar actions are not new because in the year of 1912 in order to maintain Adolfo Díaz in the presidency of Nicaragua against the national will large marine forces of the US as at present invaded our national territory; upon the repetition of the intervention at the solicitation of the same A. Díaz it is fitting to inquire and define for once what is the international status of Nicaragua. Is she a free, sovereign and independent nation, capable, therefore, of assuming her own government, or must we arrive at the painful conclusion that she is a colony or a protectorate? Have, perchance, the US, forgotten that small peoples have a right to independent life in the society of nations? Who determines the personnel of the Government of Nicaragua? The Nicaraguan people at the polls or the Government of the US by its recognition? (US Department of State Records, 817.00/4570).

Although Sandino sympathized with the Liberal cause he did not immediately join the Liberal forces. Rather, after arriving in Nicaragua following the failed Liberal revolt in Bluefields, Sandino headed straight for the mountainous Segovias and accepted a job in a US-owned mine, where he lectured employees about their exploitation at the hands of management. Sandino recalled:

> I explained to them the system of [workers'] cooperatives in other countries and the sad fact that we were exploited and that we ought

to have a government really concerned for the people to stop the vile exploitation by the capitalists and big foreign enterprises....I explained that I was not a Communist [bolshevik], but rather a socialist (quoted in Hodges 1986: 9).

Cutting short his efforts as a labor agitator, Sandino organized a paramilitary unit that attacked a government garrison close to the mines (Macaulay 1967: 54). The attack was repulsed, frustrating Sandino's attempt at leading an independent army.

On August 26, 1926, Liberal forces in a steamer launched from Mexico "flying the red flag" captured Puerto Cabezas after a brief battle (US Department of State Records 817.00/3896). In December of 1926 Sacasa returned from exile in Costa Rica and declared Puerto Cabezas capital of the provisional Constitutionalist Government. The United States was determined to stifle the efforts of Sacasa, who Mexico immediately recognized as the legitimate president of Nicaragua. However, Sacasa's minister of war, José María Moncada, was simultaneously waging a successful war against the Conservative garrisons of the Atlantic Coast. The US State Department feared that unless US intervention was escalated, the Conservative government would fall and the pro-Mexican Liberal forces would triumph. Encouraged by the Liberal takeover of Puerto Cabezas, Sandino descended from the Segovian highlands to the Caribbean port in order to join the Constitutionalist movement.

In contrast to the route taken by other Constitutionalist leaders and their troops, who typically traveled to Puerto Cabezas by sea from other Caribbean ports, Sandino traveled by land and river through the lowland jungles. Sandino relied on rural *Costeño* guides, who, with their knowledge and skill in navigating their canoes (*pipantes*) down the Coco River, carried Sandino to Cape Gracias a Dios. This was the first time that Sandino became acquainted with both this great river, the longest in Nicaragua, and the *Costeños* who lived on its banks. Sandino described his first impressions on arriving to the provisional Liberal capital of Puerto Cabezas:

> The morning was foggy and cold. The houses of the port looked depressed from the torrential downpour of the previous night. The small boat in which I was traveling with my five men docked at the fiscal peer.
>
> We jumped up on the peer and discovered some men armed with new carbine rifles and rounds in great abundance. They weren't in

military clothes and they gave me the impression of the mexican agrarianists [agraristas mexicanos].

The day was december 1, 1926.... [my translation, Wünderich 1989: 34).

Sandino's illusions as to the parallels between the Mexican revolution and the Nicaraguan Liberal revolution were soon shattered as both Sacasa in Puerto Cabezas and Moncada, who had established his headquarters to the south, in Prinzapolka, denied Sandino's request for arms and men. Moncada distrusted Sandino's political philosophies, which he considered far more radical than his own Liberal Party doctrines. Moncada wrote of this meeting with Sandino:

> At this time Sandino submitted to me a manuscript he had written that contained some of his ideas. It ended with the phrase "PROP-ERTY IS THEFT." Naturally this showed me what kind of man San-dino was and I refused to give him arms....Sandino's ideas go beyond socialism. His lifelong emblem is the red-and-black flag with a skull and crossbones. It seems that in Mexico he came into contact with anarchist elements [elementos ácratas]...and I believe these are the elements which are helping Sandino. (My translation; quoted in So-moza 1936: 83-4).

Rejection by the Liberals humiliated Sandino, who described the expe-rience as his "first political surprise." The next political surprise for San-dino, which he also perceived as an assault on his personal and civic honor, occurred three weeks after his arrival in Puerto Cabezas when US forces landed at Puerto Cabezas and declared it a neutral zone.

On December 23, 1926, the USS Cleveland and USS Denver landed 200 troops at Puerto Cabezas. The Bragmans Bluff Lumber Company along with other US companies in eastern Nicaragua had for months been requesting military protection from the US government.[1] When the US government finally did authorize the occupation of Puerto Cabezas, the company, which

---

1 Since August of the same year, US companies on the Atlantic Coast had been swamping the State Department with requests for US warships to be dispatched to the region. After the Liberal takeover of Puerto Cabezas the USS Rochester had been sent to the port but was not instructed to invade. In response to the requests by US lumber, banana and commercial companies, the USS Galveston was also sent to the Mosquito Coast. The following companies made requests to Washing-ton: the Otis Manufacturing Company of New Orleans, the Freiberg Mahogany Company of Cincinnati, the Mengel Company of Louisville, the A.W. Tedcaste Company of Boston, the Astoria Importing and Manufacturing Company of Long Island, the Chicago Bridge and Iron Works Company, the American Dyewood Company of New York and, of course, the Standard Fruit and Shipping Company of New Orleans. The above-mentioned La Luz and Los Angeles Mining Company

had been notified previously of the planned invasion, graciously provided "an engine and flat cars on the dock to assist the transportation of the landing force and equipment" (USS Cleveland Commanding Officer, United States Department of State Records 817.00/4570). The US military force instructed Sacasa's forces, which did not resist the landing, that "within twenty-four hours all armed forces must be withdrawn or the arms turned in" (USS Cleveland Commanding Officer, United States Department of State Records 817.00/4570). The majority of those Liberal forces that chose to evacuate the city before being disarmed went south to join Moncada's army at Prinzapolka. Sandino, an eyewitness, described these events in the following manner:

> Having received this rude order [for disarmament], the Constitutionalists began to abandon the town within the brief specified period. Since they were unable to remove all the weapons stored there, many of were thrown into the sea by the Yankees. As a result of this terrible humiliation, Sacasa's forces abandoned forty rifles and seven thousand rounds of ammunition along the stretch of coast from Puerto Cabezas to Prinzapolka.

> My six aides and I didn't want to go another step without taking those abandoned weapons with us. With the help of some natives of the Mosquitia we transported the weapons and ammunition by land to Prinzapolka (Conrad 1990: 44).

This time Moncada grudgingly accepted Sandino's bid for a command in the Liberal army. Prevented from maintaining their isolated strongholds on the Atlantic Coast, the Liberal army took the war to the central highlands where Sandino's column, on Moncada's right flank, demonstrated its effectiveness in battle.

Although the Liberal army first established itself on the Atlantic Coast, very few *Costeños* participated in the uprising. The only feature of the Coast that attracted the Liberal leadership was its isolation from the Nicaraguan government of the Pacific Coast. The Pacific Nicaraguan leadership, as well as most of the rank and file, had almost no experience with the lowland tropical forest environment of the Atlantic Coast. They were only familiar with the coastal ports which they traveled to and from by boat - never by land. In many ways the Atlantic Coast represented a foreign and unexplored country to Pacific Nicaraguans.

---

also complained to Washington that revolutionary forces were disrupting production (US Department of State Records 817.00/4515).

The lowland sub-tropical jungles of the Atlantic Coast inspired awe and fear in the hearts of Pacific Nicaraguans, who were accustomed to the deforested and heavily settled savannas of the Pacific. This image of the region is clear in Moncada's recollection of the Liberal march out of the Atlantic Coast neutral zones:

> Bottled in, the Constitutionalist Army...with nothing more on the horizon than the utter darkness of those jungles, the virgin forest, gloomy, labyrinthine, with deep swamps and dangerous trails, impenetrable rivers...only forked rapids on the horizon, a waiting tomb... (my translation; Moncada 1942: 108).

In the Pacific Nicaraguan imagination the people of the Atlantic Coast were thought to parallel the wild and uncivilized nature of its geography. The government in Managua had historically despised the British-backed Mosquito government that existed until 1894, often using racial epithets to disparage Costeño leaders. The Creole and Miskitu leaders of the Coast were often describe as savage and ignorant puppets of the British. Moncada followed in this tradition when he wrote: "The creoles of the coast have an extreme love for their lands. Pearl Lagoon was the capital of the Mosco King — that man that England had crowned who celebrated his monarchy hanging from a tree" (Moncada 1942: 98).

For the Constitutionalist Army, the Atlantic Coast represented a forbidding backwater region, inhabited by people who they commonly described as uncivilized Indians and traitorous West Indians. It was a region that could give them shelter long enough to organize an attack on the Pacific. Sandino adopted a different stance towards the Coast, however he still shared many of the same prejudices held by his Pacific brethren.

Sandino returned to the Segovias, the northern section of the mountain range which divides Nicaragua in half, via the Coco River; a journey that lasted an entire month. Along the way Sandino named new leaders and civil functionaries, who would be loyal to the Liberal Party, in the small villages that lined the Coco River. Some Costeños joined Sandino's armies as they traveled west (Wünderich 1989: 37). In February of 1927 Sandino captured San Rafael del Norte, a relatively isolated Segovian town. In March Sandino marched south and captured a more important mountain city, Jinotega. Sandino then joined with other Constitutionalist columns in the push to Managua. The United States, fearing an outright Liberal victory, sent Secretary of State Stimson to negotiate a settlement of the civil war. On May 12, the Liberals, represented by general Moncada, accepted the US peace proposal which guaranteed Liberal control of six departments and US supervised elections in 1928, in exchange for a complete cease-fire and disarmament. Sandino, the only Liberal general to refuse to accept the terms of agreement, retreated to his Segovian strongholds where he prepared to continue the struggle, which was now conceived as a war against the US marines and all of their Nicaraguan conspirators, regardless of their political affiliation. This marked the end of the Nicaraguan civil war and the beginning of what Sandino called the "war for national liberation" (Macaulay 1967: 58-60). This was a war that Sandino would wage independently, without having to make his ideas palatable to the Liberal leadership. The actions and pronouncements that Sandino made during this war provide the clearest example of his actual views with regard to the "Yankee invader," the Atlantic Coast and the "Indo-Hispanic race."

The main theater of operations for Sandino's armies was the Segovias and the northern Atlantic Coast, as well as adjacent districts along the Honduran border. These regions were the least populated and most impoverished regions of the country (Wall 1993: 2). Not coincidentally they both were the areas with the highest level of export-oriented production, all of which was controlled by the US. Sandino looted mines in both regions in order to raise money for his army, which was now being actively pursued by the marines (Macaulay 1967: 73). During 1927 and 1928 Sandinista and US troops met in several violent confrontations that caused significant casualties on both sides. The marines were greatly aided by the bombing and strafing runs of US warplanes. As Sandino's guerrilla tactics continued to have limited success, the undeclared war became increasingly unpopular in the United States. In only the first year of military occupation, the marine force in Nicaragua numbered over 5,000 and the US military spent over US$3.5 million (Dozier 1985: 207).

In the presidential elections of 1928, a much reduced Nicaraguan electorate elected Jose María Moncada, the minister of war under whom Sandino served in the Constitutionalist War. When the marines refused to fulfill their promise to withdraw from Nicaragua, Sandino resolved to continue the war against the United States, despite the fact that a Liberal was now in power. At this time the marines started to form the infamous National Guard, which was supposedly intended to be a neutral force composed of Liberals and Conservatives. This National Guard, and the family of dictators it propped up, would not be overthrown until the 1979 Sandinista revolution. Sandino and his armies, whose chief demand was the withdrawal of all US troops, continued to fight until 1933 when the marines withdrew without having defeated them.

Conclusion

Why should we focus our attention on Sandino again, after authors from every generation since his assassination, including his assassin, Anastasio Somoza himself, have written essays and books chronicling his legacy?[1] In addition there have been a number of works that have focused specifically on his dealings with and in the Atlantic Coast (Brooks 1998, Wunderich 1989). I believe that Sandino's life and writings put on tragic display both the failures and potential successes of the construction of a Nicaraguan nationalism and pan-americanism that is still a work in progress. Sandino was a border crosser who grew up in an agrarian world of the Nicaraguan *campo* as well as the industrial world of American-owned mines, plantations and oil fields in Nicaragua, Mexico, Guatemala and Honduras. He was an angry warrior in the "clash of civilizations" between the Anglo-Saxon and the Hispanic world that continues to collide between the Pacific and Atlantic of Nicaragua and beyond. He is a political figure whose legacy continues to be fought over among the decision makers of Nicaragua today as the, perhaps trivial, example of the naming, un-naming and renaming of Managua's Augusto César Sandino Airport illustrates. He was an original race traitor: a bastard son of a humble *campesina* and a Spanish-descended *patrón* who struggled to assume the inherited class position that was denied to him and, when he achieved this "recognition," he walked away from it. He was the *general de hombres libres*; a man obsessed with masculinity and Nicaragua's emasculation at the hands of the Yankee's "machos," and a classic caudillo who honestly and openly struggled to wage war without the sexualized violence that typified the rural warfare of his time (Schroeder

---

1  See Alemán Bolaños (1952); Baylen (1951); Beals (1983) [1932]; Belausteguigoitea (1981) [1934]; Bendaña (1994, 2007); Hodges (1986, 1992); Grossman (1996, 2006); Macaulay (1985) [1967]; Schroeder (1996, 1998) Selser (1979) [1966], Navarro-Genie (2002); Román (1983); Somoza (1976) [1936]; Torres Espinosa (1983); Ramírez (1988); Salvatierra (1934). With such exhaustive biographical coverage of Sandino, I cannot pretend to offer any new data on the life of Sandino. I rely mostly on secondary sources and collections/reprints of primary sources, with the exception of some documents on Sandino that are found in the records of the United States Consular Office in Puerto Cabezas, which are held in the National Archives in Washington DC.

1996: 412, Román 1983: 86, Torres Espinosa 1983: 81). He is the foundational hero for a new Sandinista administration that, unlike Sandino, has a second chance to build a just relationship between Atlantic and Pacific.

## References

Alemán Bolaños, G. (1952) *Sandino, el libertador* (Mexico, D.F, Ediciones del Caribe).

Anaya, S.J. and Grossman, C. (2002) 'The Case of Awas Tingni v. Nicaragua: A New Step in the International Law of Indigenous Peoples' in *Arizona Journal of International and Comparative Law* Vol. 19, pp. 1-15.

Baylen, J. (1951) 'Sandino: Patriot or Bandit?' in *Hispanic American Historical Review* Vol. 31, pp. 394-419.

Beals, C. (1983) [1932] *Banana Gold* (Managua, Editorial Nueva Nicaragua).

Belausteguigoitia, R. (1981) [1934] *Con Sandino en Nicaragua, la hora de la paz* (Managua, Nueva Nicaragua).

Bendaña, A. (1994) *La Mística de Sandino* (Managua, Centro de Estudios Internacionales).

Bendaña, A. (2007) *Sandino: Mística, Libertád y Socialismo* (Managua, Centro de Estudios Internacionales).

Brooks, D. (1998) *Rebellion from Without: Culture and Politics along Nicaragua's Atlantic Coast in the Time of the Sandino Revolt, 1926-1934* (Ph.D. Dissertation, University of Connecticut).

Brysk, A. (2000) *From Tribal Village to Global Village: Indian Rights and International Relations in Latin America* (Palo Alto, Stanford University Press).

Dennis, P. (2004) *The Miskitu People of Awastara* (Austin, University of Texas Press).

Dozier, C. (1985) *Nicaragua's Mosquito Shore: The Years of British and American Presence* (Tuscaloosa, The University of Alabama Press).

Finley-Brook, M. and Offen, K. (2009) 'Bounding the Commons: Land Demarcation in Northeastern Nicaragua' in *Bulletin of Latin American Research* Vol. 28, No. 3, pp. 343–363.

Frühling, P., González, M. and Buvollen, H. (2007) *Etnicidad y Nación: El Desarrollo de la Autonomía de la Costa Atlántica de Nicaragua, 1987-2007* (Guatemala, F&G Editores).

Gould, J. (1993) ' "Vana Ilusión!" The Highlands Indians and the Myth of Nicaragua Mestiza, 1880-1925' in *Hispanic American Historical Review* No. 73, pp. 393-429.

Grossman, R. (1996) 'Hermanos en la Patria',Nationalism, Honor and Rebellion: Augusto Sandino and the Army in Defense of the National Sovereignty of Nicaragua,1927-1934 (Ph.D. Dissertation, University of Chicago).

Grossman, R. 'Augusto César Sandino of Nicaragua: The Hero Never Dies' in Brunk, S. and Fallaw, B. (Eds) (2006) *Heroes & Hero Cults in Latin America* (Austin, University of Texas Press).

Hale, C. R. (2002) 'Does Multiculturalism Menace? Governance, Cultural Rights and the Politics of Identity in Guatemala' in *Journal of Latin American Studies* Vol. 34, No. 3, pp. 485-524.

Hodges, D. (1986) *Intellectual Foundations of the Nicaragua Revolution* (Austin, University of Texas Press).

Hodges, D. (1992) *Sandino's Communism: Spiritual Politics for the Twenty-First Century* (Austin, University of Texas Press).

Holm, J. (1978) *The Creole English of Nicaragua's Mosquito Coast: Its Sociolinguistic History and a Comparative Study of its Lexicon and Syntax* (Ph.D. Dissertation, University of London).

Hooker, J. (2005a) ' "Beloved Enemies": Race and Official Mestizo Nationalism in Nicaragua' in *Latin American Research Review* Vol. 40, No. 3, pp. 14-39.

Hooker, J. (2005b) 'Indigenous Inclusion/Black Exclusion: Race, Ethnicity and Multicultural Citizenship in Latin America' in *Journal of Latin American Studies* Vol. 37, No. 2, pp. 285–310.

Hooker, J. (2009) *Race and the Politics of Solidarity* (New York, Oxford University Press USA).

Horton, L. (1998) *Peasants in Arms: War and Peace in the Mountains of Nicaragua, 1979-1994* (Athens, Ohio University Center for International Studies).

Howe, C. 'Gender, Sexuality, and Revolution: Making Histories and Cultural Politics, 1979-2001' in French, W. and Bliss, K. (Eds) (2007) *Gender, Sexuality, and Power in Latin American since Independence* (New York, Rowman & Littlefield Publishers, Inc.), pp. 230-260.

Kepner, C. (1935) *The Banana Empire: A Case Study of Economic Imperialism. A Case Study of Economic Imperialism* (New York, The Vanguard Press).

Macaulay, N. (1985) [1967] *The Sandino Affair* (Durham, Duke University Press).

Mollett, S. (2006) 'Race and Natural Resource Conflicts in Honduras: The Miskito and Garifuna Struggle for Lasa Pulan' in *Latin American Research Review* Vol. 41, No. 1, pp. 76-101.

Moncada, J. (1942) *Estados Unidos en Nicaragua* (Managua, Tipografía Atenas).

Navarro-Génie, Marco Aurelio (2002) *Augusto 'César' Sandino: Messiah of Light and Truth* (Syracuse, Syracuse University Press).

Pineda, B. (2006) *Shipwrecked Identities: Navigating Race on Nicaragua's Mosquito Coast* (New Brunswick, Rutgers University Press).

Ramírez, S. (1988) *Pensamiento Político* (Caracas, Biblioteca Ayacucho).

Román, J. (1983) *Maldito País* (Managua, Editorial Union).

Salvatierra, S. (1934) *Sandino o Tragedia de un Pueblo* (Madrid: Talleres Tipograficos Europa Libertad).

Schroeder, M. (1996) 'Horse Thieves to Rebels to Dogs: Political Gang Violence and the State in the Western Segovias, Nicaragua, in the Time of Sandino, 1926-1934' in *Journal of Latin American Studies* Vol. 28, No. 2, pp. 383-434.

Schroeder, M. 'The Sandino Rebellion Revisited: Civil War, Imperialism, Popular Nationalism, and State Formation Muddied Up Together in the Segovias of Nicaragua, 1926-1934' in Joseph, G. and LeGrand, C. (Eds) (1998) *Close Encounters of Empire: Writing the Cultural History of U.S.-Latin American relations* (Durham, Duke University Press).

Selser, G. (1979) [1966] *Sandino, General de Hombres Libres* (San Jose, Costa Rica, Editorial Universitaria Centroamericana).

Somoza A. (1976) [1936] *El Verdadero Sandino o El Calavario de las Segovias.* (Managua, Editorial San Jose).

Torres Espinosa, E. (1983) *Sandino y sus Pares* (Managua: Editorial Nueva Nicaragua).

United States Department of State Records. Records of Foreign Service Posts. Managua, Bluefields, and Puerto Cabezas. Washington DC, National Archives.

Weismantel, M. (2000) 'Race Rape: White Masculinity in Andean Pishtaco Tales' in *Identities* Vol. 7, pp. 407-440.

Wunderich, V. (1989) *Sandino en la Costa: De las Segovias al Litoral Atlántico* (Managua, Editorial Nueva Nicaragua).

# CHAPTER 4. FROM DEVELOPMENTALISM TO AUTONOMY: THE SANDINISTA REVOLUTION AND THE ATLANTIC COAST OF NICARAGUA

*Luciano Baracco*

> The angel would like to stay, awaken the dead, and make whole what has been smashed. But a storm is blowing in from Paradise; it has got caught in his wings with such violence that the angel can no longer close them. This storm irresistibly propels him into the future to which his back is turned, while the pile of debris before him grows skyward. This storm is what we call progress.

Walter Benjamin

The revolutionary triumph of the Sandinista National Liberation Front (FSLN) in July 1979 brought an end to the increasingly brutal Somoza dictatorship that had ruled Nicaragua since 1937. Although few links existed between the Sandinistas and Costeños, the revolutionary government gave a commitment to establish programs to protect and promote the diverse local cultures of the region. However, despite the successful implementation of a number of these projects, by 1981 the region became the centre of a crisis signaled by a sudden and unexpected rupture between the Miskitu Indians and the revolutionary state. In order to understand the emergence and nature of this conflict this chapter will discuss the construction of indigenous Costeño political identities in Sandinista discourses, demonstrating how such discourses functioned to deny the Miskitu any political agency of their own and rendered their demands for autonomy a result of manipulation by counter-revolutionary forces. It will then discuss the Miskitu rejection of the Sandinista revolution through the analytical concept of "Anglo cultural affinities," developed by Hale (1994). Rejecting Hale's approach, this chapter will examine the Miskitu struggle against the Sandinistas in terms of an emergent ethnonationalism sparked by an increasingly invasive national state that embodied a strongly assimilating modernization project, the growing saliency amongst the Miskitu of the idea of self-determination as a consequence of the Sandinistas' own anti-imperialist rhetoric and the influence of Fourth World pan-indigenist ideology, and a region-wide intensification of communications between Miskitu communities consequent on the Literacy Project in Languages (1981). By examining the combined impact of these factors, the analysis will move beyond the focus on ideological manipulation and "backwardness" common to the explanatory models of both the Sandinistas and Hale, to demonstrate how the Miskitu acted as conscious political agents bearing their own national project.

Company Time

The period of the Somoza dictatorship coincided with the economic boom of the 1950s, commonly referred to on the Coast as Company Time, when US logging and mining interests offered Costeños lucrative employment and access to well-stocked company stores. During this period, the repression that became the hallmark of the dictatorship's National Guard remained largely unknown to the inhabitants of the Coast. US companies had established a number of economic enclaves centered on the extraction of natural resources that were highly integrated into the world market and, consequently, highly susceptible to boom-and-bust cycles of world trade (Helms: 1971, Vilas: 1989). The region's limited infrastructural and industrial development was restricted almost exclusively to the areas around these enclaves, leading to a significantly different form of economic development than in the rest of the country (Ramírez 1982: 6, Gordon 1985: 131).

As Hale (1994: 119) points out, the 1960s witnessed a new development in the coastal economy as national capital began to be invested in the region. State development initiatives facilitated the colonization of forested lands by land-hungry mestizo peasants from Pacific Nicaragua, as well as the exploitation of coastal resources. Such initiatives were integrationist in character, with an underlying belief that regional development and national integration were mutually reinforcing (Vilas 1989: 61). However, the modernizing intent of these initiatives was undermined by the patrimonial character of the Somocista state itself, for, whatever the modernizing rhetoric, the Somoza clique was rapaciously plundering the region's resources with little regard to national development (Vilas 1989: 79).

The increasing presence of the national state in the region coincided with political and social changes that led to a degree of mobilization amongst Costeños. In 1967 Miskitu farmers set up the Association of Agricultural Clubs of the Coco River (ACARIC) which by 1974 had evolved into the larger indigenous organization, the Alliance for the Progress of the Miskitu and Sumu (ALPROMISU). This mobilization was helped by the nativization of the Moravian Church, with Costeños replacing North American pastors and adopting a more progressive social agenda. Working together with Capuchin missionaries who had themselves been radicalized by the advent of liberation theology, both churches played a critical role in the establishment of ALPROMISU as an organization that promoted ethnic demands (Hale 1994: 126). In its early days ALPROMISU engaged in covert activities to garner support amongst both the Miskitu and Sumu-Mayagna Indians for the recognition of their communal lands: work that went unnoticed by both Somocistas and Sandinistas owing to its clandestine nature.[1] By the late 1970s, however, the organization suffered the same fate as many mestizo organizations, having been effectively co-opted by the Somocista state (Hale 1994: 128).

Social activism was also on the rise amongst the Coast's Creole population. By the 1970s Creole activism had become increasingly radical as a new focus on mestizo racism became a perceptible current of thought amongst a number of nascent Creole organizations. Influenced by the rising Black Power movement from the United States and the nativization of the Moravian Church, Creoles formed the Southern Indigenous Creole Community (SICC) which published a number of letters in the Bluefields paper *La Información* that were openly critical of the dictatorship (Gordon 1998: 172178). In 1977, Creole students based at the National Autonomous University of Nicaragua (UNAN) in Managua set up a Costeño political studies group,

---

1 Interviews with Julian Holmes, Puerto Cabezas 07/09/09; David Rodriquez, Puerto Cabezas 07/13/09.

with one member of this group, Dexter Hooker, making contact with San-dinista commanders in Costa Rica to persuade them that he could form a revolutionary front on the Atlantic Coast (Hooker 2008: 19).[1] Although Dexter's first approach was not well received, on a second visit he received military training and was sent back to Bluefields with radio equipment and instructions to recruit Bluefileños to the Sandinista cause.[2]

This activism remained largely unacknowledged by the Sandinistas in the elaboration of their revolutionary program. From its inception in 1961, the FSLN was a class-based mestizo-dominated organization with little ideological awareness of ethnic issues. As Gordon (1998) points out, the *Historic Program of the FSLN* (1969) is the only pre-revolutionary official party document that makes sustained reference to the Coast. In common with well established mestizo nationalist discourses, the *Historic Program* empha-sized the need to reincorporate the region into the nation's life and was es-sentially developmentalist in terms of the means to achieve this objective. It also stated a willingness to strengthen those original local cultural values that had their provenance in the region (Borge et al. 1982: 19). Beyond this party document, references to the Atlantic Coast were periodically made in the more literary works of Sandinista intellectuals, such as the poetry of Ernesto Cardenal and the academic studies of Jaime Wheelock. Yet such references were overwhelmingly disparaging, with Miskitu and Sumu In-dians depicted as living in a state of nature with no political consciousness and easy prey for imperialist manipulation.[3] It is also evident that Atlantic Coast Creoles are entirely absent from Sandinista texts, apart from one brief reference in the *Historic Program* to the need to wipe out "odious discrimina-tion" against blacks (Borge et al. 1982: 19).

Despite this negative portrayal, evidence suggests that at the dawn of the revolutionary triumph Costeños had begun to exhibit a greater degree of mobilization. Although ALPROMISU had been co-opted into Somoza's patronage networks by the late 1970s, a younger generation of politically active university-educated Miskitu was agitating for the adoption of a more

---

1 Interview with Dexter Hooker, Managua 06/30/05.
2 Interview with Jaime Wheelock, Managua 07/12/05.
3 See for example Cardenal's *Mosquito Kingdom* (1972) and *Zero Hour* (1956) reprinted in Walsh, D. (1980) *Ernesto Cardenal: Zero Hour and Other Documentary Poems* (New York, New Directions Books); and Wheelock, J. (1974) *Raíces indígenas de la lucha anti-colonialista en Nicaragua: de Gil González a Joaquín Zavala 1523 a 1881* (Siglo XXI Edi-tores, Mexico), chapter 2.

radical agenda. At the same time, Creole militant mobilization had led to the emergence of an anti-Somocista movement in Bluefields, with a small group of Creoles aligning themselves directly with the Sandinistas and engaging in armed actions against the dictatorship.

The Revolutionary Triumph on the Coast

By July 1979, the once bustling coastal ports of Puerto Cabezas, Bluefields and El Bluff, remained relatively forgotten backwaters as the boom of Company Time drew to an end with the global economic slump of the 1970s. Neither the dictatorship nor the Sandinistas had a significant military presence in the region. While the main northern city of Puerto Cabezas remained peaceful when the dictatorship finally collapsed, the southern city of Bluefields saw a number of military operations conducted by both mestizos and Creoles who had rallied to the Sandinista cause. From the outset, Sandinista sympathizers in Bluefields were divided along racial lines, with Creole Sandinistas commanded by Dexter Hooker occupying the National Guard's barracks, while a predominantly mestizo Sandinista group took over the Palacio, the city's main administrative building. Although Dexter Hooker's Creole group managed to disarm the Palacio group with military assistance from an international brigade that had arrived from Costa Rica, they too were subsequently disarmed on the orders of the Sandinista National Directorate over fears that they were promoting Black Power.[1] Mestizo Sandinistas sent from Managua tended to aggravate growing racial tensions by re-establishing what was seen by many Creoles as mestizo control of the city, replacing Creoles with mestizos in local government institutions.[2] By October 1980 Creole discontent erupted into mass demonstrations which were broken up by a contingent of military police sent from Managua (Hooker 2008: 91).

Despite this greater propensity amongst Creoles for militant mobilization, it was the Coast's Miskitu population that came to pose the greater problem for the revolutionary state. By 1981 the Miskitu, who had acquiesced throughout the Somoza years and who had failed to mobilize during the insurrection, mounted a full-scale military rebellion. Unlike the other armed groups opposing the revolutionary state, many of whose leaders were

---

1 Interview with Jaime Wheelock, Managua 07/12/05.
2 Interview with Hugo Sujo, Bluefields 07/16/09.

former members of Somoza's National Guard, the counter-revolutionary content of the Miskitu rebellion focused on its portrayal as a separatist movement that aimed to re-establish the Mosquitia: a project that challenged the very image of the Nicaraguan nation held by mestizos since the Reincorporación of 1894.

MISURASATA and Miskitu Political Consciousness

Given ALPROMISU's lack of belligerence during the Somocista period, the Sandinistas appear to have been genuinely surprised when the organization presented extensive demands only one week after the fall of the dictatorship (Carrión 1983: 250). After detailed negotiations, the director of the Junta Government of National Reconstruction (JGRN), Daniel Ortega, abandoned plans to integrate coastal Indians into existing mass organizations that had their provenance in Pacific Nicaragua and recognized a new Indian mass organization. At the fifth congress of ALPROMISU in November 1979, the organization was renamed MISURASATA: Miskitu, Sumu, Rama and Sandinistas Working Together.[1] The leadership of the new organization was composed of young Miskitu university students: Steadman Fagoth, who became MISURASATA's General Director, Hazel Lau, and Brooklyn Rivera.

MISURASATA's founding document *General Directions* (1980) represents a very strong anti-imperialist statement that aligns the new organization with the Sandinistas' anti-imperialist ideology and egalitarian values. Conversations with its main authors suggest that this pro-Sandinista stance was genuine rather than an attempt by the organization to ingratiate itself with the new regime.[2] The document portrays coastal Indians as "pure" Nicaraguans given their ancestral provenance in the region, while identifying their historic enemies as Nicaragua's liberal-conservative oligarchy and the general category of "foreigners," who are accused of the "merciless exploitation" of the region and its population. Despite the accommodation that had existed between Atlantic Coast Indians and Somoza, the dictatorship

---

1  Although Bourgois (1981: 33) states that no Rama representatives were present, Hazel Lau confirmed to me that the Rama did have one representative at the meeting. E-mail correspondence with Hazel Lau 27/12/09.

2  Interview with Hazel Lau, Puerto Cabezas 08/07/09. In July 2009, I managed to have a brief conversation with Steadman Fagoth in Managua. As one of the main authors of the document, he claimed its content was a genuine expression of support for the revolution at that time.

is singled out for particularly harsh criticism, with accusations of ethnocide being made against it (MISUARASATA 1983: 50).

The document contains an elaborate portrayal of coastal Indians as political protagonists who possess an "inherent revolutionary vocation and a capacity to resist conquest and domination" (MISURASATA 1983: 51). This capacity had developed over centuries of resistance against imperialism, which made them *sui generis* anti-imperialist subjects. There is also a criticism of "dogmatic Marxism" for denying the possibility of ethnic consciousness acting as a basis for political consciousness, implying an awareness of the negative characterization of ethnicity by the Left (MISURASATA 1983: 60). Contesting such negative characterizations, the revolutionary potential of indigenous people is underlined by presenting their cultural traditions as being "useful in the task of building a more brotherly, human and egalitarian society" in line with the Sandinistas' project of a classless society (MISURASATA 1983: 52). Being vulnerable to the same kind of exploitation by imperialism as the workers and peasants, indigenous peoples are depicted as analogous to these "broad groups," providing a legitimate space for Indians in the revolutionary process (MISURASATA 1983: 59). References to the right of Indians to participate in the revolution on their own terms are accompanied by a condemnation of the kind of official state indigenist cultural policies for amounting to no more than mestizo reconstructions of indigenity that "take away from indigenous people the role of being the protagonist in the formation of their destiny" (MISURASATA 1983: 60).

However, *General Directions* also underlines the indigenity of MISURASATA's claims, as its interpretation of themes such as imperialism and egalitarianism contained subtle differences from Sandinista interpretations. For Indians, the struggle against imperialism also included the need for "internal decolonization," while the notion of egalitarianism contained in the document was clearly at odds with the Sandinistas' developmentalism (MISURASATA 1983: 50-52). The celebration of subsistence production, coupled with a distain for "making a profit," suggests a model of production inimitable to the growth-oriented developmentalism so central to the Sandinistas' project of national modernization. Beneath these differences lay two mutually exclusive epistemic views of the world. Whatever the intent of the document to establish a space for coastal Indians within the revolutionary process, it did so without compromising their indigenous identity. Indians remained distinct from workers and peasants even though they saw themselves as bound together with these broad groups by a shared experience of exploitation by imperialism. Given the Sandinistas tendency to use the more nebulous dichotomy of "exploited" and "exploiters" alongside more specific class-based terminology in their populist appeals, MISURASATA claimed a legitimate place for Indians within the revolutionary process on the grounds of being an exploited group, regardless of their non-class identity.

*Asla Takanka* (Working Together): The Literacy Project, Plan 81 and Map Making

As the principal mass organization on the Coast, MISURASATA became responsible for implementing the revolutionary government's policies amongst the Coast's Indian communities. After negotiations with the government, work began on three major projects that ran concurrently: the Literacy Project in Languages, the promotion and organizational consolidation of MISURASATA itself, and a mapping project to define the land claims of Indian communities. The Literacy Project mirrored many aspects of the National Literacy Crusade in Spanish, that had reduced illiteracy rates amongst Spanish speakers to 12.96% (Ministerio de Educación 1980: 2). Government plans for a similar project on the Coast were changed after MISURASATA persuaded the Ministry of Education (MED) that literacy should be taught in indigenous languages and English rather than Spanish (Rivera 1983: 211).[1] Moravian schools had taught in English and Miskitu until the Reincorporación, when Spanish was imposed as the sole language of instruction. Although the prohibition on the use of local languages in schools was lifted after 1909, Somoza re-imposed it in state-funded schools (Freeland 1988: 26, 80). Given this history, the reintroduction of education in local languages formed an historic demand on the part of both indigenous and Creole Costeños.[2]

The negotiations between MISURASATA and the MED appear to have been characterized by a degree of confrontation. Hazel Lau, one of the architects of the Literacy Project, described the Sandinistas' original plans as manifesting a "Pacific vision" and demonstrating a "lack of confidence

---

1 See also chapter 8 of this volume.
2 Interviews with Hugo Sujo, Bluefields 9/04/99; Hazel Lau, Puerto Cabezas 07/08/09.

between the Pacific and Atlantic."[1] This lack of confidence appears to have been aggravated when the subsequent decision to teach literacy in coastal languages was portrayed as a victory over the Sandinistas (Gurdián and Hale 1985: 141). However, the discussion did not simply exhibit a mestizo-Costeño divide, as MISURASATA opposed the inclusion of Sumu in the project as an expression of the Miskitu's dominant position within MIS-URASATA, as well as the fact that the written form of Sumu was still in its infancy.[2]

As with the National Literacy Crusade in Spanish, the project followed a radical conscientizising pedagogy heavily influenced by the Brazilian educator Pablo Freire, which linked education to a wider humanistic agenda of social and political liberation. It soon became apparent that the content of the project contained fundamental contradictions with Costeño consciousness. The literacy primers were a direct translation of the Spanish version and focused on the historic struggle of Sandino, the revolution against Somoza and the role of imperialism in exploiting the country. Thus, the themes and symbolism of the project either had no resonance amongst Costeños or contradicted their collective memories of Company Time and the positive role played by the US on the Coast. The alien content of the lessons led many brigadistas (literacy teachers) to see the project as indoctrination, with the eulogization of Sandino being particularly alienating given his portrayal by the Moravian Church as a communist and bandit.[3]

Despite these negative aspects, the Miskitu were generally positive about the Literacy Project. Empowered by the revolution's pronouncements on ethnic rights and the formation of their own mass organization, Miskitu brigadistas were dispersed across communities, engaging in a process of conscientization that went well beyond the task of teaching literacy. Interview data collected from former brigadistas and técnicos (organizers) suggests that the ideological content of the Literacy Project was rejected by Costeños, yet detailed questioning revealed that they did not believe an alternative ethnic content emerged to replace it. This conclusion contrasts with accusations made by the Sandinistas that the project had been manipulated by MISURASATA to support its agenda of ethnic rights. Interviewees explained the failure of such an agenda to emerge on the grounds of

---

1  Interview with Hazel Lau, Puerto Cabezas 07/08/09.
2  Email correspondence with Jane Freeland 12/28/09.
3  Interview with Hugo Sujo, Bluefields 07/16/09.

a general lack of historical knowledge, the authoritarian manner in which the Sandinistas imposed the project, and a pragmatic silence that allowed Costeños to take advantage of the educational aspects of the project without in any way endorsing its political content.[1]

Throughout the Literacy Project, MISURASATA experienced a significant increase in importance and membership. The organization now had a regional presence with brigadistas in every community; a development that significantly improved MISURASATA's organizational coherence and communications with its base constituency.[2] Such an outcome began to raise questions that MISURASATA had deliberately manipulated the Literacy Project to increase its power on the Coast vis-à-vis the revolutionary government (Ramírez 1982: 7).

At the beginning of 1981, MISURASATA prepared to publish its *Plan of Action 1981* (Plan 81), which reflected the recent transformations within the organization consequent on its participation in the Literacy Project. While *Plan 81* included demands on well-established themes such as land, education, and cultural survival, the document contained a new focus on organizational questions designed to increase MISURASATA's mobilizational capacity. These moves appear to have raised the political-administrative status of MISURASATA in the eyes of its General Directorate, as *Plan 81* also proposed that the organization be given a seat on the JGRN, the highest governmental body in the country. The General Directorate felt justified in making such demands as the organization had become one of the biggest mass organizations in the country. They also believed that their claims were justified further by the presence of one JGRN-member, Rafael Córdova Rivas, who did not represent any mass organization.[3] In relation to regional government institutions, *Plan 81* stated MISURASATA's intention to take over the political-administrative functions of the Nicaraguan Institute for the Atlantic Coast (INNCA), the governmental department established to administer the Coast (MISURASATA 1983: 90).

*Plan 81* also disclosed preparations for the submission of land claims which would be based around the amorphous idea of "areas of domination" rather than the more usual term of "community," with support for such claims being fostered by an intensive consciousness-raising campaign and

---

1 Interviews with Julian Holmes, Puerto Cabezas 07/09/09; Anon, Puerto Cabezas 07/08/09; Anon, Puerto Cabezas 07/10/09; Hugo Sujo, Bluefields 07/16/09.
2 Interview with Hazel Lau, Puerto Cabezas 07/08/09.
3 Interview with Hazel Lau, Puerto Cabezas 07/08/09.

mass demonstrations (MISURASATA 1983: 92). On the basis of Costeño's long-held grievances over community lands lost after the Reincorporación, the JGRN had agreed to MISURASATA's proposal for a land demarcation project. The objective of the project was to establish the historic boundaries of the communal lands of coastal Indian communities. The Reincorporación had radically altered the legal status of the land on the Coast, with the national state claiming a monopoly of landownership. Under pressure from the British, Nicaragua signed the Harrison-Altamirano Treaty (1905) which gave Costeños two years to legally register land titles granted during the Kingdom of Mosquitia and the Mosquito Reserve. In reality, the treaty led to the granting of virtually no land titles and had failed to protect the long-established land arrangements practiced by Costeños (Hale 1994: 48, Pineda 2006: 65).[1]

In formulating its policy on land claims, MISURASATA appears to have been specifically concerned to avoid the imposition of an agrarian reform program based around the private ownership of "parcelized" land that mirrored a similar process occurring in Pacific Nicaragua (Rivera 1983: 215). With support from the pan-indigenous organization, Cultural Survival, Steadman Fagoth, together with a Salvadorian geographer named Mauricio Polanco, traveled along the River Coco collecting communal land titles from Miskitu villages to provide the data for a cartographic representation of the Miskitu's historic lands (Bryan 2007: 14). The map, which quickly became known as the Polanco Map, was completed shortly before the untimely death of its author who drowned during one of his expeditions on the River Coco. Although the many Costeños whom I have spoken to about the map told me that they knew of its existence at the time, only two people, Steadman Fagoth and Hazel Lau, confirmed that they had seen it. The elusiveness of the eagerly-awaited map appears to have encouraged rumors that it went well beyond the boundaries of communal lands to include a large strip of contiguous territory roughly corresponding to the boundaries of the Kingdom of Mosquitia.[2]

---

1 The Harrison-Altamirano Treaty also exempted Costeños born before the Reincorporación from military service for 55 years, in contrast to the Treaty of Managua which exempted indigenous people from military service in perpetuity. Interview with Julian Holmes, Puerto Cabezas 07/09/09.
2 MISURASATA subsequently published a map reputedly similar to the Polanco Map that covered 45,407km² of territory. This map also contained Creole lands. A copy of this map can be found in Ohland and Schneider (1983: 171).

The Breakdown

It was in this environment of increasing mistrust that the projects of land demarcation and literacy teaching reached their completion. As both had run simultaneously, MISURASATA's directorate decided on a joint ceremony to mark their completion, which would take place in Puerto Cabezas around February 25th 1981. Daniel Ortega was invited to conclude the Literacy Project, and Jaime Wheelock, as Minister for Agrarian Reform and Agriculture, was invited to receive the Polanco Map.[1] As a large crowd of recently conscientizised brigadistas would be in attendance, it was felt that if the map were to be presented under these circumstances its acceptance would be a *fait accompli*. Given the rumors that had already begun to circulate about the nature of the map, the Sandinistas ordered the pre-emptive arrest of MISURASATA's directorate and many of the tecnicos and brigadistas involved in the Literacy Project. Brooklyn Rivera and Hazel Lau were arrested on their return to Puerto Cabezas from Waspám on February 19th. Steadman Fagoth was already in custody for his role in a strike that had paralyzed Puerto Cabezas over disputed forestry commission payments made to Miskitu communities on the sale of timber cut on their land.[2]

By resorting to mass arrests, the Sandinistas avoided addressing the fundamental disjunction between mestizo and Miskitu conceptualizations of the land that remained so inimitable from one another. MISURASATA's approached to the land was doubly alienating for the Sandinistas, as it simultaneously threatened the long-settled mestizo population of the region, whilst also running counter to the developmental objectives held by the regime, particularly those emanating from the Ministry for Agrarian Reform and Agriculture, that saw the agricultural sector as the engine of a dynamic growth-oriented economy. Anxiety over what were seen as "selfish" Miskitu land claims was not restricted to mestizos, as they also generated significant fears amongst the large Creole population living in and around Bluefields that they would be "cast out" of their homes.[3]

During the mass arrests that followed the detention of MISURASATA's directorate, Sandinista security forces deliberately targeted tecnicos working on the Literacy Project. One interviewee who had worked as a brigadista informed me that, given their regular visits to communities spread

---

1 Interview with Hazel Lau, Puerto Cabezas 08/07/09.
2 Interview with Hazel Lau, Puerto Cabezas 08/07/09.
3 Interview with Hugo Sujo, Bluefields 07/16/09.

across the region, tecnicos were able to spread the news of the arrests in Puerto Cabezas.[1] It was during the pursuit of a tecnico named Elmer Prado that the first violent confrontation erupted. According to a number of informants who took part in the confrontation, Prado left Puerto Cabezas and headed for the mining town of Bonanza, spreading the news of the arrests of Steadman Fagoth, Brooklyn Rivera and Hazel Lau. Being pursued by state security troops, Prado traveled to Alamikamba and then to the small town of Prinzapolka.

State security troops arrived in Prinzapolka on the afternoon of the 23rd February, and that evening surrounded the Moravian church where a ceremony to mark the end of the Literacy Project was being held. Four armed troops entered the church demanding that Prado give himself up. The Moravian pastor attempted to negotiate with them, but the troops insisted on carrying out their mission.[2] One of the troops was then assailed by members of the congregation, during which the soldier's gun accidentally fired, killing the soldier instantly. In the developing chaos, the three remaining troops appear to have panicked and opened fire on what was an unarmed congregation before they, too, were killed. The national press reported four state security troops and four worshippers killed, with one of the dead soldiers reportedly having been beheaded (*El Nuevo Diario* 02/24/81: front page). The following account was given to me by a participant in the incident:

> On the 23 February, with the end of the literacy campaign in languages we returned from Puerto Cabezas and that night we held a mass in the Moravian church presided over by pastor Nanivan Wilson, who still lives in Puerto Cabezas. Then state security arrived in Prinzapolka in the morning investigating where Elmer Prado was. In the evening they came to the church looking for Elmer and came inside; they entered the church in the middle of the mass. They didn't respect the fact that the reverend was in the middle of mass. They told him they wanted to take Elmer from the church to prison.

> Well, Elmer was there and one of the state security known as Tiger entered the church followed by someone called Víctor from Managua. At this moment we went to say that they weren't going to stop the mass and that they should respect the place. We took their arms because we were in the church so we didn't have any. We were defending ourselves: an armed group entered the church with hundreds of people in it. We took their arms and killed Tiger

1  Interview with Anon, Puerto Cabezas 07/10/09.
2  Interview with David Rodriguez, Puerto Cabezas 07/13/09

and Victor with them. Two Miskitu were killed because they [the troops] started shooting as they ran away.[1]

Prado and one of my informants, both of whom were wounded in the incident, fled to the community of Kuamwatla, and later arrived at the hospital in Puerto Cabezas where they were arrested by Sandinista troops. The doctor who treated them during their convalescence in hospital was a Moravian pastor who provided them with women's clothing and make-up, and the pair subsequently escaped dressed as women. On their escape, they traveled north, eventually crossing the Honduran border and arriving in the port town of Lempira where they met up with other Miskitu who had fled Nicaragua.[2]

Accusations of separatism had already begun to be made against MISURASATA, in response to *Plan 81* (*El Nuevo Diario* 02/22/81: 9 and 02/25/81: 10, *Barricada* 02/24/81: 7). The Sandinistas claimed the document provided evidence that MISURASATA intended to break up the institutional unity of Nicaragua by monopolizing power in the region and to act as a parallel state that would declare independence and "seek annexation to England" (Sandinista People's Army 1983: 99-100). The incident in Prinzapolka was reported as part of an ongoing operation taking place on the Coast against a separatist faction within MISURASATA led by Steadman Fagoth, who was portrayed as a Somocista with links to counter-revolutionary forces in Honduras. Fagoth had recently been exposed as a former agent of Somoza's Office of National Security when intelligence reports written by Fagoth under the pseudonym of Saúl Torres were published, showing that he had informed on Brooklyn Rivera and other members of ALPROMISU for their supposed separatist activities (*Barricada* 02/21/81: front page, *El Nuevo Diario* 02/22/81: 9).[3] Identified as the main author of *Plan 81* in which he is accused of implicitly proposing himself to be appointed to the JGRN, Fagoth was depicted as a manipulative political opportunist who, as a member of the JGRN, would act like a Trojan Horse and betray the inner workings of the revolution to its imperialist enemies in pursuit of his personal aspirations to become a modern-day Mosquito King (*El Nuevo Diario* 02/22/81: front page, *Barricada* 02/24/81: 7).

---

1  Interview with David Rodriguez, Puerto Cabezas 07/13/09. Many of the people who were present at the incident whom I interviewed told me that they were convinced that Prado would be taken away and killed.
2  Interview with Anon, Puerto Cabezas 07/10/09. Elmer Prado died in Miami in the mid-1990s in a road traffic accident.
3  It was later claimed that Fagoth was acting as a double agent for the Nicaraguan Socialist Party. See *El Nuevo Diario* (02/28/81: 5).

After the release of most MISURASATA prisoners, government attempts to negotiate on any issue with Miskitu communities were summar-
ily rejected until Fagoth had been released from custody.[1] Fagoth had accepted an offer to study at a university in Bulgaria, and was permitted to
visit his ailing parents on the Coast before his departure. Accompanied by
only a light guard owing to the humanitarian nature of the visit, he escaped
and made his way over the Honduran border from where he began broad-
casting calls on *Radio Septiembre 15*[th] for the Miskitu to join him in his fight
against communism.[2] Responding to these calls, Miskitu began to cross
over to Honduras to be recruited into the ranks of a CIA-backed counter-
revolutionary force named MISURA, commanded by Fagoth.

In December 1981, the Sandinistas claimed to have discovered a CIA plot
referred to as "Red Christmas" involving a general uprising of Miskitu communities along the River Coco that would be joined by MISURA fighters
crossing into Nicaragua from Honduras. The uprising would declare the
region's independence, and invite recognition and military support from
foreign governments (Carrión 1983: 259). On the basis of these suspicions,
the Sandinistas removed the entire Miskitu population from the River Coco
region, destroying their villages and resettling them in the new inland settlement of Tasba Pri. The trauma involved in the removal of the Miskitu
from the centre of their ancestral homeland was wholly counterproductive,
significantly increasing the number of recruits to MISURA, whose ranks
swelled to an estimated 12000 (Carrión 1983: 235).

### The Sandinista Response: Indigenous Consciousness and Imperialist Manipulation

Responding to the crisis developing on the Coast, the JGRN published
a document entitled *Declaración de Principios de la Revolución Popular Sandinista
sobre las Comunidades Indígenas de la Costa Atlántica*, which restated an essentially integrationist and nationalizing perspective by underlining the territorial integrity of the nation and the need to integrate the Coast in national
economic development programs (JGRN 1982: 20). Although the document

---

1 Interview with Hazel Lau, Puerto Cabezas 07/08/09.
2 Interviews with Luis Carrión, Managua 05/08/05; and Hazel Lau, Puerto Cabezas
08/07/09. Hazel Lau informed me that she had visited Fagoth in prison, and he had
told her that he was tired of the situation and wanted to take up the offer to study
abroad made by the vice-minister of the Interior, Luis Carrión.

acknowledges the rights of Indians to exercise their distinctive cultural practices, the document makes clear that patterns of landownership will be determined by where communities "have traditionally lived" rather than by reference to historic territory (JGRN 1982: 19). The document also states that problems between the revolutionary state and the Miskitu were due to confusion deliberately spread throughout the communities by counter-revolutionary and imperialist forces (JGRN 1982: 19).

Subsequent announcements following the growing crisis on the Coast elaborated further on the peculiar vulnerability of coastal Indians to the counter-revolutionary tactic of confusion. In a speech entitled *La Amenaza Imperialista y el Problema Indígena en Nicaragua*, the minister for the Atlantic Coast, William Ramírez, stated that Nicaragua was essentially a mestizo nation despite the persistence of ethnic minorities. The fact that miscegenation between indigenous and Spanish colonizers had not taken place on the Atlantic Coast as it had done in the Pacific was attributed to the mercantile nature of British colonialism and the enclave nature of the extractive economic activities of US companies that had operated in the region. This model of colonialism and exploitation had limited economic development to the small enclaves that acted as economic hubs linked exclusively to the US market, rather than the rest of Nicaragua. Both British colonialism and US companies were accused of instituting a system of apartheid amongst the local workforce that had deliberately sustained indigenous identities as a strategy of "divide and rule" (Ramírez 1982: 6). In political terms, by sustaining indigenous identities, the enclave economy had retarded the growth of the kind of class consciousness developed by mestizos that had allowed them to play a significant role in Nicaragua's historic struggle against imperialism. This absence of class consciousness was identified as an explanatory factor for the complete lack of participation in the revolutionary struggle amongst the Miskitu (Ramírez 1982: 6). Given the "backward political consciousness of the coastal population," then, it had proved relatively easy for certain leaders within MISURASATA to manipulate them to take an antagonistic position towards the national government (Ramírez 1982: 7).

Sandinista attempts to explain the breakdown in relations with MISURASATA remained rooted in their conception of the backwards nature of Indians that they had held prior to the revolutionary triumph. Looking through the prism of this analysis, the Sandinistas had always been reluctant to support requests for the formation of a new Indian mass organization, as such a move would only sustain a political consciousness vulnerable to manipulation (Ramírez 1982: 9). The alternative would have been to include Indians in the class-based mass organizations that had developed during the revolutionary struggle in Pacific Nicaragua, which would enable the Indians to develop the kind of class consciousness that had led mestizo Nicaraguans to become active political agents (Calderon 1983: 147). By contrast, the inherently non-political nature of what the Sandinistas referred to as "ethnic" consciousness had left the Miskitu incapable of participating in any form of political life whatsoever (Calderon 1983: 152). While Ramírez notes the example of Miskitu participation in Sandino's army during his campaign against the US marines during the 1920s, he does so solely to underline the fact that Miskitu resistance had been wholly dependent on contacts with mestizo political actors: prior to this contact, the Miskitu had failed to offer any resistance to the foreign invader (Ramírez 1982: 6).

Given the perceived lack of political agency, it seemed inconceivable that the proposal for autonomy made by MISURASATA was a genuine expression of the Miskitu people. Historically, autonomy had its roots in the period of British colonialism which had created the Kingdom of Mosquitia to facilitate British imperial commerce in the region (Wheelock 1985: 47). This form of autonomy had continued under US colonialism as a strategy of divide and rule that had permitted the rapacious exploitation of the Coast's resources by US companies. From the perspective of the Sandinistas, by resurrecting a form of autonomy that appeared to emulate the Kingdom of Mosquitia, the Miskitu once again demonstrated their vulnerability to imperialist manipulation: they were now claiming as their own a system that had been created to serve the interests of British and US colonialism and which had left them in a severely underdeveloped state. In light of such a negative characterization, the Miskitu appear to have been presented with a binary choice: to maintain their identity as Indians and remain outside the revolution, or develop a class consciousness and, by the same token, become mestizo. Without such class consciousness, they would remain the kind of objects of imperialist manipulation that they had been ever since the times of British colonialism. Following such conclusions, Sandinista policies towards the Coast began to exhibit an overriding developmentalist and integrationist character as a means of instilling a class consciousness into the local population.

Miskitu Resistance and Anglo-American Affinities

While the Miskitu had acquiesced in the face of the abandonment and periodic repression characteristic of the Somoza period, the more progressive Sandinistas policies of cultural revival and economic assistance had been met with a militant ethnic mobilization that, by 1981, had developed into an armed insurgency. Hale (1994) has attempted to explain this paradox through the analytical concept of "Anglo cultural affinity," which depicts the Miskitu's embrace of Anglo-American culture and institutions as an act of resistance to the mestizoising pretensions of the Nicaraguan national state. Specifically, Hale argues that the Miskitu's adoption of Anglo-American affinities acted as a means of distinguishing themselves from "Spaniard" Nicaraguans (Hale 1994: 49, 83). However, this form of resistance became problematic during the Somoza period because of the dictatorship's close relations with the US and its emulation of North American anti-communism, all of which acted to obscure the exploitative nature of the dictatorship (Hale 1994: 139-40). In contrast, not only did the Sandinistas' essentially mestizoizing policies make them unmistakably "Spaniard," but their peculiar brand of anti-imperialist nationalism proved doubly alienating given its explicit condemnation of Anglo-American culture and institutions (Baracco 2005: 148). Thus, whilst Hale's thesis suggests Miskitu Anglo affinities acted as a break on ethnic militancy during the Somoza period, under the new conditions prevailing after the revolutionary triumph these same elements became the lodestones around which ethnic militancy coalesced (Hale 1994: 162).

This form of resistance was laden with contradictions, however, for the Miskitu adoption of Anglo culture and institutions as their own in their resistance against the colonizing pretensions of Spaniard Nicaraguans led to the substitution of one form of colonial subordination for another. Whatever the empowering affect of the Anglo-American presence on the Coast vis-à-vis mestizo Nicaraguans, the Miskitu's Anglo allies nonetheless subjected them to extreme forms of economic exploitation as well as political and cultural oppression by banishing many of their cultural practices and denying them the right to nationhood on multiple occasions. These features are exemplified by the Protestant Moravian mission, which many Miskitu came to see as the centre and protector of their cultural world. Documentary evidence from Moravian missionaries discloses a strongly negative characterization of the Miskitu, who were commonly described as "heathens" and "child-like": a distain that gave rise to a determination to civilize the Indians through a form of evangelization that strongly condemned almost every aspect of the Miskitu's traditional way of life (Hale 1994: 49). Thus, by exerting their distinctiveness vis-à-vis "Spaniard" Nicaraguans, the Miskitu drew on those very Anglo-cultured institutions that had condemned them: "Miskitu people were subordinated to both the Nicaraguan state and the institutions of Anglo-American neocolonialism. They resisted the former, while largely accepting the hegemonic premises of the latter" (Hale 1994: 27). This feature demonstrates that Miskitu consciousness was inherently contradictory, simultaneously resisting and accommodating forms of rule that were detrimental to their identity.

Although Hale seeks to demonstrate the rationality informing Miskitu reactions towards the Sandinista revolution, his analysis ultimately reinforces well established ideas concerning the irrational, backwards nature of Miskitu political consciousness. For Pineda (2006: 215), by suggesting that the Miskitu resisted mestizo oppression by internalizing Anglo-American hegemonic beliefs that were equally subordinating, Hale's analysis hardly moves beyond that of the Sandinistas in terms of his focus on the Miskitu's ideological confusion which made them incapable of recognizing the exploitative nature of their relations with the British and the US (Pineda 2006: 215-216). While Hale demonstrates the strong presence of Anglo cultural affinities amongst the Miskitu, his analysis continues to portray them as confused and manipulated objects of imperialism.

## Miskitu Resistance and the Sandinista Revolution: An Ethnonationalist Interpretation

An alternative explanation of the Miskitu rejection of the Sandinista revolution can be gained by seeing it as an expression of an emerging ethnonationalism.[1] The Miskitu insurgency against the Sandinistas did not occur because of ideological confusion rooted in political backwardness, but instead had its roots in the proto-nationalist imaginings awakened by the

---

1 Ethnonationalism is described by Connor (2004) as loyalty to one's own national group rather than to a state. Most states are multinational rather than nation states, as they contain within their borders multiple nations, or multiple ethnic groups that could develop their own distinctive national consciousness. It is loyalty to this national group rather than the state that ethnonationalism refers to (Connor 2004: 24-25).

increasingly invasive national Nicaraguan state, the demonstration effect arising from the Sandinistas' nationalist rhetoric on the rights of peoples to national self-determination, and qualitative and quantitative developments in communication between Miskitu communities consequent on the Literacy Project. From an ethnonationalist perspective, the Miskitu can be viewed as autonomous, active political agents who had begun to bear a national project that competed directly with mestizo Nicaraguan nationalism.

The Sandinistas' policy objectives of national integration through economic development disclose a nation-building agenda rooted in a teleological interpretation of modernization theory. Modernization theory has attempted to provide a systematic account of the gradual commodification of land, resources, labor and exchange relations characteristic of what Marx referred to as "primitive accumulation" that suppresses traditional relations of production by population expulsions and the expropriation and privatization of land and other forms of property formally held in common. Subjected to such pressures, the subsistence economies of traditional societies are expected to undergo a transformation that results in a "take off" of dynamic, perpetual, growth-orientated development characteristic of modern economic relations. This economic transformation is accompanied by a radical disenchantment and disembedding of society more generally, the essence of which is captured by Marx and Engels in the *Communist Manifesto* (1848) as the "uninterrupted disturbance of all social conditions" that sweeps away "All fixed fast-frozen relations, with their train of ancient and venerable prejudices and opinion" (Marx and Engels 1977: 39).

It is within these processes of disenchantment and disembedding that many scholars of nationalism locate the germination of modern nations. In the European context, the disintegrative impact characteristic of the initial phase of modernization was acutely observed in Durkheim's early elaboration of anomie. The moral disintegration of society wrought by modernization, and its corresponding psychological impact on the individual, impelled a search for new forms of social solidarity in which nationalism proved to be the most potent (Giddens 1984: 215, Delanty and O'Mahony 2002: 44-45). Resolving the disintegrative impact of modernization became so urgent precisely because of the historically peculiar need of modernization for a tremendous, continuous, coordinated, yet highly differentiated, human effort. With such an effort being seen as beyond the capacity of the mechanistic solidarity found in traditional village, caste and tribal societies, nationalism offered the possibility of fostering a more complex organic form of solidarity through the creation of a mass, generic, literate "high culture," capable of achieving integration regardless of the high levels of differentiation that constitute an inherent feature of modern societies (Gellner 1983). Nationalism represented a necessary component of modernization, allowing for the re-enchantment and de-disembedding of society under structural arrangements that were radically differentiating and destructive of the pre-existing moral universe: "...it has often been a form of modern re-enchantment in the sense of building the forms of identification that overcome the psychological emptiness that follows differentiation" (Delanty and O'Mahony 2002: 44).

Encountering modernization, the ethnic groups of traditional societies find themselves irresistibly caught up in its urbanizing, industrializing impulse, as well as its mass communications networks. This encounter is seen to erode the ethnic and cultural distinctiveness of small-scale collectivities by connecting them to each other, a process that leads, ultimately, to their assimilation into the growing generic national society which urbanization and industrialization embodies (Deutsch 1966: 188, Delanty and O'Mahony 2002: 106). And once the encounter has taken place, there is no turning back. Like Benjamin's depiction of the angel of history, pre-national people can attempt to "make whole what has been smashed," but the violence of modernization acts like a "storm blowing from Paradise" which irresistibly propels them into a future towards which their back is so often turned.

In the Nicaraguan case, this process of assimilation has commonly been referred to as "mestizaje" a miscegenation between the indigenous population and Iberian settlers that established the dominance of white, Spanish-speaking mestizos. Having broken their ties with their indigenous ancestral identity, mestizos bore an essentially national identity: becoming mestizo was analogous to becoming Nicaraguan. In the Pacific, mestizaje is commonly seen to have been completed at the end of the *War of the Indians* (1881), with the defeat of the last remnants of Indian resistance to the emerging national Nicaraguan society. On the Atlantic Coast, however, mestizaje had been blocked by the presence of British and US colonialism, which had established mercantilist and enclave economic activities that proved minimally disruptive to established ways of life amongst the indigenous population and thus permitting their survival into the mid-twentieth century.

These non-invasive relations continued until the end of Company Time, when the decline of the enclave economy brought a wave of mestizo immigration into the region encouraged by a new, though ineffective, modernization intent fostered by the national state. However ineffective Somocista modernization proved to be, the increasing presence of the national state appears to have encouraged limited mobilization amongst Costeño Indians, with the formation of ACARCI and ALPROMISU. This presence increased exponentially after the revolutionary triumph, when the new government engaged in an unprecedented modernization drive congruent with key aspects of modernization theory. Miskitu fears over the disintegrative impact that such modernization would have on their communities were not misplaced and demonstrate an acute consciousness of its assimilationist character, leading to significant resistance and, ultimately, to the emergence of a Miskitu national consciousness. For the Sandinistas, however, the nature of this resistance, seemingly rejecting modernization and drawing on culture and institutions introduced to the region during the colonial period, only confirmed the Miskitu as ideologically confused and objects of imperialism; a conclusion that led to an intensification of development-cum-nationalization policies.

A number of conclusions can be drawn from these observations. The critical explanatory factor behind Miskitu acquiescence or mobilization appears to have been the absence or presence of the national state in their daily lives, rather than hegemonic subordination. The abandonment of the region characteristic of the Somoza era proved minimally disruptive for Miskitu communities, suggesting that the absence of a cultural Other meant that there was nothing to resist. The exponential increase in the presence of the national state after the revolutionary triumph appears to produce a corresponding intensification of the Miskitu's militant mobilization and a strong assertion of their ethnic distinctiveness. Here modernization itself appears to have played a constitutive role in the formation of the Miskitu's self-awareness of their distinctive identity. Rather than promoting assimilation, modernization commonly sparks a self-awareness amongst ethnic groups concerning their distinctiveness, as improvements in transport and communications networks bring the increasingly pervasive presence of an alien national state and cultural Others into their life-worlds, often resulting in xenophobic conflict rather than assimilation (Connor 2004: 40). Self awareness is also dual-edged, as contrasts with an alien Other induce a reciprocal recognition of shared identity amongst members of the same ethnic group (Connor 1994: 37).

This observation becomes particularly pertinent in the context of the Literacy Project. One important factor arising from this project which remained relatively unnoticed was the role played by tecnicos in the region-wide coalescence of an increasingly coherent, and exclusively Miskitu, group identity. The continuous travel undertaken by tecnicos in their role as literacy coordinators that was originally designed to maintain the Literacy Project's momentum, acted as a medium through which to imagine a sense of connectedness amongst tecnicos and brigadistas who experienced each other as "traveling-companions," who shared the same mission within the same territorially limited space. More generally, the coordination of the Literacy Project facilitated unprecedented levels of inter-community communications. This appears inadvertently to have generated a horizontal sense of "temporal coincidence" across Miskitu communities despite their geographical isolation from one another, through which communities were made aware of their simultaneous progression through time, together, measured by the unfolding of the Literacy Project. It was this mundane, organizational feature that held the potential to imagine a novel sense of communion between geographically dispersed communities and their largely anonymous inhabitants, creating a sense analogous to what Anderson (1991) described as "that remarkable confidence of community in anonymity that is the hallmark of modern nations" (Anderson 1991: 36). The Sandinistas interpreted growing demands for autonomy amongst the Miskitu as the result of ideological confusion owing to the manipulation of the Literacy Project by agents of imperialism within MISURASATA. However, it appears that the emergence of such collective sentiments was an inherent feature of this mass-mobilizational campaign, suggesting that the process of participating in the project, rather than the conscious manipulation of its educational content, played a critical role in the formation of Miskitu group self-awareness (Baracco 2004: 646).

Focusing on analogies with colonial-era culture and institutions as the grounds for rejecting Miskitu demands for autonomy, the Sandinistas failed to recognize the essentially modern nature of this demand. Despite the historical precedent of the Mosquitia, the demand for autonomy was rooted in the revolutionary state's invasive modernization policies and the national imagining qualities of the Literacy Project. In no sense should the demand for autonomy be taken to represent a resurrection of the past. The Miskitu had long been Other-defined, yet perhaps for the first time the Literacy Project enabled them to become self-defined by creating a collective, inter-community self-awareness amongst the Miskitu of their unique group iden-tity. With the publication of the Polanco Map, this collective self-awareness would have gained an existential presence, with the discourse of cartogra-phy allowing for the imagining of a tightly-bounded geographical domain purportedly sharing a unique antiquity with the Miskitu people. Having disappeared from paper history, the precise form of Polanco's map will per-haps remain forever unknown, yet a similar map of the Coast published by MISURASATA in 1982 demonstrates the striking modernity of such spatial representations, with the depiction of a measured space bounded by con-tinuous and precisely-drawn lines that is entirely absent from cartographic representations of the Mosquitia.

The condemnation of autonomy as illegitimate owing to its perceived provenance in the colonial era also suggests the Sandinistas replicated the tendency within modernization theory to treat ethnicity as a primordial category characterized by ancient, autochthonous origins. The clause ad-dressing the Atlantic Coast in the *Historic Program* states the intention to "stimulate the flowering of the local cultural values of the region" yet re-stricts the definition of these values to those "that stem from the original aspects of its historic traditions" (Borge et al. 1982: 19). Such an approach denies the process of ethnogenesis that anthropologists have identified as an inevitable experience of ethnic groups (Eriksen 2002: 130). Acknowledg-ing that ethnic groups undergo significant evolution, rather than assimila-tion, makes the possibility of distinguishing "original" elements within their culture problematic. But in their treatment of the Miskitu, the Sandinistas maintained the primordialism implicit in the *Historic Program*, leading to a thorough rejection of autonomy on the grounds that it was not an "authen-tic" element of the region's traditions.

It is important to observe that this growing self-awareness amongst the Miskitu over their distinctive group identity occurred in an environment likely to transform such sentiments into a national imagining process. In-fluenced by the links established with pan-indigenist Fourth World orga-nizations such as Cultural Survival and the Indian Law Resource Centre throughout the 1970s, MISURASATA adopted a rights-based discourse that articulated Miskitu demands within the framework of the rights of peoples to national self-determination (Pineda 2006: 199-200, MISURASA-TA 1983: 163). These sentiments mirrored precisely elements within the Sandinistas' brand of anti-imperialist nationalism, producing what Connor (2004) describes as a demonstration effect: "If they have the right, why do not my people also?" (Connor 2004: 32). Once established by Sandinista nationalism, the idea of national self-determination was, to quote Anderson (1991), "available for pirating" in a modular fashion (Anderson 1991: 81). The Sandinistas were correct to assume that their policies of modernization towards the Coast would induce a national imagining process, but their belief that the nation to be imagined would be Nicaragua could not have been more wrong. The disenchanting effects of an increasingly pervasive alien national state, coupled with a perceptible sense of temporal coincidence amongst Miskitu communities as a consequence of the Literacy Project, played a critical role in enabling the Miskitu to recognize for themselves their unique collective group identity. Yet the transformation of group self-awareness into a national consciousness was made possible by the currency of the political ideal of national self-determination introduced by the Sandinista revolution itself. Attributions of backwardness as an underlying explanation of Miskitu resistance to the modernizing pretensions of the Sandinista revolution appear to be as misplaced as Hale's explanatory concept of Anglo cultural affinities, both of which deny the essentially modern, nationalist nature of this resistance. The Miskitu resisted assimilation into the Nicaraguan nation because they had begun to bear a competing national imagining process of their own.

This explanation leaves a question mark over the status of the Miskitu's Anglo cultural affinities. As Hale (1994) suggested, these affinities acted as highly visible group markers, which maintained a sense of distinctiveness vis-à-vis Nicaraguan mestizos whilst simultaneously providing the basis for self-recognition amongst the Miskitu themselves. However, the interpretation of the Miskitu's Anglo cultural affinities should not go beyond this symbolic level. While ethnic groups that have developed a national consciousness commonly assert their linguistic, religious and economic differences as a strategy of differentiation, these characteristics should not be taken to constitute the essence of their national consciousness (Connor 1994: 43). This is because national consciousness is psychological, rather than tangible, being based around a fictive, yet strongly held, belief of ancestral kinship (Connor 1994: 202). Ethnic groups that have developed a

national consciousness commonly draw upon history and cultural practices ethnosymbolically to reinforce group boundaries, but these do not in
themselves represent the essence of the nation which remains an essentially
psychological and attitudinal sentiment (Connor 1994: 43).[1] Given the symbolic nature of the Miskitu's Anglo cultural affinities, their existence should
not be taken to represent any form of ideological subordination.

## Conclusion

This chapter has located the roots of the Miskitu rebellion in the Sandinistas' anti-imperialist nationalism and national modernization policies.
What emerged from this program was not the assumed assimilation of
coastal Indians into the Nicaraguan nation, but what Connor (1994, 2004)
refers to as ethnonationalism: a minority nationalism that competed directly
with a pre-existing, dominant, Nicaraguan nationalism of a larger mestizo
population. Being restrained in their analysis of the situation by strongly-
held notions of the non-political and backwards nature of what they referred to as ethnic consciousness, the Sandinistas only saw the malign influence of their international enemies when confronted with Miskitu demands
for autonomy. Seen in terms of an imperialist plot, autonomy was soundly
rejected as a strategy to undermine the revolution through destroying the
territorial integrity of the Nicaraguan nation. Yet the status of Miskitu demands for autonomy as a separatist movement is questionable. According
to Connor (1994), the majority of ethnonational movements are concerned
with freedom from other, dominant, national groups, rather than becoming
an actor within the interstate system, leading them to favor "meaningful
autonomy" over independence (Connor 1994: 82-83). This observation appears to reflect many aspects of an emergent Miskitu nationalism during
the 1980s. Sandinista fears about separatism were inflamed by the actions
and rhetoric of a number of Miskitu leaders, particularly Steadman Fagoth,
whose role in channeling the frustration of Miskitu national consciousness

---

1 Connor (1994: 104-105) cites the example of Irish nationalism to demonstrate this
point. Although the Gaelic language became a rallying point for Irish nationalism
in its early years, the loss of the Gaelic language to English in no way diminished
the sense of nationhood amongst the Irish. The Catholic religion continues to play
a significant role in contemporary Irish nationalism, yet this role remains symbolic
rather than essential. Describing oneself as Catholic in Northern Ireland provides
a distinguishing marker against the predominantly Protestant British rather than
denoting any kind of deep religious conviction to the Catholic faith.

into armed opposition cannot be underestimated. However, his leadership status gradually diminished as a result of his intention to align the Miskitu struggle with the anti-communist ideology of mestizo counter-revolutionary forces. Many former Miskitu fighters informed me that they never saw their struggle as having anything to do with the anti-communist objectives of their CIA backers.[1] Much of the testimony given to me articulated the struggle against the Sandinistas in terms of resisting the authoritarian imposition of what they saw as a foreign way of life and a denial of rights. Fagoth's pursuit of a stridently anti-communist agenda marginalized these original demands and, in doing so, he appears to have alienated many Miskitu fighters who felt increasingly betrayed by this turn of events.[2]

By 1985, Sandinista proposals to negotiate a peace settlement provided a space for each side to reassess the situation. Fagoth's refusal to negotiate led factions within MISURA to form breakaway groups that conducted their own peace negotiations.[3] The negotiations were also joined by what remained of MISURASATA, under the leadership of Brooklyn Rivera. The critical issue arising from these faltering and intermittent negotiations was the increasingly clear distinction between the ethnic agenda of Miskitu fighters and the CIA-backed counter-revolution; a recognition that allowed the Sandinistas to conceptually separate demands for regional autonomy from the counter-revolution, making it an acceptable basis for peace negotiations.[4] For the Miskitu, autonomy held out the prospects of freedom from a dominant national Other; an objective they shared with so many other ethnonational movements and one which, if achieved, would allow them to negotiate with modernization on their own terms, autonomous from the hegemonic pretensions of both Nicaraguan nationalism and US neo-imperialism to which they had been subjected, and actively resisted, from the beginning of the revolution.

---

1 Interviews with Anon, Puerto Cabezas 07/10/09; Anon, Puerto Cabezas 08/07/10; David Rodriguez, Puerto Cabezas 07/13/09.
2 Interviews with Anon, Puerto Cabezas 08/07/10; David Rodriguez, Puerto Cabezas 07/13/09.
3 Interview with Anon, Puerto Cabezas 08/07/10. These groups continued to attack Sandinista patrols and also engaged in a number of ambushes of MISURA forces to take their weapons.
4 Interviews with Luis Carrión, Managua 05/08/05; Anon, Puerto Cabezas 08/07/10; David Rodriguez, Puerto Cabezas 07/13/09.

## Acknowledgements

I would like to thank the Middle East Technical University Northern Cyprus Campus Research Support Fund which financed fieldwork in Nicaragua in 2009.

## References

Anderson, B. (1991) *Imagined Communities: Reflections On The Origin And Spread Of Nationalism* (2nd edition) (London, Verso).

Baracco, L. (2004) 'Sandinista Anti-Imperialist Nationalism and the Atlantic Coast of Nicaragua: An Analysis of Sandinista-Miskitu Relations' in *Nationalism and Ethnic Politics* Vol. 10, No. 4, pp. 625-55.

Baracco, L. (2005) *Nicaragua: The Imaging of a Nation. From Nineteenth-Century Liberals to Twentieth-Century Sandinistas* (New York, Algora Publishing).

Benjamin, W. (1973) *Illuminations* (London, Fontana).

Borge, T. et al. (1982) 'The Historic Program of the FSLN' in *Sandinistas Speak* (New York, Pathfinder Press).

Bourgois, P. (1981) 'Class, Ethnicity, and the State Among the Miskitu Amerindians of Northeastern Nicaragua' in *Latin American Perspectives* Vol.8 No.2 pp 22-39.

Bryan, J. (2007) ' "We Fought the War to Defend Our Land" ' unpublished manuscript, Department of Geography, University of California, Berkeley.

Calderon, M. 'We Have The Job of Forging a Class Consciousness' in Ohland, K. and Schneider, R. (Eds) (1983) *National Revolution And Indigenous Identity: The Conflict between Sandinistas and Miskito Indians on Nicaragua's Atlantic Coast* (Copenhagen, IWGIA) pp. 142-152.

Carrión, L. 'The Truth about the Atlantic Coast' in Ohland, K. and Schneider, R. (Eds) (1983) *National Revolution And Indigenous Identity: The Conflict between Sandinistas and Miskito Indians on Nicaragua's Atlantic Coast* (Copenhagen, IWGIA) pp. 235-268.

Connor, W. (1994) *Ethnonationalism: The Quest for Understanding* (Princeton, Princeton University Press).

Connor, W. 'Nationalism and Political Illegitimacy' in Conversi, D. (Ed) (2004) *Ethnonationalism in the Contemporary World: Walker Connor and the Study of Nationalism* (London, Routledge), pp. 24-49.

Conversi, D. (Ed) (2004) *Ethnonationalism in the Contemporary World: Walker Connor and the Study of Nationalism* (London, Routledge).

Delanty, G. and O'Mahony, P. (2002) *Nationalism and Social Theory: Modernity and the Recalcitrance of the Nation* (London, Sage Publications).

Deutsch, K. (1966) *Nationalism and Social Communication: An Inquiry into the Foundations of Nationality* (2nd edition) (Cambridge, MIT Press).

Eriksen, T.H. (2002) *Ethnicity and Nationalism: Anthropological Perspectives* (2nd edition) (London, Pluto Press).

Freeland, J. (1988) *A Special Place In History: The Atlantic Coast In The Nicaraguan Revolution* (London, Nicaragua Solidarity Campaign).

Gellner, E. (1983) *Nations and Nationalism* (London, Basil Blackwell).

Giddens, A. (1984) *The Nation-State And Violence: A Contemporary Critique of Historical Materialism* Volume II (Cambridge, Polity Press).

Gordon, E. (1998) *Disparate Diasporas: Identity and Politics In An African-Nicaraguan Community* (Austin, University of Texas Press).

Gordon, E. (April–Sept 1985) 'Etnicidad, conciencia y revolucion: la cuestion miskito-creole en nicaragua' in *Encuentro* No. 24-25, pp. 117-138.

Gurdián, G. and Hale, C. R. (Sept 1985) '¿Integracion o participacion? El proyecto de autonomia costeña en la revolucion popular sandinista' in *Encuentro* No. 24-25, pp. 139-149.

Hale, C. R. (1994) *Resistance and Contradiction: Miskitu Indians and the Nicaraguan State, 1894–1987* (Stanford, Stanford University Press).

Helms, M. (1971) *Asang: Adaptations to Culture Context in a Miskito Community* (Gainville, University of Florida Press).

Hooker Kain, D. (2008) ¿La costa atlántica es parte de *nicaragua*? *Situación previa a la insurrección* (Copy Express, Managua).

JGRN (Oct 1982) 'Declaración de Principios de la Revolución Popular Sandinista sobre las Comunidades Indígenas de las Costa Atlántica' in *Nicaráuac* No. 8, pp. 19-20.

Marx, K. & Engels, F. (1977) *The Manifesto of the Communist Party* (Moscow, Progress Publishers).

Ministerio de EducaciÓn (1980) *La Cruzada en Marcha* No. 16.

MISURASATA 'General Directions' in Ohland, K. and Schneider, R. (Eds) (1983) *National Revolution And Indigenous Identity: The Conflict between Sandinistas and Miskito Indians on Nicaragua's Atlantic Coast* (Copenhagen, IWGIA), pp. 48-63.

MISURASATA 'Plan of Action 1981' in Ohland, K. and Schneider, R. (Eds) (1983) *National Revolution And Indigenous Identity: The Conflict between Sandinistas and Miskito Indians on Nicaragua's Atlantic Coast* (Copenhagen, IWGIA), pp. 89-94.

MISURASATA 'Proposal on Land-Holding in the Indigenous and Creole Communities of the Atlantic Coast' in Ohland, K. and Schneider, R. (Eds) (1983) *National Revolution And Indigenous Identity: The Conflict between Sandinistas and Miskito Indians on Nicaragua's Atlantic Coast* (Copenhagen, IWGIA), pp. 163-177.

Pineda, B. (2006) *Shipwrecked Identities: Navigating Race on Nicaragua's Mosquito Coast* (New Jersey, Rutgers University Press).

Ramírez, W. (Oct 1982) 'La Amenaza Imperialista y el Problema Indígena en Nicaragua' in *Nicaráuac* No. 8, pp. 3-10.

Rivera, B. (1983) 'We Are Part of This Revolution' in Ohland, K. and Schneider, R. (Eds) (1983) *National Revolution And Indigenous Identity: The Conflict between Sand-*

*inistas and Miskito Indians on Nicaragua's Atlantic Coast* (Copenhagen, IWGIA), pp. 120-130.

Rivera, B. (1983) 'Problems of the Indians with the Sandinista Revolution' in Ohland, K. and Schneider, R. (Eds) (1983) *National Revolution And Indigenous Identity: The Conflict between Sandinistas and Miskito Indians on Nicaragua's Atlantic Coast* (Copenhagen, IWGIA), pp. 203-217.

Sandinista Popular Army 'Counter-Revolutionary Plan Subdued in the Atlantic Coast' in Ohland, K. and Schneider, R. (Eds) (1983) *National Revolution And Indigenous Identity: The Conflict between Sandinistas and Miskito Indians on Nicaragua's Atlantic Coast* (Copenhagen, IWGIA), pp. 99-104.

Vilas, C. (1989) *State, Class, and Ethnicity in Nicaragua: Capitalist Modernization and Revolutionary Change on the Atlantic Coast* (Boulder, Lynne Rienner Publishers).

Walsh, D. (1980) *Ernesto Cardenal: Zero Hour and Other Documentary Poems* (New York, New Directions Books).

Wheelock, J. (1974) *Raíces indígenas de la lucha anti-colonialista en Nicaragua: de Gil González a Joaquín Zavala 1523 a 1881* (Siglo XXI Editores, Mexico).

# CHAPTER 5. EL GIGANTE QUE DESPIERTA (THE AWAKENING GIANT): PARTIES AND ELECTIONS IN THE LIFE OF THE AUTONOMOUS REGIONAL COUNCILS

*Miguel González*

The February 1990 general elections in Nicaragua chose the first regional autonomous councils of the Caribbean Coast, in addition to national authorities. The beginning of the councils' mandate coincided with the electoral defeat of the *Frente Sandinista de Liberación Nacional* (FSLN) at the national level and in the two autonomous regions. This created a totally new political situation throughout the country. The war ended and a reconciliation process got underway. It included a reform of the state and a reduction of the size of the public sector. Nicaragua was launched into an abrupt program to favor a market economy and a democratic representative system, abandoning the state that had acted as a centralizer of power despite being fragmented and weakened by war (Pérez-Baltodano 2003: 648-51). Some authors have called this initial stage a triple transition in Nicaragua: to a democratic regime, to a market economy, and to the construction of a new legal framework (Cruz 2001: 79). In the midst of this shifting ground at the national level, the Costeño population had tremendous expectations, especially about the autonomy statute, approved in 1987 under a polarized political context. In this chapter I would argue that autonomy has been held captive by the difficulties of democratic consolidation of post-war Nicaragua. By the same token, the meaning of autonomy for the heterogeneous population of the Coast is still a contentious issue and consequently needs to be scrutinized.

The Autonomy Statute: A Legitimate Though Still Contentious Accord

In January 1985, in parallel with negotiations with MISURASATA and in the same period when trends towards internal ruptures in the ranks of MISURA could be seen, the government began a consultative process on the conditions for autonomy through Regional Commissions headquartered in Puerto Cabezas and Bluefields. In June 1985, the National Autonomy Commission published a document entitled *Principios y políticas para el ejercicio de los derechos de autonomía de los pueblos indígenas y comunidades de la Costa Atlántica de Nicaragua*. It was a basic document designed to facilitate a direct consultation with the grassroots, to take place in every Atlantic Coast community (Comisión Nacional de Autonomía 1985).[1] At that time there was very limited knowledge among the various levels of central government institutions regarding models of autonomy established in other countries to resolve demands for autonomy through legislation and political-structural administrative measures.

In January 1987, the National Assembly approved a new political constitution, which for the first time explicitly recognized that the Nicaraguan people are "by nature multiethnic" (Asamblea Nacional de Nicaragua 2000: article 8). For the first time legal recognition were given to the communities of the Atlantic Coast over the right to preserve their languages, religions, art, and culture, as well as the right to "adopt their own forms of social organization and to administer local affairs in accord with their own traditions." Furthermore, "the state recognizes the communal property forms of land holding of the communities of the Atlantic Coast. Equally, it recognizes their enjoyment, use, and derivation of benefit from the waters and forests of their communal lands" (Asamblea Nacional de Nicaragua 2000: articles 89, 90, 91).[2]

---

1 Between September and December 1985, the most intensive phase of the consultation, some 1,200 volunteers got involved in promoting discussion in the communities. That led to the formation of almost 100 local autonomy commissions in Miskitu communities alone.

2 These three articles constitute a separate chapter in the 1987 constitution, entitled *Derechos de las Comunidades de la Costa Atlántica*.

In April 1987, a consensus was finally reached on a draft autonomy statute by the two Regional Commissions. Their proposal was put to debate in
an multi-ethnic assembly of 220 delegates, with each delegate representing a community from the two regions. This assembly gave its stamp of approval to the draft law or bill, culminating in the drafting of the autonomy
statute. A few days later the text was issued publicly in Spanish, English,
Miskitu, and Sumu-Mayangna.

In February 1989, in response to that publication, MISURASATA, while
still in exile in Costa Rica, presented a counter proposal entitled *Tratado de
Paz entre la República de Nicaragua y las Naciones Indígenas de Yapti Tasba* (YATA-
MA, 1989). It directly challenged the autonomy statute adopted by the
FSLN government. In its document — also unilateral and not the result
of consultations on the Coast, at least not among non-Miskitu people —
YATAMA presented,

> [the] fundamental matters of indigenous demands which...are the
> basis for a solution of peace with justice within the *Yapti Tasba:*
>
> • The traditional territory of Mother Earth, based on recognition
> of the historical rights of her people over the conglomerate of their com-
> munal lands;
> • Indigenous Autonomy in *Yapti Tasba*, based on recognition of the
> rights to internal self-determination of her peoples;
> • *Yapti Tasba*'s natural resources, through recognition of collective
> property rights over forests and water as well as usufruct of subsoil and
> the sea;
> • organization of the peoples of *Yapti Tasba* with guarantees for
> their complete freedom of movement, organization, and operation,
> within and without the country;
> • self-defense of the peoples of *Yapti Tasba* in which indigenous
> troops will have to continue to have responsibility for internal order and
> security of traditional communities and areas of the region (YATAMA
> 1989).

YATAMA's peace initiative saw the autonomy statute as a unilateral decision of the Sandinistas. But it conceded that both its proposal for a Peace
Treaty[1] and the statute could serve as a basis for defining indigenous autonomy, and hence for a definitive agreement between the parties.[2] Given its characteristics, MISURASATA's counterproposal did not prosper. With some

---

1 The *Tratado de Paz* was given to the government negotiating team in 1988.
2 Charles Hale identified the consistency of those demands then coming from ethnic militants. Hale grouped them into four categories, expressed as a platform for
rights. They included demands regarding territory, control of economic activities,
and authority over cultural and political norms in areas where indigenous autonomy would prevail (Hale 1994: 192).

modifications, the draft law backed by the Asamblea Multiétnica was introduced into the National Assembly in September 1987 and finally approved as
the *Estatuto de Autonomía de las Regiones de la Costa Atlántica de Nicaragua.*

Both the texts of the statute presented by the Sandinista government
and those by YATAMA, such as their proposed peace treaty, became para-
digmatic documents in the contest over the scope of desired rights for the
Atlantic Coast. They also became opposing visions that would be in ongoing dispute at varying levels of intensity during the contentious period
when the regional councils came into being.

YATAMA's conception of autonomy tends to have the character of an ethnic and territorial autonomy aimed to guarantee the rights of indigenous people in *Yapti Tasba.* In contrast, the Sandinista government proposed a regional
autonomy that, while territorially based, would take in the entire multiethnic
array of the Coast population. One of the factors of greatest importance for
the contentious nature of the autonomy regime can be seen in the political
tug-of-war over the legitimacy of each of these counterpoised visions, and in
the unachieved and disputed normative framework established.

In sum, severe changes in economic, social, and political life impacted
on the Costeño environment at the end of the 1980s. The war, the impossibility of carrying out economic projects, and the demoralizing impact of
displacement of populations imposed by war, would deeply alter daily life
on the Coast. Probing the magnitude of those changes is important in order
to evaluate what would be the real challenges of the autonomy process, not
only in terms of creating convivial social relations, but also in terms of finding an appropriate development model and fostering the wellbeing of Caribbean society.

Efforts Toward Unity and Reconciliation in the Coast

During the election campaign in the North Atlantic Autonomous Region (RAAN) the main leaders of the indigenous movement YATAMA assumed ambivalent postures, due to their questioning of the legitimacy of the
process of formulating and adopting the autonomy statute. YATAMA had
broad support in Mískitu communities. However, its leaders did not manage to define a strategy to enable the movement to participate and find allies in the elections. This caused a great deal of confusion on the Coast that
was aggravated by the fact that those leaders appeared to prefer to remain

outside Nicaragua. They did not really assume leadership as political figures, and they lost the opportunity to run as candidates.[1] There was consent
within YATAMA that its historic leaders, Brooklyn Rivera and Steadman
Fagoth, should come back in time to be nominated as their main candidates.
When that did not happen, a climate of uncertainty and doubt began to
cloud the coastal political environment. YATAMA's electoral slate for the
regional autonomous council was weak because their highest profile leaders were out of the race, and many other militants had insufficient time as
residents in the region to be eligible to run. The principal merit of most of
its candidates was their participation in the armed struggle, but they lacked
experience in democratic civic processes.

Brooklyn Rivera returned just before the elections, in time to help
YATAMA form two different national level electoral alliances. One was
with the Social Christian Party (PSC) for the election of National Assembly deputies. The second was with the large anti-Sandinista coalition, the
National Opposition Union (UNO) in the vote for president and vice-president of the country (Equipo Envío 1991a). This arrangement was motivated
by a strategy aimed to win as much support as possible in different levels
of the political-administrative ambit. It combined YATAMA's own political strength on the Coast with support from "friendly" political parties at
the national level in order to gain influence in the legislative and executive
branches of government in Managua. This seemed to be the correct strategy to be able to obtain support for subsequent reforms of the autonomy
statute that YATAMA had called for. These arrangements, however, meant
that YATAMA had to prepare its supporters to follow a complicated ballot
choice while its main political competitor in the region, the Sandinistas,
had a simple option for its supporters — voting Sandinista on all three ballots; presidential, national assembly, and regional council.

In the RAAN, the political options continued to mirror the polarization
between those who had been rivals during the 80s: the Sandinistas and the
Miskitu resistance grouped in YATAMA. The Sandinistas definitely came

---

1 Electoral law regulations establish that candidates and voters in regional elections must have resided for a certain period on the Atlantic Coast. Already in
1989 the Sandinista commander Tomás Borge had called on several occasions for
Brooklyn Rivera to return so he could participate in the elections. This would have
assured broader participation and candidates with appeal. According to Brooklyn
Rivera, Borge even offered him the Sandinista nomination for National Assembly
deputy, which demonstrates the high opinion held by the Sandinista of his leadership capacity (Interview with Brooklyn Rivera, Managua, February 2003).

out as more pluri-ethnic, with its Mískitu, mestizo, and Creole candidates. That diversity became a part of its appeal and mirrored the ideal presented in the autonomy statute. YATAMA's electoral rhetoric, by contrast, exhibited an ethno-political discourse charged with Biblical language and metaphors. It recalled the wartime suffering and the bloody relationship between the Mískitu people and the Sandinista government (Rizo 1990: 34-35). YATAMA did not seem to have illusions about winning votes from non Mískitu people, as its list of candidates was almost exclusively Mískitu. The UNO, however, ended up with only mestizo candidates on its RAAN ballot. It did not promote autonomy and had little presence in the campaign.

In the South Atlantic Autonomous Region (RAAS), by contrast, the UNO drew in the main forces aligned against the Sandinista revolution, above all in the urban Bluefields area. The Sandinistas ran several candidates who were members of the Creole intelligentsia and had played an important role in the formulation of the autonomy statute. The party presented a fairly coherent discourse on autonomy and multi-ethnicity, and it counted on local leaders with considerable political experience and appeal.

In summary, the contest to form the first regional autonomous council in the RAAN was between YATAMA and the Sandinistas. In the RAAS the main contestants were the UNO and the Sandinistas. In the north the elections took on a greater regional importance related to the issue of the autonomous system and distinct visions regarding the disputed normative framework and the legitimacy of the autonomy statute. In the south, however, interest was mostly focused on the national government and the polarization between Sandinistas and anti-Sandinistas, putting the regional elections on the back burner, and consequently tending to reflect national options.

However, the different dimensions of the contest — formerly fought out in armed action — had finally entered into the democratic civic and electoral arenas. In that context it would become possible to observe how different actors related to the normative framework of autonomy adapted to it, built their options and alternative alliances, and sought consensus. This stage in the contest also allows us to interpret how the different visions intertwined, and above all how people would try to apply them in practice, whether in the regional councils or in relation to national political figures.

The results of the first regional elections on the Atlantic Coast were in many ways surprising. First, the complicated voting formula offered by

YATAMA succeeded, as its sympathizers had to vote for different symbols on each of the three ballots, especially in the North Atlantic region (Rizo 1990: 36). There, thanks to YATAMA support, the UNO coalition won the majority in the presidential contest and the Social Christian Party, supported by YATAMA, won its only deputy in the entire country. In the regional elections YATAMA won a majority in its own name.[1] Second, the Sandinistas, although defeated in both regions, obtained a strong representation in both regional councils. Their vote mirrored the national tendency, where the anti-Sandinista forces were victorious (Equipo Envío, 1991b). But their regional vote suggests that the Sandinistas' discourse on autonomy and its pluri-ethnic slate of candidates had an impact on voters. The final distribution of seats in the regional councils, in political and ethnic terms is shown in the Table 5.1 below. It also summarizes the results for the six successive periods of the regional councils, with one table for each autonomous region, north and south.

Table 5.1. North Atlantic Autonomous Region (RAAN), Political and Ethnic Distribution of Seats, Regional Autonomous Council, 1990–2014[2]

| Period/ party | Ethnic group | | | | |
|---|---|---|---|---|---|
| 1990–1994 | Mestizo | Mískitu | Creole | Sumu-Mayangna | Total |
| YATAMA | 0 | 22 | 0 | 1 | 23 |
| FSLN | 15 | 3 | 2 | 2 | 22 |
| UNO | 3 | 0 | 0 | 0 | 3 |
| Sub-total | 18 | 25 | 2 | 3 | 48 |
| 1994–1998 | | | | | |
| YATAMA | 0 | 7 | 1 | 0 | 8 |
| FSLN | 9 | 9 | 1 | 1 | 20 |

---

1  A large portion of votes were annulled in the RAAN (20 percent). The usual reason was that voters marked more than one option on each ballot. It is likely that most of those votes came from YATAMA sympathizers who had not understood how to mark their ballots. YATAMA's complicated electoral tactic worked in large measure because of the enormous support it enjoyed, so strong that it could even lose 20 percent of the votes cast and still win a majority of seats on the regional council.
2  Tables 5.1 and 5.2 are based on data from the Supreme Electoral Council (1991). *Elecciones 1990*, República de Nicaragua: Managua; Consejo Supremo Electoral (1995). *Elecciones 1994, RAAN-RAAS*, Managua: Consejo Supremo Electoral

| | | | | | |
|---|---|---|---|---|---|
| PLC | 11 | 7 | 1 | 1 | 20 |
| Sub-total | 20 | 23 | 3 | 2 | 48 |
| | | | | | |
| 1998–2002 | | | | | |
| YATAMA | 0 | 8 | 0 | 0 | 8 |
| FSLN | 8 | 5 | 2 | 0 | 15 |
| PLC | 15 | 8 | 0 | 2 | 25 |
| Sub-total | 23 | 21 | 2 | 2 | 48 |
| | | | | | |
| 2002–2006 | | | | | |
| YATAMA | 0 | 11 | 0 | 0 | 11 |
| FSLN | 10 | 4 | 1 | 1 | 16 |
| PLC | 15 | 5 | 0 | 0 | 20 |
| PAMUC | 0 | 1 | 0 | 0 | 1 |
| Sub-total | 25 | 21 | 1 | 1 | 48 |
| | | | | | |
| 2006–2010 | | | | | |
| YATAMA | 0 | 11 | 2 | 0 | 13 |
| FSLN | 8 | 5 | 2 | 2 | 17 |
| PLC | 14 | 2 | 1 | 1 | 18 |
| Sub-total | 22 | 18 | 5 | 3 | 48 |
| | | | | | |
| 2010–2014 | | | | | |
| YATAMA | 0 | 12 | 1 | 0 | 13 |
| FSLN | 13 | 7 | 2 | 2 | 24 |
| PLC | 9 | 2 | 0 | 0 | 10 |
| Sub-total | 22 | 21 | 3 | 2 | 48 |
| | | | | | |
| Total | 130 | 129 | 16 | 13 | 288 |
| % | 45 | 45 | 5.6 | 4.5 | 100 |

*YATAMA — *Yapti Tasba Masrika Nanih Asla Takanka*; FSLN — *Frente Sandinista de Liberacion Nacional*; PLC — *Partido Liberal Constitucionalista*; PAMUC — *Partido Movimiento de Unidad Costeña*;[1] UNO — *Unión Nacional Opositora*.

The figure for Yatama in the RAAN includes the one and only councilor elected by the PSC (a Mískitu), with support from Yatama.

The departure of the Sandinistas from government at the national level symbolized the arrival of peace. The new central government (allied with YATAMA) was committed to support the development of Costeño au-

---

1 The PAMUC was founded in 1997. The party's foundation was preceded by another organization, the MUC — *Movimiento de Unidad Costeña* (Movement for Costeño Unity). The MUC was a Popular Subscription Association which had been founded by former YATAMA dissidents. The MUC had participated for the first time in the 1996 municipal elections; it won a seat in Waspám's municipal council. The 1995 electoral law instituted the Popular Subscription Associations as a flexible political organization able to compete for office in municipal elections. In addition to the municipal level, in the Atlantic Coast they were also entitled to compete for the regional autonomous councils.

tonomy (Matamoros 1992: 12-13). The evident regional base of this alliance appeared strong since the combined seats held by YATAMA and the UNO made up a majority in both councils. The hard times of the Costeño struggle seemed to be over, and the task now was to build the autonomous regime.

Table 5.2. South Atlantic Autonomous Region. Political and Ethnic Distribution of Seats. Regional Autonomous Council, 1990–2014

| Period/party | Ethnic group | | | | | | Total |
|---|---|---|---|---|---|---|---|
| 1990–1994 | Mestizo | Miskitu | Creole | Sumu-Mayangna | Garifuna | Rama | |
| YATAMA | 0 | 1 | 2 | 2 | 0 | 0 | 5 |
| FSLN | 9 | 1 | 6 | 1 | 1 | 1 | 19 |
| UNO | 8 | 2 | 10 | 0 | 2 | 1 | 23 |
| Sub-total | 17 | 4 | 18 | 3 | 3 | 2 | 47 |
| 1994–1998 | | | | | | | |
| YATAMA | 0 | 4 | 1 | 0 | 0 | 0 | 5 |
| FSLN | 7 | 0 | 6 | 0 | 1 | 1 | 15 |
| PLC | 15 | 0 | 1 | 1 | 1 | 1 | 19 |
| ADECO | 0 | 0 | 1 | 0 | 0 | 0 | 1 |
| UNO | 2 | 0 | 2 | 1 | 0 | 0 | 5 |
| MAAC | 0 | 0 | 2 | 0 | 0 | 0 | 2 |
| Sub-total | 24 | 4 | 13 | 2 | 2 | 2 | 47 |
| 1998–2002 | | | | | | | |
| YATAMA | 0 | 3 | 1 | 0 | 0 | 0 | 4 |
| FSLN | 9 | 0 | 1 | 1 | 1 | 0 | 12 |
| PLC | 14 | 1 | 3 | 1 | 1 | 1 | 21 |
| PIM | 2 | 1 | 3 | 1 | 0 | 1 | 8 |
| ALIANZA COSTENA | 0 | 0 | 1 | 0 | 1 | 0 | 2 |
| Sub-total | 25 | 5 | 9 | 3 | 3 | 2 | 47 |
| 2002–2006 | | | | | | | |
| YATAMA | 0 | 0 | 1 | 1 | 0 | 0 | 2 |
| FSLN | 6 | 4 | 1 | 1 | 1 | 1 | 14 |
| PLC | 22 | 2 | 4 | 0 | 2 | 1 | 31 |
| Sub-total | 28 | 6 | 6 | 2 | 3 | 2 | 47 |
| 2006–2010 | | | | | | | |
| YATAMA/ Coast Power | 0 | 2 | 4 | 0 | 0 | 0 | 6 |
| FSLN | 7 | 1 | 1 | 0 | 1 | 1 | 11 |

| | | | | | | | |
|---|---|---|---|---|---|---|---|
| PLC | 16 | 1 | 3 | 0 | 2 | 2 | 24 |
| ALIANZA LIBERAL | 5 | 0 | 1 | 0 | 0 | 0 | 6 |
| Sub-total | 28 | 4 | 9 | 0 | 3 | 3 | 47 |
| | | | | | | | |
| 2010–2014 | | | | | | | |
| YATAMA | 0 | 3 | 0 | 0 | 0 | 0 | 3 |
| FSLN | 9 | 0 | 6 | 1 | 1 | 1 | 18 |
| PLC | 15 | 0 | 4 | 1 | 1 | 1 | 22 |
| APRE | 0 | 0 | 1 | 0 | 0 | 0 | 1 |
| ALN | 2 | 0 | 0 | 0 | 0 | 1 | 3 |
| Sub-total | 26 | 3 | 11 | 2 | 2 | 3 | 47 |
| | | | | | | | |
| Total | 148 | 26 | 66 | 12 | 16 | 14 | 282 |
| % | 52 | 9.2 | 23 | 4.3 | 5.7 | 5 | 100 |

The parties are: PIM — Partido Indígena Multiétnico;[1] ADECO, Asociación para el Desarrollo de la Costa Atlántica;[2] Coast Power, The Coast People Political Movement — Movimiento Político del Pueblo Costeño;[3] MAAC, Movimiento Autónomo Auténtico de la Costa;[4] APRE, Alianza por la República; and ALN — Alianza Liberal Nicaragüense.

---

1 The Partido Indígena Multiétnico (PIM—Multi-ethnic Indigenous Party) was founded in 1997 by the Reverend Rayfield Hodgson Bobb.

2 The ADECO was founded in 1994 by Alvin Guthrie, a former union leader, first regional coordinator of the RAAS, and congressmen for the UNO organization in the 1990–1996 period. The organization had become inactive by mid 1995.

3 Coast Power was funded in 2005 by prominent Creole politicians, foremost among them Owyn Hodgson, a lawyer and former president of the Bluefields Indian and Caribbean University (BICU). Among the mainly Creole executive committee of Coast Power are: Weady Hawkins, Stanford Cash, Ruth De León, and Carrol Harrison. Owyn Hodgson was also Vice Minister of INDERA in the government of Violeta Barrios de Chamorro.

  The Alianza Liberal Nacional (ALN) was a national political organization founded by PLC dissidents headed by Eduardo Montealegre. They had become dissatisfied with Arnoldo Alemán's leadership. The ALN was able to recruit regional PLC members in both autonomous regions who were also dissatisfied with their regional PLC party leadership.

4 The MAAC was founded in April 1993 in Pearl Lagoon and headed by Faran Dometz, the well-known leader of the Moravian Church. Dometz had performed a key role as a peace mediator during the peace negotiations in the 1980s. For the 1994 regional elections the MAAC registered candidates in 10 of the 15 electoral districts of the RAAS.

Table 5.3. *Juntas Directivas* of the Regional Autonomous Councils Political Composition, 1990–2007, RAAN

| Period | Political Organization | | |
|--------|------|------|--------|
|        | FSLN | PLC  | YATAMA |
| 1990–1994 | 0 | n/a | 7 |
| 1994–1998 | 2 | 0 | 5 |
| 1998–2002 | 0 | 7 | 0 |
| 2002–2006 | 3 | 0 | 4 |
| 2006–2010 | 4 | 0 | 3 |
| 2010– | 4 | 0 | 3 |

Table 5.4. *Juntas Directivas* of the Regional Autonomous Councils. Political Composition, 1990–2007, RAAS

| Period | Political Organization | | | | |
|--------|------|-----|-----|--------|--------|
|        | FSLN | UN0 | PLC | YATAMA | Others |
| 1990–1994 | 0 | 7 | 0 | 0 | 0 |
| 1994–1998 | 0 | 1 | 5 | 0 | 1 |
| 1998–2002 | 0 | 0 | 5 | 2 | 0 |
| 2002–2006* | 0 | 0 | 7 | 0 | 0 |
| 2006–2010 | 0 | 0 | 7 | 0 | 0 |
| 2010– | 0 | 0 | 4 | 0 | 3 |

*\* During this period, two Juntas Directivas disputed their legality in the politicized courts. It was not until May 2004 that the dispute was resolved in favor of president Enrique Bolaños. The data included here refer to that faction.*

## Political Composition of the Regional Councils: Contentious Alliances and Exclusionary Politics from the Outset

The first regional councils were sworn in on May 4, 1990. The Sandinistas were excluded from the executive Junta Directiva of the council in both regions. In the RAAN, YATAMA took exclusive possession of the executive. The RAAN council also named a YATAMA member as government coordinator.[1] Old adversaries of the armed struggle thus predominated in the

---

1 The Junta Directiva was headed by the ex-military commander Uriel Vanegas, the council president; the first Coordinator of the regional government was Leonel

RAAN regional council. The three UNO councilors came from the Mines Zone, had no previous political experience, and had little knowledge of autonomy. In the RAAS the Junta was made up only of UNO members.[1]

Given the exclusion of the Sandinistas from the Juntas Directivas of the two recently established autonomous regions, the UNO and YATAMA became the protagonists in the first regional councils and regional governments.[2] Allying to form a government was a reasonable decision on the part of UNO and YATAMA leaders (Fonseca 1991). YATAMA saw the UNO-led central government as an ally while the UNO knew that support from YATAMA in the presidential campaign on the Coast had been very useful. Finally, everything seemed to suggest that, for the first time, conditions existed to build a "positive relationship" between the Coast and the central government. This might have opened the way to reformulate the framework for autonomy elaborated under the political hegemony. The total exclusion of the Frente Sandinista in the regional councils, however, would likely result in postponing and making more difficult the necessary regional reconciliation and consensus. But that factor was not considered. Or at least it did not manage to take on much weight in the considerations of the opponents. But it would impact greatly on how politics evolved inside the two councils: that is, through pragmatic and short-term alliances and through exclusion of opposition forces. Some improvement in party relations occurred in the next electoral period, though in the context of a growing role and pressure of national party politics on the life of the councils.

Engaging Collaboration in the Midst of Nationally-Driven Party Politics: Electoral Results and Political Consequences, 1994-2002

The scenario for the second regional elections, held early in 1994, was very different from that of 1989/1990 (Butler 1994). This time the elections were held only on the Coast and did not coincide with other elections

---

Pantin, administrator of the Moravian Church"s humanitarian organization.

1  Lawyer Alvin Guthrie, who had been elected National Assembly deputy for the UNO and hence automatically gained a seat on the regional council, was elected to the important post of government coordinator. The Junta Directiva included a member of YATAMA, originally from the *Desembocadura de Río Grande* community where political support from that organization was important.

2  Exclusion also took place in the working commissions of the regional councils. The Sandinistas were only awarded two important positions in coordination work.

throughout the country. Second, the war was over and relations with the United States, under president Violeta Barrios de Chamorro, had become normalized. Hence, the UNO coalition, whose only shared goal was to defeat the Sandinistas, had already begun to break up. Some of the organizations that had been part of this bloc went into the second elections on their own. Third, taking advantage of the erosion in both the Sandinistas and the UNO, a third political option was organized on the national level — the Constitutionalist Liberal Party (PLC). It arose from fusions between the various liberal parties of the country and under the leadership of the then mayor of Managua, Arnoldo Alemán. The 1994 Costeño elections, in fact, became an important trial run for the 1996 presidential election. Fourth, YATAMA suffered from a revival of the old internal struggle among its leaders. This was fostered by the new political context in which autonomy was underway, and new national political actors were becoming electorally interested in the Atlantic Coast. YATAMA thus entered the election campaign with serious divisions. Although the first two above mentioned factors meant that the election campaign could be held in a less conflictive and polarized ambience than in 1989/90, the last two factors would lead to significant changes in coastal politics for some time to come.

The Coast's regional elections were strategically important for the PLC. They were both a test of its capacity to reach local power in the regions and a step towards erecting its platform for the 1996 presidential elections. Hence, the party tried hard to get into every nook and cranny in both regions. From July 1993 on, the PLC energetically presented itself as a new political alternative by launching Arnoldo Alemán as national leader and future president, and by celebrating the centennial of the liberal revolution of president José Santos Zelaya.

The reference to Zelaya represented something positive in "Spanish Nicaragua"; economic advance, modernization, and consolidation of the country. However, in the Atlantic Coast, Zelaya was a negative symbol because he led the forced reincorporation in 1894. Despite all that, many Costeños were impressed by this effort on the part of the PLC. Although the PLC's discourse on autonomy for Costeños was not based on conviction, it was in fact the only national party that gave importance to the regional elections. It was consequently fairly successful in establishing a local power base and loyalties among some important Costeño leaders.[1] In part, this fact is also explained by the strong disenchantment of the entire Atlantic Coast population with the central government formed by the UNO coalition that had promised so much in the 1990 election. At the same time the Sandinistas did not seem to give much priority to the Coast elections and only managed to consolidate its traditional base of support and passively reap some benefit from the attrition of the UNO government.[2] The possibility of Arnoldo Alemán becoming the next president was obviously attractive to many Costeños who had seen that autonomy was an empty concept without a collaborative central government. This image of Alemán as a future national leader was also re-enforced by the alliance with leaders of the indigenous movement who, in a surprising move, emerged from an internal YATAMA dispute.

Brooklyn Rivera's leadership in YATAMA had been strongly affected by his role as the Minister Director of the Nicaraguan Institute of Development of Autonomous Regions (INDERA). Because of that, not only was his stature as YATAMA leader weakened, but also his period of convivial relations with YATAMA's other historic leader, Steadman Fagoth, had ended. That gave rise to a renewal of traditional rivalry between the two leaders. The final outcome — catalyzed by the dispute before the Supreme Electoral Council over who had the right to the official name and symbol of YATAMA for the election campaign — was that a faction of YATAMA led by Fagoth allied with the PLC and registered its candidates on the lists of that party, leaving Rivera with YATAMA's legal representation. This division in YATAMA was reflected tangibly in the electoral results and the seats obtained in the regional councils.

The political conjuncture of the 1994 elections, that saw a relatively low level of polarization and still high level of citizen participation,[3] favored both the proliferation of genuinely local electoral initiatives, under the rubric of the still permitted popular subscription association, and participation by

---

1  In fact, the PLC program in 1996 referred to "minorities of the Atlantic Coast" when referring to indigenous and Afro-descendant people.

2  Part of this fairly passive attitude on the part of the FSLN was probably due to preparations underway for its National Congress that took place in 1994 amidst strong internal tensions.

3  The 1990 elections were historic contests about the destiny of Nicaragua — war or peace. They drew the participation of seventy eight percent of the electorate at the regional level. The uniquely regional 1994 elections mobilized seventy four percent of those of voting age, a still impressive figure.

small political parties.[1] There were fourteen electoral options in the RAAS (ten parties and four popular subscription associations) and twelve in the RAAN (seven parties and five popular subscription associations). Of these, however, only three won seats in the RAAN council and six in the RAAS. In general terms, the results (see Table 5.1 in this chapter) confirmed the success of the PLC electoral strategy and the relative failure of YATAMA, due to its internal crisis. The FSLN maintained its stable place in opposition. Unlike 1990, only one party, the PLC, obtained victory in both regions although it did not have an absolute majority in either.

The PLC success in the regional elections on the Atlantic Coast surprised various observers of Nicaraguan national politics who had emphasized that the Liberal Party had no historic tradition in that part of the country. For Costeños, however, the high vote for the PLC was no mystery. It was due to attrition in support for the party of the central government (UNO) and the low profile of the FSLN in the campaign. It was also due to the personal alliance between Steadman Fagoth, leading a faction of YATAMA, and Arnoldo Alemán. Comparing the 1990 electoral results (in the same ridings) with those of 1994, there is no doubt that PLC votes, especially in the RAAN, were not for a "Liberal Party" but an expression of direct support for the Mískitu leader Fagoth. Hence, a large percentage of these PLC votes were in reality votes in favor of an indigenous electoral option that could be called "YATAMA-Fagoth."

Both in the RAAN and in the RAAS, the distribution of seats in the regional councils described above gave rise to complicated negotiations. As late as the eve of May 4, 1994, the date the new regional authorities would assume their posts, neither the composition of the new Juntas nor the deci-

---

1  To found a political party, the 1995 electoral law only called for the formation of a national directorate of nine members, and executives of seven members in the seventeen departments and autonomous regions. To form executives, the law stipulated at least five members in at least half of the one hundred and forty seven municipalities of the country. In summary, a political party could be founded with fewer than five hundred sympathizers or members, something that without a doubt helped to encourage the proliferation of mini parties at that time. At the national level, the result of this legislation was the formation of twenty-seven national political parties with a consequent parliamentary overrepresentation. In the 1996 elections, nine small national parties obtained sixteen percent of the seats in the National Assembly with only ten percent of the vote. Some observers have noted that: "the 1995 electoral system allowed party sub-division, fragmentation in the parliament, and provided extraordinary benefits to small parties" (ASDI 2000: 2).

sion about who would become Coordinator of each regional government was clear.

In the RAAN, the equal number of seats obtained by the Sandinistas and the PLC made YATAMA the key actor in decisions about members of the Junta and the government coordinator. After much vacillation and intense negotiation, the faction of YATAMA led by Brooklyn Rivera decided to ally with the Sandinistas, leaving the PLC completely out of the Junta Directiva.[1] Old warring enemies found themselves together in the common task of defending autonomy against the project of Arnoldo Alemán whose electoral victory on the Atlantic Coast only had importance as a first step towards political hegemony at the national level. The same forces would re-enact this initial alliance later (in 2002), on the basis of a greater pragmatic convergence that excluded other contenders from the political arena.

In the RAAS the multiparty composition of the council demanded negotiations at various levels. Initially there were possibilities of forming a pluralist Junta Directiva and electing regional government authorities by consensus. However, here the PLC had greater success and managed to form an alliance with ADECO and UNO, which enabled them to exclude Costeño organizations with lesser representation, such as YATAMA and MAAC.[2] UNO and ADECO each obtained one member in the Junta that was dominated by PLC members.

## YATAMA: Contentious Politics of an Internal Struggles for Legitimacy and Leadership

YATAMA's transition from a political-military organization to a civic organization was indeed complex. It had to take part in free elections, construct alliances with established parties and with the government, govern and administer the autonomous regional institutions, and also conserve legitimacy among its grassroots as the main political organization of the Mískitu people. With the difficult experience of governing the RAAN and being a minority in the RAAS during the 1990-1994 period, YATAMA was conscious of the necessity to consult with its grassroots about its strategic role and to maintain itself as a real and strong alternative for the Mískitu

---

1   Choosing Alta Hooker (FSLN) as president of the Junta Directiva and Marcos Hoppington (YATAMA) as regional Coordinator.

2   Rayfield Hodgson was elected as government coordinator and Augusto César de la Rocha as president of the Junta Directiva, both from the PLC.

population in the 1994 regional elections. YATAMA was originally constituted in Honduras in 1987 in an effort to reunify the armed Mískitu movement. The organization still had not confirmed its legitimacy as a civic expression. From exile, the collective leadership of Brooklyn Rivera, Steadman Fagoth, and Wycliff Diego had handled the military affairs of the indigenous organization. Now, with experience as a political force and the expectations generated among the Mískitu population that it would become a key force in defense of autonomy, YATAMA had to reconstitute itself and democratically choose its leadership. There were big differences in perspectives and strategies between the Fagoth and the Rivera factions, differences that constantly weakened YATAMA's efforts.

To deal with that situation, the Council of Elders, that still constituted the maximum authority among the Mískitu, proclaimed in February 1993 the necessity to convene among the Mískitu and Sumu-Mayangna peoples the first General Assembly of YATAMA on Nicaraguan soil. It would gather their opinions on autonomy and obtain their participation in the 1994 elections. Steadman Fagoth and Wycliffe Diego seemed to promote the assembly in order to strengthen the democratic character of YATAMA, but Brooklyn Rivera tried to deny legitimacy to this initiative.[1] Nevertheless, Rivera's effort had little success and when the assembly convened in May 1993 in Waspám, Río Coco, one hundred and forty one of the one hundred and seventy communities registered in the two regions were present. There were nine hundred delegates. The twenty nine absent communities were mainly those of Río Coco Abajo, where leaders loyal to Rivera had "reported" that the assembly had been cancelled.

The General Assembly produced an analysis of autonomy and important discussions took place about the management of natural resources and preparations for the 1994 elections. Because Brooklyn Rivera and his closest collaborators had not responded to the convocation of the Council of Elders, they could not, by definition, be candidates for the new YATAMA executive body. In that situation, Fagoth also declined his candidacy, opening up an opportunity to completely renew the leadership of the organization. However, Wycliffe Diego was finally elected as the new president, a lamentable fact given that he did not reside in the country and had not participated in

---

1 Rivera's faction also questioned the legitimacy of the Council of Elders. It argued that the representatives of the Council were not the same as those in 1987, and that this body was being manipulated by Fagoth.

the autonomy process.[1] Fagoth was elected as YATAMA's representative to the Supreme Electoral Council and to take charge of inscribing YATAMA in the 1994 elections.

The majority of delegates from the communities, along with important YATAMA leaders, felt that the assembly had resolved the crisis of representativity and leadership of the organization. Rivera, however, denounced the event as insignificant and "only based on the participation of Fagoth loyalists from sixty Rio Coco communities."[2] He announced that there would be other assemblies, again sewing doubts about the true leadership of YATAMA.

As a Popular Subscription Association, YATAMA had to re-register to participate in the regional elections. In November 1993, the Supreme Electoral Council received two distinct lists of signatures for YATAMA's registration: one presented by Fagoth and another by Rivera. Both claimed the legitimate representation of YATAMA. In its observations, the Supreme Electoral Council stated that YATAMA did not have legal status in Nicaragua, as it did not have approved statutes, it lacked decision-making bodies and accredited legal representation, and there were no minutes that documented the election of its leadership (Consejo Supremo Electoral, *Resolución*, December 10th, 1993). Given this situation, the Electoral Council suggested that both factions run in the elections, but not under the same name and symbol — each one would have to add something that would serve to make clear the difference between the options. Not long afterwards, Fagoth withdrew his petition and allied his candidates with the PLC campaign. That left Brooklyn Rivera with YATAMA's legal representation.

The complex transition of YATAMA would bring about significant changes in the organization, from social movement to ethnic political party, as well as ups and downs in its capacity to represent a unified indigenous movement. At the root of the internal struggle between Fagoth and Rivera's leaderships were: a fierce quarrel over political control of YATAMA and deep-seated disputes as to who should be the legitimate interlocutor vis-à-vis the national government. There were also power struggles for control-

---

1 Wycliffe Diego was originally an evangelical pastor and a controversial member of the Miskitu resistance in Honduras. He kept close relations with the US military and intelligence organizations. His residence was in Miami, Florida. He returned there following the YATAMA General Assembly and never returned to assume his responsibilities as president of the organization.

2 Interview with Brooklyn Rivera, Managua, April 2003.

ling governmental appointments in regional institutions (Matamoros 1992: 12-13; González 2007: 478). The erratic process of alliances in the 1990s was in part the result of an effort to combine the search for strategic agreements about that vision of autonomy with pragmatic goals that would enable it to maintain — through alliances with national political parties — its spaces of power in the political life of the autonomous regions. However, YATAMA's demand for a not yet realized indigenous autonomy would continue to be present in the discourse of the organization throughout the decade.

The 1996 National Elections: Alemán and the PLC, a Rising Power Against Autonomy

Arnoldo Alemán and his Alianza Liberal (still on the way to constituting itself as the PLC) won a very clear victory in the 1996 elections. Alemán won the presidency in the first round with 51 percent, while the FSLN got 38 percent. In the National Assembly elections the difference between the PLC and the FSLN was less sweeping, 46 percent for the PLC and 36.5 percent for the FSLN. That translated into 42 deputies for the PLC and 36 for the FSLN. The remaining 15 seats were shared among eleven other political parties. It was obvious from this distribution of seats that neither of the two big parties could count on a minimum number of deputies to obtain a simple majority in the National Assembly. That would require 48 votes. It therefore became evident that the next political period would be characterized by strenuous negotiations in the National Assembly to construct solid blocs and avoid changing majorities.

In the Atlantic Coast, YATAMA, led by Brooklyn Rivera, had allied with a new party, PRONAL, led by Antonio Lacayo, minister of the presidency of the Chamorro government. In the RAAN, the YATAMA faction led by Fagoth had given its support to the PLC. As in the regional elections in 1994, Fagoth's support generated positive results for the PLC, which won more than 50 percent of the votes, both in the RAAN and the RAAS. It won a similar vote in the National Assembly contest. The PLC victory in the municipal elections was simply a steamroller — with almost 67 percent of votes in the RAAN and more than 71 percent in the RAAS. The PLC won nine municipal governments, while the FSLN was left with only four.[1]

---

1  In the RAAN, the PLC won the municipalities of Waspám, Rosita, Prinzapolka, and Siuna; the FSLN won in Puerto Cabezas and Bonanza. In the RAAS, the liber-

Arnoldo Alemán's presidential victory in October 1996 led to a sharp increase in the influence of national parties in general, and of the PLC in particular, on the political and institutional life o the Atlantic Coast. The changes in the Junta Directiva and the coordinator of the RAAN that were taken over by PLC allies in 1996 were a reflection of Arnoldo Alemán's new strategy of assuming direct control of the regional governments, once having gained a predominant position in the municipalities of the Coast.[1]

Meanwhile, political agreements between the PLC and the FSLN at the national level began to close participation spaces to regional political organizations, initiating bipartisan control. In September 1997, the FSLN and the PLC collaborated to reform the electoral law in such a way that they shared between themselves the executive bodies of the regional electoral councils, excluding all the local organizations.[2] The formula was immediately applied in the regional elections on the Atlantic Coast in March 1998.

Since the PLC had its own members presiding over regional authorities, that should have led to a better relationship and understandings between the different levels of government. But this second period (1996–1998) witnessed an impasse in the initiatives and performance of Costeño authorities. Although Fagoth was formally a PLC deputy, his alliance with Arnoldo Alemán was weak and was very pragmatic and personal in nature. Only that makes it possible to understand the local contradictions in which the RAAN Regional Council was immersed in that period. Moreover, the caucus led by Fagoth, the group officially allied with President Arnoldo Alemán, continued to demand for itself the official representation of YATAMA in open dispute with Brooklyn Rivera and the YATAMA members of the regional council.

---

als won Bluefields, la Cruz de Rio Grande, el Tortuguero, Kukra Hill, and Pearl Lagoon; the FSLN was left with Corn Island and the Desembocadura de Río Grande.

1  Amidst strong rumors about "juicy payoffs" the PLC managed to place Steadman Fagoth in the post of regional government coordinator. Alemán also appointed Fagoth collaborators to posts in the national government. One was named vice-minister of mines; another became vice-minister of INPESCA, the Nicaraguan Fishing Institute. Both institutions were of great importance to the Coast.

2  According to Article 3 of the law, "The president and respective alternate of the two regional electoral councils will be designated alternately from a party in the Atlantic Coast regions, between the parties in first and second place in the 1994 regional elections. The first member and alternate will be designated in the same way" (Asamblea Nacional de Nicaragua 1997b). They (electoral council members) would now have to be chosen from lists presented by the political parties.This reform immediately put members of the FSLN and the PLC in charge, alternately, in each regional electoral council in both autonomous regions.

Both in the RAAN and in the RAAS, the inoperability of the councils increased considerably. During the entire two year period, both regional councils managed to hold only 13 regular sessions, while the property of the regional authorities was poorly managed. That fact included political attrition and loss for legitimacy of the actions of the regional councils. [1] It was in that context that the central government increased its level of intervention in making decisions about Coast affairs.

1998: Regional Elections with Many Parties and Scant Participation

The third regional elections were held in March 1998. They took place amidst marked disenchantment and loss of confidence in the functioning of the autonomous institutions on the part of the Costeño population. Three elements contributed to that sentiment within Costeño society. First, the heavy handed interference by national political parties, especially the PLC, in the functioning of the regional councils. Secondly, the lack of will or interest on the part of national authorities to commit to dealing with Costeño problems and to promote autonomous rights. Finally, the dissociation of councilors from the communities where they had been elected. Those three factors helped to create a record abstention level in the 1998 regional elections: 58 percent of those registered on the voters' lists. That was twice the level of any previous regional election.

A total of 18 political groupings participated in those elections. Six were national political parties. There was a regional political alliance (Alianza Costeña)[2] and four regional political parties (including the Partido Indígena Multiétnico, PIM). Furthermore, seven popular subscription organizations ran, including YATAMA which presented candidates in both autonomous regions (Wani 1998: 6).[3] The PLC won most seats in the RAAN, followed by the FSLN and YATAMA (Table 5.1). The advantage gained by the PLC enabled it to set up a Junta composed only of liberals, excluding the FSLN and YATAMA, whose councilors were left with only minor tasks in the coun-

---

1  One example was the sale of the BLUPESCA firm in the RAAS in April 1998. Administrative and legal irregularities in the deal finally forced the Auditor General to declare the sale null and void and, at the same time charge ten regional councilors with responsibility.

2  *Alianza Costeña* was formed by the Coastal Peoples Party (PPC), a regional political organization founded in 1997, and other small national parties.

3  Due to the 2000 electoral law reforms this was the last time that popular subscription organizations could present candidates.

cil's work commissions. The RAAS results also favored the PLC, with the FSLN coming second. The PIM won an important number of seats despite being new (Table 5.1).[1] The PLC elected a Junta in alliance with YATAMA and some PIM dissidents. Of the seven posts, the PLC took five, including the presidency of the council and YATAMA got two. The FSLN and the Alianza Costeña were excluded.

In contrast to Violeta Chamorro, Arnoldo Alemán's governing style involved direct instrumental use of power and central government resources to wage a permanent political campaign aimed at maintaining his support base in forthcoming elections, including the presidential campaign at the end of his term. When circumstances permitted, as in the case of the RAAN, it was convenient for him to have a counterpart in a strong regional executive (the regional government) that, to the detriment of the regional council, was capable of acting autonomously without accounting for its actions to the council, the municipalities, or the communities. In the RAAS, Alemán initially took the same approach, but quickly lost confidence in the first Coordinator of the regional government and promoted his firing in mid 2001. Relations between the national executive power and autonomous regional authorities were autocratic and bossy. Partisan politics prevailed.

### Bi-partisan and Exclusionary Politics at the National Level

From 1996 onwards, the top leaderships in Managua strengthened their control over Costeño politics. This was an issue that came under scrutiny and criticism from different sectors of Coast society. In effect, a good part of the discussions of the "Third International Symposium on Autonomy," held in Managua in October 1997, was focused on analyzing the strong influence of national parties on, and their role in, "obstructing" autonomous life. Hugo Sujo, a well known *Costeño* intellectual, noted this problem in his presentation to the round table on political parties and autonomy:

---

1 The PIM participated for the first time as a regional political party in the 1998 election and obtained good results. The Reverend Hodgson had been a PLC councilor in the 94–98 period, but he was not chosen to be a PLC candidate for deputy in the 1996 election. Rejecting the impositions of president Alemán, he decided to create a dissident PLC group with a "Costeño" face. The PIM had an anti-central government discourse against the control that Alemán exercised over the autonomous process. It took advantage of the discontent, especially in urban Bluefields. However, once elected to the regional council, PIM councilors rarely acted independently and in practice tended to ally with the PLC.

> [The] predominance of national political parties was extended to
> the autonomous regions with a corresponding obstruction of prog-
> ress in the process of regional autonomy [....] disrespect on the part
> of national political parties for the *Costeño* autonomous process and
> their colonialist behaviour reached into all levels: from the allocation
> of natural resources to approval of laws injurious to autonomy, and
> even the imposition of the names of their heroes on regional pub-
> lic institutions, humiliating names that injured the feelings of the
> Costeño parties (Sujo 1997: 73).

That predominance of partisan politics and exclusion was soon accompanied by the consequences of the first pact between Arnoldo Alemán and
Daniel Ortega, announced publicly near the end of 1999. Nevertheless, both
the anti-Sandinista rhetoric of Alemán and Ortega's ferocious anti-PLC discourse remained vibrant on the political stage, minimizing or negating any
suggestion that they were secretly carrying on an intense bilateral dialogue.
It was not until June of 1999 that both *caudillos*[1] began to admit publicly that
talks between the two parties were underway, and now in a mutually con-
ciliatory tone. Ortega affirmed:

> I would not go so far as to call this a pact because making a pact
> is when you get closer to a dictator in order to make personal gain,
> as happened in the past. President Alemán is a democratic president
> who was elected by the citizenry and his government is a civil gov-
> ernment. Alemán is not Somoza (Equipo Envío 2006).

That same day, Alemán responded, declaring: "Ortega has changed enor-
mously; he is a sensible man" (Equipo Envío 2006).

On the evening of August 17, 1999 the thirty-three agreements that defined the pact were made public. Great debates and criticism burst out over
the following months, but they could not restrain the pact or change its
main content. Yet neither this criticism nor the protest from various social
sectors restrain or change the content of the pact. On January 18, 2000, the
pact agreements were ratified in the second session of the National Assembly and became reforms to a series of laws, including the Electoral Law and
the national constitution.[2]

In official events both *caudillos* presented the pact as "a quest for convergence" and the means to create "governability in the country" after a period
of constant conflict and the destruction caused by Hurricane Mitch. But the

---

1   By *caudillo* I refer to charismatic party leaders who often have a strong, personal
    command over their political organizations, and engage in cronyism in order to
    maintain their power and influence. See Démelas (2001: 67).
2   The constitutional reforms had to be approved in two subsequent legislatures.

real shared goals had been obvious from the beginning: that is, to establish bi-partisan and exclusive control in the electoral arena, and obtain control of the key institutions of the state and share posts according to the same bipartisan scheme (Pérez-Baltodano 2003: 705).

Internally, both parties to the pact could present specific issues on which they had made considerable gains "for themselves." Most important for the FSLN, for example, was the reduction, established in the electoral law, in the percentage of the vote required for a presidential candidate to win on the first round. With the pact and subsequent legal reforms it was reduced from 45 to 40 percent. That would lead eventually to the electoral victory of Daniel Ortega when he confronted a divided PLC in the 2006 elections.[1] The big emblematic gain for the PLC was the agreement that the outgoing president Alemán would automatically have a seat in the incoming National Assembly, without having to be elected by popular vote. The PLC said that this would guarantee the presence in national politics of its main leader and maintain the strength of the liberal party.[2] The pact, however, meant a serious setback for the democratic process of the country in general and the Atlantic Coast specifically.[3] It had negative consequences in almost all political and institutional spheres. It also affected the nature of a law-based state.[4]

---

1  The reduction could go as low as 35 percent in the event that the runner up did not obtain 30 percent or more of the vote. Ortega's initial objective was to completely eliminate the need for a second round, but he failed to get that.

2  Another key aspect was that it would grant five more years of legal immunity to Alemán who had already been accused of severe acts of corruption. In this context the necessity of a qualified vote (two thirds of the deputies) to suspend the immunity of the President of the Republic was also established. This was a favorable decision for both Alemán and for Ortega as a possible future president. Alemán's initial goal of eliminating the prohibition on re-election of an outgoing president was not achieved.

3  Alemán's presidential style relied on his PLC party as a system of clientelism, which also characterized his relationships with other municipalities in the rest of the country. Overall, scholars have observed that as a consequence of the PLC–FSLN pact, the 1997–2000 period, "besides the institutional setback [of the state], another effect has been the strengthening of a *caudillo* style, looting-ridden, and centralist political culture" (Ortega & Wallace 2001: 503).

4  Overall, the 1997 electoral reforms were followed by a more comprehensive package of constitutional reforms agreed upon by the FSLN and the PLC in the years 2000 and 2004. The reforms resulted in "a vehicle by the dominant groups to make their agreements operational" (Montenegro et. al. 2005: 103). In practical terms, the reforms resulted in: using legality and jurisprudence in order to strengthen the hegemony of the dominant groups; closure of the political system to alternatives not controlled by the dominant groups (namely, the PLC and the FSLN);

In summary, the pact reformed the electoral law so as to always favor the two big parties. It made the participation of other political actors difficult and ended the possibility for local groups or parties to run for office.[1] Finally, the reforms to the electoral law were clearly designed to enable their authors to take complete control of the Supreme Electoral Council and "oligopolize" the electoral-political space: "The new rules of the game have two goals: bipartisan domination of the electoral bodies and the forceful channeling of the will of voters towards the bipartisan arrangement. And their sole philosophy is: majorities impose themselves and do not respect minorities" (Equipo Envío 2000).

Along the same lines, the pact deepened and legalized open bipartisan control of other important national institutions like the Supreme Judicial Court (CSJ) and the Auditor General of the Republic (CGR).[2] The new rules and exclusionary procedures of the reformed electoral law took force at the beginning of 2000 and were applied without delay. They produced dramatic results in both the municipal elections that same year and in the presidential elections at the end of 2001. Twenty-seven political parties campaigned in the 1996 elections. Only four political groupings participat-

---

the creation of a new legal framework that acts in response to the interests of the dominant groups; control of the state's public institutions, especially by the FSLN; and undermining of the national executive so as to subordinate it to the political control of both parties [the PLC and the FSLN] (Montenegro, et. al., 2005: 104). For a thorough discussion of the far-reaching implications of the FSLN–PLC pact over the Nicaraguan political system, see Montenegro et. al. (2005: 92-93); also Pérez-Baltodano (2003: 704-53).

1   The rules of the January 2000 Electoral Law were motivated by an exclusionary agenda. First, it demanded that a new party present a document carrying the signatures of at least three percent of registered voters in the national elections, affirming their support. In 2000, that would be 73,000 signatures. The same rules established that a citizen could only support one party in this way. Second, the rules required that in order for a group to get recognition and legal status as a political party it had to have a national executive of nine members, departmental executives of seven members, and municipal executives of seven members in each and every department and municipality in the country. Those executives had to be constituted in the presence of an observer from the Supreme Electoral Council, making it a long process. The combination of these requirements generated both economic and "class" exclusion. The mere cost of collecting signatures implied that the process is not socially neutral. The requirement of forming executives in all departments and municipalities also involved a prohibitive cost.

2   The *Contraloría General de la República* (Auditor General of the Republic) would have five controllers instead of just one, all nominated by the dominant national political parties on the basis of their loyalty to each candidate.

ed in the 2000 municipal elections — the PLC, the FSLN, the Conservative Party, and the Christian Road party.[1]

The latter two groups were "allowed" to run by the pact operators. But the only parties that might have represented real competition were eliminated by the Supreme Electoral Council (SEC) in arbitrary, clouded decisions. It was not by accident that the SEC magistrates, before taking those decisions, asked that their headquarters be guarded by anti-riot troops, a rare occurrence in Managua. Representatives of the parties that were eliminated declared that the pact partners had obviously agreed to a strategy of pre-electoral fraud. By excluding other contestants, they could proceed to carry out technically cleaner elections.

The SEC on the Atlantic Coast even excluded YATAMA from the municipal elections, falsely alleging that it had not complied with all the new requirements. That decision provoked a strong reaction from Costeños and YATAMA supporters who declared that it amounted to a "declaration of war on the indigenous peoples" (Butler 2000: 37). To fight that exclusion, YATAMA introduced a complaint in the Inter-American Court of Human Rights (IACHR). In June 2005, the IACHR issued its decision. It condemned the Nicaraguan state for having violated political and other rights guaranteed by the American Human Rights Convention.[2] Moreover, the IACHR demanded that Nicaragua reform its electoral law to guarantee the political

---

1   Finally for the Atlantic Coast, the electoral law recognized the right to form regional political parties based on traditional organizations of the indigenous communities. However, they too had to collect signatures from a highly illiterate electorate. As regional parties they would only be allowed to run candidates at the municipal and regional level on the Coast, as well as for regional deputies at the National Assembly, and not for the national elections for president or for the Central American elections (Parlacen) (Consejo Supremo Electoral 2004: 44). See in particular article 71 of Electoral Law 331.

2   As observed by legal scholars, the IACHR decision on "YATAMA vs. Nicaragua" has a decisive relevance for the international legislation concerning the rights of indigenous peoples. Campbell notes that the decision "authoritatively interprets the general human right to political participation to include for indigenous peoples the more specific rights to (1) special remedial measures and procedural safeguards to ensure effective participation and (2) participate in national political systems according to indigenous traditional systems. The decision adds to the developing norms in international law and domestic legal systems that also support these rights. By recognizing the rights of indigenous peoples to *effectively* participate in the national politics of the dominant society, in accordance with their traditional forms of organization and practices, *YATAMA v. Nicaragua* advances the rights to self-determination and equality for indigenous peoples" (Campbell 2007: 500).

participation of indigenous peoples, respecting their traditional forms of organization (González 2007: 480; Campbell, 2007: 523; CIDH 2005: 105-6).

Voting day in the RAAN took place under a lot of tension and some acts of violence. Voter turnout was a very low, with abstention rate on the Coast varying from 65 to 70 percent, while the national abstention rate reached 40 percent. Costeño activists saw the pact as an obstacle to any autonomous and independent movement that might want to participate in elections. Forging a broad front of Costeños was very difficult in the past when the Coast had been under centralized control from Managua. So it would be once more. Allying with the two political parties was the other option, but that generally meant that Costeño priorities could be easily put on the back burner or simply ignored.

Contradictory Trends, 2002–2006

Preparations for the fourth round of regional elections, held at the beginning of March 2002, were marked by internal conflicts in the Supreme Electoral Council, along with the application of the reforms to the electoral law with their exclusionary character.[1] Moreover, Enrique Bolaños, who had been elected to the presidency of the republic on a PLC ticket, launched a legal case against ex-president Alemán for acts of corruption.[2] This reflected an important division in the governing party and within the elites of the Nicaraguan right. Bolaños's allegiances were with the traditional Conservative party, but he had joined the PLC as part of an effort to build an anti-FSLN political force. As we will see, Bolaños's stance would have local implications for the functioning of the regional councils.

The 1998 elections had witnessed an abundance of political parties in the race, 18 in all. But in 2002 only four participated: PLC, allied with Camino Cristiano, the FSLN, and the two regional parties, YATAMA and PAMUC. Both parties had to undergo an intense organizational process in order to meet the conditions imposed by the revised electoral law. In the case of YATAMA, besides transforming it into a regional political party,

---

1 The SEC internal conflict was mostly a fight between the PLC and the FSLN, reflected by the magistrates from those two parties, over control of the SEC. It also had to do with the issue of the exclusionary character of the reformed electoral law.

2 The legislation states that it is the Supreme Electoral Council in plenary that has to swear in the elected authorities of the regional councils.

the new electoral regulations hindered its possibilities to forge alliances with other regional political organizations, such as the Coastal People's Party (PPC), or the Indigenous Multiethnic Party (PIM).[1] Electoral apathy remained unchanged although the proportion of abstention climbed even higher — from 58 percent in 1998 to 62 percent in 2002. In political terms, the election results gave hegemony to the PLC in the RAAS, while the FSLN and YATAMA were strengthened in the RAAN.

In the RAAN, the PLC could no longer act alone as in 1998 when it was able to form the Junta Directiva and the council without the need for any alliance. The new situation allowed for a political agreement between the FSLN and YATAMA that together held a majority. They could elect from their members the top autonomous authorities to the exclusion of the PLC. According to YATAMA leader Brooklyn Rivera, that decision was based on the fact that: "The PLC in six years in the RAAN Regional government has only promoted the exclusion and abuse of the indigenous movement and its ranks. This party has never respected the identity and right of indigenous people to their own space and organization" (Rivera 2002). Hence it was reasonable for YATAMA to reach an agreement with the FSLN in order to "recover and defend the identity and autonomy of the peoples and communities of our Moskitia" (Rivera 2002).

Fifteen sessions took place during the first two years of the work of the fourth RAAN Regional Council that began in September 2002.[2] The new Junta Directiva was elected in May 2004, based on a FSLN–YATAMA alliance. Because of that, there were no major tensions or shocks that interrupted the flow of the regional council's work in this period.[3] In the RAAS, however, the PLC decided to erect an alliance with YATAMA to assure a

---

1  In particular, the possibilities for creating alliances further imposed additional restrictions on political parties. According to the law, a party alliance "should specify the political party that leads the alliance, and should participate under its name, emblem and flag. In practical matters, this translates the alliance into an adhesion to the stronger political force" (ASDI 2000: 10). The electoral law, in particular Articles 77 and 80, discouraged political alliances (Consejo Supremo Electoral 2004). As a consequence of these changes, on August 15, 2000, the SEC denied YATAMA its request to register its candidates under the YATAMA/PPC alliance (Consejo Supremo Electoral 2000: 2).

2  In September because it was not until them that the Junta Directiva and the Coordinator was finally sworn in by the plenary of the Supreme Electoral Council.

3  A new *Junta Directiva* president, Juan González, was elected by the FSLN, and another term was ratified for Hurtado García Becker of YATAMA as government Coordinator.

solid majority in the regional council. That would allow the two to totally exclude the FSLN from any important posts. Up to a certain point it was contradictory for YATAMA to ally with the FSLN in the north while allying itself with the PLC in the south in order to exclude the FSLN. This is to be explained both by the pragmatic approach taken by YATAMA in its policy of alliances during the period under analysis and by the different relationship of forces prevailing in each regional council.

These political decisions on the Atlantic Coast had not taken into account the new way the Supreme Electoral Council worked. Formerly it had been a professional body. However, since the PLC–FSLN pact it had become permeated with partisan politics and subjected to circumstantial policies, that is, to the kind of relations prevailing between the PLC and the FSLN. At that very moment, in May 2002, the fight for control of various state institutions had resulted in very conflictive Liberal-Sandinista relations. In that situation, the decision by YATAMA and the FSLN to govern the RAAN in alliance — a completely legitimate decision supported by the voters of the region — meant an open fight with the SEC which was controlled by PLC magistrates disinclined to bless the political accord. The SEC refused to swear in the new council authorities. In Bilwi, shortly after the solemn inaugural session of the RAAN council got underway on Many 4, 2002, the president of the SEC decided to abruptly abandon the hall. His place was occupied by Sandinista SEC magistrates who, in an "extraordinary session," organized in the heat of partisan tensions, swore in the new Junta Directiva.[1]

The Liberal magistrates challenged the swearing in act. They believed it was illegal and appealed for an injunction against it in the Supreme Court. The Court ruled in favor of a new session to swear in the RAAN authorities and called on the SEC to preside over the ceremony in plenary, as they had done on former occasions ever since 1990. Despite pressure from the Coast, the SEC did not carry out this mandate until September when it confirmed the election of the new Junta Directiva and government coordinator chosen by the FSLN–YATAMA Alliance: the same formula that had been sworn in unofficially by Sandinista SEC magistrates on May 4.

Developments in the RAAS were much more chaotic and would remain so for a long time. Frustrated by the morning events in the RAAN on May

---

1 This Junta was chaired by Juan Saballos of the FSLN, and Hurtado García Becker of YATAMA, as government coordinator (Sandoval, 2002).

4, the SEC Liberal magistrates decided to travel to Bluefields that same day and swear in the Junta Directiva and government coordinator chosen by the PLC–YATAMA alliance. Faced with this action, the FSLN regional council members refused to be sworn in. They argued that the regular FSLN and SEC magistrates, who were still in the RAAN, had been illegally replaced by alternate magistrates favorable to the interests of the PLC. The swearing in ceremony was repeatedly disrupted by the Sandinistas who alleged that the event was illegal. Faced with this disorder and protests, SEC president Roberto Rivas called for the intervention of the riot squad.

Following this failed session to install the regional authorities, a long and barren period of two years went by during which the regional coun-cil met only twice. From February, 2003 until May 2004, two Juntas Di-rectivas, one controlled by the FSLN–PLC linked with President Enrique Bolaños, and another controlled by a PLC faction tied to Arnoldo Alemán,[1] fought over who represented the regional council. They submitted innu-merable complaints and suits for injunctions to the courts in Bluefields and Managua, each claiming to be the legitimate authority (Miller 2004). Despite everything, they did not manage to persuade the authorities of the SEC to hold a plenary session to deal with the dispute and give legitimacy to the elected RAAS authorities.[2] Clearly, the partisan interests and agendas of Managua had priority over democratic legitimacy and governability in the Atlantic Coast.[3]

The central government initially manifested a lack of concern in the governability crisis in the RAAS and was not interested in smoothing out the internal conflicts. It unofficially said that this was "their problem. We are not going to let them drag our government into their internal problem.

---

1 The first year of Enrique Bolaños's government was marked by a strong and un-expected campaign against Alemán and his collaborators over acts of corruption. This initiative by Bolaños won strong popular support and hence generated ten-sions and divisions within the PLC.

2 A fairly detailed report of those legal conflicts and controversies can be read in Miller (2004). Various newspapers also reported on the internal tensions in the RAAS. See, for example, Centeno (2003)

3 The regional government, however, was led continuously by Guy Cox, of the PLC, for a two year period, from mid 2002 to September 2004. That at least allowed for a regular pace of activities by this regional authority. During a four month lapse between May and September 2004, two different people claimed to be the legiti-mate coordinator of the RAAS

Either the elected leaders resolve this problem among themselves or the people will have their necks."[1]

Once a second Junta Directiva had been formed that was linked to the Bolaños administration, the latter began to transfer resources for the work of the council, despite having to defy resolutions of the courts that questioned the legitimacy of both rival Juntas. The transfer payments enabled some kind of functioning by the council and its commissions, and above all by the regional government. However, they brought with them another dimension to the conflict and thus helped to prolong the stalemate. During the entire period from 2002 to 2005, the political contradictions at the national level impacted strongly on the ability of the regional authorities to carry out their mandates.[2]

Table 5.5. Political Affiliations. Regional Coordinators and Presidents of the Regional Councils. RAAN and RAAS, 1990–2010

| Period | RAAN | | RAAS | |
|---|---|---|---|---|
| | Coordinator | President | Coordinator | President |
| 1990–1994 | Yatama | Yatama | UNO | UNO |
| 1994–1996 | Yatama | FSLN | PLC | PLC |
| 1996–1998 | PLC | FSLN | PLC | Yatama |
| 1998–2002 | PLC | PLC | PLC | PLC |
| 2002–2006 | Yatama | FSLN | PLC | PLC |
| 2006–2010 | Yatama | FSLN | PLC | PLC |
| 2010– | Yatama | FSLN | PLC | PLC |

2006: Participants, Results, and New Alliances

On March 5, 2006 the people of the Atlantic Coast were called to the polls to elect their regional authorities for the fifth time since 1990. Never before were *Costeños* exposed to so much pressure from the head offices of

---

1  Interview with Carlos Hurtado, presidential advisor on Atlantic Coast affairs, Managua, 02/18/04.
2  Finally, in September 2004, a new majority was formed by the PLC. It elected Rayfield Hodgson as president of the Junta Directiva of the RAAS, and Alejandro Mejía, as coordinator of the regional government. Both officials completed their terms in office.

national political parties as in this election. Those parties saw the regional elections as a dress rehearsal for the coming presidential elections scheduled for November 2006. This time it was not just a matter of traditional political polarization between two big national *caudillos*, Daniel Ortega and Arnoldo Alemán, and their respective parties, the FSLN and the PLC. Pressure had increased because of the new challenges both *caudillos* were confronting, coming from other leaders who until only recently had been part of their own political families.

In this new situation, Daniel Ortega and the FSLN would not only have to confront the PLC of Arnoldo Alemán, but also the former mayor of Managua, Herty Lewites, who had obtained support from many historic leaders of the Frente. Meanwhile, Arnoldo Alemán[1] and his PLC would have to defeat not just the FSLN but also the new Liberal Alliance (ALN), led by the well known banker and ex minister, Eduardo Montealegre. The latter had insisted openly that Arnoldo Alemán should not be able to name the PLC presidential candidate. On both fronts, the bipartisan arrangements of the FSLN–PLC pact were being challenged. Because of those circumstances, a very costly campaign developed on the Coast with the heavy presence of cadres and political managers from the capital, producing a campaign that for the first time had broad coverage in the national media. However, for the same reason, it was also a campaign that will be remembered for the relative absence of issues linked to daily life and felt needs of Costeños. The priority for almost all the national parties was to take advantage of the opportunity to publicize their presidential candidates for the election half a year away, relegating "autonomous" themes to the back burner.

On the eve of the elections, Alta Hooker, URACCAN rector, called on national parties to show some respect for the regional process and to take seriously the agenda of Costeño problems that the main sectors of the autonomous regions had developed through consensus: "The regional elections are held to make the indigenous peoples, with their demands and aspirations, visible. But the national parties are making us invisible" (Equipo Envío 2006).

Since the national political situation involved a ruthless struggle for power, this complaint and very reasonable request found no echo. One factor that added to the deafness and contributed to the deterioration of the

---

1 Because of his court sentence for corruption, Alemán would have to find another person to run as the PLC's main candidate, but at bottom that changed nothing.

political climate to the point where the contest was nearly called off was the open conflict inside the Supreme Electoral Council. In the home stretch of the electoral preparations, it was completely paralyzed.[1]

Another problem involved strictly technical issues, related to the accuracy of the electoral rolls. They were quite vexing, but no realistic proposal, in terms of timelines, on how to purge the rolls could prosper, given the seriously divided and inoperable electoral council. The defects in the voters list covered almost every possible facet: the overall list was small compared to the vote-age population; dead persons and people who had emigrated still appeared on the rolls; and often the data on registered voters were invalid.[2] As well, there were quarrels over distances between voting stations and the number of voters per station. The struggle was so bitter that people often doubted that the regional elections would actually take place. Such doubts were even expressed by SEC magistrates. Talk began about possible violent disturbances on voting day and of massive numbers of challenges to the procedures the next day. Just one week before the election, Etica y Transparencia publically warned that:

> SEC partisanship has eroded its credibility and capacity to function. Far from being an entity that resolves and adjudicates normal problems between parties, it has become an institution that reproduces and magnifies them. For some time battles have been taking place inside the SEC for partisan control and to find a way to give legal cover to manoeuvres motivated solely for party convenience. Since that time, the two characteristics essential to the tribunal — neutrality and independence — have been abandoned completely, even in its discourse. This is the basis of the problem and the main

---

1  The cause of his expulsion was simply having insisted on democratic internal elections to select the presidential candidate of the party (PLC). That collided with the *caudillo* tradition whereby the right to appoint and take away positions was solely reserved for Arnoldo Alemán. This new round of contradictions within the SEC was a direct result of the expulsion of Montealegre from the PLC and the formation of the Alianza Liberal. It managed to attract SEC president Roberto Rivas (formerly loyal to Alemán's PLC) who began to lean towards supporting proposals coming from FSLN magistrates, thus placing the PLC in a minority position on that body. With Rivas's decisive vote, the SEC allowed Eduardo Montealegre to run under the denomination of the Alianza Liberal, as well as to use the red flag (the liberal color), something that enraged the magistrates loyal to the PLC who then almost permanently boycotted SEC sessions.

2  Just before the regional elections, the Instituto para la Promoción y Desarrollo de la Democracia (IPADE) did an "audit" of the electoral lists. They found that 60,000 electors (28 percent) had since moved, but this was not noted in the registry. 21,000 names on the list (10 percent) could not be located, and no one in the neighborhoods or communities knew of them. Furthermore, almost 8,000 registered voters had died (IPADE 2006).

---

threat to the March and November 2006 electoral processes (Grupo Cívico Ética y Transparencia 2006).

Finally, the SEC majority managed to make a decision regarding the technical issues without resolving anything more. The voting took place as planned and transpired without violence, disturbances, or any major incidents.

Six national parties and two regional parties or movements participated in the March regional elections. The national parties, which were often appeared in multiple alliances, were: i) the *Partido Liberal Constitucionalista*, PLC, in alliance with the *Partido Indígena Multiétnico* (PIM), the *Partido Neoliberal*, the *Partido Liberal Nacionalista*, and the *Partido Unionista Centroamericano* (PUCA). ; ii) the *Alianza del Frente Sandinista de Liberación Nacional*, FSLN, made up of the *Partido Unión Demócrata Cristiana*, and the *Partido Movimiento de Unidad Cristiana*; iii) the *Alianza del Partido Renovador Sandinista*, also known as the *Alianza Herty 2006*, in alliance with the *Partido Alternativa Cristiana*; iv) the *Alianza Liberal Nicaragüense*, ALN-PC, in alliance with the *Partido Liberal Independiente* (PLI), the Partido de la Resistencia Nicaragüense (PRN), and the *Partido Conservador* (PC); v) the *Partido Alianza Por la República*, APRE, that participated in union with the *Partido de Acción Ciudadana*; and finally, vi) the *Partido Camino Cristiano de Nicaragua* (CCN), the only national party not to present itself under the umbrella of some kind of alliance.

The two regional parties that participated did not do so as part of any alliance with national parties. They were the *Partido Multiétnico de Unidad Costeña* (PAMUC) and YATAMA which in the RAAS ran as part of a coalition with the local *Coast Power* organization.[1] Just as in the 1998 and 2002 elections, people who abstained constituted the largest sector of the registered voters, some 55 percent. That was, however, a slight reduction from previous levels.

As can be noted in Table 5.1, the FSLN managed to conserve and slightly improve its standing in the RAAN. In the RAAS, however, it lost three seats compared with 2002. The divided liberals presented themselves through two options in the regional elections. That resulted in the PLC losing four seats in the RAAN and nine in the RAAS. The Alianza Liberal won six seats in the RAAS, but none in the RAAN. YATAMA's results represented a suc-

---

1   The Coast Peoples Political Movement — *Movimiento Político del Pueblo Costeño* was founded in 2005. Its main leaders included Owyn Hodgson, ex-vice minister of the disbanded INDERA, and Weady Hawkins, a local Bluefields businessman.

cess as the party managed to make advances in both regions. Compared with 2002, YATAMA gained two more seats in the RAAN and its best vote ever in the RAAS, with six councilors, a gain of two over its 2002 results. This improvement in YATAMA's position in the RAAS is partly explained by its strategy of alliances with Afro-descendant sectors in the South, mainly Creoles organized in the *Coast Power* movement. The latter had undertaken organizational efforts in the Bluefields Creole community and some communities in Pearl Lagoon, an area where YATAMA had no traditional support.[1] The *Alianza Herty 2006*, APRE, and *Camino Cristiano*, despite winning a significant number of votes, did not elect any candidates to the two regional councils.

On May 5, 2006, two months after the elections, the new regional councils were sworn in by the SEC. Each proceeded to elect its president and its Junta Directiva, as well as the coordinator of its regional government. This event in the RAAN had generally been characterized by uncertainty and high drama up until the last moment. But this time it was carried out in a totally tranquil manner, despite the presence of the PLC and FSLN presidential candidates, José Rizo and Daniel Ortega, respectively. The reason is simple: the elections had been agreed to two days before by Daniel Ortega and Brooklyn Rivera, who that same day had formed an alliance for the coming presidential election.[2] While the FSLN won the job of council president and a majority of the Junta Directiva, YATAMA got the post of government coordinator and the other members of the Junta Directiva. As well, YATAMA gained half the working commissions. This time, the PLC was left without a single member in the Junta and with no posts in the commissions.

The same event was carried out a few hours later in the RAAS. The atmosphere was less relaxed. Tactical maneuvering took place inside the council right up to the last minute before the vote. Finally, the PLC took all seven posts in the new Junta Directiva, including the post of council president and the regional government coordinator.

---

1 YATAMA's traditional support in the RAAS mainly comes from the Desembocadura de Río Grande zone and Corn Island, where significant Miskitu communities are located.

2 Returning to Managua on the evening of May 5, Brooklyn Rivera described this Alliance between YATAMA and the FSLN as "an act that without doubt has transcendent importance in the life of indigenous peoples and ethnic communities of the Coast" (FSLN 2006).

Parties and Elections in the Life of the Autonomous Council: A Preliminary Assessment

The description of six consecutive electoral periods of the regional councils allow for an interesting assessment of the newly embraced self-governing political institutions. Two interrelated aspects worth discussing: the extent democratic advancement in the life of Coast society as a result of the autonomy regime, and the level of political representation of formerly disfranchised indigenous and Afro-descendant peoples, including the representation of women in regional councils.

Overall, multiethnic representation and democratic inclusion have occurred as the result of the inauguration of autonomy. Nonetheless, the data on ethnic representation shows an overrepresentation of mestizo and Mískitu peoples in the autonomous councils in the RAAN, and of mestizos and Creoles in the RAAS. Compared to population makeup, the under representation of Sumu-Mayangnas is noticeable in the RAAN, in which they make-up 6 percent of the population. It is also noticeable that Creoles, who constitute 1.55 percent of the RAAN population, were able to secure 5.4 per cent of seats in the autonomous council. In the RAAS, mestizos have controlled more than 50 percent of the seats over the study period. The Creole community secured 24.6 percent of the seats in a region in which they constitute 6 percent of the population. Other ethnic groups also gained important representation, reflecting a higher representation relative to their actual numbers in the total population in the region.

In terms of political and ethnic representation, YATAMA, for the most part, has elected Mískitus to the regional councils, though a differing trend appears in the last elections toward the inclusion of other ethnic groups. Meanwhile, the PLC has generally been represented by mestizos in both autonomous regions. The FSLN, on the other hand has been the organization with the most multiethnic representation. Ethnicity, as an indicator of social cleavage and rationale for alignment of voters to specific political parties is still a powerful influence. This is clearly the experience of YATAMA, which has consolidated its position as an indigenous party among the Mískitu, although it may be increasing its inclusiveness and representation among Afro-descendant peoples.

As for the representation of women, the data show a less positive outcome. Taken together, in both autonomous regions women secured only 17 percent of the seats in five regional councils:15.6 percent in the RAAN and

18.4 percent in the RAAS. Women were better represented by the FSLN in the RAAN, while the PLC achieved better representation of women in the RAAS. Women's representation in both autonomous regions reproduced a pattern of relative exclusion based on the combination of gender and ethnicity. This process is more noticeable in the case of the Sumu-Mayangna: only one woman from that group was elected to the RAAN council, while in the RAAS no Mayangna women have ever been elected in the course of its electoral history.

Table 5.6. Women, Ethnicity and Political Parties, RAAN 1990–2010

| Ethnic Group | Political Organization | | | Total |
|---|---|---|---|---|
| | FSLN | PLC | YATAMA | |
| Miskitu | 5 | 2 | 12 | 19 |
| Mestizo | 11 | 7 | 0 | 18 |
| Sumu-mayangna | 1 | 0 | 0 | 1 |
| Creole | 5 | 1 | 1 | 7 |
| Total | 22 | 10 | 13 | 45 |

Source: Figueroa, 2006: 14

Table 5.7. Women, Ethnicity and Political Parties, RAAS 1990–2010

| Ethnic Group | Political Organization | | | | | | Total |
|---|---|---|---|---|---|---|---|
| | FSLN | PIM | Alianza Liberal | PLC | UNO | YATAMA | |
| Miskitu | 0 | 0 | 0 | 1 | 0 | 2 | 3 |
| Mestiza | 10 | 1 | 2 | 14 | 2 | 0 | 29 |
| Creole | 5 | 0 | 2 | 7 | 2 | 1 | 17 |
| Rama | 1 | 0 | 0 | 1 | 0 | 0 | 2 |
| Garífuna | 0 | 0 | 0 | 0 | 0 | 1 | 1 |
| Total | 16 | 1 | 4 | 23 | 4 | 4 | 52 |

Source: Figueroa 2006: 15

Another dimension through which one can assess political representation and participation in the decision-making process is by looking at the extent to which local indigenous and Afro-descendant communities and their authorities were able to make their voices heard in the regional councils. Unfortunately, after the autonomy statute was approved, a rather limited effective articulation between communities and the councils was visible. This fact was surprising since local communities were instrumental in the efforts to secure peace, autonomy, and reconciliation (Hale 1994: 166). However, once autonomy came into effect, politics shifted from being locally-based to being regionally and nationally based. From then on, key discussions about regional issues, such as policies on land, natural resources management, and large-scale development projects, would become a matter of debates solely in regional bodies. In some cases these debates would reproduce political tensions that originated at the national level, with local priorities often being displaced in favor of national concerns. The level of disillusionment and sense of powerlessness among indigenous communities were intensified by the fact that their demands were not being addressed in a timely way by autonomous institutions.[1]

Exclusionary practices in the organization of each consecutive regional council, shifting and unstable alliances, more evident in the first two periods, 1990 - 1998, and the limited consensus between 1996 and 2002, resulted in polarization and long periods of inactivity in both councils. Periods of inactivity, and, in turn, political clientelism, made the possibilities for multiparty cooperation less likely. The likelihood of cooperation within the councils was also influenced by national parties, *caudillo* practices, and their specific agendas. The overall result was popular dissatisfaction with the functioning of autonomy, as represented by the regional councils' paltry performance, among Coastal society, evident in the trend toward decreasing turnout in regional elections.

The last four regional elections have been characterized by a high percentage of abstention as compared to the first two electoral processes. Although people would not reject autonomy as a symbol of aspirations for self-determination, their disappointment with autonomous institutions, regional councils and regional administrations / coordination, is considerable. Data from national figures for municipal and presidential elections clearly show that levels of abstention have been consistently more significant in the Atlantic Coast.

---

1 Legal titling over collective land has been an historical demand of indigenous peoples. The fact that the land surveillance law (*Ley de Demarcacion*) was not approved until 2002 is an indication of the delay of autonomous institutions in addressing key indigenous demands.

Table 8.1: Abstention in Municipal, Regional, And Presidential Elections in the Autonomous Regions 1990–2006 (percentages)

| Year/ Elections | Municipal | | Regional | Presidential | |
|---|---|---|---|---|---|
| | Coast | Nicaragua | Coast | Coast | Nicaragua |
| 1990 | | | 22 | 21 | 13.3 |
| 1996 | 43 | 23.6 | | 43 | 23.3 |
| 1998 | | | 43 | | |
| 2000 | 62 | 42 | | | |
| 2001 | | | | 33 | 28 |
| 2002 | | | 59 | | |
| 2004 | 57 | 56 | | | |
| 2006 | | | 55 | 54.5 | 25 |

Data from the *Consejo Supremo Electoral* (2006). Municipal, Regional and Presidential series from 1990 through 2002, cited in Chavez (2002: 36), based on data from the CSE (http://www.cse.gob.ni/)

In relation to its political stance and alliances vis-à-vis autonomy, over-all, YATAMA was consistent in challenging the *status quo* and contesting the legitimacy and regulatory framework of the autonomy regime. This long-term position was illustrated by its defiance and reluctance to enter into meaningful multiparty cooperation with regard to autonomy's enabling legislation, and the various initiatives proposed by regional institutions in order to approve autonomy's by-laws. Instead, YATAMA constantly emphasized the need for a "deep reform" of the autonomy statute and pursued unstable political alliances with national political parties in exchange for promises by those parties to reform the legal framework. In 2002 YATAMA supported the passing of a bill on indigenous land demarcation because it had fully participated in its design, had promoted and achieved significant consultation among indigenous communities, and sought the law as a strategic legal instrument to fulfill its vision of indigenous community-based territorial autonomy and self-determination.

The FSLN on the other hand, tended to support the preservation of the *status quo*, avoiding reform of the autonomy statute. At the same time, the FSLN was engaged in developing enabling legislation to advance the realization of autonomy. For this purpose, the FSLN was often pushed by organizations from the Coast's civil society, such as universities, communities, and local NGOs, rather than itself promoting enabling legislation. It might also be argued that FSLN support for autonomy was mediated by its overall political strategy at the national level. For instance, the bi-partisan pact agreed upon with the PLC in 1998 resulted in the exclusion of YATAMA from the 2001 municipal elections and precluded other local political organizations from participating in the municipal and regional elections. One year after the FSLN had agreed to ally with YATAMA to oppose the PLC in the RAAN, they both promised to promote democratic governance and autonomy in the RAAN. The upcoming 2006 national elections, the FSLN's efforts to win the presidency, and YATAMA's dissatisfaction with the PLC may have all functioned as a powerful incentive for that alliance. [1]

The PLC on the other hand, since it became a political force in the life of the autonomous regions, has opposed autonomy and has represented the interests of the governing elites in the national government. Since its inception in mid 1990s, the PLC's national leadership has promoted a discourse of "national integration" and "incorporation," and it has taken actions accordingly to advance this vision. Interestingly enough, the PLC has also gained a stronghold among voters in the Coast, in particular among the large mestizo population in the south autonomous region among whom nationalistic discourse resonates. Though this backing may be changing due to the split in the liberal party, voters' support for the PLC since 1994 may also be explained by the importance that Coastal society places on a supportive central government. This is seen as a chief condition for the realization of autonomy.

As political competitors, the PLC and YATAMA have coincided as contending forces against the FSLN in various electoral processes since 1990. Their mutual rejection of the existing autonomy arrangement as a legitimate framework has also brought them together for short-term, pragmatic alliances aimed to control access to regional institutions, the central state's budgetary allocations to these institutions, and representation in the regional councils. However, the rationale behind their opposition to the

---

1  In the electoral contest of 2006 YATAMA and the FSLN galvanized their political alliance. These accords envisioned a mutual understanding on a series of reforms needed to strengthen the autonomy regime. Five areas were considered in the accords: i) implementation of enabling legislation, in particular the law on land demarcation, reforms to the electoral law and the autonomy statute; ii) reforms of the state and indigenous participation; iii) the implementation of socioeconomic programs; iv) increases in the funding of regional governments; and finally, vi) organization of the regional councils under a bi-partisan scheme. In addition, the FSLN included YATAMA's representatives in its electoral list for the National Assembly (YATAMA-FSLN 2006: 3-10).

contested autonomy regime is rather different. The PLC has constantly opposed effective autonomy rights from being granted to indigenous and Afro-
descendant peoples, and it has pursued an image of autonomy that is politically and administratively subordinated to the national state. Alternatively,
YATAMA has tried to advance a vision in which the meaningful self-determination of indigenous communities can be exercised. In its perspective,
the existing framework of autonomy rights blocks the effective realization
of collective rights and indigenous autonomy. It then seems that the occasional alliances, in which both the PLC and YATAMA were engaged, revealed an uneasy tension between a conception of autonomy subordinated
to the central state, clearly put forward by the PLC, and a vision of an indigenous territorial autonomy aimed at empowering the indigenous peoples.

Since 2002, the FSLN and YATAMA have coincided in the need to
consolidate their position as political forces by excluding other electoral
competitors, in particular the PLC. For YATAMA, the frustrating alliances
with the PLC have corroborated the PLC's lack of interest in reforming the
contested autonomy regime in such a way that it will eventually meet indigenous self-determination demands. The FSLN in turn, for reasons related to
its national race for gaining the presidency, crafted alliances with various
political organizations, including YATAMA. In a radical contrast to its previous position, the FSLN promised YATAMA its support for reforming the
autonomy statute. It remains to be seen whether this process of reform will
eventually result in a democratic experience or instead be characterized by
top-down decision-making.

Conclusion

Having assessed the political life of autonomous institutions over almost two decades (1990–2007), crucial elements emerge in the analysis.
First, consensus on the autonomy regulatory construct has been difficult to
achieve between regional political actors. Secondly, it has been difficult to
advance autonomy, meaning enduring coalitions between competing forces
as well as multiparty collaboration. Some of the reasons that can explain
the paucity of sustained cooperation can be found in the institutional design of autonomous institutions. Also, another reason might be explained
by the effect of the meddling of national political parties in autonomous
institutions. Such meddling has discouraged instances of cooperation be-

tween autonomous councils and their executive administrations. It has also excluded political competitors regionally and inhibited local participation. This interference has intensified, and might get even stronger in the future because the Nicaraguan political system has been moving from an incipient multiparty democracy to a bi-partisan pact that threatens to foreclose previous political rights. It should also be pointed out that the negative effects of the PLC–FSLN pact on municipal government performance and citizen participation have not been unique to the Atlantic Coast. Scholars have noted that the PLC–FSLN agreement at the national level resulted in "a hostile and restrictive climate to participation, which did not favour the development of an informed and critical participation on the [municipal] government's performance" (Ortega & Wallace, 2001: 469).

In synthesis, autonomy in the Atlantic Coast has been held captive by the problems of democratic consolidation of post-war Nicaragua. Recurrent disputes, mainly due to access to resources and political power, are a factor that has inhibited consensus building within autonomous institutions. However, the most compelling reasons can be found at the level of the contested meaning that autonomy conveys to the heterogeneous population of the Atlantic Coast societies.

## References

Asamblea Nacional de Nicaragua (1997b) Ley de Reforma Parcial a la Ley Electoral. Ley 266. *La Gaceta*, Número 174, 11 de Septiembre (Managua: Nicaragua).

———. ( 2000) *Constitución Política de Nicaragua* (Managua: Editorial Jurídica).

ASDI (Agencia Sueca para el Desarrollo Internacional) (2000) 'La Reforma Electoral Nicaragüense: ¿Gobernabilidad o Exclusión?' Report Commisioned by SIDA (Managua).

Butler, J. (1994) 'Nuevos gobiernos costeños, viejos problemas abiertos' in *Envío* 148 UCA (Managua).

———. (2000) 'YATAMA: Rebellion with a Cause?' in *Envío* 19, 232/3 (Managua), pp. 37-40.

Campbell, M. S. (2007) 'The Rights of Indigenous Peoples to Political Participation and the Case of YATAMA V. Nicaragua' in *Arizona Journal of International & Comparative Law* 24, 2, pp. 499–540.

Centeno, M. (2003) 'Consejo Regional de la RAAS nada en corrupción' in *El Nuevo Diario*, February 19.

Comisión Nacional de Autonomía (1985) Principios y Políticas Para el Ejercicio de los Derechos de Autonomía de los Pueblos Indígenas y Comunidades de la Costa Atlántica de Nicaragua (Managua: DEPEP).

Consejo Supremo Electoral (1991) *Elecciones 1990* (República de Nicaragua: Managua).

———. (1993) *Resolución* (10 de diciembre) (Managua).

———. (1995) *Elecciones 1994, RAAN-RAAS* (Managua: Consejo Supremo Electoral).

———. (2000) *Cedula de Notificación.* (15 de Agosto) (Managua).

———. (2004) *Ley Electoral.* Ley 331 (Managua: Consejo Supremo Electoral).

———. (2006) *Elecciones Regionales 2006.* Resultados Electorales (Managua, Consejo Supremo Electoral) (http://www.cse.gob.ni/).

Corte Interamericana de Derechos Humanos, CIDH (2005) *Caso YATAMA versus Nicaragua. Sentencia 23 de Junio, 2005* (San José, Costa Rica) (http://www.corteidh.or.cr/)

Cruz, A. (2001) 'Nicaragua: La transición hacia una economía de Mercado' in *El PNUD y Nicaragua ante el Tercer Milenio. Una visión Nicaragüense sobre Gobernabilidad y Desarrollo.* (PNUD: Managua), pp. 75–80.

Chavez, H. (2002) 'La Participación Electoral en la Costa Caribe' in *WANI* 29, UCA, pp. 28 - 37.

Démelas, M. (2001) 'El Nacimiento De Una Forma Autoritaria de Poder: Los Caudillos', in *Fundamentos de Antropología* Vol. 10-11, pp. 65-70.

Equipo Envío (1991a) 'La Costa en su laberinto: Qué está sucediendo realmente?' in *Envío* 116 (june).

———. (1991b) 'Autonomía de la Costa a Pesar de la UNO' in *Envío* 122, UCA, (december).

———. (1999) 'Nicaragua: Se Prepara el Pacto' in *Envío* 208, UCA, (July) (http://www.envio.org.ni/articulo/2367)

———. (2000) 'Nicaragua: Después del pacto: la suerte está echada' in Envío 214, UCA, (January) (http://www.envio.org.ni/articulo/985).

———. (2006) 'Elecciones en el Caribe: ¿termómetro de cuáles calenturas?' in *Envío* 288, UCA, (marzo).

Figueroa, D. (2006) 'The Quest for Gender Equality: The Participation of Miskitu Indigenous Women in the Autonomous Regional Elections,' (paper delivered at the CPSA Annual Conference: York University, May).

Fonseca, R. (1991) 'En la Costa: ¿la frustración mediatizara la democracia?' in *Wani,* 9, UCA, (enero-abril).

FSLN (Frente Sandinista de Liberación Nacional) (2006) *El Frente es el Mejor Aliado para los Pueblos Indígenas* (Secretaría de Comunicación del FSLN) (Transcription of Words delivered by Brooklyn Rivera at 100% Noticias radio program) (May 5).

González, M. (2007) 'Los Caminos de *Yapti Tasba*: Autonomía Regional en Nicaragua', in Marti i Puig, S. ed. *Pueblos Indígenas y Política en América Latina. El Reconocimiento de sus Derechos y el Impacto de sus Demandas a Inicios del Siglo XXI* (Barcelona: CIDOB), pp. 469-497

Grupo Cívico Ética y Transparencia (2006) *Sexto Informe Por la Transparencia y Seguridad de los Comicios electorales de Marzo y Noviembre 2006* (Managua, Febrero) (http://www.eyt.org.ni/recurso1.htm).

Hale, C. R. (1994) *Resistance and Contradiction, Miskitu Indians and the Nicaraguan State, 1894-1987* (Stanford, Stanford University Press).

Instituto para la Promocion y Desarrollo de la Democracia (2006) *Principales Hallazgos de la Verificación Técnica de Doble Vía al Padrón Electoral de la Costa Caribe de Nicaragua* (Managua, Febrero). (http://www.ipade.org.ni/index.php?cat=728)

Matamoros, J. (1992) 'Las fracciones de Yatama y la Situación Política de la RAAN' in *Wani* 13, UCA, pp. 1-19

Miller, D. (2004) *Informe Actualizado sobre el Consejo Regional del Atlantico Sur, correspondiente al periodo 2002-2006* (Programa de Fortalecimiento Institucional RAAN-ASDI-RAAS) (Bluefields: Unpublished document).

Montenegro, Sofía, Cuadra, E, Saldomando, A. and Zamora, Y. (2005) *Nicaragua: La Gobernabilidad Al Servicio de las Reformas* (Managua: Centro de Investigaciones de la Comunicación, CINCO).

Ortega Hegg, M. and Wallace Salinas, G. (2001) *Nicaragua: Experiencias de Gestión Municipal* (El Salvador: FUNDAUNGO).

Pérez-Baltodano, A. (2003) *Entre el Estado Conquistador y el Estado Nación: Providencialismo, Pensamiento Político y Estructuras de Poder en el Desarrollo Histórico de Nicaragua* (Managua: Instituto de Historia de Nicaragua y Centroamérica & Fundación Friedrich Ebert).

Rivera, B. (2002) 'La Resistencia de la Autonomia,' in *El Nuevo Diario* (Managua, May 25).

Rizo, M. (1990) 'La Identidad Étnica y Elecciones: El Caso de la RAAN' in *Wani* 8, UCA, pp. 28-51.

Sandoval, C. (2002) 'Trasladan a la RAAN conflicto del Pacifico', in *La Prensa*, (Managua, May 4).

Sujo Wilson, H. (1997) 'Los Partidos Políticos y el Proceso de Autonomía en la Costa Atlántica de Nicaragua' (Paper delivered at the *IV Simposio de Autonomía de las Regiones Autónomas de la Costa Atlántica*) (Managua: FADCANIC) (October 12-15).

Wani (1998) 'Panorama General de las Elecciones en la Costa' in *Wani* 23, UCA, pp. 5-12.

YATAMA. (1989) *YATAMA Peace Initiative* (February, San Jose, Costa Rica) (http://cwis.org/fwdp/Americas/yatpeace.txt)

YATAMA-FSLN (2006) *Acuerdos YATAMA-FSLN con la Autonomía. Plan de Gobierno de la Unidad Nicaragua Triunfa para la Costa Caribe* (Bilwi, 2 de Mayo).

# CHAPTER 6. NEOLIBERALISM, PATRIARCHAL RULE, AND CULTURAL CHANGE AT THE TURN OF THE TWENTIETH CENTURY: THE CASE OF TASBAPAUNI

*Ken Henriksen & Christopher Kindblad*

This chapter studies the cultural impact of neo-liberal adjustment in Tasbapauni, a Miskitu community located in the Southern Autonomous Atlantic Region (RAAS). In Nicaragua, neo-liberal reforms began with the electoral defeat of the Sandinistas in 1990, and since then an epoch with subsequent governments ideologically dedicated to neo-liberalism deepened the adjustment policies, until the Sandinistas were restored to power after the elections of 2006. In Tasbapauni, as well as in other communities on the Atlantic Coast, neo-liberal policies incited a double trend in local development. On the one hand a state in retreat created a cutback in state-sponsored services and an institutional vacuum. The failure to develop a framework for the implementation of the autonomy statute, a laissez-faire attitude in critical matters, such as the ongoing land conflicts, the extension of the agricultural frontier, and the illegal exploitation of land and water, are just a few signs of this vacuum (Mordt 2001). A general feeling of alienation and isolation, and a widespread perception among Costeños that the central government is neglecting the Atlantic Coast is also an indication of this absence of government institutions (Sánchez 2007). On the other hand, the absence of the state created a space for an expansion of the market. The lower priority given to control and regulation of commercial activities resulted in a rapid and intense commercial exploitation of land and marine species, which in turn threatened to increase internal competition over communal property. In accordance with this argument, neo-liberal changes were likely to provoke a cultural change towards individualism and increasing competition between households.

Miskitu culture has always been heterogeneous, malleable, and subject to change. In fact, some authors have argued that the Miskitu culture is a result of cultural contact, first with British and Caribbean civilizations, and later with the Nicaraguan state (Helms 1971; Hale & Gordon 1987; Hale 1994). The Miskitu population, thus, seems to have a long history of successful interaction with the surrounding world. Miskitu culture could be described as a *matriztic* culture (Maturana & Verden-Zöller 2003), which in this case refers to a network of conversation characterized by food gifts between matrilocal households, collaboration between men and women in child rearing, bride service, mutual help in agricultural work, participation in community matters, and co-inspiration as a way to solve communal problems when families or the entire community face social and material problems. This culture has developed as a result of the diverse strategies community members have resorted to in their encounters with the outside world. In the beginning of the twentieth century Tasbapauni received collective land-titles, and since then the community has developed a culture based on communal ownership, mutual help and practices of labor exchange in agricultural work. The communal property regime, together with the matrilocal and social organization of community life, has been central for the development of a collective identity in Tasbapauni, and on the Atlantic Coast in general, which community members have seen as different from the surrounding patriarchal culture.

However, the matriztic culture of the Miskitu is not static. Just as in previous times, Miskitu culture is subjected to different situational contingencies, including the instauration of neo-liberal and patriarchal rule in Nicaragua. In this chapter we will focus on cultural change in Tasbapauni in the 1990s and the beginning of the new century. We argue that the combination of global capitalist penetration and the institutional withdrawal of the central state resulted in a cultural dilemma in Tasbapauni (Henriksen & Kindblad 2005). On the one hand, the penetration of capitalist modes of exchange motivated community members to exploit communal property for individual purposes. On the other hand, the continuous arrival of foreign entrepreneurs and companies constituted an external threat to the communal property regime, which was likely to generate a collective reaction. This dilemma, between resorting to an individual rationality or developing the pre-existing collective spirit, makes it possible to distinguish two paths of cultural change: one that we call a *disruptive change*, which would imply a disruption of the matriztic culture, and a disintegration of the social organization, and another that we refer to as a *transformative change*, which would transform the culture in such a way that the social organization is conserved. The aim of this chapter is thus to cast light over, and account for, the actual path of change that took place in Tasbapauni as a result of neo-liberal penetration.

Methodological Considerations

The chapter weaves together the insights from two independent ethnographic studies done in the community of Tasbapauni. Based upon fieldwork in 1994, 1995-96 and 1999 Christopher Kindblad has made historical-comparative research into the processes of economic change and continuity in Tasbapauni (Kindblad 2010). Ken Henriksen did his fieldwork in the same community in 1997, 1998-1999 and again in 2001. His research focuses on the politicization of ethnic identities after the electoral defeat of the Sandinistas in 1990, and thus on what he calls ethno-political practice in the neo-liberal era (Henriksen 2002, 2008). In our view, a cross-disciplinary combination of an economic-historical approach with an ethno-political perspective provides a deeper and more nuanced understanding of cultural change in Tasbapauni than a more narrow study of either economic or ethno-political matters would generate. One main reason for this is that the main economic asset in this community, land, has for many years also been a main ingredient in local constructions of ethnicity and ethno-political identities. Accordingly, in Tasbapauni, just as in many other indigenous communities in Latin America, the study of economic and cultural aspects must be inseparable.

The combination of these two approaches can help us understand the character of the cultural transformations which took place in the second half of the 1990s and the beginning of this century. Kindblad (1995; 2010) has argued that a particular economic culture has developed in Tasbapauni, which combines two different transactional orders: a long-term order of exchange mainly among women, which is based on gift-relations and rituals, and a short-term order of exchange, which consists of individualistic competition among men. The transition to commercial exploitation of communal property after the 1960s, which started to compete with the custom of food gifts in the 1970s, led to the development of a contradiction between long-term gift relations and short-term exchange. In the 1990s, population increase, external exploitation and few wage labour opportunities threatened to intensify the contradiction. Henriksen (2002) has focused on how a general retreat of the central state in the 1990s has given room for the mobilization of community members in formal and informal types of ethnopolitical activity. Although the neo-liberal call for individual rationality has for many years been the dominant credo in Nicaragua, he argues that a particular collective orientation was formed in the community of Tasbapauni.

Background

The community of Tasbapauni received collective land titles at the beginning of the twentieth century as noted above. The Harrison-Altamirano Treaty of 1905 had established the legal conditions for the recognition of indigenous and Creole lands, and after a coordinated effort between British diplomacy and a Nicaraguan Land Title Commission, Tasbapauni and many other communities received their first collective land title around 1916 (Henriksen 2008; Kindblad and Henriksen 2005). Evidence suggests that the establishment of a communal property regime has contributed to deepening the collective orientation in Tasbapauni, and, thus, to institutionalizing the matriztic culture based on mutual help, labour exchange and participation. The social organization of the community has thus been central for the formation of a collective identity in Tasbapauni, which is underscored by the fact that the community has a long history of being one of the most belligerent in terms of safeguarding its communal lands (Henriksen 2008). It is interesting that this collective spirit has mostly been expressed locally and only on rare occasions as a regional or ethnic mobilization.

The Sandinista insurrection of the 1980s represents a critical moment in which pan-local alliances were formed in the quest for territorial autonomy and political self-determination. In Tasbapauni a large number of community members decided to leave the community to join the Contra-movement based in Honduras and Costa Rica (Hale 1994). In part, for this reason, the inhabitants are known to be perhaps the most militantly anti-Sandinista ex-combatants in the entire country. This also suggests that the collective identity of Tasbapauni is not static, but shifting and always in flux. In the 1980s, the combination of a developmentalist and paternalistic central state, and the pan-ethnic mobilization supported by powerful indigenous organizations, can be seen as some of the most important factors in transforming local identities in Tasbapauni.

However, if we focus on the economic history of Tasbapauni it is possible to discern additional and more individualistic transformations. At the end of the 1960s a number of fishing companies established plants along the Coast, and the demand for lobster, turtle and other fishery produce increased. In Tasbapauni, which is favorably located on a narrow land tongue between the Pearl Lagoon Basin and the Caribbean Sea, some community members were attracted by the new economic opportunities and began to commercially exploit communal property (Kindblad 2010). Bernard Nietschmann, who did extended periods of fieldwork in Tasbapauni during this era, noted that the community was on the rise. The green turtle became a particularly important source of growth, but many other species, such as wild and domestic animals, coconuts and other locally grown vegetables were now also sold on the market (Nietschmann 1973, 1979).

The economic boom undoubtedly resulted in cultural changes. Nietschmann (1973) argues that new meanings were added to the old perception of communal land and water as simply a source of subsistence. Now many community members began to view communal land and water as a resource that could supply a monetary income, and for this reason the community experienced increasing economic inequality. In the late 1970s some indications of a growing inequality were emerging as many fishermen began to catch lobster rather than turtle, which had become scarce because of overexploitation and were subject to occasional closed seasons and other restrictions. With the greater disparity and changing mentality among some groups in the community, Tasbapauni also experienced more internal conflicts between different social groups, such as the younger and older generations, and between more and less economically successful community members. In addition to these changes, Hale has argued that those groups experiencing upward mobility started to increasingly identify as Creoles rather than as Miskitu Indians (Hale 1994:121ff). Although evidence suggests that this conversion began much earlier (Henriksen & Kindblad 2005), the socio-economic changes that Tasbapauni was experiencing also gave rise to emerging ethnic discrepancies within the community.

In the 1980s, the escalation of the war between the Sandinista government and the US-backed Contras had damaging effects on all types of economic activities in the community. For a long period it was extremely dangerous to leave the community to work on farmland or fishing. The Sandinista cadres stationed in Tasbapauni also restricted or prohibited access to the plantations in the hinterland for extended periods because they feared that community members would supply the Contras with food and equipment. The restrictions on hunting, fishing and farming led many people to keep domestic animals in the community and to maintain a small vegetable patch close to their home. The severe economic and social crisis meant that those who stayed in the community began to increasingly rely on old customs, such as mutual help and solidarity between households.

As mentioned above, the return to peace also implied the establishment and the institutionalization of neo-liberal and patriarchal rule, which took full force in the wake of the victory of Violeta Chamorro and the UNO-coalition in national elections in 1990. In this situation, we argue, the community of Tasbapauni, along with other ethnic communities on the Atlantic Coast, began to face a cultural dilemma initiated by the double trend in local and regional development: a neo-liberal laissez-faire politics, which included decentralization and privatization of social and political responsibility, combined with an aggressive expansion of the capitalist market and an agricultural colonization of the Coast. These macro-economic changes gave rise to a critical situation in Tasbapauni in which the community members faced a number of external threats, including the settlement and deforestation by campesinos and the arrival of foreign fishing fleets. In our view, this situation could trigger contradictory responses between the Miskitu and Creoles, where either communal identity would flourish in an attempt to defend communal territory, or where individualistic competition, local entrepreneurship and individual accumulation could develop in the commercial exploitation of the commons.

This situation could be analyzed in terms of a conflict between a collective and individual rationality, which is something that has been heavily discussed since Garrett Harding first published his famous article *The Tragedy of the Commons* (1968). Harding describes a situation in which multiple individuals, acting independently and rationally in accordance with their own self-interest, will ultimately deplete a common property, even if it is not in anyone's long-term interest for this to happen. The "tragedy of the commons" has often been formalized with reference to game theory as a prisoner's dilemma, which demonstrates why two groups of people might not cooperate even if it is in both their interests to do so. The fundamental problem is thus to account for collective action, or collaboration, from the body of premises that underlies this game-situation. Most of the existing literature suggests that a tragic scenario can only be avoided through effective normative regulation of individuals pursuing their own self-interest (Harding 1968; Ostrom 1998). According to this view, social norms and values are external to social actors and, thus, something that regulates or constrains individual behavior from above or from without. Tragedies are therefore only avoided if a regulatory body, from within or from without, imposes the "right" norms on deviating individuals.

Instead, we suggest that the cultural dilemma generated two possible processes of cultural change in Tasbapauni. One very plausible scenario would be the penetration of the capitalist market and a concomitant increase in internal as well as external competition over local land and water. The motivation to exploit communal property for the benefit of individual households would contribute to increasing economic differentiation within the community and to the development of a new capitalist culture based on an individual rationality. We argue that such a path of change would have disrupting effects on social life in the community. Firstly, traditional forms of social organization would disintegrate, and, secondly, and perhaps more seriously, because individuals within the community would now begin to act independently based mainly on their own self-interest, any forms of communal mobilization against outside threats would be unlikely to occur. In a situation with little government involvement in matters such as the illegal exploitation of communal land and water, this would ultimately lead to the destruction of common goods. This is what we refer to as a disruptive change.

However, in the absence of state institutions community members themselves may also mobilize communal forms of political authority. The state's failure to pursue a fair development strategy, including the absence of a genuine political will to create a just multi-ethnic society, generated an institutional vacuum that had to be filled out. With the extension of the agricultural frontier and many other sources of externally generated problems, community members would also be likely to act upon a communal spirit. Rather than attempting to maximize individual utility, community members would self-organize collectively against the threats. Although such a mobilization would not necessarily put an end to the destruction of the communal property, we argue that it would generate a transformative change by which traditional forms of social organization would be preserved.

### The Communal Spirit in Tasbapauni

The aim of this section is to point out some of the important cultural changes that took place in the community during the 1990s and the beginning of the new millennium, and discuss in depth what type of transformations actually occurred. In accordance with our observations, the community members in Tasbapauni wanted to conserve a communal identity, and in our view this was also what determined their response to the cultural dilemma that we have described above. The most salient feature of this local response was what we call a communal spirit among local villagers, and in particular certain members of local institutions, such as the Communal Board. This communal spirit could be described as a strong motivation for participation, collaboration and mutual help, for the shared purpose of communal development, and as a way to handle problems relating to community land, such as external exploitation and internal competition over common property.

### Communal Development in the Early 1990s

With the return to peace in the early 1990s, people in Tasbapauni wanted to see progress, because of the destruction of infrastructure during the war, divided families, and the threats that arose because of commercial exploitation. There was a feeling among many families that they had to start all over again, and that many of the problems had to be solved together. Most families in the village were facing severe material needs. Houses had to be built or restored, farms had to be re-organized and new farmland prepared. The main focus was on the possibilities offered by the local fishing industry, which formed the backbone of the local cash economy. But this industry faced a number of problems, such as the lack of facilities for catching, storing, transporting and selling fish, turtle and lobster. The young and middle-aged men who returned from the Contra war, or from exile, turned to commercial fishing, but many of them also agreed to the need to develop the community (Kindblad 2010).

In our view, a certain communal spirit developed in Tasbapauni in the beginning of the 1990s, which could be characterized as a shared purpose among community members to develop and re-build the community.

There were several identified groups who clearly wanted this to happen. These included young and middle-aged men who had joined the Contras during the war, old men and women who had stayed in the village during the same period, and two groups of women involved in projects like the reconstruction of the wharf. Another very influential group was constituted by the lay pastors of seven different churches present in the community. The lay pastor of the Moravian church had taken the initiative for ecumenical collaboration between the churches. Importantly, he got support from many church members in the community. There were certainly disagreements, and conflicts, concerning how the community should develop, because of hatred, distrust and suspicion after the war. For instance, a small group of relatives who wanted to take charge of land affairs argued for the exploitation of the forest, which could provide an income for the village, so that members in important positions like the Communal Board could get payment for their work, rather than working almost for free. Other influential groups opposed this, arguing that they should exploit the forest for their own benefit. There was also distrust between different people with regard to the use of marine resources, which for instance led to a split in the fishing cooperative in 1994 (Kindblad 1995).

However, groups of community members who wanted to work together for the development of the community took the initiative, and below we want to say something more about the motives of the different groups. The older generation, who had stayed in the community, had seen the traditional Miskitu way of life being disrupted during the war. This was mainly due to the restrictions in farming and fishing. Many of these old men and women were parents, relatives or neighbors of the young and middle-aged men who were involved in the Contra. There is no doubt that the social ties between these two groups were conserved during the war to a large extent. Through these measures the Sandinistas became even more of a common enemy, which strengthened, rather than weakened, the social ties between families, neighbors and friends. This older generation was still living in Tasbapauni at the end of the 1990s, and could provide vivid and detailed accounts of the difference between "Somoza-time" and "Sandinista-time" (Kindblad 2010).

Many of the young and middle-aged men who returned as ex-Contras to the village after the war, as well as some men who returned from exile in Costa Rica, the United States and Managua, were influenced by the experiences of the revolution, the war, ethno-political mobilization and Fourth World ideologies. The experiences that they had shared during the turbulent period of the 1980s make it possible to argue that they constituted a social generation (Kindblad 2010). These men were very influential in local development. Some of these persons could also be described as charismatic, in the sense that they were extraordinarily involved in communal development, and determined to make sacrifices for the community, sometimes even at the cost of their own family. This included some members of the Communal Board, who worked constantly initiating different projects, participating in meetings, making forestry inventories, and travelling extensively between Tasbapauni and Bluefields in order to handle critical issues. This also included some of the middle-aged men who had joined the Contras, and who had a cynical and distrustful attitude against national politicians and powerful and wealthy people in general, who "only see to their own benefit."

In Tasbapauni there were also two groups of women, which were active in different local projects. They worked in collaboration with some of these groups of men, for instance in the wharf project. The significance of women participating in local projects can hardly be exaggerated. Household work and child-rearing is often carried out in collaboration between women from different households, which means that they tend to be present in the community, and they also attend the local churches regularly. This means that their participation in local projects is often on a continuous and uninterrupted basis. In contrast, men are often absent for extended periods because of activities outside the community, such as travelling to Bluefields and other places, fishing, hunting and farming. There was also a common perception among many women that young and middle-aged men are often involved in internal conflicts and competition, which they felt does not benefit the development of the community. These women often accused the men of being responsible for a perceived lack of unity in Tasbapauni (Kindblad 1995). However, the group of women that we refer to also collaborated with men who had aspirations to become elected representatives of the town. These men included one who had studied in Costa Rica while living in exile in the 1980s and another man who had been involved in several projects in Managua.

## The Transformation of Local Institutions

There were many signs of a renewed collective spirit, and a strong sense of community and indigenous identity in the middle of the 1990s, which had consequences for local institutions. In order to understand the persistence of this spirit in Tasbapauni, it is important to stress the participation of the major bulk of the young and middle-aged men in the ethnic mobilization against the Sandinista revolution in the 1980s. This mobilization was closely linked to ideas of self-determination, and political and territorial autonomy (Henriksen and Kindblad 2005, Hale 1994). The anti-Sandinista insurrection occurred alongside an ethnic revival and the emergence of a new sense of belonging, which was linked to the political construction of a collective ethnic project based on indigenous and historical rights (Henriksen 2008). With the participation of men from Tasbapauni, as well as members from most other communities, this mobilization contributed to the formation of pan-ethnic alliances that were constructed against the Nicaraguan state and for territorial rights. With the introduction and deepening of neoliberal rule in the 1990s, this collective orientation seems to have taken a new course in the community of Tasbapauni.

We argue that the ethno-political ideas of self-determination and autonomy have been left intact, but in Tasbapauni the regional, multiethnic alliances receded into the background, and a local and a spatially more narrow orientation emerged, which was closely linked to local institutions. This means that ideas about collective land rights and self-determination might have changed, but they have not dissipated or given precedence to an individualistic attitude. This could best be illustrated by focusing on the role of some of the political institutions in the community. During fieldwork throughout 1998-99 attempts were made to clarify the responsibility of each of the many political institutions in Tasbapauni. However, when asking community members about their perceptions of the responsibility of the main institutions in the community, they often preferred to talk about origins. There appeared to be two kinds of institutions: "those from here"

(Tasbapauni or the Atlantic Coast) and "those from the outside" (state institutions). State institutions, such as the *alcalde* [mayor], were mostly referred to using the Spanish term, and they were only attributed minor importance:

> The *alcalde* is a government man. That is a government man. The *alcalde* is the one who collect in taxes. He don't have nothing to do with community property, you see. Through all those things he don't have no right to touch community property. He is for the government, you know the government business. The *alcalde* is different. He is not with us, he is apart.[1]

The person serving as the mayor[2] in 1998–1999 was a respected community member. Many people appreciated what he had done for the community, and the fact that he was part of the Contra movement added to his reputation. The term "government man," therefore, referred to the institution and not to the person in charge of the position. This institution was seen as alien and as an entity that had not grown out of communal interests. It is therefore important to stress that the deprecation of this and a couple of other institutions that were perceived to be from without, was rooted in a localist and collective idea of the community. It can in fact be argued that the rejection of government institutions was based on a communal identity, which distinguished between an organic collective Self and an external Other.

In contrast to the office of mayor, the Council of Elders was appreciated as an important local institution. The role of the Council of Elders can best be described as an advisory organ for the Community Board, another politically important institution. The president of the council was sometimes counseled and often took part as an observer in Community Board meetings, but apart from this there are reasons to believe that the power of the Council of Elders should be found in its symbolic value. In 1999, none of the informants in Tasbapauni was really able to remember when the Council of Elders was established. While some people said that it was an old Miskitu organization, others held that it was established during the war. However, interviews with leaders of YATAMA revealed that this organization had advised the communities to establish the council around 1995, confirming

---

1  Interview Anon, Tasbapauni 1998.
2  Importantly, he was in fact just the vice-mayor. Since Tasbapauni is part of the municipality of Pearl Lagoon, the mayor lives and works in the larger town of Pearl Lagoon.

that the Council of Elders was a fairly new institution. They explained: "Indian communities need elder councils to be more Indian." Influenced by the global discourses on indigenous rights, the leadership of YATAMA probably considers the Council of Elders to be a powerful political and symbolic tool, which serves to construct indigenous identity and which can reinforce claims about rights and entitlements. Although the governors in Tasbapauni had been unable to integrate the council into formal political structures, it was widely accepted as one of the principal institutions in the community, and most people clearly viewed this institution as "one from here."

However, the most important political figure in Tasbapauni in the 1990s was beyond doubt the síndico. In 1919, a government decree (Decreto No. 61, 13 de marzo de 1919) established the position of síndico in the communities that in the years before had been granted collective land titles. According to the decree, the síndico is a government appointee whose main responsibility is to represent the community in all matters concerning communal land and he is the overseer of that land, as well as the guardian of the land title documents. Community members often claimed that the position of síndico is the most important in the community and almost everybody agreed that, in view of all the land problems that the community was facing, the importance of the síndico was growing. As mentioned previously, these problems have to do with the illegal exploitation of communal land and water, especially lumber, the deliberate selling of land that belongs to the community, and the extension of the agricultural frontier, which implies that a huge area of community land has been cleared and cultivated by poor mestizo immigrants. People steadily emphasized the ongoing aggravation of the land situation. The síndico, for example, stated that the situation had worsened in recent years:

> In Somoza time there wasn't too much problem about the land. The changing of government bring these problem. Especially with this government right now, the Alemán government. He want to take away land, you see!... First time it was not like this. The changing of government is bringing these problems. The problem is from my take over. So I received the problem. It's hard and you see what I fight for, and I win it. And right now I think I get it clear...we [unintelligible] with the Spaniard them. No more people can go in and cut no land, you see, no more cutting of these big woods there I am fighting for. You see, on the next side, the Wawashang, I have to see what I can. I have to have meeting there, talk to the people them, I will be running around there and if I capture anything I taking them out, I just tell them move out, giving them some time, maybe they

have something planted to eat; when they done take that out, OK, leave out. Sorry but what to do....Those people who are there they don't come under a good "acuerdo," under a good position to come and situate there. Because they didn't come to aks [ask] for no land to live there. They just come in "mala fe." I can take them out, that my job. That is my position to fight for the land, as a síndico. In San-dinista time another kind of problem: the war.[1]

According to Hale (1994), the síndico of a nearby community took up the role of promoting dialogue and reconciliation between local Contras and the government during the war, as well as in the subsequent autonomy process. He therefore developed close working relations with government officials (Hale 1994: 149f and 181f.). This type of cooperation is absent from the síndico's narrative above and outweighed by a discourse that stresses his, and the community's, capacity and right to handle their own commu-nal affairs. Consider this account about the nearby mestizo-village, Pueblo Nuevo:

If them [the people of Pueblo Nuevo] go to the government to aks [ask] for help the government don't have nothing to do with our community land... They have to come here; they have to come here the Pueblo Nuevo people and the government if they want. The central government he don't have nothing to do with us, what he is looking is war, he is dangerous, it is very delicate...We don't want no more war.[2]

This discourse of self-governance, present in many townspeople's idea about Tasbapauni as a discrete and autonomous entity, had a temporal di-mension as well. Projects for the future mainly focused on prosperity for the community, rather than for the nation, the Atlantic Coast or an ethnic group as a whole. But the discourse of self-governance was also rooted in images of a common communal past. The síndico's explanation of his duties and responsibilities was founded on such a moral link with the past:

A síndico he elected by the community... The síndico is from the com-munity.... (He) is the responsible one for the community property, he is the one that take caring about the whole community land property. He have to take care of the whole community property: land, sea, and everything. The town elect you, the town, not no one else, the town elect you. That is from our ancestors' time, you see. Those land our ancestors get them working for the Miskitu king. So all those land what my old ancestors have those 'mo-

---

1 Interview with the síndico, Tasbapauni January 1999.
2 Interview with the síndico, Tasbapauni January 1999.

jones' put we owning them. Through that we have our land 'ubicated.' And from our own ancestor time we have síndico in this community. That is the one who see about the welfare of this whole territory, land, water, sea and everything, the land for the community.[1]

The Threats against the Community

The community of Tasbapauni faced a series of threats in the 1990s that we want to describe before discussing the response by members of local institutions, such as the síndico. The main factor behind these changes was the general turn to neo-liberal policies in the aftermath of the Sandinista electoral defeat in 1990. These policies, with a general retreat of the state and a simultaneous expansion of the market and the private sector, led to a series of externally generated changes in and around Tasbapauni. First, an increase in immigration of landless campesinos and other poor sectors from Spanish-speaking Nicaragua has given rise to ethnic conflicts and growing pressure on land and natural habitats. Second, there has been a steady increase in the commercial exploitation by outsiders of communal property, especially in the fishing sector. These changes did of course give rise to a number of threats, especially those associated with deforestation and over-exploitation of marina resources, which will be described here.

The expansion of the agricultural frontier on the Atlantic Coast was probably the most pressing problem in the 1990s (Mordt 2001; Acosta 2000; Howard 1996, 1997). The processes of modernization and liberalization in central and western Nicaragua have forced many landless campesinos to migration into the agrarian frontier areas, which include land belonging to Tasbapauni. In addition, in recent years the large number of timber industries and other private parties that are staking out claims to huge tracks of land reflect the governments' general failure to demarcate and distribute land (Vanden 1997; Howard 1997; Mordt 2001). The autonomy statute could have been an effective institution for the regulation and control of these incursions. Passed by the Sandinista government in 1987, but not taken into effect until after the electoral defeat of the Sandinistas in 1990, the autonomy statute introduces a set of collective rights for the ethnic communities living on the Atlantic Coast, including the right to control communal land. It is stipulated that "communal property is constituted by the communal

---

1  Interview Anon, Tasbapauni October 1998.

lands, waters and forests that have traditionally belonged to the communities" and that these communities are entitled to "their own forms of communal, collective, or individual ownership and transfer of land." Nevertheless, the state has not yet developed a framework for implementing the autonomy statute.

In the case of Tasbapauni this development has been detrimental. According to most community members, the community possesses a relatively large territory compared with other villages in the Pearl Lagoon region.[1] Perhaps for this reason, most families have traditionally practiced swidden agriculture, either along the beaches or along the rivers and creeks of the Pearl Lagoon basin. However, large areas of land have been cleared and cultivated by a growing number of landless campesino families. In 1996, community leaders estimated that about 1500–2000 individuals were staying illegally on land belonging to the community, and more recent estimates suggest that there could be more than 4000 Spanish-speaking campesinos in the area; a number twice as high as the Tasbapauni population itself. The large unprotected territory, with its abundance of mahogany, has also made it attractive to commercial interests. In some cases companies simply exploit the land illegally, in other cases they have been able to purchase or provide themselves with land titles in Managua, evading the principles laid out in the autonomy statute (Kindblad 2010, Henriksen & Kindblad 2005).

In this epoch the Atlantic Coast became internationally known for the abundance of natural resources, the lack of control and the inefficient means of regulation, which among many other things resulted in an over-exploitation of marine and forestry species (Henriksen 2002; Kindblad 2010). In the case of fisheries, the sea has for many years provided access to turtle, lobster and scalefish. But, in addition to these challenges, Tasbapauni has been facing a serious problem since the beginning of the 1990s. The construction of five processing plants and the presence of national and foreign fishing fleets operating close to the community have resulted in over-exploitation of especially lobsters and shrimps stocks. The Nicaraguan government pursued an investment friendly policy which threatened the artisanal fishermen in Tasbapauni, but the arrival of illegal pirate boats from Colombia, Panama and Honduras became a new source of frustration. Many informants in Tasbapauni expressed annoyance and concern with the operations of the foreign boats:

---

1  The size equals 58000 hectares according to some informants.

> Most of them come from Honduras and Panama, and that is a big effect. When they come and fish there, they put out a thousand traps, two thousand traps and they surround large areas. Whatever they drop off there we don't catch anything, because they are stopping everything from coming to us. I have heard that they fish shrimp in the night and I believe it, because sometimes when we are sleeping on the cays we get up and see a light, but very dim. That light is working all night, and when the day clear you don't hear that boat anymore. He is gone. So well, we know that they are working as pirates.[1]

Neo-liberal policies were also a source of new opportunities for some community members. Many of the young and middle-aged men began to fish lobster, which gave easier access to money[2], and other community members earned a living as loggers working for timber companies. This resulted in a general commercialization of the local economy and increasing economic inequality: a process which can be seen as a continuation of the development pointed out by Nietschmann in the 1970s. In addition, because most of the younger people had turned to commercial fishing, many of the traditional subsistence activities had been disrupted. Most significantly, still fewer community members wanted to engage in farming. Members of the older generation decried the changing mentality, the decline in agricultural productivity as well as the emergence of what they perceived as a short-sighted, individualistic attitude. For them it reflects an erosion of the very meaning of community, and in more practical terms, an erosion of long-term social and economic security:

> In working, everybody used to work in those days. So if you had your little place to work you would have people go and help you, chop the place and get it fixed so that maybe you can plant your provision. Because you always had help, but in these times that is not there again. Even the young people them they don't want to work — they don't work. They rather are using the 'one day money.' Like to say if they go out and haul their trap and catch their little lobster and come with it, and that is sufficient. Or they go and dive about in the water and that is different, something else again. So nobody would be preparing for tomorrow. Everybody is just for today, but in the olden time they always try to prepare for tomorrow.[3]

---

1  Interview Anon, Tasbapauni June 1994.
2  In 1992, the company Promarblue began to buy fish and lobster from Tasbapauni fishermen.
3  Interview Anon, Tasbapauni March 1996.

However, many households remained dependent on the yields from the "farm." The locally based production system continued to provide the key staples of coconuts, breadfruit, cassava, dasheen (taro), plantains, and rice. But with the introduction of cash and the increased purchasing power of some community members, the traditional rituals of gift giving were no longer as frequent as it used to be. Instead, the perceived obligation to share with other community members was limited to close siblings and relatives. But the changes have not yet resulted in a complete commodification of local culture. Whereas the foods "from without" such as sugar, flower and soft drinks are sold at their market value, the prices on local items are fixed by the Communal Board.[1] According to one member of the community board in 1999, the reason for this is that "everything that grows on community land is a common good" and it is therefore considered morally wrong to sell the yields at too high a price.

Now we have described some of the social, political and economic changes that took place in Tasbapauni in the 1990s. Together these changes constitute a serious threat to the community, and a number of internal changes in the community further aggravate the impact of neoliberal policies. As mentioned above, due to returning emigrants and refugees, the community of Tasbapauni experienced some population growth in the 1990s. The returnees left the community during the war, but with peace restored they began to come back. Many returnees have developed new consumption habits while living in exile, and in part for this reason, there seems to be a growing need for money in the community. One of the results is the emergence of cultural conflicts between returnees and those who stayed in the community during the war. Yet cultural conflicts are also occurring between younger people, who desire easy access to money, and the older generation, who often decry the negative influence of the new habits. There has thus been a decline in subsistence economy and practices, with relatively fewer people engaged in agriculture and more people working for fishing companies. The reduction in practices such as gift giving and mutual help has had the consequence that wage labour is more common today. Many community members, especially returnees and the wealthiest part of the population, have to pay a salary if they need help.

---

1 However, the presence of only two or three stores limits the competition.

Local Institutional Responses

Despite these developments the communal spirit that emerged in Tasba-pauni in the 1990s seems to have made possible adequate responses to these threats against communal life, in particular as they were conducted by a few charismatic persons in and outside the Communal Board, like the síndico and the communal coordinator. Local institutions, such as the Communal Board, Council of the Elders and the women's groups, could recruit experi-enced members from groups like the ex-Contras, men returning from exile, and respected old members of the community. The majority of the popula-tion was aware of the problems that the community faced, and they were steadily engaged in the discussions concerning how to find solutions. The main attitude was one of democratic decision making in town meetings, where all adult members could express their opinions, concerning such top-ics as the arrival of an eco-tourist project, the influx of campesino settlers, and projects concerning the fishing industry. Members of the Communal Board, in particular the síndico, were certainly seen as responsible for han-dling issues concerning the land, and took initiatives in this direction, but there was also a constant dialogue between the síndico and coordinator, other members of the Communal Board, and the local villagers.

The síndico, along with other governors of the community, had taken a range of initiatives to reduce the influx of campesino settlers. The creation of a cartographic map of the communal territory was one of them. This map includes local place names in Miskitu that are unknown to outsiders. But from the point of view of the community members, they function to embed local history in the landscape and as a medium for the mobilization and maintenance of belonging and attachment to local territory. The elabora-tion of the cartographic map can be viewed as an important step. Apart from visualizing the communal land possessions, the map strengthens col-lective selves and local belonging, and it contributes to the construction of a communal ethnic territory through the inscription of a history and a shared community on local space. On some occasions the síndico along with the coordinator and other community members also arranged a trip into dif-ferent parts of the communal forest. The purpose was to overhaul the land, to control the illegal exploitation of the land, and to make a survey of the influx of mestizo campesinos, as well as to review the damage caused by swidden agriculture. This is not a business without risks. Because of mutual distrust and the illegal character of many of the foreigners' activities, the encounter between townspeople and settlers can easily provoke violent and armed confrontations.

The problems in Tasbapauni were further aggravated by local villagers themselves, because of the rapid development of commercial fishing in the 1990s, which led to increasing competition between different families involved in the local industry. The combination of these factors - the expansion of the market, the growing influence of capitalistic modes of exchange and production, and the emergence of conflicts and competition between households and other small economic units in the community — was an indication of a tendency towards disruptive change in the community. The disruption would take place not only because a new individual rationality endangered the social modes of living of the matriztic culture, but also because of over-exploitation of communal property by internal and external actors. Some of the empirical observations presented above do suggest that the cultural dilemma that the community faced in the 1990s did have some negative consequences. The increasing economic inequality arising out of the newly established fishing industry, and the conflicts between different social groups in the community, have led to some social fragmentation in Tasbapauni. Importantly, the negative influence of drugs, both in terms of violence, health problems, and the circulation of "illegal money," adds a new and very serious dimension to these changes.

This leads us to the following questions: What impeded the development of a modern entrepreneurial spirit in Tasbapauni? Given the favorable political and ideological conditions in the country, how come the emerging entrepreneurial spirit, which Nietschmann described in the 1970s, did not resurface in the 1990s? Or to put it another way, if we accept the premise established at the beginning of this chapter that Tasbapauni was facing a cultural dilemma in the 1990s, what prevented the destructive change from taking place?

The communal spirit that developed in the community, which strengthened and modernized collective identity in Tasbapauni, constituted an effective bulwark against individualistic and selfish attitudes. The majority of young and middle-aged men involved in the fishing industry were aware of the threats that the community was facing. There were also older men who retained an interest in fishing, as a part-time activity besides farming, who did not want uninhibited commercial development. There were certainly serious conflicts that arose in the fishing industry, because of attempts to initiate entrepreneurial development, like the case of the president in the fishing cooperative, a shopowner and restaurateur, who decided to use divers to catch lobsters. This practice makes it possible to earn larger amounts of money, but may destroy the lobster nests. The introduction of this method led to a split in the cooperative, where a new group consisting of older men in the village showed their discontent against this practice (Kindblad 1995). The communal spirit among older men, and most of the men involved in the fishing industry, seems to have limited the scope for entrepreneurial development in the village. Therefore, even under economic conditions that tended to be more favorable to entrepreneurial development, the new and reinforced collective orientation would probably prevent a full-blown tragedy of the commons.

The conservation of a communal identity in Tasbapauni, which provided the inspiration for a communal spirit to develop, seems to have been rather successful in finding effective ways of handling the threats against community life. The different groups involved in these processes; old men and women, ex-contras and other returnees, and groups of women, which shared a common goal of communal development, seem to have limited the scope for entrepreneurial activity and individual accumulation. We therefore argue that, rather than resulting in destruction, the impact of the neoliberal policies in the 1980s has been one of transformation and modernization of traditional institutions. By modernization we wish to refer to the incorporation and appropriation of global ideas on ethnic identity and solidarity, which have been skillfully employed in political conflicts over communal land and water, and in the development of already existing forms of collective organization. We will return to this modernization of indigenous culture below.

The Transformative Change in Tasbapauni

In this section we argue that the spirit of community, which we found among the population in Tasbapauni, made possible the transformative change that we could observe in the second half of the 1990s. This communal spirit was to a large extent characterized by collaboration and mutual help in a wide range of matters related to community life among the members who participated in local institutions, such as the Communal Board. Active participation and town meetings, map-making, demarcation of communal possessions and collective defense against intruders, social control against families with entrepreneurial ambitions, communication with "Spaniards," legal actions, denouncement of exploitation on the radio, and in sharing the economic costs associated with these activities are just some of the manifestations of this communal spirit. In our view, this spirit of community constitutes a necessary condition for explaining the transformative change, but it is not sufficient as an explanation in its own right. We must also pay attention to how this spirit could emerge in the first place. We will emphasize one additional factor, which has contributed to the emergence of the collective spirit in Tasbapauni: the influence of the Moravian Church. This influence, however, cannot be viewed as a stable factor unaffected by larger dynamics in the national and international context. The impact of the Moravian Church can be assessed in terms of how a local Moravian ethics has developed during the Sandinista revolution and as a result of the process of globalization.

The Moravian Church

We suggest that a Moravian ethic has played a key role for the strengthening of the communal spirit, which has made possible communal solidarity, or unity, in the village, and a shared communal identity and moral building during the war in the 1980s. The Moravian Church has had a marked presence on the Atlantic Coast since the *Great Awakening* in the 1880s, where thousands of Miskitu and members of other ethnic minorities converted. This happened at a moment when the Atlantic Coast was experiencing large-scale transformations. The British rule and influence in the region had been declining for about thirty years, and North American companies had begun to make their presence felt. Much of the existing literature about this era suggests that the Moravian Church played a central role in communal development on the Atlantic Coast, in particular because it offered social services, and promoted communal development in different areas, such as education and health care (Hale 1994; Garcia 1995; Kindblad 2010). In an important appendix to Mary Helms's ethnographic study of Asang (1971), she describes the Moravian doctrine in some detail, arguing that the Moravian Church emphasizes ethical conduct rather than theological arguments, the value of emotions in religious practices rather than thought, and real life experiences rather than doctrines (Helms 1971: 240-241). The framework for ethical behavior is provided by the example of the life of Jesus, as it is told in the Bible, rather than the Pope and clergy. The faithful are united in a community of brotherly love, where the "social character of religious experience provided a powerful ethical basis for cooperation as a group. Individuals were taught to subordinate their own interests to the demands of the community, and they generally did" (Helms 1971: 241). The ethics of the Moravian Church also emphasizes hard work, not because it is associated with salvation, but in order to maintain a state of grace. The Moravian religion is often described as a "religion of the heart."

In order to tell the history of how this ethics came to influence local development in Tasbapauni in the 1990s, we agree with Garcia (1995) that the separation of the Moravian Church in Nicaragua from the head quarters in United States in 1974 was an important decision (Garcia 1995: 99-104). The Church became an associated province of Unitas Fratrum from this point onwards. This institutional reorganization happened at the same time as the Somoza dictatorship began to undertake a major national modernization project. This led to an increasing commercialization of communal property in Tasbapauni and in an extension of the agricultural frontier. The Rio Coco Pilot project, which had as its aim to homogenize the nation through mestizoization, can also be seen as part of the modernization plans. However, many Costeños saw this as a threat to their original ways of living and being. Now separated from the United States, many lay pastors and ordinary members of the Moravian Church were provided with an impetus to ethno-political activism. One of the many manifest responses was the creation of ALPROMISU in 1974 (Garcia 1995: 99-104).

The Sandinista Revolution

According to García (1995), this process of defending ethnic identity was given new strength when the Sandinista revolution initiated a wave of political discussions and became a new source of self-reflection among many members of the ethnic communities on the Atlantic Coast:

> By using religious symbolism, the discourse of the Church legitimated the political discourse of the indigenous organisation...the revolutionary triumph generated changes in individual´s lives but almost all Miskitu took advantage of the new situation and began a process of self-reflection about their distinctiveness. The Church became the locus where this process was carried out, and it resulted

in the strengthening of their collective self-consciousness as Indians (García 1995: 118).

Carlos Vilas's analysis of the ethnic mobilization in the 1980s can provide us with additional insights into the institutional aspects of this development (Vilas 1990). His main focus is on the role of ethnic and indigenous organizations in the anti-Sandinista mobilization. Vilas asserts that the demands of MISURASATA rapidly radicalized in the first years after its formation (Vilas 1990: 79ff.). From the outset the organization took an ethnic stance, but the initial statements focused mainly on protection and integration. However, in December 1980, only little more than a year after the first statements had been published, MISURASATA issued the *Plan of Action 1981*, revealing a much stronger and qualitatively different position (MISURASATA 1981, reprinted in Ohland & Schneider 1983:89-94). This document introduced the discourse of indigenous nations and former demands of communal land-titles had now been replaced by territorial claims.[1]

As mentioned previously, the majority of younger men in Tasbapauni joined the Contras as well as MISURASATA and other ethnic organizations that became part of this anti-Sandinista movement. Thus, many community members established personal relations with other MISURASATA members, and later with MISURA cadres. In this way, ideas associated with ethnic militancy formed on a regional and international level were disseminated to most ordinary members of Tasbapauni and other communities. Although the militant indigenous rhetoric of MISURATA/MISURA, with an emphasis on autonomy, self-determination, and indigenous nations, was a radical development, we argue that it resonated with the Moravian ethics and the values associated with unity, and the focus on collective rather than individual matters.

The leadership of MISURASATA and other organizations consisted of local intellectuals, often educated at universities in Managua or abroad. They were thus familiar with the emergent focus on the fourth world and on the global movement for indigenous and historical rights. It is our basic contention that the ethnic mobilization in the 1980s has contributed to the formation of a strong ethnic and collective consciousness in Tasbapauni. This consciousness permits community members to exercise indigenous and historical rights and encourages them to act as social and collective subjects. In particular the ideas of rights play a lead role in upholding a strong

---

1  See also chapter 4 of this volume.

ethnic consciousness in the community. But whereas rights were associated with the establishment of regional autonomy on the Coast in the 1980s, they were conceived of as a more or less broad permission to tend to community affairs by the end of the 1990s. People in Tasbapauni continued to decry the absence of a real autonomous regime, and they often expressed anger about the governmental neglect of the autonomy law. But in most day-to-day parlance, autonomy had come to be linked to more immediate land problems, and ideas of self-determination were mostly expressed when the focus was on the defense of *communal* landholdings. Compared to the 1980s, the collective orientation had thus narrowed, but the ethno-political ideas of ethnic membership and the sense of belonging to a collective community had been largely undamaged.

Moravian Ethics in the Post-War Era

The major point that we want to make here is thus that the Moravian ethics, which had infused the development of an ethno-political ideology during the 1980s, became the impetus for the communal spirit of local development in the post-war period. The electoral defeat of the Sandinistas in 1990s meant that Costeños did not feel the need to mobilize against a common enemy, and most people invested most of their available resource building up what had been destroyed during the war, as we have argued above. The desire to "build up the community became a common ground for ex-Contras, families who had stayed in Tasbapauni, and persons who had returned from their exile in Managua, Costa Rica or the United States. From the mid 1990s and onwards the concern with new sources of external threats against the community, e.g. the arrival of capitalist entrepreneurs, Spanish-speaking campesinos and foreign fishing fleets, emerged. The ethno-political ideology, which had developed on the basis of Moravian ethics, had influenced the young and middle-aged men during the war, and became the basis for the interpretation of local traditional institutions, like the Communal Board with the Síndico and co-ordinator and the Council of Elders.

The importance of Moravian ethics can also be found in the role that they played in the process of healing the wounds of the war, where the lay pastor in the Moravian church in Tasbapauni took the initiative to work in ecumenical collaboration with other churches in the community. The war had brought hatred and resentment between different families who had taken different sides in the political-military conflict. The Moravian church took a lead in the process of reconciliation between these families. Some informants stated that participation in the church had increased with the arrival of lay Moravian pastor. In religious life there appeared a clear desire to work together ecumenically for the community: "In religious work there is the belief that things can be done together...Unity is a central word coming up when informants speak about the churches. The pastors are often addressing issues in their sermons, that are directly or indirectly related to needs in the community" (Kindblad 1995: 23). In our view the ecumenical collaboration between churches was possible because of a Moravian ethic, which was the relational basis for the spirit of community that arose in Tasbapauni in the 1990s.

What must also be mentioned in this context is the difference between the world of men and women in Tasbapauni. As noted above, there are two separate orders of exchange, where men are involved in short-term exchanges within the market economy, as in the case of lobster and turtle fishing, and women mainly sustain a long-term order of exchange through matrilocally related households. The short-term exchange of men is characterized by individualistic competition, division and rivalry, and the long-term order of women provides the stability and order of the community, where women historically are the more regular members of church congregations. There is a pattern in Tasbapauni where men hand over money to women, who use this money for collective consumption between households. This means that women are involved in symbolic and ritualistic exchanges, and play a key role in the socialization of children and young people into the Moravian ethics within a network of matrilocally related households (Kindblad 2010). It is not surprising, thus, that a group of women, who were working on a project concerning the wharf, collaborated closely with some of the members of the Communal Board. The local development that happened in Tasbapauni may, in fact, have its roots in the matriztic ethic of women, as it has been conserved in the long-term order of exchange. This analysis suggests that a Moravian ethic is the mechanism that explains the communal spirit in Tasbapauni in the 1990s, which made possible the transformative change. But there is one piece missing in this explanation.

The religious framework of the Moravian Church has been conserved among most of the community members in Tasbapauni since the turbulent history from the 1960s onwards. Moravian ethics played a key role not only for ethno-political mobilization on a national level, but also for development and reconstruction in local communities after the war, where it has influenced work within local political institutions like the Communal Board. This ethics provided the basis for the conservation of a communal identity, or spirit, which has been important for social solidarity, collaboration and morale building. There is no doubt that there was a potential for a disruptive change in Tasbapauni, because of competitive individualistic, entrepreneurial development, but the villagers who were influenced by the Moravian ethic constituted the cognitive majority as a consequence of the regional history since the 1970s. The religious framework of the Moravian Church had developed into an ethno-political ideology, which had influenced several politically militant groups in Tasbapauni in the 1990s. In alliance with local villagers, these groups successfully conserved a communal identity, which meant that there was very limited space for other groups to engage in an alternative capitalist-led development project for the locality in line with the neo-liberal policies of the post-Sandinista national governments.

Conclusion

In this study we have argued that the processes of neo-liberal adjustment in the 1990s did not lead to a disruptive change in Tasbapauni. Although there were some signs of a growing individualistic culture with more community members and families pursuing their own self-interest, we argue that the general trend in Tasbapauni was one of a transformative change. By transformative change we wish to pay attention to what we have termed the "communal spirit," which has proven to constitute an effective bulwark against a competitive and commercially oriented mentality. However, this communal culture, developed throughout the last two centuries as a result of external contact, has not been left unaffected. We have argued that the dissemination of ideas associated with indigenous identities and rights have played a crucial role in transforming the more narrow-minded communal attitude dominant in the 1970s. The indigenous organizations played a key role in this transformation during the anti-Sandinista uprising. But, perhaps most importantly, the Moravian Church, which has a long history in Tasbapauni and on the Atlantic Coast in general, has instituted a communal mindset, which is central if we want to adequately understand the transformative change that has taken place in Tasbapauni throughout the 1990s.

References

Acosta, M.L. (2001) 'The State and Indigenous Lands in the Autonomous Regions of Nicaragua: The Case of the Mayagna Community of Awas Tingn' in W. Assies. et al. (2001) *The Challenge of Diversity. Indigenous Peoples and Reform of the State in Latin America* (Amsterdam, Thela Thesis).

Assies, W. et al. (2001) *The Challenge of Diversity. Indigenous Peoples and Reform of the State in Latin America* (Amsterdam: Thela Thesis).

García C. (1995) *The Making of the Miskitu People in Nicaragua. The Social Construction of Ethnic Identity* Studia Sociologica Usaliensia 41 (Uppsala, University of Uppsala).

Hale, C.R. (1994) *Resistance and Contradiction. Miskitu Indians and the Nicaraguan State, 1894-1987* (Stanford California, Stanford University Press).

Hale, C.R. and Gordon, E.T. (1987) 'Costeño Demography: Historical and Contemporary Demography of Nicaragua's Atlantic Coast' in CIDCA/Development Study Unit, *Ethnic Groups and the Nation State. The Case of the Atlantic Coast in Nicaragua* (Stockholm, University of Stockhom).

Hardin, G. (1968) 'The Tragedy of the Commons' in *Science* Vol. 162, pp. 1243-1248.

Helms, M. (1971) *Asang: Adaptations to Cultural Contact in a Miskito Community* (Gainsville, University of Florida Press).

Henriksen, K. (2002) *The Construction of Ethnic and Spatial Identities. Everyday Forms of State Mutation on Nicaragua's Atlantic Coast* (PhD thesis, Copenhagen, Copenhagen Business School).

Henriksen, K. (2008) 'Ethnic Self-regulation and Democratic Instability on Nicaragua's Atlantic Coast: The Case of Ratisuna' in *European Review of Latin American and Caribbean Studies* Vol. 85, pp. 23-41.

Henriksen, K. and Kindblad, C. (2005) 'El dilema colectivo de los pueblos miskitos de Nicaragua en los años 90. El caso de Tasbapauni' in *Wani*, Vol. 42. pp. 6-39.

Herlihy, L. H. (2007) 'Matrifocality and Women's Power on the Miskito Coast' in *Ethnology*, Vol. 46, No. 2, pp. 133-149.

Howard, S. (1996) 'Autonomía y Derechos territoriales delos Sumos en Bosawás: El Caso de Sikilta' in *Wani*, No. 18, CIDCA.

Howard, S. (1997) 'Conflict and Mayangna Territorial Rights in Nicaragua's Bosawás Reserve' in *Bulletin of Latin American Research* Vol. 17, No. 1.

Kindblad, C. (1995) 'Community Under Threat — A Restudy of Tasbapauni, an Atlantic Coastal Village, Nicaragua' Report from a Minor Field Study, April-June 1994 (Lund, Prop Reports No. 6).

Kindblad, C. (2010 [2001]) *Gift and Exchange among the Miskitu on the Atlantic Coast, Nicaragua. A Historical-Comparative Study on Cultural Change, 29th Century.* (Saarbrücken, Lambert Academic Publishing).

Maturana, H. R., Verden-Zöller, G. and Dávila Yáñez, X. (2003 [1993]) *Amor y Juego. Fundamentos Olvidados de lo Humano desde Patriarcado a la Democracia.* (Santiago de Chile, J.C. Sáez Editor).

Mordt, M. (2001) *Livelihoods and Sustainability at the Agrarian Frontier. The Evolution of the Frontier in Southeastern Nicaragua* (Göteborg, Department of Human and Economic Geography, Goteborg University).

Nietschmann, B. (1973) *Between Land and Water. The Subsistence Ecology of the Miskito Indians, Easten Nicaragua* (New York & London, Seminar Press).

Nietschmann, B. (1979) *Caribbean Edge. The Coming of Modern Times to Isolated Peoples and Wildlife* (Bobbs-Merill Co).

Ohland, K. and Schneider, K (Eds) (1983) *National Revolution and Indigenous Identity: The Conflict Between Sandinistas and Miskitu Indians of Nicaragua's Atlantic Coast.* (Copenhagen, IWGIA).

Ostrom, E. (1998) 'A Behavioral Approach to the Rational Choice Theory of Collective Action' in *American Political Review* Vol. 92, No. 1, pp. 1-22.

Plant, R. (2001) 'Indigenous Rights and Latin American Multiculturalism: Lessons from the Guatemalan Peace Process' in Assies, W. et al. (Eds) (2001) *The Challenge of Diversity. Indigenous Peoples and Reform of the State in Latin America* (Amsterdam, Thela Thesis).

Sánchez, L. (2007) 'Splitting the Country: the case of the Atlantic Coast of Nicaragua' *Journal of Latin American Geography* Vol. 6, No. 1, pp. 7-23.

Vanden, H.E. (1997) 'Democracy Derailed: The 1990 Elections and After' in Prevost & Vanden (Eds) (1997) *The Undermining of the Sandinista Revolution* (MacMillan Press and St. Martin's Press).

Vilas, C.M. (1990) *Del Colonialismo a la Autonomía. Modernización Capitalista y Revolución Social en la Costa Atlántica* (Managua: Editorial Nueva).

Wilson, R (Ed) (1997) *Human Rights, Culture and Context. Anthropological Perspectives.* (London, Pluto Press).

# CHAPTER 7. RISING UP? INDIGENOUS AND AFRO-DESCENDANT WOMEN'S POLITICAL LEADERSHIP IN THE RAAN

*Laura Hobson Herlihy*

> The main accomplishment of women in the last twenty-five years is that they have become more visible. Women have become secretaries, directors of agencies, and have progressed more in education. For these reasons I say that at the legal level, this is pretty good, but everyday life still is not favorable, for example, regarding women's level of political participation.
>
> —Myrna Cunningham Kain

Based on historical precedence of cultural difference, the Sandinista government passed the autonomy law in 1987, creating two autonomous regions on the Atlantic Coast, the North Autonomous Region (RAAN) and the South Atlantic Autonomous Region (RAAS). The regional governments in RAAN and RAAS have implemented a quota system to ensure proportional democratic representation to all indigenous and ethnic groups present in both regions. These democratic practices render the Atlantic Coast a model throughout Latin America for pluri-ethnic, autonomous homelands (de la Pena 2006; Hale 1996). The autonomy process, along with cultural pluralism and equality in inter-ethnic relations, is also concerned with gender equity. Article 14 of the autonomy law (Law 28) guarantees equality of men and women in economic, political, social, and cultural aspects. Yet, the way in which the regional government interprets the laws for gender equality has not been favorable for Atlantic Coast women, who continue to experience violations of their individual human rights regarding their land and inheritance rights, issues of domestic violence, and political participation.[1] This chapter addresses one of the main challenges for women within the autonomy project on the Atlantic Coast: their right to full political participation. Specifically, the chapter examines indigenous and minority women's access to political leadership in the North Atlantic Autonomous Region (RAAN).

## Methods

When I first arrived in Bilwi-Puerto Cabezas (population 58,000), the capital of Nicaragua's North Atlantic Autonomous Region, I was struck by the high visibility of women in professional and political positions. Women served as chancellors of universities, professors, NGO directors, congresswomen, judges, attorneys, and more.[2] I learned that women first entered leadership posts after the granting of the autonomous region. Indeed, the Sandinistas inspired minority women in 1987 by selecting Myrna Cunningham as the first governor of the North Atlantic Coast.[3] The Sandinistas mainly selected Creole women as leaders in the new autonomous region, rewarding them, as it were, for their loyalty to the Sandinista party during the revolutionary and war-torn years of the 1980s. Admittedly, Creole

---

1 Interview with Myrna Cunningham Kain, Bilwi-Puerto Cabezas 08/07/07. Myrna Cunningham went on to say that the autonomy law was ratified in 2003, calling for *instancias* to make sure the regional government is fulfilling its obligation to women regarding gender equity. She also explained that women's rights are represented within the RAAN regional government by the Secretaria de la mujer in the executive branch (GRAAN); the Comisión de la Mujer in the legislative branch (CRAAN); and the Foro de Mujeres de la RAAN, a multiethnic group representing twenty to twenty-five women's organizations created by a resolution within CRAAN in 2005 (see, also Antonio 2006: 8,9). However, Myrna maintained that women's access to their rights, guaranteed by article 14, is hindered by the many inconsistencies between the Foro de Mujeres, the Comisión de la Mujer, and the Comisaría de la Mujer y Niñez, the Nicaraguan state agency for women that is located in the Puerto Cabezas Police station. Myrna believes that the Comisaría de la Mujer y Niñez should oversee the Foro and the Comisión de la Mujer.
2 Significantly, Hazel Law is Magistrate to the Appeal Tribunal in the RAAN, an appointment made by the Nicaraguan Supreme Court of Justice.
3 From 1998-2002, another woman, Alva Rivera (PLC), served as governor of the RAAN. Like Myrna, Rivera served two terms of two years each term. In 2010, a third woman was selected as governor, the Yatama candidate Mara Rivas.

women were more prepared than the other minority women to take on new roles as leaders, as they historically have held a higher socio-economic status and had more access to education than their Miskitu, Sumu-Mayangna, and Garífuna neighbors on the Coast (Gabbert 2006).

By the time of my study in 2006-2007, however, indigenous Miskitu women of Yatama and other political parties, such as the PLC, were breaking down impressive political barriers. Nancy Elizabeth Henríquez was elected mayor of Puerto Cabezas; Rosa Wilson was elected *síndica* (Trustee) of Puerto Cabezas and served as president of the powerful political organization *Diez Comunidades*, which controls the finances of communally owned resources in RAAN. Perhaps most significantly, Cora Antonio was named superintendent of the Moravian Church for all of Nicaragua. Creole women aligned with the Sandinistas continued to enter public positions of leadership. Raquel Dixon, for example, was elected as one of the three RAAN representatives to the Nicaraguan National Assembly. Both Creole and Miskitu women directed government agencies, such as the Ministry of Health (MINSA) and municipal and regional government commissions.

As my interests progressed in RAAN women's leadership, I realized that at the same time that women were becoming more visible in the public arena and making advances as political and civic leaders, their overall participation in the autonomous region's government was decreasing.[1] This contradiction, RAAN women's increasing visibility as leaders but decreasing participation in the regional government, became the main focus of this research.

My research and interviews focused on the factors that have facilitated indigenous and Afro-descendant women's ascent to public office, and also the factors that impede their access to leadership roles, especially in the regional government. The factors that have helped RAAN women's participation as leaders present a compelling case study, where indigenous and Afro-descendent women are rising up, shifting their domain of power from the matrigroup to more legitimate political arenas. The factors that have hurt women's leadership reflect the challenges minority women face in their quest to democratize political participation within the Latin American nation-state. Analysis of the data will help determine the women's views of their own empowerment and oppression, thus broadening our un-

---

1  See also González, Figueroa, and Barbeyto (2006: 10-23). I would like to thank Miguel González for his help and guidance in my own research.

derstanding of the RAAN women's movement and an emerging indigenous feminism on the Nicaraguan Atlantic Coast. I refer to indigenous feminism as a new kind of transnational feminism, which stresses the combination of individual and collective rights to culture, language, land, and resources (Green 2007; Ouellete 2002).[1]

While in Bilwi-Puerto Cabezas, I completed ethnographic research and interviewed twenty-five women who were government, religious, and civil-society leaders. In this chapter, I especially highlight an interview that I completed with Myrna Cunningham Kain, just before Hurricane Felix hit the north coast. The interview was conducted at the Casa Museo, the Cunningham home in Bilwi-Puerto Cabezas, which also serves as a hotel, arts and craft museum, and NGO headquarters.[2]

The individual story of Myrna Cunningham tells of how she has risen up to become one of the most important political leaders on the Nicaraguan Atlantic Coast and a person of international recognition. Myrna was born in the Miskitu community of Waspám and raised in a mother-centered, extended family. Her family's ties with the Moravian hospital and Moravian nursing school in Bilwaskarma provided her with the opportunity to become a nurse, train as a surgeon, and to later earn a Master's of Public Health. Stemming from her involvement with the Sandinistas during the revolution and US-backed war, Myrna was appointed to serve as the minister of health in RAAN, the first governor of the North Atlantic Coast, the founding chancellor of the University of the Autonomous Regions of the Caribbean Coast of Nicaragua (URACCAN), and an elected member to the Nicaraguan National Assembly.

Today, Myrna is a leading social activist for indigenous peoples around the globe. She founded and is director of the NGO, The Center for Indigenous Peoples' Autonomy and Development (CADPI) and is vice-president of the Indigenous Peace Initiative. Working for indigenous women's rights, Myrna helped plan the first Indigenous Women's Summit in Oaxaca, Mex-

---

1 Indigenous feminism developed along with the global indigenous women's movement, which began to flourish in 1992 when Rigoberta Menchú was awarded the Nobel Peace Prize. This new kind of transnational feminism blends aspects of women's rights, human rights, and indigenous rights. Indigenous feminists view indigenous women's oppression as coming from the nation state, colonialism, and neoliberal economics; and their empowerment, as being tied to women mobilizing for their individual rights within the broader struggle for indigenous autonomy or self-determination (IIWF 2006:25).

2 All interviews are translated by the author.

ico in 2002, and the International Indigenous Women's Forum in New York in February 2005, where women demanded the right to equal political participation as leaders (IIWF 2006). Most recently, Myrna was elected a member of the United Nations Permanent Forum on Indigenous Issues for Latin America. The remarkable story of how she came to power, through her socialization in a female-centered domestic group, participation in the Moravian Church, the Sandinista revolution, and projects with NGOs, reflects the experiences of many other women leaders who have risen up from the matrigroup to public office.

Factors in Favor of Women's Leadership: Matrifocality

Anthropologists have detailed matrilocality among the Nicaraguan Miskitu. Garcia (1996), Helms (1971), and Peter (2002) noted that post-marital residence amongst Nicaragua's Miskitu is matrilocal, where women pass down Miskitu language and kinship practices to the children while the men are away working in wage-labor activities. Miskitu women typically move into their own households after having children, yet the woman's household is part of a larger matrigroup under the control of a grandmother or "kuka" (Herlihy 2006; 2007). Sonia Pedro contends that today, RAAN women continue to raise their children without a man in the husband-father role, and that about thirty-five percent of the households in Puerto Cabezas are female-headed.[1] Pedro stated that the high number of female-headed households in RAAN communities can be attributed to migrant wage-labor and to the one-thousand, seven-hundred men that died in the revolution and Contra war.

The Creoles have the highest level of female-headed households on the Coast and live in multi-generational, extended family households that are headed by grandmothers (CEIMM 2008: 4). Creole and Miskitu women leaders interviewed first and foremost mentioned that being raised in a

1  Interview with Sonia Pedro, Bilwi-Puerto Cabezas 08/02/07. Other sources state that female headed-households in RAAN were 30 percent in 2001 (Antonio 2006: 3) and 21.6 percent in 2008 (CEIMM 2008: 4, 5). Pedro's higher estimate may relate to the fact that female-headed households are higher in the urban areas like Bilwi-Puerto Cabezas. However, the author contends that census data underestimates female-headed households among the Miskitu people. For example, there are many Miskitu households that claim permanent male members in the husband-father role, when in fact the men are absent on a daily basis, working in migrant subsistence and migrant wage-labor activities, such as lobster-diving (Herlihy 2006; 2007).

female-centered domestic group helped them to become leaders. Many women claimed to have acquired and developed their leadership abilities by watching senior women in their roles as heads of families and households. Beginning my open-ended interview with Myrna Cunningham, I asked why so many women had become leaders on the Atlantic Coast?

> The first reason that there are so many female leaders is because the Miskitu culture is matriarchal. Culturally, the older woman of the Miskitu *raza* is who assumes the important role in the cultural reproduction and this is a type of living together that is truly matrilocal. After marriage, as is established by tradition, the spouse of the daughter moves into or buys the house of the wife's family, so there is in the culture, if in a reduced way, a kind of *matriarcalismo*. Maybe the woman does not make as many economic decisions, because of limitations to work, but from the cultural perspective, the older woman's voice has a lot of weight here. Many polls have been carried out and when someone asks (in a Miskitu home) who is in charge, the usual answer is the elder woman, which is different from the mestizo culture. When you ask who the boss is in a mestizo home, it is the man; and in the Creole culture also, the answer has been the older woman. I believe that there is a kind of matriarchal culture that competes with the machista culture imposed through the Catholic Church on the Pacific side. In a way, matriarchality fortifies women leaders because women do not have a rejection within the heart of the family to assume a leadership role.[1]

Myrna's comments bring out some important aspects of women's status and gender identities along the Coast. She stated that both indigenous and Afro-descendant Creole women live in matrifocal domestic groups where women made household economic and child-rearing decisions, suggesting a regional matrifocal culture exists. Myrna views Costeño women's power and status as being tied to their roles as mothers and family leaders, similar to gender-power relations in Caribbean societies. Afro-Caribbean women's views of leadership often engage notions of family and community and tie into their female-dominant gender ideology, including what it means to be a woman, mother, daughter, and sister (Collins 1994). Mohammed (1986) and Wekker (2006) have noted that Caribbean women have a maternally-based vision of leadership and empowerment. These views of empowerment diverge from western feminism and align themselves with black feminist thought, revealing a defining feature of indigenous feminism along the Nicaraguan Atlantic Coast.

---

1 Interview with Myrna Cunningham Kain, Bilwi-Puerto Cabezas 08/07/07.

The Moravian Church

Many women leaders interviewed related to me that the Moravian Church has played a key role in promoting women. Yolanda Dimitri claimed that by the 1970s, Moravian women's organizations opened spaces for both Creole and Miskitu women to become trained in the fields of education and health, which prepared them to become educators, nurses, and leaders in their local churches.[1] Dimitri explained that women were allowed to take the pulpit as pastors in churches by the early 1990s, and since then, have ascended the hierarchy. I asked Myrna how religion helped to empower women.

> Religion has been interesting also. You see a pretty good recognition of women within the Moravian Church. For example, here in the region it was notorious when Cora Antonio won as superintendent of the Moravian Church. This was the first time in nearly one-hundred and fifty years to elect a female superintendent in Nicaragua...Yet, many symbolic and cultural symbols are still impeding women's participation. Even in the case of Cora Antonio, the Church was worried about her still being a menstruating woman, which they thought made her more vulnerable than a menopausal woman. They also believed that because she was married, that her husband would be the power behind the throne.[2]

Myrna agreed that the Moravian Church has given women opportunity for professional advancement. She pointed out, quite significantly, that the Moravian Church appointed Cora Antonio in 2007 to the position of superintendant for all of Nicaragua. Yet, Myrna also stated that Moravian Church leaders continue to possess machista ideologies. Following Corinthians, the Moravian Church believes that a woman is inferior to the man, that her main role is to attend to her husband and children, and that a woman should be taught proper behavior and corrected by her husband (Herman 2006: 81-83). Despite the Moravians' male-dominant views on gender and power, the women leaders interviewed claimed that women experience more gender-based discrimination within the Catholic Church, which arrived on the Coast almost a century later than the Moravians. The long-term presence of the Moravian Church on the Atlantic Coast, according to RAAN women, has provided them with an alternative to the more patriarchal structures and rigid hierarchy of the Catholic Church.

---

1  Interview with Yolanda Dimitri, Bilwi-Puerto Cabezas 05/08/07.
2  Interview with Myrna Cunningham Kain, Bilwi-Puerto Cabezas 08/07/07.

The Sandinista Revolution

Nicaragua became a model for gender equity in Latin America after the gains that took place for women's rights during the Sandinista revolution (Chinchilla 1994).[1] In 1979 under new Sandinista rule, the Nicaraguan government for the first time took responsibility for the health and education of the marginalized coastal region, significantly helping single mothers struggling to raise and care for their children and grandchildren. They also abolished the distinction between legitimate and illegitimate children. The Sandinista movement, then, connected with Creole and Miskitu women by building on their gender ideology that values motherhood and does not assume a husband-father's presence in the household.

One of the most striking parts of the revolution was women's involvement with the revolution, including their heightened political participation and their entrance into roles of political leadership (Randall 1981). Atlantic Coast women contributed radically to the revolution and the war. Women served as nearly 30 percent of the military combatants on the Sandinista side and between 7 and 15 percent on the Contra side; however, many more contributed as nurses, information providers, and other supportive roles in the revolution and struggle for autonomy (Davis 2006; Kampwirth 2001). Women also contributed to the peace process and several played formal roles on the autonomy commission, established during peace negotiations between the national Sandinista government and the Contras.[2]

---

1   The Sandinistas called for the emancipation of women and the FSLN women's organization, AMNLAE (Asociación de Mujeres Nicaraguenses Luisa Amanda Espinoza), assisted and promoted the cause (Molyneux 1985). The main slogan of AMNLAE during the revolution was "no revolution without emancipation and no emancipation without revolution." However, women's mobilization efforts became suppressed within the larger group struggle to remove Somoza from power (Randall 1992). Women's rights in Nicaragua regressed under the neo-liberal presidents that took office in the 1990s. Even though Sandinista president Daniel Ortega was elected into office in 2006, Myrna explained that women's rights regarding reproduction and sexuality have reversed due to the criminalization of therapeutic abortion, which is now being reviewed by the international court. Interview with Myrna Cunningham, Bilwi-Puerto Cabezas 07/08/07.

2   On the autonomy commission for the Sandinistas were Myrna Cunningham and Hazel Law, and for the Contras, Reyna Jack (Sasha Jannel Marley, personal communication, 03/06/10). Yolanda Dimitri, who works within the Pastoral de la mujer de la Iglesia Morava, explained that the Moravian church helped women to become involved with the peace-making process for the autonomous regions. Many wives and mothers, who first heard about the peace process in Moravian church meetings, initially convinced their husbands and sons to put down their arms. Rose Cunningham claimed that many Miskitu women used *sihka*, plant-

---

The RAAN women leaders interviewed underlined the importance of the Sandinista revolution as a major factor that enabled them to play more prominent roles as leaders and public officials. I questioned Myrna about how the Sandinista revolution empowered women as leaders.

> I believe that the second major cause of women becoming leaders is the impact of the war years. During the 80s, the majority of men were involved in military activities, so that much of the social life and cultural life was assumed directly by the women. The advantage that women had was that they were preparing themselves from the educational perspective, so that by the time the men returned, the women didn't want to return totally to their traditional role in the home. The ex-military men could not put their system of military control over the communities because it competed with women's traditional organization.

> Here there was a high rate of men that were in the army. All of the youth that did not fight in the counter revolution, when they reached seventeen or eighteen years old, had to go do (Nicaraguan) military service because it was mandatory on both sides. So we are talking about, I would say, 90 percent of the men became soldiers. We could say between one and two-thousand men died. So we have a high rate of single women and besides that, the women that already were assuming responsibilities during the ten years of war also contributed to create female leadership.[1]

Myrna also underlined the fact that in the 1980s, women assumed much of the preservation of Miskitu culture and social life and took on more visible roles. After autonomy was granted and the men returned home, Myrna believes that RAAN women did not want to return to their more traditional roles in the home.

RAAN women also emphasized that Sandinismo provided women with equal access to education for the first time. This education prepared women to become professionals and political and civic leaders. I asked Myrna how Sandinismo promoted women.

> Another reason for the many female leaders is education, which also is tied to Sandinismo. Sandinismo was decisive because it began the democratization of the educational model. Before, education was limited to a certain sector of the population. Within the revolution in the 1980s, however, the right to education and literacy was given

---

based healing remedies, to manipulate men's emotions. This example details the way RAAN women were able to use their knowledge of *sihka* (magic potions) and leadership, originally learned in matrilocal groups, to help negotiate for the autonomous regions. Interview with Rose Cunningham, Bilwi-Puerto Cabezas 07/08/07.

1  Interview with Myrna Cunningham, Bilwi-Puerto Cabezas 07/08/07.

to the whole population, as much as in Spanish as in the different in-digenous languages. Programs of adult education and intercultural and bi-lingual education all began during the Sandinista revolution. And obviously in the 1980s, they opened the universities, permitting many more women to enter and to achieve literacy to the point that today there is a degree in education, which has contributed enor-mously to the leadership of women....There are many female leaders in positions of leadership because of the education process that is promoting them.

At the present time, bi-lingual intercultural education has been established in the region for more than twenty years and it has given women an opening through the universities and technical schools. There are more women studying now and, therefore, women have more opportunities for work. There are more women participating as students, who are entering all levels, elementary schools, high schools, and universities; and they are also gaining technical skills. This has created a large group (*una cantera*) of women with a certain level of educational formation that also incites women leaders. This is a reason for there being many female leaders here.[1]

The Sandinista revolution made educational advancement available for all Atlantic Coast women, including those of different ethnic backgrounds and political party affiliation. Myrna stated that RAAN women particu-larly benefitted from the Intercultural Bilingual Education Program (PEBI) with indigenous language instruction.[2] She mentioned that the Sandinistas helped to begin the pluri-ethnic University of the Autonomous Regions of the Caribbean Coast (URACCAN), where nearly 50 percent of the admin-istrators, professors, and students are women; and two women, Myrna her-self followed by Alta Hooker, have held the highest position of chancellor since the university was founded in 1994. Ultimately, she maintained that the heightened level of male-absenteeism during the war-torn years pro-pelled women into leadership roles, and that the democratization of the education model prepared them for these new roles.

Post-1990 NGOs

Government programs pulled out of the Atlantic Coast region after the 1990 electoral defeat of the Sandinistas. At the same time, neo-liberal eco-nomic policies and extreme structural adjustment measures emerged that forced cut-backs in the public sector (Mendez 2005). Single mothers, aban-

---

1  Interview with Myrna Cunningham, Bilwi-Puerto Cabezas 07/08/07.
2  See Dennis and Herlihy (2004: 46) and chapter 8 of this volume.

doned by the state, were called upon to provide more health and education services for their children. While conditions of poverty flourished, NGO and development organizations established projects in the region to replace government programs (Babb 2001). RAAN women welcomed the assistance and have benefited greatly from many NGO and civil society programs, especially the Yatama women's organization, the La Asociación de Mujeres Indígena de la Costa Atlántica (AMICA); and the Sandinista women's organizations, Movimiento de Mujeres Nidia White, Gaviota, a CIDCA-based organization, and CEIMM (Centro de Estudios y Información de Mujeres Multiétnicas), which is part of the URACCAN.

RAAN women leaders interviewed claimed that NGOs have promoted women as leaders because they have primarily selected women to become directors of their organizations. Miskitu, Afro-descendant, and Mayangna women were selected as directors for the most high-profile NGOs in RAAN, including Centro de Investigación y Documentación de la Costa Atlántica (CIDCA); Centro de Derechos Humanos Cuidadanos y Autonómicos (CEDEHCA); Programa de la Naciones Unidas para el Desarrollo (PNUD); Plan Mundial de Alimentos (PMA); Cruz Roja (Red Cross); Casa de Cultura Teneniska (Teneniska Culture House); and the Fondo de las Naciones Unidas para la Infancia (UNICEF).[1] Creole women since the 1990s generally have held more directorships of NGOS and government organizations than Miskitu women. However, this was beginning to change.

During interviews with NGO directors and women in public office, many women told me that NGOs, as well as the national government, prefer working with women because they viewed RAAN women as being more responsible with money, and less corrupt, than the local men. Debby Hodgson stated, "there were men as directors previously, but they had too many girlfriends and spent too much money entertaining them." Debby Hodgson also commented that the universities, URACCAN and the privately funded Bluefields Indian and Caribbean University (BICU), have given RAAN women the same access to education as the men. She added, "We are just as educated now and more responsible, so we do a better job." Debby went on to explain that of those with graduate degrees, the women tended to stay locally because they are the primary care and economic providers for

---

1 PNUD was headed by Betty Rigby; PMA, by Laura Chow; UNICEF, by Daisy George; Cruz Roja, by Christina Sosa; CIDCA, by Melba McLean; CEDEHCA, by Debby Hodgson; and Teneniska, by Celia Mueller.

their family members.[1] During my interview with Myrna, she delved into the more structural and causal reasons behind why women flourished as directors of NGOs.

> Many NGOs have female directors and this probably has to do with the role that NGOs play, replacing the role of the state and state agencies. Women are dominating NGO directorships because women continue doing work previously done by the state agencies, especially in education, health, and various other domains.[2]

Myrna argued that women's involvement with NGOs represents a general shift for women in Nicaragua, and in Latin America more generally, who increasingly are taking on responsibilities formerly assumed by state agencies.[3] Despite the negative economic and political situation that created the need for women to work with NGO programs, women's involvement with NGOs along the Atlantic Coast has positioned them into highly visible leadership roles.

Factors Working Against Women's Leadership: National Political Parties and Popular Elections

RAAN women have a low level of participation in the regional and municipal government. Women leaders interviewed claimed that government positions elected by popular vote were the most difficult for women to attain, with women having the lowest level of political participation within the legislative branch of the regional government.[4] The forty-five councilors that comprise RAAN's regional council, the main legislative body, constitute the only members of the autonomous government whom are elected by popular vote. González, Figueroa, and Barbeyto (2006: 16) found that in the first four elections (1990-2006) since the autonomous regions were founded, women's participation in the regional council has never acceded

---

1  Interview with Debby Hodgson, Bilwi-Puerto Cabezas 08/08/07.
2  Interview with Myrna Cunningham, Bilwi-Puerto Cabezas 07/08/07.
3  See also Metoyer (2000).
4  In the regional government, women were most visible in the judicial branch, where they accounted for nearly 40 percent of the judges. Within the executive branch, less than 15 percent of the thirty-five highest level positions were occupied by women. In the second tier of the executive branch, women directed two of the twelve secretarías, including the Secretaría de la Mujer, Niñez, Adolescencia y Familia, (Marina Ingram) and the Secretaría de Salud (Dra. Silvia Malespin). The highest position of governor was held by Reynaldo Francis, a former Contra leader and loyal member of the Yatama party. Interview with Vilma Patterson, Bilwi-Puerto Cabezas 02/08/07.

20 percent. My research shows that from 2006–2010, women's participation plummeted to just over 4 percent. Of the forty-five elected councilors in the regional council between 2006-2010, only two were women; Juana Chow and Marisol Carlson, both of whom were Miskitu affiliated to Yatama.[1] This gender inequity has important consequences, as the legislative branch is arguably the most powerful branch of the government. The legislative branch, guided by the regional council's Board of Directors, appoints the governor and all others serving in RAAN's executive and judicial branches. One woman, Juana Chow, sat on the regional council's Board of Directors from 2006-2010.

Research by González, Figueroa, and Barbeyto (2006:12-13) found that RAAN women are at a disadvantage in popular elections when national political parties are involved. I asked Myrna about women's decreasing presence in the Regional Council and the affect of national political parties on voting patterns. I also asked her about the status of women's political participation in the legislative branch of the RAAN government.

> Over the last twenty years, political participation of women in the main legislative body of the autonomous region, the *consejo regional*, has dropped....Women also have a low participation in municipal level elections as well. Although Nancie Elizabeth was elected mayor in Puerto Cabezas, this doesn't reflect broader patterns in women's political participation.

> Women are limited by political parties that economically back men more than women in popular elections. Loyal party men primarily are elected to leadership positions within the political parties. Many times women candidate's names are listed at the bottom of the list on the voting ballot, with only men's names in top positions on the ticket, which attracts more votes for the leading men candidates.

National political parties, according to Myrna, influenced local voting patterns to the detriment of women candidates. She claimed that national political parties based in Managua influence municipal and regional elections by choosing to support and provide campaign finances exclusively to men's campaigns. This was echoed by Liliette Campbell, who said, "on the more machista Pacific side of the country, those with decision making

---

1 González, Figueroa, and Barbeyto (2006: 17) found that in popular elections for the regional council, Miskitu women have had more success than Creole women, and that Sumu-Mayangna women have only had one elected member to the regional council.

power believe that women can not win elections."[1] Myrna also mentioned that national parties placed women's names at lower positions on the voting ballot, suggesting that women running for office were not serious candidates. By denying economic support to female candidates and placing their names lower on the ballot, national political parties block women out of offices elected by popular vote.

Local Gender Ideology

The women leaders interviewed pointed out that gender-based discrimination at the local level also impedes their access to offices elected by popular vote. Women leaders blamed both local men and women for not yet being comfortable voting for women in popular elections. They attributed this to culturally-based perceptions of motherhood, as Miskitu and Creole societies in particular view women's primary role in society as mothers and motherhood entails being the care-giver and protector of children. Miskitu and Creole men and women believe that mothers should not expose their families to the public life of a politician, where negative campaigns are pitched against families during public elections. Interestingly, while motherhood was cited previously as the source of women's power and leadership abilities, local perceptions of motherhood, as protectors of children, simultaneously hinders women's participation and success in popular elections. Myrna commented on how local gender ideologies have hurt women's access to elected office.

> A significant reason why women's participation has declined [in popular elections] is that women are often denigrated in negative campaigns. In this way, the political process of campaigns runs contrary to communitarian values and communal politics. Women do not want to subject themselves and their families to public scrutiny and criticism and they opt for a more harmonious home-life. Another reason is that married women have to negotiate gender relations with their husbands, who are often in a position of power in the household.[2]

Running for public office, Myrna later explained, leaves the candidate's entire family, the children included, open to criticism and gossip within the community to the point where entire families may become socially ostracized. She also discussed why married women are not considered good can-

---

1  Interview with Liliette "Ashanti" Campbell, Bilwi-Puerto Cabezas 06/08/07.
2  Interview with Myrna Cunningham, Bilwi-Puerto Cabezas 07/08/07.

didates in popular elections: local voters believe that a married woman run-ning for public office needs the complete emotional and economic support of her husband. More commonly, the community is aware that men will not support their wife, by refusing to step into domestic roles at home. This situation has often deteriorated into marital discord and domestic violence. Additionally, Myrna related to me that if a woman is married and serving as a government official, locals tend to believe that her husband will influence her position and tell her which way to vote.

That a husband would refuse to help with domestic chores, physically abuse his wife, and control the way she votes on issues, seems counterin-tuitive to the fact that Miskitu and Creole societies are organized around matrilocal residential and matrifocal domestic patterns, where women have high status vis-à-vis men. Anthropologists have noted that ambigu-ous power relations exist in matrifocal domestic groups cross-culturally, where men traditionally maintain economic authority through their access to wage-labor, and the women control social relations and make household economic decisions (Menon 1995). These kinds of contradictory gender-power relations may have led to high rates of intra-familial violence on the Atlantic Coast.

Intra-familial violence is a serious problem on the Atlantic Coast and the Miskitu have the highest rate of intra-familial violence in the RAAN (Herman 2006: 76-77). Following the gendered division of labor in Miskitu society, Miskitu women's work revolves around the household, while men typically work for wages. Married Miskitu women who work away from the home upset deeply inscribed gender relations and increase their risk of being victims of violent acts perpetrated by their husbands (Olivera 2006). Additionally, violence is normalized in Miskitu society and is seen as a nat-ural part of Miskitu marriage, as the family, Church, and community expect men to correct their wife for "bad" or non-traditional behavior (Herman 2006: 86).[1] Miskitu women who mobilize for their rights are particularly susceptible to violence, given that most men perceive women's mobiliza-

---

[1] During my fieldwork, many Miskitu women claimed that if a man does not beat her, he does not love her. I witnessed women taking pride in their bruises and proudly showing them off to family and friends. Most strikingly, the word for love in the Miskitu language is "latwan kaikaia," which literally translates as, "to see pain" or "it hurts me to see you." Exploring the ethno-poetics of the word latwan kaikaia underscores the fact that violence is not just a woman's issue, but that it is a problem within the community.

tion as running counter to communitarian values and the autonomy process (Figueroa 2006: 625).[1]

Under the legal system known as *usos y costumbres* (customary law), part of the autonomy law passed by the Nicaraguan nation-state, cases of gender violence are resolved by a communal judge or "wihta." The communal judge often does not punish the offender, who commonly gets off lightly and pays a small fine. Wihtas are less concerned with punishing the offender and more concerned with restoring the community to harmony. Customary law, then, institutionalizes gender violence by promoting a justice system that seeks resolutions to insure harmonious relations in the community. Myrna explained women's rights regarding gender violence under customary law.

> That is a truly complicated topic because effectively, *usos y cos-tumbres* at some level accepts the oppression of women as normal beneath the argument of communal culture. And beneath the argument of culture it isn't necessary to go beyond the heart of the community to find justification for the oppression of women. In our case, usos y costumbres is partially responsible for women's oppression regarding violence against women. Our autonomy law establishes the administration of a communitary judge.

> Yes, the wihta and the system where the wihta coordinates those in charge of justice within the community and includes the penal code of Nicaragua. This establishes that in the case of violence against indigenous women in the heart of the community that this should be handled by traditional means; that is to say that there are cases of violence within the community that are not resolved by the community because the community decides that women should put up with violence to make community life harmonious. And so to confront this problem, women in communities are increasingly using part of their system of usos y costumbre but when they cannot stand (*soportar*) the oppressive situation they are using the state system of administration. Then they come to the Comisaria de la Mujer and they file a complaint (*denuncia*) and even call in another judge, the state judge, to resolve the situation. For these reasons, I say that the problem is not that we demand respect for tradition and customary law, but the truth is that at times this very tradition oppresses women.

Myrna explained how customary law creates the situation where violence often goes unpunished by local law. Women are called upon to put up with (*aguantar*) violence for the supposed benefit of the community. In

1  For women to be successful in their struggle for their individual rights on the Atlantic Coast, Myrna believes that their demands must not be seen as being disruptive to the autonomy process or as upsetting the gender and power equilibrium in society (Figueroa 2006: 625).

some cases of violence, RAAN women turned to Nicaraguan law for access to social justice denied to them locally. State judges and the Nicaraguan Comisaria de la Mujer, located at the police station in Puerto Cabezas, resolved their cases. This situation in the RAAN shows that customary law has negative effects on women's everyday lives and reinforces women's inability to work away from the home as professionals, serve as political leaders, and, especially, enter popular elections. Significantly, autochthonous gender ideologies work against women's full political participation by normalizing community gossip and domestic violence against women who seek elected office.

The Atlantic Coast sits within the circum-Caribbean culture area, where women have high status living in female-centered domestic groups, yet geopolitically the Atlantic Coast is positioned within the patriarchal Latin American nation-state. As a result, contradictory and competing discourses of gender and power relations exist. Atlantic Coast women must negotiate their identities and status between the local discourse arising from their domestic and kinship groups and the national discourse emanating from the patriarchal state. The interviews and my research show, however, that women's oppression did not result only from interactions with the patriarchal nation state. Oppressive patriarchal ideologies revolving around perceptions of motherhood and womanhood also arise at the local and regional level, which discourage women from entering leadership positions.

Conclusions

This chapter focused on the current status of indigenous and Afro-descendant women's political participation and their access to leadership positions. My research began by exploring the process in which Miskitu and Creole women in Nicaragua have catapulted from positions of leadership in the matrilocal group to high political office. Data collected in Bilwi-Puerto Cabezas shows that Miskitu and Creole women leaders in the last twenty-five years have gained access to positions of political leadership through their involvement with the Moravian Church, the Sandinista revolution, and post-1990s development organizations that have worked in the region. These stages of empowerment, through religious organizations, a political movement, and development projects, may provide a model for the process in which minority and indigenous women have en-gendered leadership throughout Latin America (Eber and Kovic 2003). These stages of empowerment may combine to favor women's leadership.

Even in progressive Nicaragua, however, where Afro-descendant and indigenous women have achieved considerable success entering leadership positions, RAAN women reach the glass ceiling during popular elections that are influenced by national political parties. National political parties choose to economically support male candidates in popular elections and put their names at the top of ballots. At the local level, slanderous and negative campaigns are also part and parcel of popular elections. Mothers are judged by the community concerning their ability to protect their children from these negative political campaigns. Married women also find it difficult to become leaders because their husbands often refuse to assume domestic tasks when women are absent from the household, which often can lead to domestic violence with few legal ramifications. These examples document the ways that indigenous women living between societies with differing gender codes are similarly excluded from leadership posts. Conclusions suggest that autonomy based on tradition combines with the patriarchal nation-state to negatively affect women's access to political leadership. Despite the progress that RAAN women have made within the revolution and the indigenous autonomy movement, different forms of discrimination against women still impede their political affirmation and participation in different arenas, especially when it comes to influential positions in decision making processes in national and regional spaces.

Gender issues and women's rights are central to discussions of indigenous self-determination throughout Latin America (Hernández de Castillo 2006; Sierra 2001). My findings coincide with the many studies that find that customary law perpetuates harmful practices and institutionalizes human rights violations toward indigenous women (IIWF 2006: 28).[1] Opponents of indigenous autonomy often use this as an argument against autonomy (Sierra 2001). Indigenous feminism, however, seems to have found a way to deconstruct the autonomy vs. rights contradiction, by demanding the right to maintain some traditions but to change those that are harmful to women.

---

1  Studying the relationship between autonomy and rights brings into focus the relativism vs. universalism debate. Merry (2003) argues that this debate is grounded in the belief that culture, and religion, oppresses women's human rights.

Since the 1994 EZLN (Zapatista Army of National Liberation) uprising, Zapatista women have remained at the forefront of gender and indigenous self-determination issues (Eber and Kovic 2003; Speed et al. 2006). Within their struggle for autonomy, Zapatista women have developed a militant indigenous feminism based on the revolutionary laws of Zapatista Women. In the laws, Zapatista women demanded the right for indigenous women to participate fully in positions of leadership (Hernández de Castillo 2006: 67-68). A quota system of gender equity now exists and 50 percent of all Zapatista government positions are currently held by women, even amongst the top positions in the EZLN army.

Following the lead of the Zaptista women's movement, Atlantic Coast women are now attempting to implement a quota system of gender equity. At a recent women's forum in Bilwi-Puerto Cabezas, twenty-four Atlantic Coast women representatives wrote a letter of intent demanding a gender-based quota system, where 40 percent of the decision making cargos in RAAN are to be filled by women. The representatives also pushed to have a municipal order approved that 40 percent of all municipal projects be designed to benefit women (Dixon 2008). RAAN women, therefore, are fighting for their individual rights to political participation within their struggle for their group rights to indigenous self-determination. Thus, RAAN women's fight for their political participation is part of a new and emerging indigenous feminism on the Atlantic Coast.

## Acknowledgements

This research was supported by the US Department of Education's Fulbright-Hays Faculty Research Abroad Program and The Wenner-Gren Foundation for Anthropological Research, Individual Research Grant.

## References

Antonio, C., Antonio, M., Blanco, E. M., Cunningham, M., Ingram, M., McClean, M., Miguel, S., Poveda, C. (2006) *Proyecto Albuergue* (propuesta de proyecto para un albergue de Mujeres, elaborado por Myrna Cunningham de CADPI con la colaboración de la red de mujeres contra la violencia) Bilwi, RAAN.

Babb, F. (2001) *After Revolution: Mapping Gender and Cultural Politics in Neoliberal Nicaragua* (Austin, University of Texas Press).

Batallion, G. (2007) 'Protestantismo moravo y establecimiento de nuevos habitus entre los misquitos nicaraguenses (1848-2000)' in *Estudios Sociológicos* Vol. 25, Núm. 73, pp. 41-68.

Centro de Estudios e Información de la Mujer Mulitétnica (CEIMM) (2008) *Serie Cuadernos de Género para Nicaragua*. Banco Mundial y Banco Interamericano de Desarrollo. Diagnóstico de género en las Regiones Autónomas de la Costa Caribe. Managua.

Chinchilla, N. 'Revolutionary Popular Feminism in Nicaragua: Ideologies, Political Transitions, and the Struggle for Autonomy,' in Bose, C. and Acosta-Belen, A. (1995) *Women in the Latin American development process* (Philadelphia: Temple University Press), pp. 242-270.

Collins, P. H. 'Shifting the Center: Race, Class, and Feminist Theorizing about Motherhood', in Glenn, E., Chang, G. and Forcey, L. (Eds) (1994) *Mothering: Ideology, Experience and Agency* (London, Routledge), pp. 45-66.

Cunningham Kain, M. (2006) 'Indigenous Women's Vision of an Inclusive Feminism' in *Development* No. 49, pp. 55-59.

(2003) 'Indigenous Women and International Law' MADRE: *An International Women's Human Rights Organization* http://www.madre.org/ (Accessed 04/10/05).

Davis, S. (2006) 'Las Mujeres Valientes del Wangki Awala: Reconstruyendo Nuestras Almas y Esperanzas' (URACCAN).

Dennis, P. (2000) 'Autonomy on the Miskito Coast of Nicaragua' in *Reviews in Anthropology* No. 29, pp. 199-210.

Dennis, P. and Herlihy, L. (2004) 'Higher Education on Nicaragua's Multicultural Atlantic Coast' in *Cultural Survival Quarterly* Vol. 27, No. 4, pp. 42-47.

Dixon, H. (2008) 'Fundacion Puntos de Encuentro Nic aragua-Para transformer la vida cotidiana, Mujeres Costeñas' in *Boletina* No. 59. [WWW document]. URL http://www.puntis.org.ni [Accessed 9/26/2008].

Eber, C. and Kovic, C. (2003) *Women of Chiapas: Making History in Times of Struggle and Hope* (New York, Routledge).

Figueroa Romero, D. (2006) 'Interview with Mirna Cunningham Kain' in *International Feminist Journal of Politics* Vol. 8, No. 4, pp. 618-626.

Gabbert, W. (2006) 'Concepts of Ethnicity' in *Latin American and Caribbean Ethnic Studies* Vol. 1, No. 1, pp. 85-103.

García, C. (1996) *The Making of the Miskitu People of Nicaragua; The Social Construction of Ethnic Identity* Acta Universitatis Upsaliensis. Studia Sociologica Upsaliensia, No. 41.

González, M., Figueroa, D., and Barbeyto, A. (2006) 'Género, etnia y partidos políticos en las elecciones regionales de la Costa Caribe: retos de la diversidad' in Revista del Caribe Nicaraguense (WANI), enero-marzo No. 44, pp 10-23.

Green, J. (2007) *Making Space for Indigenous Women* (London: Zed Books).

Hale, C. (1996) 'Mestizaje, Hybridity, and the Cultural Politics of Difference in Post-Revolutionary Central America' in *Journal of Latin American Anthropology* Vol. 2, No. 1, pp. 34-61.

Helms, M. (1971) *Asang; Adaptation to Culture Contact in a Miskito Community* (Gainesville, University of Florida Press).

Herlihy, L. (2007) 'Matrifocality and Women's Power on the Miskito Coast' in *Ethnology* Vol. 46, No. 2, pp. 133-150.

(2006) 'Sexual Magic and Money: Miskitu Women's Strategies in Northern Honduras' in *Ethnology* Vol. 45, No. 2, pp. 43-59.

Herman Sálomon, C. (2006) Violencia intrafamiliar y cultura: Un estudio comparativo de las comunidades étnicas de Bilwi. Tesis de maestria en Antropología Social. Universidad de las Regiones Autónomas de la Costa Caribe Nicaraguense (URACCAN).

Hernández de Castillo, R. 'Between Feminist Ethnocentricity and Ethnic Essentialism: The Zapatistas' Demands and the National Indigenous Women's Movement.' in Speed, S., Hernández de Castillo, R. and Stephen, L. (Eds) (2006) *Dissident Women; Gender and Politics in Chiapas* (Austin, University of Texas Press), pp. 57-73.

International Indigenous Women's Forum (2006) *Mairin Iwanka Raya: Indigenous Women Stand Against Violence*. A report on violence against indigenous women by the Secretary General of the United Nations (New York, FIMI/IIWF).

Kampwirth, K. 'Women in the Armed Struggles in Nicaragua: Sandinistas and Contras Compared' in González, V. and Kampwirth, K. (Eds) (2001) *Radical Women in Latin America: Left and Right*. (University Park, Pennsylvania: The Pennsylvania State University Press).

Mendez, J. B. (2005) *From the Revolution to the Maquiladoras: Gender, Labor, and Globalization in Nicaragua* (Durham, NC: Duke University Press).

Menon, S. 'Male Authority and Female Autonomy: A Study of the Matrilineal Nayars of Kerala, South India' in Maynes, M., Waltner, A., Soland, B. and Strasser, U. (Eds) (1995) *Gender, Kinship, Power: A Comparative and Interdisciplinary History* (New York: Routledge), pp. 131-145.

Merry, S. (2003) 'Human Rights Law and the Demonization of Culture (and Anthropology Along the Way)' in *POLAR* Vol. 26, No. I, pp. 55-77.

Metoyer, C. (2000) *Women and the State in Post-Sandinista Nicaragua* (Colorado: Lynne Rienner).

Mohammed, P. 'The Caribbean Family Revisited' in Mohammed, P. and Shepherd, C. (Eds) (1986) *Gender in Caribbean Development* (Jamaica, University of the West Indies), pp. 170-182.

Molyneux, M. (1985) 'Mobilization without Emancipation? Women's Interests, the State, and Revolution in Nicaragua' in *Feminist Studies* Vol. 11, No. 2, pp. 227-254.

Olivera, M. (2006) 'Violence Against Women and Mexico's Structural Crisis' in *Latin American Perspectives* Issue 147, Vol. 33, No. 2, pp. 104-114.

Ouellette, G. (2002) *The Fourth World: An Indigenous Perspective on Feminism and Aboriginal Women's Activism* (Halifax, Fernwood Publishing).

Peter Espinoza, M. (2006) 'Parentesco y grupo doméstico de los miskitos: Los casos de Auhya Pihni y Santa Martha' in *WANI* No. 44, pp. 30- 36.

Pineda, B. (2006) *Shipwrecked Identities: Navigating Race on Nicaragua's Mosquito Coast* (New Brunswick, Rutger's University Press).

Randall, M. (1981) *Sandino's Daughters: Testimionies of Nicaraguan Women in Struggle* (Vancouver, BC: New Star Books).

(1992) *Gathering Rage: The Failure of Twentieth Century Revolutions to Develop Feminist Agenda* (New York: Monthly Review Press).

Sierra, M. (2001) 'Human Rights, Gender and Ethnicity: Legal Claims and Anthropological Challenges in Mexico' in *POLAR* Vol. 23, No. 2, pp. 76-92.

Speed, S. 'Rights at the Intersection: Gender and Ethnicity in Neoliberal Mexico' in Speed, S., Hernández de Castillo, A., and Stephen, L. (Eds) (2006) *Dissident Women: Gender and Cultural Politics in Chiapas* (Austin, University of Texas Press), pp. 203-221.

Wekker, G. (2006) *The Politics of Passion; Women's Sexual Culture in the Afro-Surinamese Diaspora* (New York, Columbia University Press).

# CHAPTER 8. GAINING AND REALIZING LANGUAGE RIGHTS IN A MULTILINGUAL REGION

*Jane Freeland*

The genuine space created for the languages of the Caribbean Coast's in-digenous and Afro-Caribbean minorities has rightly been praised as a major and enduring achievement of the 1979 Sandinista revolution. Especially in the early years, the provision of the Literacy Campaign in Native Languages (1980–81) and the passing of a bilingual education law (1980) were cited as firm proof of early Sandinista commitment to pluralism (Bourgois 1982; Rediske and Schneider 1983; Dunbar Ortiz 1984; Vilas, 1989), and bilingual education programs became an important part of the autonomy process. Later, as the neo-liberal governments that followed the Sandinistas after 1990 procrastinated over implementing this law and undermined many of its key principles, these programs became an emblem of autonomy in action (Ortega Hegg 1997, González Pérez 1997: 193, Muñoz Cruz 2001, McLean Herrera 2001: 121).

Nevertheless, as this chapter will show, these developments were not nearly as straightforward as the above narrative suggests. Given their very different historical experiences and the language ideologies they generated, the Sandinistas and the Costeño minorities had very different conceptions of linguistic rights. Although both parties drew on the contemporary in-ternational discourse on linguistic human rights, their different interpretations of some of its key concepts generated misunderstandings and conflict. Consequently, like other areas of Sandinista policy for the Coast, language policy was shaped in the difficult dialectic between Sandinista and Costeño ideologies which culminated in the 1987 autonomy law. The language rights it granted were among the most progressive in Latin America. Yet, as their broad permissive framework encountered the intricate sociolinguistic realities of the Coast, unexpected limitations were revealed to its founding assumptions, which offer valuable lessons not only for Nicaragua, but for the implementation of language rights in general.

There are three main sections. The first section in this chapter describes those sociolinguistic realities and traces their historical evolution. The second analyzes the development of language rights policy in two main phases, up to and following the outbreak of war in 1981. The third section explores through selected case studies the problems of realizing the rights it granted, in the Coast's complex multilingual circumstances and how they have been approached. Centering mainly on the bilingual programs, it draws some broad conclusions from Nicaragua's particular experience.

The chapter draws on my work in the region since 1980, as a researcher and teacher in the sociolinguistics of multilingualism. It is grounded in recent sociolinguistic and ethnographic concerns with "language/linguistic ideologies." These are "the abstract (and often implicit) belief systems related to language and linguistic behavior that affect speakers' choices and interpretations of communicative interaction" (Silverstein 1998, summarized by McGroarty 2010: 3) which can acquire particular importance in relation to protecting minority languages. Since they are constructed from specific political and economic perspectives language ideologies are also multiple (Field and Kroskrity 2009: 11) and come into conflict.[1] Whilst they evidently inform explicit state policy and legislation about language, they are also found in people's casual talk about language and are implicit in daily communicative practice.

The Caribbean Coast — A "Contact Zone"

Any language policy for Nicaragua's Caribbean Coast region must take account of its ethnic and linguistic pluralism and of complex relationships

---

1  Changing definitions of language ideology in this developing field are explored in Blommaert (1999); Schieffelin, Woolard and Kroskrity (1998); Kroskrity (2004), and McGroarty (2010).

between language and group identity. The Coast is home to three indigenous groups — the Miskitu (125,869), the Sumu/Mayangna (19,370) of which the Ulwa are a sub-group of about 600 (Green 1996), and the Rama (1,290). There are two African-Caribbean groups — the Creoles (27,197), and the Garífuna (3,440),[1] and a growing mestizo population, which as a result of state-encouraged peasant migration since the 1960s now constitutes almost 76% of the Coast population.[2]

In much of the region different combinations of groups interact within contiguous or sometimes shared territories; in both the South and North Atlantic Autonomous Regions (RAAS and RAAN), the main towns are multi-ethnic, whilst ethnically mixed rural communities are quite common. These interactions take place through four main languages: Spanish, the official national language, the regional *lingua franca*, and the first language of the mestizos; Creole English (and some Standard Caribbean English); and two related but distinct indigenous languages, Miskitu, and Sumu/Mayangna. Three further languages, Ulwa (related to Sumu), Rama, and Garífuna, are no longer in daily use.

Consequently, although language does mark ethnic boundaries, it also mediates complex inter-ethnic relations; the link between language and identity is therefore not simple or absolute. Many Costeños acquire dynamic bi-, tri- and even quadrilingual repertoires, and often switch and mix codes to construct and express complex, equally dynamic identities (Freeland 2003; Gurdián 2001; Jamieson 1998, 2001, 2003). These have de-

---

1 Group names have been contentious (González Pérez 1997: 193-216). Coast people (including Mestizos) call themselves *Costeños* when opposing a common, regional identity against the Pacific Coast region. Official documents, such as the Nicaraguan Constitution (1987) and the Autonomy law, use the expression "indigenous and ethnic groups" to acknowledge differences between aboriginal inhabitants of the region and the later-arrived African-Caribbeans and mestizos, and I adopt this usage here.

Until the mid-1990s, the Mayangna self-identified and were referred to as Sumu, which included the Ulwa. To escape the pejorative connotations of this name, especially in Miskitu usage, they adopted the name Mayangna, which is still not universally accepted; the Ulwa, for instance, regard themselves as part of the Sumu family but not as Mayangna (Benedicto and Hale 2004). With members of this group I adopt a hyphenated form — "Mayangna-Sumu" — to indicate respect for both positions. Linguists generally refer to the Sumu language, distinguishing Southern Sumu (Ulwa) from Northern Sumu, spoken by the Mayangna; Mayangna non-linguists refer to their language, as to themselves, as both Sumu and Mayangna.

2 Population figures based on McLean (2008) and PNUD (2005).

---

veloped over centuries through complex processes of ethnogenesis which began long before the entry of Europeans into Central America (Offen 1999; González Pérez 1997; Romero Vargas, 1995; Gurdián 2001) and were further shaped by subsequent processes of globalization, Hispanic and Anglo colonial interventions, and modern Nicaraguan nation-building.[1]

One product of these processes is a hierarchy of power which is reflected in and maintained by a corresponding hierarchy in the symbolic power of the Coast's languages. In the eighteenth century, the Miskitu's special alliance with the British not only gave them economic and military power over other indigenous groups; as they mediated trade between these groups and British settlers, or exacted tributes to the Miskitu king, Miskitu became an indigenous *lingua franca*. Nevertheless, they also took pride in speaking English, to mark their status as a "European-like people" different from the "wild Indians" (Holm 1978: 39, 50). As Dennis observes, today's Miskitu still value both English and multilingualism (Dennis 2004: 173, 177).

Miskitu dominance, especially over the Mayangna, was further cemented in the nineteenth century by Moravian missionaries who translated the Bible into Miskitu, taught Miskitu lay pastors to read and even write their language, and later trained Miskitu to lead the indigenous church. As Miskitu was used to evangelize among the Mayanga, it became the official church language, gaining power and prestige and expanding its scope and range. However, as its dominance grew in this powerful domain, it excluded Sumu, simultaneously lowering its prestige and limiting its evolution.

Among the Creoles and the Rama in the south of the region, the Moravians evangelized in English, then the quasi-official language there. The literate skills the Creoles could acquire in the Moravians' English-medium schools fitted them for clerical and management jobs in the US enclaves and contributed to their gradual ascendancy over other non-white groups. In contrast, evangelization in English caused Rama to be virtually replaced by English in a single generation. However, Creoles quickly lost their dominant position after 1894 when the Coast was "re-incorporated" into the Nicaraguan state. To foster national unity, strict Hispanization policies were imposed, education in other languages was proscribed, forcing the Mora-

---

1 Hill (1996) defines ethnogenesis as the dynamic process by which ethnic and indigenous groups maintain "enduring identities in general contexts of radical change and discontinuity...a synthesis of people's cultural and political struggles to exist as well as their historical consciousness of those struggles" as expressed in their myths and oral histories (Hill 1996: 2).

vian schools to adopt Spanish as their medium of instruction. This reduced English to minority status, though it remained important in the US economic enclaves.[1]

By 1979, Spanish was incontestably the dominant regional language and the region's *lingua franca.* "English" ran it a close second, though its position was more complicated. In Coast parlance, "English" denoted both Standard (Caribbean) English and the English-Kriol vernaculars spoken by the Creoles, Rama and Garífuna.[2] Although Kriol was a key marker of Creole identity, it was discouraged in schools as "bad English," as in many Caribbean countries (Freeland 1993, 1999, 2004). As section four will show, this internal division has caused complications for Creole bilingual education. Other groups continued to value "English" (usually Kriol) as a passport to better-paid jobs in the US enclaves or on cruise ships. Third in the hierarchy came Miskitu; although now subordinated to both Spanish and "English," it retained its role in the indigenous Moravian Church and remained the only written indigenous language. Sumu-Mayangna was thus multiply subordinated, not only to Spanish and English, but also to Miskitu.

Such ethnolinguistic hierarchies are common in post-colonial multilingual regions. They not only reflect unequal structures of social and economic power but maintain them through self-confirming processes that affect both speakers and languages themselves. Firstly, such linguistic stratification imposes unequal burdens of language learning: the more domains a language is excluded from, the more its speakers need other languages to operate in those domains. Whilst mestizos could choose to remain monolingual (Holm 1978), "English"-speakers needed to become bilingual, and the Miskitu trilingual to become economically mobile. At the bottom of the pile, the Sumu-Mayangna needed Miskitu, Spanish, and possibly some "English." Yet in the absence of planned bi- or multilingual education, acquisition of these multilingual competences was informal, contingent on social opportunity, and therefore limited.

Secondly, languages excluded from specific domains do not naturally develop the expressive resources (vocabulary, specialist discourses, social

---

1  For fuller accounts of these processes and their socio-economic, political and ethnolinguistic consequences within various ideological and methodological frameworks, see Dunbar Ortiz (1985); González Pérez (1997); Gordon (1998); Hale (1994); Offen (1999), and Vilas (1989).

2  I use here the orthography developed in 2004 through a series of URACCAN workshops and subsequently adopted for writing Nicaraguan Creole.

---

routines, styles of speech and writing) needed for such domains. Speakers of dominant languages then use this lack of resources to justify the continued exclusion of these languages, as though the failure were inherent in the languages themselves, rather than the product of socio-historical barriers.

Thirdly, through the semiotic process of "iconization" (Irvine and Gal 2001), the supposed "backwardness" of a language becomes associated with its speakers. In face of such self-confirming forces, speakers themselves come to internalize this association. Gradually, these combined pressures push minority speakers towards "language shift" (Fishman 1991): they abandon their own language in favor of another in order to "pass" among a more economically or socially advantaged group. One Garífuna father offered exactly this explanation for the loss of Garífuna in Nicaragua: "the old people them consider, well maybe you'll be better, in order to...survive among these people, if we could drop this language and then pick up these people [speak their language]... in order to pass, to get on" (Orinoco parents' meeting, 1994). Even so, language shift is not inevitable: even severely subordinated languages can survive within a multilingual repertoire if they retain meaningful social functions for their speakers (Dorian 1998; Mulhäusler 1995; Kroskrity 1993).

By 1979, many Coast communities were experiencing marked language shift, whose direction depended on local inter-group contacts and pressures. Some communities of all ethnias were shifting towards Spanish, whilst many Miskitu communities, especially in the south of the region, were shifting towards "English," which had become the first language of the Garífuna and the Rama. Meanwhile, the Ulwa and some Mayangna communities were shifting towards Miskitu, under pressure from the influx of Miskitu workers to the US gold mines and the lumber camps in their vicinities (Holm 1978; Green 1996; Green and Hale 1998).

The upshot of these processes is that Costeño indigenous/ethnic groups were not discrete, internally homogeneous blocs, inhabiting clearly bounded territories and speaking similarly bounded, discrete languages that corresponded to and defined their identities. Over centuries, the region had become what Pratt calls a "contact zone": a social space "where disparate cultures meet, clash, and grapple with each other, often in highly asymmetrical relations of domination and subordination — like colonialism, slavery, or their aftermaths as they are lived out across the globe today" (Pratt 1992: 4; Dunbar Ortiz 1984: 206f.). Correspondingly, Costeños used the languages in their environment to construct multi-faceted social identities negotiated in complex intercultural relationships (Freeland 2003).[1]

When the Sandinistas took power in 1979, they were broadly aware of the Coast's plurilingualism, and that some languages were dying or nearly extinct, but not of these sociolinguistic complexities.

Negotiating Language Rights

The Sandinistas' approach to the Coast's linguistic pluralism has typically been analyzed separately from other aspects of Sandinista policy for the Coast. The early literature narrates a relatively conflict-free development towards the bilingual education programs instituted in 1985, whilst subsequent studies have focused primarily on the practical problems of those programs since 1985 in a similarly neutral vein (Shapiro 1987; Docherty 1988; Amadio 1989; Freeland and McLean 1994; Muñoz 2001; Rizo Zeledón 1996; Venezia Mauceri 1996, 2001).

Yet, as Anderson (1993) shows, for Western nation-builders language has been a key tool for uniting diverse groups into unified national "imagined communities" through a common language, primarily through education. Language policy, then, is almost by definition ideological. This is particularly true of Latin America, with its Spanish inheritance of "one-language-one-nation" nationalism (Mar-Molinero 2000) which as we saw in the previous section, was central to attempts to "reincorporate" the Coast from 1894 and throughout the Somoza period.

This section links the development of Sandinista language policy to the broader transformation in Sandinista thinking on diversity from the centralist developmentalism of the early years (1979-1981) towards the concept of the multi-ethnic nation, a transformation entailing a significant broadening of their concept of culture and of language within it. Development followed a course in which politically driven, often improvised responses to Costeño demands were followed by policy statements and legislation that codified principles learned through practice.

---

1   That this is not a new phenomenon is suggested by Benedicto and Hale's (2000: 97) description of the region as a long-established and well-defined "linguistic area" where "the syntactic structures of the present-day [Miskitu and Sumu] languages exhibit the characteristics of grammatical "merger" not uncommon in such areas". See also Jamieson (2001, 2003) and Gurdián (2001) on the deep historical roots of these processes.

Conflicting Concepts of Diversity (1979–1981)

As Hale (1994), Gould (1998) and Gordon (1998) have argued, the San-dinistas' approach to the Coast was rooted in a Marxist re-working of the Latin American *indigenismo* that had inspired Sandino.[1] *Indigenismo*, "the hall-mark of progressive thinking on the part of liberal and revolutionary gov-ernments until well into the second half of the [twentieth] century" (Adams 1991: 202-3), envisaged national unity as a new blend of the Hispanic and the indigenous, which would "integrate" indigenous people into the mod-ern nation-state, whilst including the "best elements" of their cultures in national culture. These "best elements" were identified with the symbolic or tangible aspects of culture (language, music, dance and artifacts) in ac-cordance with Western notions of "high" culture and disarticulated from the economic, political and organizational systems to which they belonged, which were dismissed as primitive or backward.

This bias is evident in early Sandinista texts about the Coast. Whilst indigenous economic practices and political consciousness were to be modernized (see chapter 4 of this volume), there was admiration for "the persistence and perpetuation of their languages and dialects," considered a "revealing measure" of the "truly impressive ... strength and vitality of these people in the face of successive invasions" (*Poder Sandinista* 1979, in Ohland and Schneider 1983: 44). Indeed, so common is the collocation "language(s) and culture(s)" [*lengua(s) y cultura(s)*] in these texts that the two terms come to operate effectively as synonyms. By the same tokens, the Creoles' Eng-lish-based language was viewed with suspicion as embodying alien values.[2]

> The conception of "language-as-culture" in fact underpinned con-temporary discourse: just as Euro-American nation-builders saw language as the essential expression of "national spirit" (Fishman 1972: 270-81), so contemporary anthropology privileged it in its cultural analysis of exotic peoples (Street 1993; Hill and Mannheim 1992; Baumann and Briggs 2003). In discussions of minority rights, too, such as the 1957 ILO Convention on Indigenous Rights and the debate around Article 27 of the 1976 UN International Conven-

---

1  On Sandino's *indigenismo*, see chapter 3 of this volume. On the significance of *indi-genismo* for Nicaragua see also Dunbar Ortiz (1984: 75-123).

2  This notion is forcefully expressed in an influential contemporary study of Nica-raguan speech. Whilst Nahuatl "a beautiful language...made for culture" has en-riched Nicaraguan Spanish, English is condemned as "the language of the future usurper of Mosquitia...of the invading Marine...the scar marking our history on the violated body of our race" (Mántica 1973: 22-34, translations from Spanish are my own unless otherwise indicated).

tion on Civil and Political Rights, culture was defined in terms of its "mental and ideological" rather than its economic or political aspects (Thornberry 1991: 188, 20f., 337-55). Indeed, so dominant was this conception at the time that *indigenista* academics were surprised by the rapid growth of indigenous organizations in the early 1980s, finding it "easier to disqualify it as a transitory phenomenon attributable to the intervention of foreign agents into indigenous communities" (Bonfil Batalla 1990: 191-2).

The Sandinistas' Marxist twist on *indigenismo* took this further, assigning symbolic culture to the superstructure and material culture to the economic base (Vilas 1989; Hale 1994). So the *Special Plan* for the Coast in their *Historic Program of the FSLN* (1969) could, seemingly without contradiction, "encourage the flowering of *the local cultural values of the region*, which derive from the original aspects of its historical tradition" (VId, my emphasis), yet plan to "develop" its economies and political consciousness.

In contrast, early indigenous claims of the revolution were couched in the discourse of the international and regional indigenous movements that so surprised the *indigenistas* (Dunbar Ortiz 1984: 32-39, 58-67, 78-86), founded on a broader, more holistic understanding of culture and a radically different understanding of integration. This discourse is the foundation of MISURASATA's 1980 *General Directions (Lineamientos Generales).*[1]

Significantly its first heading was "Land," under which MISURASATA demands that "our revolutionary government recognize and guarantee each community...its *territory*, registering it...as continuous, collective, inalienable property, sufficiently extensive to assure population growth" (MISURASATA n.d.: 7, my emphasis). Language first appeared under heading two, "Education," which proposed a bilingual-bicultural education system designed to give children "knowledge of their own culture...to strengthen their ethnic identity, as well as a wide knowledge of our country," to be delivered "in the mother tongue of our respective peoples, in the first years, moving gradually towards a bilingual system" (MISURASATA n.d.: 8). To this end, "national history should be taught beginning with the authentic history of the native cultures, to contribute to the creation of a national consciousness" (MISURASAT n.d.: 14). Finally, MISURASATA proposed that Miskitu be rec-

---

1  MISURASATA was a Miskitu-dominated organization which represented the Sumu and Rama only nominally and eventually turned against the Sumu (von Houwald, 2003: 553, n.2). See also Dunbar Ortiz (1984: 268, n. 195) on Miskitu dominance of the pre-revolutionary organization ALPROMISU, from which MISURASATA was formed.

ognized as the second official national language with Spanish, and Miskitu and Sumu as co-official regional languages.[1] Then "the native (and so national) languages should be taught within the national education system... to promote *a genuine integration*" (MISURASATA n.d.: 14, my emphasis).

What is envisaged here is not a unidirectional education to assimilate minorities to the dominant culture, but a nation-wide "bilingual-bicultural" education system based on mutual cultural exchange to achieve "*genuine* integration."[2] Language also appears under the third heading, "Culture," broadly defined as the right "to be, to live according to our customs" as well as "to preserve and promote *our cultures, languages and traditions*" (MISURASATA n.d.: 14, my emphasis). This includes, under the heading "Organization," the first (albeit indirect) claim to political autonomy: the right "*to organize and rule themselves* according to their *cultural, social, economic and political* necessities, without restriction to our rights of citizenship" within their own territories (MISURASATA n.d.: 14, my emphasis). In this manifesto, then, language is integral to culture but not its primary manifestation.

MISURASATA's manifesto set the tone of early negotiations, and theoretically spoke for all the indigenous groups. However, the Mayangna, ever wary of Miskitu control, had their own organization, SUKAWALA, founded in 1974 (Jenkins Molieri 1986: 254), which initially became a sub-division of MISURASATA.[3] In 1980, SUKAWALA presented to government officials and MISURASATA leaders some quite modest demands more in keeping with Sandinista thinking. Mayangna priorities were "to plan goals...for the development of our communities in accordance with the principles of the Sandinista Revolution" and for "communal titles to the lands they currently occupy" (*Barricada* 14 and 15 March 1980, quoted von Houwald 2003: 571).

---

1 "Official" status is a slippery term; it generally indicates that a language is to be used in all key public contexts.

2 Indeed, the *General Directions* explicitly rejects "the 'progressivist' *indigenista* (paternalist) concept of integration" as well as the tendency of "a certain dogmatic Marxism" to conflate ethnicity with class (MISURASATA 1980:13).

3 SUKAWALA stands for *Sumu Kalpanka Wahaine Lani/Asociación Nacional de Comunidades Sumus* (ANCS: National Association of Sumu Communities). The organization initially operated under the aegis of MISURASATA, though Sumu who tried to work in this way fairly quickly withdrew. In 1981, SUKAWALA distanced itself from the Miskitu-Sandinista conflict and escaped proscription (von Houwald 2003: 622-3). It continued to operate among Mayangna-Sumu in exile, survived to lead the autonomy process from 1984 (von Houwald 2003: 622-3), and is still in existence.

On language, they wanted "literacy to be carried out in the Sumu mother tongue" (ANCS 1980: Section 1-A-2), as well as in Spanish "to take [learners] to third grade of primary in coordination with the government's national adult literacy plan" (ANCS 1980: Section 1-A-2). However, they had to defend this claim against MISURASATA arguments that indigenous literacy be carried out in Miskitu (Jenkins Molieri 1986: 254, von Houwald 2003:570), arguments clearly aimed at defending Miskitu's privileged position.

The Creoles had yet other expectations of the revolution, focused not on land but on the recovery of "their long-held racially and culturally based demands" (Gordon 1998: 203), indispensable to which was the restoration of the English-based education denied them since the Reincorporation (Guillermo McLean, personal communication, 1994). This aim, however, conflicted with the need expressed by Minister of Education Tünnerman "to rid education of all it contains of foreign intervention" (Tünnerman 1980).[1]

Practical Responses

Almost immediately, the Ministry of Culture began cultivating the symbolic aspects of Coast cultures with an assiduity that Dunbar Ortiz found "somewhat baffling, considering the extreme poverty and crisis conditions" (Dunbar Ortiz 1984: 243), always within their framework of economic and political integration. Throughout the 1980s it "subsidized the establishment of crafts and folklore co-operatives in the indigenous communities, and acted as a market for their production. Within a year, musical and dance groups had formed and were taken to events throughout Nicaragua and abroad, under the aegis of the ministry" (Dunbar Ortiz 1984: 243).

Yet simultaneously, and despite MISURASATA demands for a campaign in Coast languages, the Ministry of Education (MED) was planning a National Literacy Crusade in Spanish only, (*Poder Sandinista* December 6, 1979, in Ohland and Schneider 1983: 47). Since its central goal was to "*contribute to national unity, integrating* the country with the city, the worker

---

1  As Gordon's subtle analysis shows (1998: Chapter 7) Sandinistas and commentators tended to view the Creoles as a "monomorphic" group and thus to miss the "ambiguous, multiple, and contradictory character of Creole political commonsense and its generative relationship to Creole politics and identity" (Gordon 1989: 205). Hence, at this stage, when in fact Creoles were well-disposed to the revolution, their demands and responses were interpreted as reactionary and pro-US.

with the student, *the Atlantic with the rest of the country*," in the Sandinista logic the national language was the natural choice (CNA/MED 1980: 3, my emphasis). Indeed, for certain mestizo sectors, "the constant presence of English-speaking imperialism ha[d] effectively turned Spanish into an anti-imperialist banner" (Norwood 1985). After three months of dialogue and a MISURASATA-organized boycott of the Literacy Crusade in Spanish, the government agreed to add mother-tongue campaigns in Miskitu, Sumu and English (Rediske & Schneider 1983: 14; Hale 1987: 108; Vilas 1989: 123; Hale 1994: 134). Inevitably, this apparent reluctance to respect Coast languages created distrust.[1]

By June, 1980, Miskitu materials were being piloted on the coast, followed by English materials in July (MED 1980: 73; Dennis 1981: 286). By the end of August 1980, materials evaluation and *brigadista* training were complete (MED 1980), and September 1980 saw literacy campaigns launched in Miskitu, Sumu and English, six months after the National Crusade opened and a month after it closed in August (Rediske and Schneider, 1983: 14).[2]

The Sandinistas now broadened their governing idea of national unity to include "the *linguistico-cultural identity* of the ethnic groups" (MED 1981: H-I, my emphasis). The political content of the mother-tongue literacy materials was to be translated from the Spanish *cartillas* (teaching manuals) into Miskitu, Sumu and English, with some local adaptations. In order "to obtain a direct participation of the Costeño element" and ostensibly to "guarantee that the materials ... *reflect, as well as national reality, that of the Coast, responding* in this way *to the real needs of the region*" (MED, 1981: H-2, my emphasis), they were developed by technical teams drawn from the three language groups. This approach enabled a rapid response to Coast demands. But in

---

1 Later, bidding for influence among the Miskitu, Brooklyn Rivera would claim the campaign as an early "victory" against the Sandinistas (Brooklyn Rivera, letter from exile in Honduras, 1981, in Ohland and Schneider 1983: 203), whilst the Sandinista press retrospectively presented the MISURASATA boycott as "counter-revolutionary" (*Barricada* 28 February 1981, in Ohland and Schneider 1983: 112-13).

2 The literature is confusing on the timing of these developments. MISURASATA's *General Directions* is undated. Ohland and Schneider date it 1982 in their introduction to the text (Ohland and Schneider 1983), but 1980 in their bibliography. I received my copy from a member of the English literacy team in early May 1980, whilst working on the methodology of the English teaching manual. So Vilas's (1989: 123) dating of the agreement on "mother-tongue" literacy to August 1980 is incorrect. According to Guillermo McLean, responsible for overall coordination of the campaign in the region: "The phases of planning, materials preparation, piloting and implementation of this campaign ran from April 1980 to January 1981" (McLean 2008: 37).

basing the literacy manuals on translation and adaptation rather than on Coast realities, the Sandinistas limited "direct participation" and "reflecting Coast reality" to simple mediation of mainstream concepts through Coast languages (Freeland 1999).[1]

Nevertheless, despite these limitations, the campaigns marked important though very different gains for all three groups. As the first books in Sumu, written by and for the Mayangna themselves, the literacy manuals to develop Sumu as a written language; for this the development team found it useful to have a model to translate.[2] Susan Norwood, a linguist working with the Sumu-Mayangna at the time, also felt the campaign was fundamental to Sumu-Mayangna participation in the later development and ratification of the autonomy statute (author's interview, Bilwi, 1987).

For the Creoles, the campaign began the restoration of the English-based education to which they felt entitled, the foundation of their former cultural leadership (Guillermo McLean, personal communication, 1994). By popular demand and in line with the Moravian educational tradition, it was taught in Standard English rather than Creole; people mainly wanted to learn to read and write "good" and were quite reluctant to engage with the politics (Searle 1984: 62).[3]

In stark contrast, the Miskitu turned their campaign into a powerful political vehicle for their ethnonationalist project (see chapter 4 of this volume and Hale 1994: 179-81). As Hale observes (1994: 264 n.46): "Here and elsewhere, the parallel between the FSLN's and MISURASATA's organizing strategies is striking," except for its pro-indigenous political orientation. As one former Miskitu *brigadista* and guerrilla fighter put it: "We put literacy within the framework of the indigenous struggle, and our main objective was to deepen the sense of indigenous autonomy" (Uriel Vanegas, interviewed in Carcache, 1988: 16-17). Indeed, MISURASATA's *Plan of Action 1981* reports high rates of desertion among literacy teachers and from the base (MISURASATA 1981: 93), suggesting that perhaps literacy skills were less important than the political campaign.

Concurrently with these developments, a draft law on Education in Indigenous Languages on the Atlantic Coast (Decree 571) was brought to

---

1  Freeland (1999) discusses in some detail the negotiation of these adaptations by the Creole team and the problems it occasioned.
2  Members of Sumu technical team, author's interview.
3  For a more detailed analysis of the Creole campaign, including issues around translating the manuals, see Freeland (1999, 2004).

the Council of State in July 1980 and passed in December. This effectively codified the principles of the *Literacy Project in Languages*, offering a purely linguistic opening towards diversity. So whilst its preamble acknowledged the importance of "mother-tongue teaching...in giving a sense of identity both to individuals and peoples," it firmly declared its purpose to further the "process of *integration and consolidation of National Unity*" (Preamble V, JRGN 1980: 81). Indeed, the words "integrate/integration" occur four times in this Preamble.

This law, an interesting mixture of *indigenismo*, ambivalence towards Costeño cultures, and regard for international human rights legislation, followed the classic Latin American pattern of "transitional" bilingual education, using indigenous languages to facilitate entry into Spanish mainstream education. There would be mother-tongue teaching in Miskitu and English from pre-school to 4th grade of primary, with Spanish introduced gradually to become the sole medium of instruction from 5th grade. Sumu and Rama were excluded because they lacked written grammars (Preamble VII, JGRN 1980: 82) and Garífuna was not mentioned. However, it did provide for the MED and the Nicaraguan Institute of the Atlantic Coast (INNICA) to "study the feasibility of providing an education in the respective indigenous languages in the future" (JRGN 1980: 82-3); in fact, work on developing writing systems for Rama and Garífuna had already begun (Dunbar Ortiz 1984: 243).

Although called "bilingual-bicultural," the model was entirely language-centered. Like the literacy project, it would use Coast languages to deliver the mainstream curriculum with mainstream methods, through "*translation* of the texts and outlines of the education programme*" (Preamble VII, my emphasis) rather than giving children "knowledge of their own culture" alongside "wide knowledge of our country" (MISURASATA 1980: 8). It therefore fell far short of MISURASATA's vision of a full national bilingual-bicultural system promoting two-way linguistic and cultural exchange.

Transitional bilingual programs of this kind can improve the early education of minority language speakers, but by easing children into the mainstream system they push them towards the dominant language and reinforce the linguistic hierarchy; minority languages are confined to the early, "homely" stages of education whilst Spanish remains the language of academia and high culture. To "preserve and develop" endangered languages as the law's preamble proposes requires "maintenance programs" that use minority languages throughout the system, enabling children to continue developing intellectually in their own languages as well as Spanish, and expanding languages accordingly into new domains (Baker 2001, Skutnabb-Kangas 1984: 125-35). Nevertheless, the law's limitations were very much of their time: the current international standards for minorities went no further and most not so far (see de Varennes 1996, 1997; Skutnabb-Kangas & Phillipson, 1995; Skutnabb-Kangas 2000, May 2001).

The law was to be implemented "gradually and in accordance with [the MED's] capabilities' (Art. 2), beginning in the academic year 1981-2. However, events at the closing ceremonies of the Miskitu literacy project dramatically escalated Miskitu-Sandinista conflict, leading directly to its militarization and the outbreak of war (see chapter 4 of this volume). The defense of national integrity and sovereignty inevitably took precedence over the pursuit of diversity and there was no further action on bilingual education until the beginnings of the autonomy process.

Language Rights in the Autonomy Process

As the Sandinistas began seeking a political solution to ethnic conflict, language rights again came to the fore. Hazel Lau, former organizer of the Miskitu literacy campaign, re-opened the question of minority languages in light of government statistics on educational failure on the Coast. In an article for a UNESCO journal, she identifies bilingual education as one among many "authentic progressive claims" possible only through the revolution, and quietly insists on making bilingual education more culturally appropriate since to impose "the norms of the dominant society...leads to clashes, inconformity and inefficiency, even when the content of the program, in political terms, is clearly liberating, as in Nicaragua" (Lau 1983: 192-96).

In 1984, bilingual programs were piloted in four Miskitu communities of the controversial Tasba Pri relocation settlements and extended in 1985 to six Creole-speaking and one Mayanga community. By 1986, the MED had assumed responsibility for the bilingual education programs, now known as the PEBI (Bilingual Intercultural Education Programs), creating a special department with technical teams of experienced Miskitu, Kriol and Sumu native-speaker teachers in Bilwi, Bluefields and Rosita respectively, led by a "central team" in Managua of mestizo teachers experienced in curriculum development but with no knowledge of the languages (Gurdián and Salamanca 1990: 361-2).

By 1987, this department was developing a new "bilingual-*intercultural*" education model:[1]

> [It will be] *bilingual*, in that it proceeds from a child's growing competence in her/his mother tongue towards gradual insertion into the National Programme; *intercultural*, because [it] recovers, develops and strengthens each ethnia's own culture, whilst fostering the acquisition of *elements of* national and universal culture; *participatory*, because the researchers, designers, methodologists and teachers are members of the ethnias; and *popular*, because it places learners at the centre of action (MED 1989c: 6-7, quoted in Amadio 1989: 74).[2]

This plan comes closer to the ideal of two-way cultural exchange propounded by MISURASATA and reiterated by Hazel Lau.

Important articles in the Constitution (Arts 11 and 90) and the autonomy law include the principles of the MED's new policy: they override all 1980 provisos about the state of development of different languages, extending to all the "inhabitants of the Atlantic Coast Communities" the right to "education in their mother tongue and in Spanish," through programs that "include their historical heritage, their value system, and the traditions and characteristics of their environment, all in accordance with the national education system" (Art. 11. 4).[3] In addition, Art. 8.2 at least in principle envisages increased regional control over the education "in coordination with the corresponding State Ministries."

Finally, Article 7 gives equal, official status to all "the languages of the Communities of the Atlantic Coast...within the Autonomous Regions." This provision responded to fears expressed early in the autonomy consultation, as claims resurfaced for Miskitu to become the second official language of the region. A poll taken in Bilwi by the independent Centre for Atlantic Coast Documentation and Research (CIDCA) produced interestingly inconclusive results: although expressing positive identification with their

---

1  See Hornberger (2000: 178-99) on the emergence and definition of the term *intercultural* as an alternative to *bicultural* from a 1980 meeting of indigenists in Patzcuaro. However, as she points out, true dialogue cannot be achieved where power remains asymmetrical (see also Aikman 1997).

2  I acquired an internal MED version of this document from the Managua development team, shortly after the ratification of the draft autonomy statute in 1987.

3  Quotations from ODACAN 1994, the official English version of the autonomy law, also published in Miskitu, Sumu and Spanish, by the Swedish-financed Office for the Development of the Autonomy of the Atlantic Coast of Nicaragua).

own languages, many voted also for languages they thought generally useful rather than their own, notably Miskitu and English, voting "within a multilingual context where...the vision of society and of the future is expressed in multilingual terms" (Norwood 1985). By giving them all equal status, the autonomy law sought to prevent the exclusion of the smaller languages.

Most importantly, these language rights are not recognized in isolation, but are supported by extensive economic (Arts. 9, 11.6), political (Art. 7) and organizational rights (Art. 4) which indicate the sea change produced in the Sandinista conception of culture through the autonomy process. This included acknowledging the fluidity of ethnic identity by investing rights in individuals as members of ethnic groups rather than in territories, and according all members of the communities of the Atlantic Coast" the right to "define and decide their own identity" (Art. 12).[1]

For the Sandinistas, the autonomy law was "a point of departure, not of arrival" (Ortega Hegg 1997: 104), a permissive framework whose development they would continue through the process of *reglamentación*,[2] working with and strengthening the projected Autonomous Regional Councils (ARCs). Of course, we can only speculate how this might have worked out. When the Sandinistas lost power in the 1990 elections it fell instead to a succession of neo-liberal governments wedded to the traditional model of the centralized, homogenized nation-state, who viewed autonomy as a Sandinista aberration and a threat to national unity, procrastinated over the *reglamentación* (completed only in 2003), and passed legislation which effectively undermined key principles of the autonomy law (see chapter 5 of this volume).

The change of government had an immediate impact on the PEBI. Like the Sandinistas before them, the Chamorro government began a root and branch ideological reform of education by withdrawing all Sandinista school texts including the hard-achieved PEBI materials, which by this time

---

1  As López notes (2008: 62, n.1), the dominant mestizo groups of Latin America have more commonly denied the right of ethnic self-ascription to indigenous or ethnic individuals with mixed blood, "in order to stress the so-called advantages of racial mixing or *mestizaje*," a central pillar of Latin American nationalisms.

2  In Nicaragua, especially in relation to laws entailing radical change, a permissive decree is passed, whose principles are then elaborated in detailed legislation or *reglamentación*. *Reglamentación* can, of course, be delayed and is not usually subject to consultation. The Sandinistas had already begun this process; until the electoral law could be modified to include election of ARCs they worked with groups constituted by the Peace and Autonomy Commissions that had led the autonomy process.

had developed up to 5th grade in English, 4th grade in Miskitu, and 3rd grade in Sumu (Amadio 1989: 77).

Early reading texts, which were increasingly based on material from the oral traditions, were now to be replaced with translations of the new national reader, *Azul y Blanco*, itself adapted to Nicaragua from a USAID-sponsored text used in much of Central America. Indeed, the Miskitu were offered an existing translation from Honduras in a Miskitu dialect not spoken in Nicaragua that was not even linguistically appropriate (Buvollen 1991). Following a well-coordinated regional and national protest in defense of the PEBI, the government was forced to recognize and support its work. For many Costeños this success made the PEBI the emblem of autonomy in practice (Ortega Hegg 1997; González Pérez 1997: 193; Muñoz Cruz 2001; McLean 2001: 121). Even so, the PEBI's status was reduced from priority program under vice-ministerial control to one among several sub-systems of Basic Education, with concomitant reductions in support of all kinds.

For neo-liberal governments, cultural diversity was no longer a resource but a problem to be dealt with through the limited, assimilative model of bilingual education of the still extant 1980 bilingual education law. Moreover, as successive governments failed to implement the territorial, economic, social and political rights provided by the autonomy law, state language policy again became disarticulated from any broader understanding of cultural diversity, so that the PEBI became the central site for the defense of Costeño language rights. Strengthened by their initial success, Costeño educational leaders continued to use the autonomy law to defend the rights they had gained.

They first pressed for the 1980 law to be revised, and in 1993, despite government reluctance to engage with *reglamentación*, a Law of Official Use of the Community Languages of the Atlantic Coast of Nicaragua (Law 162, 1993) was agreed, though it did not come into force until 1996. In the main, it ratifies and clarifies the autonomy law provisions on language, including the commitment of state resources, but expands them in two important ways. It provides for a "maintenance" model of bilingual education like that developed by the Sandinista MED, which extends "mother-tongue" education to the end of primary school (Art. 7.2c) and into adult education (Art. 7.5), requires "the official languages of the communities" to be "taught in courses in intermediate education" (Art. 7.3c) (though not used as the medium of instruction), and provides for "bilingual-intercultural" teacher training (Art. 7.4).[1] This extension of bilingual teaching, although not yet a full bilingual system, had the potential to reduce the subordination of minority languages. The law also clarifies the definition of official language status by specifying specific contexts of use,[2] and ratifies all the other language provisions of the autonomy law, including the commitment of state resources.

Realizing Language Rights

Nicaragua's language legislation, forged in the dialectic between Costeño and state conceptions of cultural diversity, was now the most advanced in Latin America. The next section shifts focus from this dialectic to the practical implementation of its product over the twenty years since 1990.

A series of evaluations and reports, many written for the several international NGOs who have supported it, offer plentiful information on many of the problems and successes of the PEBI (e.g. Amadio 1989; Buvollen et al. 1992; Freeland and McLean 1994; Rizo Zeledón 1996; Venezia 1996, 2001; Muñoz 2001; McLean Herrera 2001, 2008: 61-66). They note the difficulties of trying to innovate under economic restrictions caused first by war and blockade and then by IMF structural readjustment programs, and of training and supporting poorly educated indigenous teachers with insecure Spanish, when Nicaragua lacked expertise in such relevant disciplines as linguistics, anthropology, and the psycholinguistics of language learning. They also record impressive achievements despite these heavy odds: expanding coverage of the target population, improvements in pupil participation, retention and progression through grades, the production of materials to meet this expansion and their growing cultural appropriacy.

Given their focus, these studies could refer only briefly to other unexpected tensions and paradoxes that arose in the process of adapting the PEBI model to the Coast's sociolinguistic complexities. Once Costeños' right to be educated in their "mother tongues" had been won in principle, it had to be realized for languages and speakers in widely different situations which rarely matched and often conflicted with the underlying assumptions (or language ideology) of the model. Indeed, the PEBI model has

---

1 Quotations from ODACAN (n.d.) official translation into English.
2 These are: in all official and legal documents (Art. 19), signage (Art. 13), contracts (Art. 14), civil registration (Art. 15), the administration of justice (Ch. III), and public administration (Ch. IV).

undergone a series of transformations in a process not unlike that by which language rights themselves were hammered out, as it has tried to meet its declared goals of providing programs rooted in Costeño cultures and values. There were two broad, interrelated sources of tension: the PEBI's emphasis on formal education and literacy, and its conception of "mother tongue" or "community language."

Language Revitalization and Formal Education

Promoting and institutionalizing languages in the powerful domain of education can certainly confer prestige, but it is also beset with complications. As Hornberger says (2000: 174), it means transforming an education system that "has been and continues to be a tool for standardization and national unification into, simultaneously, a vehicle for diversification and emancipation. The paradox is fundamentally an ideological one about roles and possibilities for multiple languages and their speakers within one national society." Indeed, it is present within Article 11.4 of the autonomy law and its various elaborations, which envisage programs that include the minorities' historical heritage, value systems, and traditions, yet require them to be "in accordance with the national education system."

An immediate question then is who will determine this "accordance," since genuinely basing the curriculum in minority values and heritage requires a considerable measure of local control. During the early 1990s, central government values prevailed absolutely; school texts were centrally vetted and cultural content, such as Miskitu traditional stories and the Garífunas' Walagallo healing ceremony, was rejected as "superstitions and witchcraft" (Buvollen 1991; Venezia 1996).[1] So once the languages law was agreed, the struggle began to gain the regional control over education stipulated in the autonomy law (McLean Herrera 2008: 40-47).

From 1995 onwards, taking advantage of small openings afforded by World Bank and IMF decentralization whose purpose was primarily economic, drawing authority from Latin American and Nicaraguan Congresses on Intercultural-Bilingual Education, especially through the newly-established URACCAN, and forming strategic political alliances in the ARCs, an Autonomous Regional Education System (SEAR) was hammered out.

---

1 See also Freeland and McLean Herrera (1994) for other, more logistical effects of centralized control.

The SEAR was incorporated in 2001 into the National Education Plan and in 2003 became an article in the National Education Law. As the following case studies show, it has provided an increasingly flexible context for curricular reform based on discussions involving all national and regional levels of education administration, the ARCs, coordinators of the PEBI programs, Normal School directors, the URACCAN, traditional authorities, parents and school pupils (ibid.).

A major source of tension, particularly among the Mayangna, has been the way the PEBI model links language revitalization so firmly to formal schooling and literacy, which creates an immediate need for some kind of standardized language. Standardization has, in fact, been actively promoted in Latin America for at least thirty years,

> as an instrument to overcome the subaltern condition of the Indig-
> enous languages...[and] to generate among [their] speakers a feeling
> of belonging to a larger linguistic community with a shared common
> heritage: the sense of belonging to a "people" who, thus, transcended
> local affiliation (López 2008: 57-8).

In other words, it applies to indigenous and ethnic minorities those Euro-American methods of fostering national unity through language. However, just like those methods, it entails choices between dialects or varieties of a language, which can reinforce hierarchical relationships and even create new ones. This is vividly illustrated in the different experiences of the Miskitu and the Mayangna.

For the Miskitu, the move towards general literacy has proved relatively straightforward. Although there is no official standard and the different Miskitu dialects do mark sub-group identity differences, Miskitu mobility and the existence of the Miskitu Bible had already produced a degree of dialectal homogeneity or at least mutual intelligibility. So the Miskitu literacy previously restricted to religious practice has expanded relatively easily into the education system, and can even begin to contribute to group unification as the Miskitu work with their Central American cousins to develop a common, transnational writing system.

In contrast, introducing literacy in Sumu has proved divisive. Firstly, the historical developments that gave Miskitu its orthography denied one to Sumu, which began to develop writing only in the 1980 Literacy Project. Sumu is also far less homogeneous than Miskitu. Indeed in Sumu linguistic ideology dialectal variation is positively valued; the two Nicaraguan Sumu dialects, Panamahka and Tuahka are strong markers of sub-group identity.

Since the Mayangna have begun to conceive themselves as a nation only relatively recently, local affiliations predominate. Consequently, both groups resist adopting the other's dialect as the standard or developing some kind of "combination" standard.

They also disagree over the mutual intelligibility of the two dialects: despite considerable linguistic overlap there are significant differences of vocabulary and morphology (Benedicto and Hale 2000). Anyway, mutual intelligibility is not solely a matter of linguistic form; its social significance is at least equally important. My discussions of this question with speakers of both varieties show people who feel their own variety is threatened insist on its differences from and *lack* of intelligibility with the other, and may emphasize them in social interaction, through "acts of identity" (Le Page and Tabouret-Keller).[1]

This defensiveness is particularly marked among the Tuahka, and seems to have grown around the development of literacy. Panamahka-speakers are more numerous, and until recently the "Sumu PEBI" was largely Panamahka-dominated, so that almost by default Panamahka became the textbook language, on economic grounds and on the (Panamahka) assumption that Tuahka-speakers could accommodate with little effort. But this choice created educational chaos, as Tuahka children, often more familiar with Miskitu, were taught by Panamahka-speaking teachers using Panamahka texts. Not surprisingly, some Tuahka feel that their "mother-tongue" is being suppressed and have rallied round it as an icon or emblem of group identity.

Various solutions have been tried so far. According to a member of the technical team for the Literacy Project (1980–81), they initially experimented with "bidialectal" readers offering variants in brackets side by side to avoid privileging either dialect. However, this did not survive into the final version of the readers, which were in Panamahka (interview with Sumu technical team, Bilwi 1987). This approach is similar to that applied in Corsica (Jaffe 1992), where dialect loyalties are similarly strong. Its aim is to avoid competition and allow dialects to converge naturally through contact towards a mutually intelligible form. Nevertheless, the French education

---

1 In "acts of identity," speakers (often unconsciously) converge with or diverge from styles or manners of speech to express their identification with or rejection of an interlocutor or the social group the speaker perceives her/him to represent (Le Page and Tabouret-Keller 1984).

system has proved resistant to such "hybrid" innovations, which violate ide-alized, imagined notions of "our language."[1]

Continuing in this vein, a common Sumu orthography was developed and disseminated in 1999 which allows each group to write in its own vari-ant (Benedicto 2000). With international support, it has been used for a bidialectal collection of Women's Stories for older readers, a First Book for kindergarten children and a children's dictionary, also bi-dialectal, de-veloped and published by Benedicto's Mayangna linguists team. Benedic-to notes the positive effects of this approach "in the interaction between the [Tuahka and Panamahka] members of the working teams [which] is changing attitudes...through knowledge of the cultural reality of the 'other'" (Benedicto 2000: 23).

This case reveals how, in linking language revitalization so firmly to for-mal education and literacy, the PEBI model overlooks and indeed underval-ues the cultural values and systems of this oral culture, except to use parts of the oral tradition as a source of written texts. This creates tensions that threaten to accelerate rather than prevent language loss, and so defeat one of the PEBI's declared purposes, helps confirm a "Western" language ideology (Dorian 1988) that places written languages at the top of a Darwinian scale of language development, and contributes to the perception, historically in-culcated into the Mayagna, that oral languages are "not proper languages." Here, I emphatically do not mean to argue against the value of literacy for the Mayangna; that would be to continue a historic denial that the Ma-yangna urgently desire to remedy. I do, though, mean to stress that in intro-ducing literacy into an oral culture, space needs to be made to allow groups to manage it according to their own linguistic ideologies.[2] In the Mayangna case, some such management has been facilitated latterly by the existence of the SEAR, but would have been impossible without external assistance.

---

1  As Pratt (1987: 49) shows, the languages that supposedly unify imagined commu-nities are themselves equally "imagined," as singular and homogeneous. Usually, it is such imagined languages that form the basis of language rights claims, partly because if subaltern groups are to be heard, they must perforce use the dominant, nationalistic discourse, and also because it is partly internalised into their own discourses.

2  See López and Jung's (1998) collection exploring how writing is valued in the context of many indigenous and other multilingual contexts, Leap's moving ac-count (1991) of how one North American indigenous group resolved it for them-selves, and Neely and Palmer's (2010) discussion of positive and negative aspects of writing in language renewal.

Multilingualism and Mother-Tongue

The Latin American "intercultural-bilingual model" on which the PEBI is based was developed in "contexts of indigenous monolingualism or of incipient bilingualism, in line with the tradition of transitional bilingual policies" (Hornberger and López 1998: 232): it therefore envisaged *bi*-lingual programs pairing an indigenous "mother-tongue," or "community language," with Spanish. Yet such pairings again assume a clear relationship between an indigenous or ethnic identity and a unified language, a relationship that is increasingly coming into question (May 2001).

Besides, in multilingual "contact zones" like the Coast, the expression "mother-tongue" carries several, sometimes conflicting meanings. Depending on the sociolinguistic history of groups or individuals, it can refer to any one of an array of languages: their first-learned, or best-known, or most-used language, or the language of ethnic identification (Skutnabb-Kangas 1981: 12-34), a usage particularly common among Costeño groups whose language had fallen into disuse. In matrilocal Mayangna and Miskitu communities it also refers to the mother's language, even if the son/daughter does not speak it.[1] For the Mayangna it denotes the variant spoken in their community; Tuahka is the "mother-tongue" of the Tuahka.

This means that the PEBI does not fulfill the perceived language rights of all communities equally. In communities of the "monolingual or incipiently bilingual" type pre-supposed by the model, such as the (Panamahka-speaking) Mayangna communities of the BOSAWAS Reserve and in many rural Miskitu communities, "mother-tongue" covers all the above meanings. Here, the PEBI (saving its difficulties) can satisfy three main language rights: giving children the cognitive advantage of learning in the language they speak; contributing to the revaluation of their culture and history through culturally appropriate teaching; and helping revitalize their language by extending it to prestigious new domains. Unsurprisingly, such communities have registered higher approval of the programs (McLean 2001; Bonilla et al. 2000).[2]

---

1 See Freeland (2003: 246-8) for discussion of these usages, and critiques of essentialist, quasi-racist uses of the term in Rampton (1995: 340-43) and Le Page (1993: 144).

2 It goes without saying that this applies only if life in these communities remains economically viable; that is, if support for language is embedded in the other rights of the autonomy law.

Elsewhere, in communities forced by history to adopt another language, or who are shifting away from their original language, or are bi- or multilingual, the PEBI fulfils only the first of these three rights. So Ulwa children are taught in Miskitu, their first-learned language, and Creole-speaking Rama and Garífuna children in their first-learned "English." The bilingual Miskitu-Creole community of Kakabila is more complex still; people mainly self-identify as Miskitu and consider Miskitu their "proper language" (Jamieson 2002: 4), but most children speak Creole at least until adolescence. Kakabila chose to take the English PEBI which the community considers the best language for literacy (Jamieson 1998: 728). However, since all these communities use learning materials that reflect the "mother-culture" of the language in which they are written rather than of their group, the PEBI functions only as a transitional program in the manner of the 1980 law; it does not assist the recovery or regeneration of their "mother-tongue" (language of ethnic identification) or its culture, but rather pushes them further towards the culture associated with the first-learned language. Many of these communities do in fact practice their original cultures despite adopting another language (Jamieson 2001) or, like Kakabila, base a complex "moral economy" on both cultures (Jamieson 2003).

In the late 1980s, the Ulwa and Rama began to claim their right under the autonomy law to be educated in their "mother-tongues" (original group languages). They were helped to realize this demand by the Massachusetts Institute of Technology (MIT) "Linguists for Nicaragua" working with these groups to document their languages.[1] They encouraged their collaborators to introduce their languages to pre-school and primary children, in oral classes running parallel with the "first language" PEBI, through play, songs and games. Despite promises in the 1993 Languages Law and the *reglamentación* of 2003, state support for this work of the kind provided by the Sandinistas ceased in the 1990s, and has since been coordinated by CIDCA and by the URACCAN's Institute for Research and Promotion of Languages and Cultures (IPILC), according to its original brief (Freeland

---

1  The late Ken Hale and Tom Green worked with the Ulwa, and Colette Grinevald (Craig) with the Rama. On the work of *Linguists for Nicaragua* and other solidarity support, much of which continues, see Rivas Gómez (2004) and the special issue of *Wani* 51, 2007 for the 25th anniversary of CIDCA. It includes documentation of languages and oral traditions, creation of grammars and dictionaries, curriculum and teaching materials development, training in mother-tongue and second-language teaching, and the professionalization of informal teachers.

and McLean 1994: 48-49). By trial and error, latterly made easier in the context of the SEAR, a parallel system is evolving broadly comparable to the "heritage programs" found in other contexts, which run outside or parallel to the formal education system and often (though not always) teach the heritage language as a second language (see e.g. Fishman, 1991, 2001; Aikman, 1996, 1998; May, 1999, Hornberger 2008). Despite its precarious funding and largely through the tenacity of its leading speakers, Ulwa is now taught up to 4th grade of primary school (McLean Herrera 2008: 56), Rama is taught on Rama Cay (Grinevald 2003: 31-35), and Garífuna in Garífuna communities, all in different ways and to different goals. These programs have several advantages: they put more firmly into community hands key decisions as to whether, when and how to bring their "mother tongue" into formal education, enabling a degree of bottom-up development, not available within the PEBI programs, which the SEAR has certainly facilitated. At present, their development depends on international support which can be precarious and discontinuous, though this is mitigated by the coordinating role taken largely by the URACCAN.

The assumptions about "mother-tongue" behind the PEBI model and its emphasis on formal education and literacy have both created particular problems for realizing Creole language rights, for which neither the solutions being tried with the Mayangna nor the "heritage" solution are appropriate.[1] As we noted in the first section of this chapter, the Creoles call their language "English," subsuming in one term both Kriol and Standard (Caribbean) English (SE). In Creole communicative practice, these are not two separate language systems but a continuum of styles ranging from "deep Creole" (rooted in slavery and the contact between several African languages and English) through to SE. Consequently, their conception of "mother-tongue" is even more variable than that of the Mayangna. In this case, though, variation does not mark separate sub-group identities. As Gordon's fine-grained analysis shows (1998: 192-93):

> Creoles historically inhabited three transnational identities simultaneously, with the popularity and salience of each varying historically. [They] can be identified by the names Creoles have called themselves...Creole black diasporic identity is signified by their calling themselves blacks (*negros*),...Creole Anglo diasporic identity...by their calling themselves Creole...and Creole indigenous identity...by their calling themselves Costeños.

---

1  This section is based on Freeland (2004), a detailed analysis of the paradoxes that have attended the Creole PEBI.

Each identity marks a different boundary from, and allows different alliances with, other Coast groups, but all signal difference from the Mestizos, the group the Creoles perceive as most distant and most threatening (Gordon 1998: 194-95). They also form a continuum; identification with different facets becomes more salient over time and/or according to the immediate social context. Creoles express them by moving their speech fluidly along the speech continuum in "acts of identity" (Le Page and Tabouret-Keller 1984).

However, this essentially fluid continuum has been split into two opposed parts by the Creole experience of education. The Moravian Mission schools, like most Anglophone Caribbean schools, taught in Standard English and educated or punished children out of their "bad" Kriol speech. In this way, SE became associated with education, literacy and refinement, and the "Anglo" facet of Creole identity, whilst Kriol remained at best a dialect, at worst "bad English," and unwritten. Yet it remained a key marker of Creole group identity outside school, used orally with verve and relish to perform an oral culture that often subverts the "Anglo" proprieties (Freeland 2004: 110). In the 1970s it became even more strongly associated with the "black" Creole identity, given value and definition in the incipient black-nationalist perspective of the SICC (Gordon 1998: 194, and chapter 6), and among a group of Black Sandinistas university students in Managua.

The Creoles adopted their "indigenous," "Costeño" identity position to claim "mother-tongue" education, but in "English," not Kriol. Yet only the Kriol end of the language continuum was their "mother-tongue" in all the senses we have explored, whereas SE was so only as the language of identification with the "Anglo" strand of the Creole identity. "Mother tongue" education in Kriol might therefore "ghettoize" them and deny them their right to the English-medium education they considered part of their heritage. Hence, in marked contrast to many Caribbean countries, where Creoles aimed to have Kriol recognized as the separate language it is, Nicaraguan Creole identity politics pushed them to insist that Kriol was a dialect of English, of which they were proud, but which was not appropriate for education. Whilst this made perfect sense within the Creole language ideology, from the essentialist, "monomorphic" Sandista conception, which associated clear-cut ethnic identities with equally clear-cut mother-tongues, it looked slippery and contradictory, a denial of Creoles' "true" identity that proved Creole sympathies with US imperialism.

Counter-arguments came from the "black" identity perspective: "to teach standard English would be to impose an alien language and culture... as is happening now with Spanish" (Yih and Slate 1985: 56), whilst both identity-positions shared the view that Kriol language and its culture would be implicitly devalued by education in SE. The terms of this argument forced people to make politicized either/or choices between what were in daily practice aspects of both a speech and an identity continuum (Freeland 2004: 118) which made it difficult to develop a clear role for Kriol in the PEBI. What Creoles really need is a trilingual system that overcomes these false antitheses, strengthening both Kriol and SE and also teaching Spanish.[1] Subsequent developments can be seen as attempts to reach such a system by trial and error, which are still ongoing.

From the outset, Creoles recognized that, as their children's first language, Kriol must enter the classroom. Initially though, it was confined to informal, oral interaction, whilst SE remained the language of literacy. However, it proved difficult to bridge the gap between the two. Teachers educated in Spanish and insecure in their SE tended to "go by the book," "correcting" children's spontaneous writing towards SE and so missing an important stage in developing writing (Hurtubise 1990). Reading texts were based on the rich Kriol story tradition, but rendered anomalously into SE. The effect was to reinforce the dichotomy Kriol=spoken dialect / SE=written language and to continue the shift away from Kriol that "black" Creoles feared.

The PEBI soon began to founder on these reefs. Progress in English reading was slow, in the teachers' opinion because it was not firmly enough grounded in children's first language; but for many parents, this simply proved the traditional view, still firmly propounded by Moravian College teachers, that Kriol was unsuitable for the classroom. Those who had the choice (for instance in Bluefields) moved their children back to Spanish-medium schools, or if they could afford it, sent them to the Moravian College.

During the Sandinista period, the popular cultural institutions promoted by the Ministry of Culture had provided alternative sites for legitimating the "black" Creole language and culture outside the school system. The last of these, Cultural Action for Autonomy, when I visited in 1989, included

---

1  See Morren (2001) on the development of such a system for the Colombian islands of San Andrés, Providencia and Santa Catalina, whose early history is similar to that of the Coast — indeed, they are still the object of territorial dispute between Nicaragua and Colombia.

an oral history project, Afro-Caribbean music, and a poetry group which both performed orally and published in a variety of orthographies, allowing "black" Creole culture to express itself in Kriol, free of the formalities of school and the shadow of SE. Experience in other contexts suggests that some such parallel development may be essential to maintain Kriol's vibrancy.[1] With the withdrawal of this support, the burden of supporting Kriol and SE fell entirely on the PEBI. Not only did its pedagogical problems continue, but the feeling grew that in this context, Kriol and its culture were being suppressed, not only by Spanish, but by SE.

One solution, actively sought since 2002 in the context of the SEAR, has been to develop Kriol as a written language, through a project sponsored jointly by URACCAN and the Finnish government's FOREIBCA program in collaboration with the Belizean Creole Council. Workshops with Creole teachers developed a Kriol orthography modeled on that of Belize that establishes some distance between Kriol and SE without making it too difficult, and a primer (FOREIBCA/IPILC 2003), and a reading primer adapted from a Belizean model, which contains a chart of orthographic symbols and illustrative words, and stories in Kriol written and illustrated by the participants.[2] It was designed to be used in teacher training, to help teachers use both Kriol and SE confidently and appropriately in the classroom.[3]

Nevertheless, this solution carries risks, insofar as it capitulates to the PEBI's underlying tendency to privilege literacy, and to the related idea that writing Kriol will make it a "proper language" — an argument I heard from many Creoles. In particular, Kriol in some quasi-standardized form which has to be "correctly" used could deprive it of its essential flexibility and vibrancy, and undermine its subversive value. If carefully handled, however, writing could be used to encourage both Kriol and its oral culture. The final workshop I attended (Bluefields 2004) was an object lesson in how this might be done. As students worked in Kriol, joyfully telling, writing down,

---

1 See e.g, Searle (1984) on the policy adopted during the Grenadian revolution (1979-83), where Kriol was revalued through official support for calypso artists, while school work recognised a quasi-bilingual situation. Spanish, of course, was not part of this context.

2 The Belizean and Nicaraguan Kriols are quite similar. The Belizean Creole Council is a voluntary body which has worked over the last fifteen years to promote Kriol writing and its use in schools. The issues around writing Kriol are discussed fully in Freeland (2004).

3 This goal is reinforced in URACCAN's *Licenciatura* in Intercultural Bilingual Education, which has workshops on the development of Creole languages and on the differences between Kriol and SE.

comparing and elaborating both stories from modern experience and the oral tradition, discovering its differences from SE, writing became a means to celebrate, strengthen and project oral Kriol.

However, traditionalists and some parents still resist the use of Kriol in the classroom. This resistance will be broken down only gradually and if increased use of Kriol proves successful. For instance, I heard at the 2004 workshop that student teachers empowered by their training in Kriol were beginning to convince their parents of its value.

Conclusions

In the Sandinista revolution, Nicaragua was in the vanguard of states attempting to open up to cultural diversity, providing a beacon for other Latin American minorities. Indeed, the Nicaraguan experience offers a crucible in which to study this difficult process. Moreover, the revolutionary context that gave Costeño minorities unusual power to destabilize also imparted an extra urgency to the process, which speeded up normally slow processes of growth, as stop-camera films accelerate the development of plants. All this applies particularly to the development of language rights, the first rights to be claimed and attended to.

Although the Caribbean Coast region is much less linguistically diverse, this small area contains languages in widely varying states, ranging from near-extinction to relative safety via various degrees of endangerment; some manifest significant internal variation, others are written and almost standardized. Importantly, the Coast's history as a "contact zone" has created intricate relationships between them so that they constitute a highly interconnected "sociolinguistic ecology" (Haugen 2001 [1972]). For language policy to succeed in such areas, then, it must find ways of treating each language according to its place within the ecology (Kaplan and Baldauf 1997: 311-320.

Nicaragua's language rights policy was not initially tailored to such variation, partly because it had hardly been studied, partly because of the terms in which it was conceived. Like most rights-oriented language legislation, Nicaragua's took for granted European-American traditions of nation-building which conceived languages as discrete, unified entities linked to comparably discrete, unified identities (Freeland and Patrick 2004a, 2004b) and sought to treat them equally. Implementing the legislation has therefore necessarily entailed a process not unlike that from which it was first forged, where government legislation and local expectations interacted in theory and practice. As my case studies show, this interaction differed for each language, according to its place in the sociolinguistic ecology, so that each case has forced a re-examination of an aspect of language policy.

So, for instance, all the case studies raise questions as to whether formal schooling can meet the needs of all groups. Both the Mayangna and the Creole cases suggest not, demonstrating the negative effects of over-emphasizing literacy or introducing it too early into oral cultures where internal variation is an important expression of identity, and where proposing a standardized form for literacy may disregard such expressions, create new relations of inequality between different varieties of the same language or exacerbate existing ones. So literacy needs to be developed in close consultation with these communities, respecting the characteristics of their oral traditions, and avoiding the sense that writing will eventually "supersede" or "develop" the oral. Otherwise, as my discussion of the easy insertion of Miskitu "church" literacy into formal schooling suggests, we risk reinforcing the old Western privileging of "written languages" over "oral dialects."

These two cases also illustrate problems associated with the concept of "mother-tongue" that underlies Nicaraguan language rights policy (and many others) which also emerged in relation to the smaller languages not in daily use, or communities whose cultures draw on two languages. To monolingual mestizos, "mother-tongue" necessarily refers to a single language that seems to relate obviously to a single, essentialized identity; to multilingual Costeños, it carries multiple meanings. The disparity can force people to make either/or choices between different aspects of multi-faceted identities.

Efforts to resolve these issues were first initiated outside the education system, through a dual system whereby the Ministry of Culture fostered the recuperation and even regeneration of emblematic mother tongues fallen into disuse, whilst the MED took responsibility for first-language education. This enabled communities like the Ulwa and the Rama to decide for themselves how to develop "mother-tongue" education. This, of course, highlights the unavoidable question of local control at the heart of the autonomy law and its stormy negotiation. On its resolution depends how far Costeños can really "promote and develop" their cultures and languages according to their own values, and how far this must be "in accordance" with those of the state. Indeed, most of the difficulties we have been examining trace back to tensions between these two competing value sets.

It is doubtful whether they could have been resolved without the autonomy law, which especially following the Sandinista defeat became a crucial powerbase in the struggle to continue to wrest control of the region's education from governments reluctant to relinquish it, through the development of the SEAR. Through this system, Costeños are gradually moving their education system towards local community values. Even so, the curriculum still "includes" or "incorporates 'cultural *elements*'" into an education organized along mainstream lines, rather than making indigenous and ethnic cultural *systems* its point of departure. As McLean notes (2008: 48), the pedagogy is still very traditional, taking little account of indigenous and ethnic "knowledge, technology, values, attitudes and behaviors," though there are moves towards making it more open and child-centered. Although the SEAR has created Community Education Councils to encourage stakeholder participation to help make the PEBI more relevant to local needs, they are top-down structures which, even after training, their members find rather obscure (Mayangna Focus group, Rosita September 2007).

Nevertheless, that so much has been achieved against these odds testifies to Costeño tenacity and coherence of vision. People are no longer ashamed to speak their languages. What survived of Ulwa and Rama is being documented under the guidance of international field linguists and so saved from total extinction; indeed documentation is providing the basis for a certain symbolic regeneration. So Rama girls, whose language is still not in daily use, are now keen to learn Rama phrases to flaunt in Bluefields as badges of their different identity (Colette Grinevald, personal communication). Bilwi has become a Miskitu-speaking town, and in the Panamahka-speaking communities of the BOSAWAS Biosphere Reserve, bilingual intercultural education both reinforces Sumu in the community and extends its range into new contexts.

The question remains, though, how much further the PEBI can be stretched to accommodate the trickier cases I have analyzed above before some more radical reform becomes necessary. In Colombia, for instance, indigenous peoples are now demanding "their 'own' education (*educación propia*) as part of the so-called *Plan de vida* (life-plan) established by each community" (López 2008: 52), whilst in Bolivia they critique the colonialism of the EIB model, and under president Evo Morales are designing and implementing an indigenous education system, rather than education for indigenous people. As López points out, they have reached these levels of analysis partly through the experience of applying and developing the very EIB approach they now critique (López 2008: 60). Developments in Nicaragua's PEBI arise from similar critiques; it will be interesting to see where they lead in the future.

## Acknowledgments

I gratefully acknowledge many sources of support for this work: Portsmouth University, UK, for paid research leave; the British Academy for a travel grant (2000) and a Small Research Grant (2005-6); the Proyecto Sahwang (developed by Terranuova (Italy), KEPA (Finland), and IBIS (Denmark) for supporting my teaching on the *Licenciatura* in Intercultural Bilingual Education of the University of the Autonomous Regions of the Caribbean Coast of Nicaragua (URACCAN); SAIH (Norway), for financing the URACCAN Community Diploma in Sociolinguistics for the Revitalization of Mayangna in which I am currently involved; URACCAN's Institute for the Promotion and Investigation of Languages and Cultures (IPILC), its director Guillermo McLean Herrera, and the co-ordinator of IPILC Rosita, Eloy Frank Gómez, for invaluable intellectual and logistical support; and above all Costeño friends, colleagues and students on my courses for their collaboration.

## References

Adams, R. N. (1991) 'Strategies of Ethnic Survival in Central America' in Urban, G. and Sherzer, J.S. (Eds) *Nation States and Indians in Latin America* (Austin, University of Texas Press) pp. 181-206.

Aikman, S. (1996) 'The Globalization of Intercultural Education and an Indigenous Venezuelan Response' in *Compare* Vol. 26, No. 2, pp. 153-65.

Aikman, S. (1998) 'Towards an Intercultural Participatory Approach to Learning for the Harakmbut' in *International Journal for Educational Development*, No. 18, pp. 463-79.

Amadio, M. (1989) 'Progresos en la educación bilingüe en situación de escasez de recursos. Experiencia y perspectiva en Nicaragua' in *Proyecto Principal de Educación en América Latina y el Caribe* Boletín 20, pp. 71-84.

ANCS (1981) *Informe de la tercera asamblea de la Asociación Nacional Comunidades Sumus* unpublished manuscript held by CIDCA, Managua.

Anderson, B (1991) *Imagined Communities: Reflections on the Origin and Spread of Nationalism* ( 2nd edition) (London, Verso).

Baker, C. (2001) *Foundations of Bilingual Education and Bilingualism* (3rd edition) (Clevedon, Multilingual Matters).

Baumann, R. and Briggs, C.L. (2003) *Voices of Modernity: Language Ideologies and the Politics of Inequality* (Cambridge, Cambridge University Press).

Benedicto, E. (2000) 'A Community's Solution to some Literacy Problems, The Mayangna of Nicaragua' in Ostler, N. and Rudes, B. (Eds) *Endangered Languages and Literacy* (Bath, Foundation for Endangered Languages), pp. 19-24.

Benedicto, E. and Hale, K. (2000) 'Mayangna, A Sumu Language, its Variants and its Status within Misumalpan' in Benedicto, E. (Ed) *The University of Massachusetts Occasional Papers, Volume on Indigenous Languages, UMOP* No. 20, pp. 75-106.

Blommaert, J. (1999) *Language Ideological Debates* (Berlin, Mouton de Gruyter).

Bonfil Batalla, G. (1990) 'Aculturación e indigenismo: La respuesta india' in Alcina Franch, J. (Ed), *Indianismo e indigenismo en América* (Madrid, Alianza Editorial), pp. 189-209.

Bonilla, C., Hansack, H. and Williams, W. (2000) *El programa intercultural-bilingüe,* unpublished student essay for the Licenciatura in Intercultural Bilingual Education, URACCAN.

Bourgois, P. (1982) 'The Problematic of Nicaragua's Indigenous Minorities' in Walker, T.W. (Ed) *Nicaragua in Revolution* (New York, Praeger).

Buvollen, H. A. (1991) 'Siakna Bara Pihni' in *Barricada,* 5 June.

Buvollen, H.A., Taylor Gil, V., Ruiz James,V., Castro, D., Escobar Thompson, F., López Sequeira, P., and Pikitle, J. (1992) *Empirismo y educación bilingüe: Un estudio de diez escuelas rurales en la RAAN.* Unpublished report (Puerto Cabezas-Bilwi)

Carcache, D. (1988) 'The Atlantic Coast — Two Leaders' Paths Rejoin' in *Envío Vol.* 7, No. 87, pp. 11-32.

CNA/MED (1980) *Manual del Brigadista* (Managua, Ministerio de Educación de Nicaragua).

Dennis, P.A. (2001) 'The Costeños and the Revolution in Nicaragua' in *Journal of Interamerican Studies and World Affairs* Vol. 23, No. 3, pp. 271-96.

Dennis, P.A. (2004) *The Miskitu People of Awastara* (Austin, University of Texas Press).

Docherty, F. J. (1988) 'Educational Provision for Ethnic Minority Groups in Nicaragua' in *Comparative Education,* Vol.24, No. 2, pp. 193-201.

Dorian, N. (1998) 'Western Language Ideologies and Small-language Prospects' in Grenoble, L.A, and Whaley, L. (Eds) (1998) *Endangered Languages, Current Issues and Future Prospects* (Cambridge, Cambridge University Press), pp. 3-21.

Dunbar Ortiz, R. (1984) *Indians of the Americas: Human Rights and Self-Determination* (London, Zed Books).

Field, M., and Kroskrity, P.V. (2008) 'Introduction: Revealing Native American Language Ideologies' in Kroskrity, P.V. and Field, M. (Eds) *Regimes of Language, Ide-*

*ologies: Politics and Identities* (Santa Fe, New Mexico/Oxford, School of American Research Press), pp. 3-28.

Fishman, J.A. (1972) 'The Ethnic Dimension in Language Planning' in Fishman, J.A. (1989) *Language and Ethnicity in Minority Sociolinguistic Perspective* (Clevedon, Multilingual Matters), pp. 265-367.

Fishman, J.A. (1991) *Reversing Language Shift* (Cleveland, Multilingual Matters).

FOREIBCA/IPILC (2003) *YOU can read and write Kriol* (Managua, FOREIBCA/IPILC).

Freeland, J. (1995) 'Why Go to School to Learn Miskitu? Changing Constructs of Bilingualism, Education and Literacy among the Miskitu of Nicaragua's Atlantic Coast in *International Journal of Educational Development* No. 15, pp. 245-62.

Freeland, J. (1999) 'Can the Grass Roots speak? The Literacy Campaign in English on Nicaragua's Atlantic Coast' in *International Journal of Bilingual Education and Bilingualism* No. 2, pp. 214-32.

Freeland, J. (2003) 'Intercultural-bilingual Education for an Interethnic-plurilingual Society? The Case of Nicaragua's Caribbean Coast' in *Comparative Education* Vol.39, No. 2, pp. 239-60.

Freeland, J. (2004) 'Linguistic Rights and Language Survival in a Creole Space, Dilemmas for Nicaragua's Caribbean Coast Creoles' in Freeland, J. and Patrick, D. *Language Rights and Language Survival, Sociolinguistic and Sociocultural Perspectives* ( Manchester, St Jerome Publishing). (2004a), pp. 103-38.

Freeland, J. and Patrick, D (2004) 'Introduction: Language Rights and Language Survival' in Freeland, J. and Patrick, D. *Language Rights and Language Survival: Sociolinguistic and Sociocultural Perspectives* (Manchester, St Jerome Publishing), pp. 1-34.

Freeland, J. and G. McLean Herrera (1994) *Informe final sobre las necesidades lingüísticas del estudiante de la Costa Caribe de Nicaragua para la elaboración de un currículum de idiomas.* Unpublished report (Managua, URACCAN/FADCANIC).

FSLN (Frente Sandinista de Liberación Nacional) (1969) 'Programa histórico' in Rosset, P. and Vandermeer, J. (Eds) (1983) *The Nicaragua Reader, Documents of a Revolution under Fire* (New York, Grove Press Inc).

González Pérez, M. (1997) *Gobiernos pluriétnicos, La constitucion de regiones autónomas en Nicaragua* (Mexico, URACCAN/Plaza y Valdés S.A).

Gordon, E.T. (1998) *Disparate Diasporas, Identity and Politics in an African-Nicaraguan Community* (Austin, University of Texas Press).

Gould, J.L. (1998) *To Die in This Way, Nicaraguan Indians and the Myth of Mestizaje, 1880-1965* (Durham/London, Duke University Press).

Green, T. (1996) 'Perspectivas demográficas e históricas del idioma y pueblo ulwa' in *Wani* No. 20, pp. 22-38.

Green, T. and. Hale, K (1998) 'Ulwa, the Language of Karawala, Eastern Nicaragua, Its Position and its Prospects in Modern Nicaragua' in *International Journal of the Sociology of Language* No. 132, pp. 185-201.

Grinevald, C. (2003) 'Educación intercultural y multilingüe, El caso de los ramas' in *Wani* No. 34, pp. 20-38.

Gurdián, G. (2001) *Mito y memoria en la construcción de la fisonomía de la comunidad de Alamikangban* unpublished Ph.D dissertation (Austin, University of Texas).

Gurdián, G., and Salamanca, D. (1990) 'Bilingual Education in Nicaragua' in *Prospects* Vol. XX, No. 3, pp. 357-64.

Hale, C. R. (1994) *Resistance and Contradiction, Miskitu Indians and the Nicaraguan State, 1894-1987* (Stanford, Stanford University Press).

Hale, K. and Benedicto, E. (2004) '¿Sumos, mayangnas, tuahka, panamahka, ulwa?' in *Wani* No. 38, pp. 6-24.

Haugen, E. (2001/1972) 'The ecology of language' in Fill, A. and P. Mühlhäusler (Eds) *The Ecolinguistics Reader* (London/New York, Continuum), pp. 57-66.

Hill, J. D. (Ed) (1996) *History, Power and Identity, Ethnogenesis in the Americas, 1492-1992* (Iowa, University of Iowa Press).

Hill, J. H. and Mannheim, B. (1992) 'Language and World View' in *Annual Review of Anthropology*, No. 21, pp. 381-406.

Holm, J. (1978) *The Creole English of Nicaragua's Miskitu Coas: Its Sociolinguistic History and a Comparative Study of its Lexicon and Syntax* Ph.D., University College, London (Ann Arbor, University Microfilms International).

Hornberger, N. H. (2000) 'Bilingual Education Policy and Practice in the Andes, Ideological Paradox and Intercultural Possibility' in *Anthropology and Education Quarterly* Vol.31, No 2, pp. 173-201.

Hornberger, N. H. and L.E. López, (1998) 'Policy, Possibility and Paradox, Indigenous Multilingualism and Education in Peru and Bolivia' in Cenoz, J and F. Genesee (Eds) *Beyond Bilingualism, Multilingualism and Multiculturalism in Education* (Clevedon, UK, Multilingual Matters) pp. 206-42.

Houwald, G. von (2003) *Mayangna: Apuntes sobre la historia de los indígenas sumu en Centroamérica* (Managua, Fundación Vida).

Hurtubise, J. (1990) *Bilingual Education in Nicaragua, Teaching Standard English to Creole Speaker* unpublished dissertation for the Diploma in Education, University of Aukland, New Zealand.

Irvine, J. and Gal, S. (2000) 'Language ideology and linguistic differentiation' in Kroskrity, P.V. (Ed) *Regimes of Language, Ideologies, Politics and Identities* (Sante Fe, School of American Research Press).

Jaffé, A. (1999) *Ideologies in Action, Language politics on Corsica* (Berlin, Mouton de Gruyter).

Jamieson, M. (1998) 'Linguistic Innovation and Relationship Terminology in the Pearl Lagoon Basin of Nicaragua' in *Journal of the Royal Anthropological Institute* No. 4, pp. 713-30.

Jamieson, M. (2001) 'Miskitu, Sumo y Tungla, Variación lingüística e identidad étnica' in *Wani* No. 27, pp. 6-12.

Jamieson, M. (2003) 'Miskitu or Creole? Ethnic Identity and the Moral Eonomy in a Nicaraguan Miskitu Village' in *Journal of the Royal Anthropological Institute* Vol. 9, No. 2, pp. 201-22.

Jenkins Molieri, J. (1986) *El desafío indígena en Nicaragua, el caso de los mískitos* (Managua, Vanguardia).

JRGN/Government of National Reconstruction (1980) *Decree No 571, Law on Education* in Indigenous Languages on the Atlantic Coast in Ohland and Schneider (1983), pp. 79-88.

Kaplan, R. B. and R.B. Baldauf (1977) *Language Planning from Practice to Theory* (Clevedon, Multilingual Matters).

Kroskrity, P. V. (2000) 'Regimenting languages, Language Ideological Perspectives' in Kroskrity, P. V. (Ed) *Regimes of Language, Ideologies, Politics and Identities* (Santa Fe, New Mexico/Oxford, School of American Research Press), pp. 1-34.

Lau, H. (1983) 'Bases metodológicas para la educación bilingüe-bicultural en Nicaragua' in Rodríguez, N.J., Masferrer, E., and Vega, R. V. (Eds) *Educación, Etnias y Descolonización: Una guía para la educación bilingüe-bicultural* (Mexico, UNESCO, Mexico), Vol. I, pp. 191-98.

Leap, W. (1991) 'Pathways and Barriers to Ancestral Language Literacy - Building on the Northern Ute Reservation' in *American Education Quarterly* No. 22, pp. 21-41.

Le Page, R.B. (1993) 'Conflicts of Metaphor in the Discussion of Language and Race' in Håkon Jahr, E. (Ed) *Language Contact and Language Planning* (Berlin/New York, Mouton de Gruyter) pp. 143-64.

Le Page, R.B. and Tabouret-Keller, A. (1985) *Acts of Identity: Creole-based Approaches to Language and Ethnicity* (Cambridge, Cambridge University Press).

López, L. E. (2008) 'Bilingual Intercultural Education in Latin America' in Hornberger, N. H. (Ed) (2008) *Can Schools Save Indigenous Languages? Policy and Practice on Four Continents* (Basingstoke, UK, Palgrave Macmillan), pp. 42-65.

López, L. E., and Jung, I. (Eds) (1998) *Sobre las huellas de la voz, Sociolingüística de la oralidad y la escritura en su relación con la educación* (Madrid/Cochabamba/Bonn, Ediciones Morata, S.L/PROEIB-Andes/DSE).

Mar-Molinero, C. (2000) *The Politics of Language in the Spanish-speaking World, From Colonization to Globalization* (London/New York, Routledge).

May, S. (1999) (Ed) *Indigenous, Community-based Education* (Clevedon, UK, Multilingual Matters).

May, S. (2001) *Language and Minority Rights: Ethnicity, Nationalism and the Politics of Language* (Harlow, Longman/Pearson Education).

McLean Herrera, G. (2001) 'Apreciación del estado del arte de la EIB en la Costa Caribe nicaragüense' in Muñoz Cruz, H. (Ed.). *Un futuro desde la autonomía y la diversidad, Experiencias y voces por la educación en contextos interculturales nicaraguenses* (Xalapa, Mexico, Universidad Veracruzana), pp. 121-34.

McLean Herrera, G. (2008) *La educación intercultural bilingüe: El caso nicaragüense* (Buenos Aires, Fundación Laboratorio de Políticas Públicas, 2008; E-book, Libros FLAPE).

McGroarty, M. E. (2010) 'Language and ideologies' in Hornberger, N.H and McKay, S.L. (Eds) *Sociolinguistics and Language Education* (Bristol/Buffalo/Toronto, Multilingual Matters).

MED/Ministerio de Educación (1980) *Congreso Nacional de Alfabetización, Héroes y Mártires por la Alfabtetización, 5-6 de septiembre 1980. Documentación del Congreso — Informe sobre el Proyecto 'Alfabetización en Lenguas de la Costa Atlántica' al Segundo Congreso Nacional de la Alfabetización* (Managua, MED).

MED/Ministerio de Educación (1981) *Documentos, 2º Congreso Nacional de la Alfabetización, Héroes y Mártires por la Alfabetización, 5-6 septiembre 1980* (Managua, MED).

MISURASATA (n.d [1980]) *Lineamientos Generales* (Managua, MISURASATA).

MISURASATA (1981) 'Plan of Action 1981' in Ohland, K. and R. Schneider (Eds) (1983) *National Revolution and Indigenous Identity, The Conflict between Sandinistas and Miskito Indians on Nicaragua's Atlantic Coast* (Copenhagen, IWGIA), pp. 89-94.

Morren, R.C. (2001) 'Creole-based Trilingual Education in the Caribbean Archipelago of San Andrés, Providencia and Santa Catalina', *Journal of Multilingual and Multicultural Development* Vol. 22, No. 3, pp. 227-41.

Muñoz Cruz, H. (2001) *Un futuro desde la autonomía y la diversidad* (Xalapa, Ver., Mexico, Universidad Veracruzana).

Neely, A.A., and Palmer, G. Jr (2010) 'Which Way is the Kiowa Way? Orthography Choices, Ideologies and Language Renewal' Kroskrity, P.V. and Field, M. (Eds) *Regimes of Language: Ideologies, Politics and Identities* (Santa Fe, New Mexico/ Oxford, School of American Research Press), pp. 271-297.

Norwood, S. (1985) *El multilingualismo y el problema de lenguas oficiales en Puerto Cabezas* unpublished MS held by CIDCA, Managua.

ODACAN (Oficina de Desarrollo de la Autonomía de la Costa Atlántica de Nicaragua) (1994) *Autonomy Statute for the Regions of the Atlantic Coast of Nicaragua* (Managua, ODACAN).

ODACAN (n.d) *Ley de Lenguas. Ley No 162 en Español, Miskitu, Sumu, Inglés* (Managua, ODACAN).

Offen, K. (1999) 'Mapping Indigenous Lands and Defining Autonomy in Northeastern Nicaragua' in Steinberg, M.K. (Ed) *Forests, Fields, and Fish, Politicized Indigenous Landscapes* (Austin, University of Texas Press).

Ohland, K. and R. Schneider (Eds) (1983) *National Revolution and Indigenous Identity, The Conflict between Sandinistas and Miskito Indians on Nicaragua's Atlantic Coast* (Copenhagen, IWGIA).

Ortega Hegg, M. (1997) 'El régimen de autonomía en Nicaragua: contradicciones históricas y debates recientes' in *Alternidades* No. 7, pp. 99-105.

PNUD (Programa de Naciones Unidas para el Desarollo) (2005) *¿Nicaragua asume su diversidad? Informe de Desarrollo Humano 2005. Las Regiones Autónomas de la Costa Caribe* (Managua, PNUD).

Pratt, M.L. (1987) 'Linguistic utopias' in Fabb, N., Attridge, D., Durant, A. and McCabe, C. (Eds) *The Linguistics of Writing, Arguments between Language and Literature* (Manchester, Manchester University Press), pp. 48-65.

Pratt, M. L. (1992) *Imperial Eyes. Travel Writing and Transculturation* (London/New York, Routledge).

Rampton, M.B.H (1995) *Crossing, Language and Ethnicity among Adolescents* (Harlow Essex, Longman)

Rediske, M. and R. Schneider (1983) 'Preface, National Revolution and Indigenous Identity. The Conflict between the Sandinist Government and the Mískito Indians 1979 to 1982', in Ohland, K. and R. Schneider (Eds) (1983) *National Revolution and Indigenous Identity, The Conflict between Sandinistas and Miskito Indians on Nicaragua's Atlantic Coast* (Copenhagen, IWGIA), pp. 3-27.

Rivas Gómez, A. (2004) 'El grupo "Lingüistas por Nicaragua" (Entrevista al Dr. Kenneth Hale)' in *Wani* No. 38, pp. 25-33.

Rizo Zeledón, M. (1996) 'Interculturalidad bilingüe en Nicaragua', in *Wani* No.18, pp. 36-44.

Romero Vargas, G. (1995) *Las sociedades del Atlántico de Nicaragua en los siglos XVII y XVIII* (Managua, Fondo de Promoción Cultural, BANIC).

Schieffelin, B., Woolard, K., and Kroskrity, P.V. (Eds) (1998) *Language Ideologies, Practice and Theory* (New York/Oxford, Oxford University Press).

Searle, C. (1984) *Words Unchained, Language and Revolution in Grenada* (London, Zed Books).

Shapiro, M. (1987) 'Bilingual-Bicultural Education in Nicaragua's Atlantic Coast Region' in *Latin American Perspectives* Vol. 14, No. 1, pp. 67-86.

Skutnabb-Kangas, T. (1981) *Bilingualism or Not: The Education of Minorities* (Clevedon, Avon, Multilingual Matters).

Skutnabb-Kangas, T. (2000) *Linguistic Genocide in Education — or Worldwide Diversity and Human Rights?* (Mahwah, NJ, Lawrence Erlbaum).

Skutnabb-Kangas, T. and Phillipson, R. (Eds, 1995) *Linguistic Human Rights, Overcoming Linguistic Discrimination* (Berlin, Mouton de Gruyter).

Street, B.V. (1993) 'Culture is a verb' in Graddol, D.L., Thompson, L. and Byram, M. (Eds) *Language and Culture* (Clevedon, Avon, BAAL/Multilingual Matters) pp. 23-43.

Thornberry, P. (1991) *Minorities and Human Rights Law* (London, Minority Rights Group).

Tunnerman, C. (1980) 'La nueva educación en el plano nacional' in *Encuentro* No. 15, p. 125-143

Varennes, F. de (1996) *Language, Minorities and Human Rights* (The Hague/Boston/London, Martinus Nijhoff Publishers).

Varennes, F. de (1997) *To Speak or not to Speak: The Rights of Persons Belonging to Linguistic Minorities, Working Paper Prepared for the UN Sub-committee on the Rights of Minorities* http,//www.unesco.org/most/ln2pol3.htm

Venezia Mauceri, P. (1996) '"Didn't you say you were not going to dig us until we were all fit?": El reto de la educación intercultural en Nicaragua', in *Wani* No. 19, pp. 3-12.

Venecia Mauceri, P. (2001) 'Los pueblos de la Costa Caribe nicaragüense y su educación, las lecciones que aprendimos' in Muñoz Cruz, H. (Ed.). *Un futuro desde la autonomía y la diversidad, Experiencias y voces por la educación en contextos interculturales nicaraguenses* (Xalapa, Mexico, Universidad Veracruzana) (Ed), pp. 135-48.

Vilas, C. M. (1989) *State, Class and Ethnicity in Nicaragua: Capitalist Modernization and Revolutionary Change on the Atlantic Coast* (Boulder, CO/London, Lynne Rienner Publishers).

Yih, K., and Slate, A. (1985) 'Bilingualism on the Atlantic Coast: Where Did it Come from and Where is it Going?' in *Wani* Nos. 2-3, pp. 23-6 and 55-56.

# CHAPTER 9. TERRITORIAL DEMARCATION AND INDIGENOUS RIGHTS IN EASTERN NICARAGUA: THE CASE OF KAKABILA

*Mark Jamieson*

The passing of the autonomy statute in 1987 ushered in a period of peace to Nicaragua's Caribbean Coast which, following the seven-year old conflict known as the Contra War, promised the Miskitu, Creoles and other minority peoples rights to lands, language, bilingual education, political participation, and control over the exploitation of resources within a new political framework defined by that statute (Gurdián 1987). This recognition of the rights of "indigenous" (including Afro-descendent) peoples was welcomed, and did much to bring these previously marginalized peoples, for whom Spanish-speakers and their institutions were regarded as distinctly Other, into the ambit of the Nicaraguan nation-state, which now came to challenge properly the previously rarely contested myth of the country's universal mestizaje (Gould 1998). In the years and decades that followed the autonomy law and the post-conflict peace that accompanied it, the indigenous and Afro-descendent communities of the region have received government-administered bilingual education programs, encouragement to engage in political processes, official recognition of indigenous languages and culture, and in 2003, with the Indigenous Land Demarcation

Law, reinforcement of indigenous claims to lands and territories (Gobierno de la República de Nicaragua 2005).

This project of bringing Nicaragua's minority peoples into the nation-state, while successful in some respects, most notably in education, has in other regards been less so, as well-intentioned laws aimed at involving these groups within projects to make them better "citizens," have floundered for various reasons at the local level. Disappointments of this kind have meant that the sense of marginalization experienced by indigenous peoples has in fact been intensified rather than reduced, as they witness one "failure" after the next in spite of these attempts to engage them.

Consequences of these perceived failures have included for some loss of faith in the rule of law (which they see at best as powerless to defend their legitimate interests), increasing dependence in some communities on the cocaine economy, rather than on programs of governmental and non-governmental development aid (Dennis 2003), and, for a few, willingness to engage in renewed hostilities with the police and army.

The Loss and Defense of Indigenous Lands

Most of Nicaragua's people identify themselves as mestizo, a group generally considered the descendents of Europeans and "acculturated" Indians. Eastern Nicaragua, however, particularly the Caribbean coastline and the Rio Coco, is home to a number of minority populations composed of speakers of other languages. These include groups of predominantly Amerindian descent: the Miskitu, Mayangna, Ulwa and Rama — and others of mixed, mainly African descent — the Creoles and Garífuna — whose ancestors arrived in the region as slaves, as independent farmers and fishermen, and as workers for the region's logging camps and banana plantations. Today many members of these groups work the land sustainably using various systems of rotational swidden farming. Some are also fishermen catching scale fish, shrimp and lobster that are sold to commercial buyers for cash. Most regard the land and waters that they exploit as the inalienable property of indigenous communities. Neither land nor waters may be sold in the absolute sense, though rights of usufruct to small parcels may be sold on the understanding that rights of usage will return to the community if they are abandoned. In most such communities the commercial exploitation of resources by members is either prohibited or frowned upon.[1]

Until the 1950s eastern Nicaragua had few Spanish-speaking residents. However, government programs in the 1950s and 1960s, designed to rationalize export agriculture in western parts of the country, set in motion an exodus of poor, landless farmers and their families that continues into the present (Jones 1988, Vilas 1989: 60-95, Everingham 2001: 62). These campesinos have sought new, apparently empty lands further east in the forests and savannas hitherto used exclusively by indigenous peoples. Once they have cleared and farmed these lands for a year or so, often to the point of soil exhaustion, many campesinos create *potreros* (cattle grazing lands) by sowing grass on the land. They then sell on these grasslands to ranchers who follow them into the region, moving further eastwards into the forest where they clear more land and repeat this process, turning more of the forest into saleable pastures (Riverstone 2004: 59-62).

Indigenous farmers, who often live far from their farms, are frequently pushed off their lands by aggressive mestizo intruders arriving in what they perceive to be underused lands in increasingly large numbers, a process well described by Riverstone (2004) for the Rama and Creoles living south of Bluefields. These campesinos often take out provisional titles from government agencies to the lands they occupy, with which they are able to intimidate indigenous peoples (many of whom lack formal title to those lands). In some instances these arrivals are prepared to offer violence to indigenous peoples (Riverstone 2004: 71-74).[2] This advance eastwards into the Caribbean watershed by thousands of these campesinos currently represents probably the greatest threat to the territorial integrity of most of eastern Nicaragua's indigenous communities (Riverstone 2004: 59-62, Hayes 2007: 737).

Commercial exploitation of the resource bases of indigenous communities by companies operating with concessions granted by government agencies and municipal authorities, offer further threats to the lands of indigenous peoples (Riverstone 2004: 69-71). These concessions constitute frequently illegal violations of the autonomy statute of 1987, which states

---

1  See Gurdián el al. (2006) and Goett (2007) for historical background of the struggle for recognition of indigenous land rights.

2  Broegaard (2003) contains discussion of the role of violence and threats in relation to property rights and transactions in other parts of the country. See also Stansfield (1995: 3-4).

that resources in the North and South Atlantic Autonomous Zones (the RAAS and the RAAN) cannot be expropriated without the consent of local communities (Gurdián 1987: 184). In a few instances the autonomy law has been enforced, most spectacularly in the case of the Mayangna community of Awas Tingni, which successfully took the Korean logging company SOLCARSA to the Inter-American Court of Human Rights in 2000 (Wiggins 2006). More often, however, indigenous communities are too poor and under-resourced to be able to take on these companies.

Land speculators have also caused indigenous communities problems. The sale and purchase of dubious titles to lands continues to worry the inhabitants of many such communities (Acosta 2006a). This is most spectacularly the case for the mixed Creole and Rama community of Monkey Point where, planners hope, the Dry Canal Mega Project, a proposed railway linking Nicaragua's two coasts, will eventually compete with the Panama Canal for control of freight across the Central American isthmus. The potential importance of this link has created a thriving market for titles of dubious constitutional validity to lands in this area which most of the Creole and Rama inhabitants regard as inalienable (Riverstone 2004: 62-66; Acosta 2006b).[1]

## Land Titles in Eastern Nicaragua

Land titles in eastern Nicaragua are of a number of kinds, and in many instances titles with different histories make competing claims to particular tracts. From the perspective of most indigenous communities the most valid have been those that were granted inalienably to communities (and not individuals) in the years following the Harrison-Altamirano Treaty of 1905 between Nicaragua and the United Kingdom, by the Land Titles Commission set up in 1915 to dispense titles to these indigenous communities (Hale 2006: 21-28; Goett 2007: 209-211). It is these titles that for many of these communities including Kakabila form the basis of claims made following Law 445.[2]

Competing with these in many places, are individually owned titles of varying provenances that were granted before the present-day Nicaraguan

---

1 See Goett (2007) for historical background of the land struggle in Monkey Point.
2 The full name is Law for the Communal Property Regime of the Indigenous Peoples and Ethnic Communities of the Autonomous Regions of the Atlantic Coast of Nicaragua and the Bocay, Coco, Indio and Maiz Rivers.

constitution of 1987 (Acosta 2006a: 115-117, Hale 2006, Howard 2006a). Many of these were issued in the years of the Somoza dictatorship, but a few are older and reportedly bear the signatures of Miskitu kings (Hale 2006 19-21). Members of indigenous communities often regard such titles as respectable (Offen 2003), and some even possess titles of this kind to lands immediately outside those of their own communities. In many cases, however, the claims of titles of this kind compete sharply with those made by indigenous communities (Acosta 2006a).

Also competing with these communal titles are those that were issued during the Sandinista administration and the period immediately afterwards. In the years following the revolution of 1979, the assets of some landowners, some of which were lands claimed by indigenous communities, were seized and redistributed. In the post-Sandinista period, however, some of these redistributed properties have been formally returned to their former owners. During this time demobilized former soldiers and Contra guerrillas in some districts have also been given lands to begin their lives anew. In a number of cases these redistributed properties and communities of the demobilized are on lands claimed by indigenous communities (Riverstone 2004: 59-60; Goett 2007: 217-218).

Most controversial are the large number of land titles of varying kinds, alluded to above, which have come to be known as *titulos supletorios*. The Nicaraguan Institute of Agrarian Reform (INRA), the Ministry of Agricultural Development and Agrarian Reform (MIDINRA), the National Privatization Corporation (CORNAP) and other governmental agencies have issued varieties of these to settlers on so-called, unpopulated "national lands."[1] Titles of this kind are often, strictly speaking, provisional, being potentially subject to annulment (Stansfield 1995: 5, 10), but this rarely happens and consequently they have acquired a legal and market value that they were not originally intended to have. The existence of these so-called *titulos supletorios* in addition to the communal titles and other forms referred to above reproduce a situation in eastern Nicaragua in which legal complexity and dispute are the norm rather than the exception.[2]

---

1  See Stansfield (1995) and Everingham (2001) for detailed accounts.
2  Complexities with regard to the formality, registration and individualization of land titles are also found in other parts of Nicaragua (Broegaard 2003: 854). Stansfield (1995: 2) makes interesting points about the state of many of the archives holding records of these titles.

Much of the land in eastern Nicaragua has also been formally incorporated into reserves such as the Bosawas (Stocks 2003, Stocks et al. 2005, Howard 2006b) and the Southeastern Nicaragua Biosphere Reserve, itself divided into four constituent reserves (Riverstone 2004: 87-97). These are intended to preserve the flora and fauna over specific parts of the region and prevent expansion of the agricultural frontier. While the Bosawas has been fairly successful in defending indigenous land rights (Stocks 2003, Jarquín 2006), these reserves are often less concerned with the occupants than with the wildlife to be found within their boundaries. At least one, The Cerro Silva Reserve, theoretically forbids any kind of settlement "unless required for the recuperative management of the forest," (quoted in Riverstone 2004: 89), owing to the perceived threat to wildlife. In some instances indigenous peoples whose families have lived in the area for generations, and who might well be considered the rightful owners and occupants of these lands, have been removed.[1]

This failure of the various administrations in Nicaragua to rationalize the terms of land ownership and rights to settlement has left eastern parts of the country with a legacy of land ownership issues which have been exceptionally complex and, in many cases, bitter (Williamson Cuthbert 2006). In January 2003, the Nicaraguan Assembly passed the Indigenous Land Demarcation Law. This legislation, known as Law 445 based on recommendations first outlined in 1998 by the Central American and Caribbean Research Council (CAARC 2006), it was hoped, would address these complex issues of land tenure as they pertained to these communities. Law 445 recognized the rights of indigenous peoples and "ethnic communities" to use and administer their traditional lands, adjacent coastal areas, and resources, and ensures that such territories would be demarcated and titled. Article 3 in particular made it clear that such land is inalienable and may not be taken by squatters because it is apparently abandoned.

In order to implement the provisions of this law, a National Demarcation and Titling Commission referred to as CONADETI, Regional Intersectoral Commissions and a Regional Technical Commission for land demarcation (Articles 41-43) were also created, while Article 45 outlined the procedural steps that were required during the demarcation and titling process. These

---

1  Naughton-Treves et al. (2005), Brandon et al. (1998) and Schlager and Ostrom (1992) contain discussion of these issues more generally. As Herlihy (2001) notes for the Río Plátano in the Honduran Mosquitia, many people are not even aware that they inhabit a reserve.

included those necessary for the formal request for demarcation, surveying, titling, the position of non-indigenous residents in indigenous territories, and procedures for conflict resolution. To this end the World Bank provided the Nicaraguan government with a substantial loan (Gordon et al. 2003). Law 445 would offer a rationalization of the indigenous land question, and, it was hoped, bring greater stability to a region where uncertainties over rights to territory and conflict had been endemic.

### Kakabila and its Neighbors

Pearl Lagoon, on whose shores Kakabila is situated, is a large, nearly land-locked body of water about twenty-five miles north of Bluefields. It is in fact an estuary with a narrow bar into which the waters of the Kurinwas, Wawashan, Patch and Ñari rivers, as well as a number of smaller creeks flow. Most of the land around the lagoon is low-lying and swampy in places, though there are a number of high banks, and it is on these that most of the lagoon's villages are situated. There are twelve towns on the lagoon's shore, all of which may be considered indigenous or ethnic in the Indigenous Land Demarcation Law's terms.[1] All these communities, often collectively referred to by residents as the Cuenca, are therefore potential beneficiaries of Law 445.

Of the twelve towns, four predominantly self-identify as Creole (the town of Pearl Lagoon, Haulover, Brown Bank and Marshall Point), three as Garífuna (Orinoco, La Fe and Square Point) and five as Miskitu (Tasbapauni, Set Net Point, Raitipura, Awas and Kakabila). Each of these towns, or communities as they are also locally known, has quite a distinctive history with regard to tenure of lands around the lagoon. The oldest of these are almost certainly Kakabila, Raitipura, Haulover and Pearl Lagoon. All four apparently date from the eighteenth century. Pearl Lagoon, originally called English Bank, was initially a settlement composed of mainly English-speaking slaves and their owners from Britain, Europe, and various parts of the English-speaking Caribbean. In the nineteenth century English Bank became a town of predominantly free, largely independent Creoles who suffered little interference from the Spanish and, later, Nicaraguan authorities, and it became known as Pearl Key Lagoon or Pearl Lagoon. Kakabila,

---

1 See Kasch et al. (1987) for a overall portrait of the Cuenca communities, which although dated in some respects is still useful.

Raitipura and Haulover were, as far as we can ascertain, communities of Miskitu-speakers whose members came south from Sandy Bay seeking better lands for horticulture as well as opportunities for the exploitation of marine resources and trade with the settlers at English Bank. The members of these communities were in time to enslave, drive away or absorb the indigenous Kukra Indians, the lagoon's original inhabitants (Jamieson 1998: 717). Tasbapauni, and its tiny neighbor Set Net Point, were founded by Miskitu settlers from Sandy Bay, as well as Cayman Islanders, who came south, perhaps a century later, in the mid nineteenth century to the Pearl Lagoon peninsula to take advantage of turtling opportunities (Nietschmann 1973: 17).

Marshall Point and Brown Bank were originally settled by English speakers from Jamaica and possibly Providence respectively. Brown Bank seems to be the older of the two, dating back to the first half of the nineteenth century. Marshall Point was apparently founded around the end of the nineteenth century by the Bennett family who came to the region to work for a logging company operation based at the mouth of the Wawashan River (Jamieson 1998: 718). Square Point, also known as San Vicente, La Fe and Orinoco were founded around the same time or shortly afterwards by Garífuna-speaking black Caribs from Honduras who also arrived to work in the logging industry (Davidson 1980).

With the exception of tiny Awas, a satellite community of Raitipura which seems to have come into existence as a distinct entity relatively recently in the mid or late twentieth century, the community map of the Cuenca had already been drawn more than half a century before the Sandinista revolution of 1979. Its inhabitants as non-mestizos are therefore justified in representing themselves as (a) indigenous or Afro-descendent, and (b) potential beneficiaries of Law 445.

The Land Titles Commission set up in 1915 in the wake of the Harrison-Altamirano Treaty of 1905, acknowledged community land titles for a number of the Cuenca's communities, and these titles represent for the most part existing claims to various land areas of the district. Miskitu communities in Kakabila, Tasbapauni, Set Net Point and Haulover, whose inhabitants then were considered Miskitu, were awarded large areas of land at that time. These included the town areas themselves and hinterlands of various sizes for the purposes of farming and hunting. Older Creole communities, such as Brown Bank and Pearl Lagoon, were awarded titles to the lands on which the towns themselves stood, but no other land. Presumably it was thought that Creoles were engaged in occupations within the cash rather than subsistence economy. Marshall Point and the Garífuna communities, including Orinoco, La Fe and Square Point, however, composed of families whose menfolk had come to work for the logging companies (Davidson 1980), were given no titles at all. This was presumably because these communities were quite recently established and it was thought that they were likely to be temporary. Their inhabitants would, it was thought, return to Honduras and other places of origin once the logging companies extracting lumber from the Wawashan and surrounding areas pulled out of the district.

In time these differing degrees of recognition to land led to both disputes and informal forms of accommodation amongst the twelve communities. The people of Orinoco, who as noted above had originally arrived to work for the logging operations, did not return to Honduras and instead began to farm and work lands that were claimed by the people of Tasbapauni, giving rise to a rivalry and a mutual enmity between these communities that persists into the present. The inhabitants of the town of Pearl Lagoon, more attuned to market forms of exchange than those of the Cuenca's other communities, soon divided their land into individually owned plots and in time attempted to export this notion of private land ownership to the people of neighboring Haulover and Raitipura who had formal title to the rich soils of the neighboring Manhattan and Rocky Point areas, many of whom continue to contest this idea. Elsewhere the people of Kakabila claimed lands that the people of La Fe and Brown Bank worked, including the town area of Brown Bank whose original title was forgotten, regarding the peoples of these villages as tenants living rent-free on Kakabila territory. Similar disputes and conflicting views between communities held for various fishing and shrimping areas around the lagoon itself, the seas adjacent to the Caribal peninsula which separates the lagoon from the sea, and the Pearl Keys to which the men of the district sailed to look for turtles and coconuts.[1] In summary even communal rights to territory were the subject of differing understandings and negotiation.

The progressive implementation of Law 445 has consequently meant that some communities have been, relatively speaking, winners, while others have been losers. Thus in the Cuenca, Marshall Point and the Garifu-

---

1  See Williamson Cuthbert (2006) for disputes between neighboring communities in the RAAN.

na towns have benefited to the extent that these communities have now received recognition to lands to which they previously had no legal title, while others, like Kakabila, have found that the lands previously given to them after Harrison-Altamirano have shrunk to a small degree with Brown Bank and La Fe finding themselves the beneficiaries. Many Kakabila people already recognized the rights of these towns to communal ownership of those lands north of Jackson Creek. Of most concern has been the CONA-DETI acknowledgement of communal ownership by Orinoco of extensive territories previously claimed by the community of Tasbapauni, for, while Kakabila, Brown Bank and La Fe enjoy mutually agreeable relations, those between Orinoco and Tasbapauni have been extremely strained for decades.

The Case of Kakabila

In spite of the fact that nobody in Kakabila owns a copy of the document dating back to the Land Titles Commission in the early years of last century, said to accord the people of the town exclusive rights to their lands, villagers themselves are on the whole quite clear about what constitutes this territory and their rights to it. In geographical terms, Kakabila territory is delineated, as far as villagers are concerned, by the lagoon to the east, Tuba Creek to the south, and the Ñari River to the west. It is only the northern border of community land that is subject to debate. For many villagers Jackson Creek between Kakabila town and Brown Bank marks the northern boundary, but for others their land extends all the way northwards to the lagoon shores at Table Point, thus incorporating Brown Bank and La Fe beyond.[1] In this latter view, the inhabitants of those two villagers are thus formally tenants on Kakabila land, permitted to live and work in their areas indefinitely as long as they recognize these as the communal property of Kakabila, and as long as they do not *cut stick* (cut down trees) for the purposes of making a profit by selling lumber to people outside the community.

---

1 Kakabila's communal title from 1915, ratified in 1917, supports the version of the community's ownership of lands north of Jackson Creek. The location of the town's lands according to this document state the boundaries of community lands as follows: N (north). Bahia y terranos nac.,: E. (east) Bahia: O. (west) T. Nacionales: S. (south) Bahia y T. titulados a favor de Royal Minex K. That the northern boundary of the community's stated 1007 hectares, 67 áreas and 50 centiáreas is situated in part on the lagoon bay suggests that lands now claimed by Brown Bank and La Fe were then indeed awarded to Kakabila (Comisión Tituladora de la Mosquitia, No. 123, Tomo unico, Folio 105-108, Date of Acquisition 4-10-15; Discreto del 21-08-05, Numero 2144, Tomo 38, Folio 150, Date of Acquisition 6-3-17).

Whether the townspeople of Brown Bank and La Fe recognize this relationship with Kakabila in these terms is unclear, but this certainly informs the view of many Kakabila people. However relations between the people of Kakabila and those other communities are entirely amicable, particularly with Brown Bank, the nearer of the two, and this ambiguity is not currently considered to be significant. It is commonly said that, in spite of the fact that these communities have different baseball teams (male and female), during such events as *set ups* (mortuary rituals) in Kakabila, which are focused to a considerable extent on community membership, townspeople from all three communities are always considered to be invited, making the people of Brown Bank and La Fe quasi-citizens of Kakabila.[1] The inhabitants of these three villages thus share membership of a moral community from which others are excluded.[2]

People from outside Kakabila are not permitted to establish residences, swiddens or *potreros* on community land. Nor are they allowed to extract from this land resources, such as lumber, for commercial exploitation. The only people permitted to do so are those legitimately considered to be community members. These include people in the following categories: first and foremost are those people who are born and raised in Kakabila or born and raised elsewhere to parents who come from the village; second are those, male or female, who are recognized as spouses (whether married, in common law unions or widowed) of Kakabila people; third are those who have by common assent of the people of the village been granted special dispensation to live in the village. In the past this third category has included people and their families, for example, who have come to work on NGO projects and have stayed on afterwards, and members of other Cuenca communities (especially Brown Bank) who have built up special relations of trust with the people of the town, leaving their own communities to live in Kakabila. There are, it should be noted, very few of these. Villagers are very clear that members of other communities in the Pearl Lagoon basin are no more given permission to live in or make use of Kakabila lands than are those from further afield.

---

1  This harmonious state of affair is conspicuous by its absence in relations between Pearl Lagoon and neighboring Haulover, and between Tasbapauni and Orinoco.

2  Whatever one's view on the question of Kakabila's northern boundary, the people of Kakabila are expected not to establish their grounds (swiddens) north of Jackson Creek. By custom and common agreement this is where villagers of Brown Bank and La Fe plant, even if ownership of this area is subject to debate.

Similar arrangements between Kakabila people and other Cuenca communities obtain with respect to the waters of the lagoon and the sea. While the community does not claim absolute ownership over any particular area of water, rights of usufruct within particular fishing, shrimping and turtling grounds are jealously guarded. While these may be waived for members of allied communities, they are, however, much more jealously protected from members of communities, especially those with whom relations in the past have been strained, notably Haulover and Tasbapauni. Members of other communities, even those considered "friendly" who set gill nets in the lagoon waters thus run the risk of these being stolen or being emptied of their catches.[1] This threat of possible theft constitutes a powerful incentive to remain in one's own waters where fellow villagers are more likely to keep watch over property. Similar arrangements obtain out at sea. Thus the turtling crews of Kakabila and Set Net Point, for example, share rights to the use of particular Cays off the shores of the Caribal Peninsula from which other people are theoretically excluded.

These special arrangements, few or none of which are encoded in the land titles that were given to some of the district's communities in the early twentieth century, are the product of decades of negotiation, the ecology of which has produced a complex mosaic of informal understandings, as well as disagreements, that inform the livelihoods of Kakabila's residents as much as it does the members of other Cuenca communities. Law 445, while welcomed insofar as it further fortifies indigenous claims to territory against outsiders, at the same time threatens to destabilize these informal arrangements (Williamson Cuthbert 2006), an issue taken up later in this chapter.

## Community or Bloque?

Communities taking advantage of the processes brought into being by Law 445 have had to consider the question of whether to propose to CONADETI simple Communal Titles or Territorial Titles. Communal Titles are those to be issued to towns or villages who wish to register claims on their own, rather than in conjunction with other communities. Territorial Titles are those to be given to Bloques, groups of two or more neighboring com-

---

1 Kakabila men similarly risk their nets being stolen if they set them in areas associated with other Cuenca communities.

munities who wish to share their ownership of a particular area of land. The advantages of making a Territorial claim is that in many cases hitherto untitled lands lying between constituent communities within the Bloque might also be claimed, whereas for those towns making Communal claims, this may not be so easy. Another obvious advantage is that a Bloque composed of several communities is likely to offer a more forceful challenge to those who would pose threats to indigenous lands (Riverston 2004: 153-160). There are, however, potential disadvantages which are apparent in the case of Kakabila and discussed below.[1]

When the twelve communities of the Cuenca were asked by CONADETI whether they wished to present Communal land or Territorial land claims, Kakabila's *coordinator* (leader responsible for external affairs) was persuaded that the community's best interests lay in joining the Bloque to which Haulover, Pearl Lagoon, Raitipura, Awas, and Set Net Point were all members. This group of communities was named the Haulover Bloque. Orinoco, La Fe, Square Point and Brown Bank formed the Garífuna Bloque, the only other such group in the Cuenca.[2] In 2006-7 the Haulover and Garífuna Bloques merged to form the new Laguna de Perlas Bloque.[3] The leaders of Tasbapauni, however, evidently suspicious of a process that might see the communities lose lands to Orinoco, and perhaps Marshall Point, elected not to join either Bloque, while the predominantly Creole community of Marshall Point, also historically at odds with neighboring Orinoco, likewise refused to join the Garífuna Bloque, and like Tasbapauni elected to pursue a claim for a Communal land title.

While membership of Bloques was clearly a good idea in some regards insofar as such units could more legitimately claim large areas of land in between constituent members (as well as those lands already considered the communal property of each), there were also problems which some Cuenca people were quick to identify, the CONADETI recognition of claims by the Garífuna Bloque and Marshall Point to lands previously claimed by Tasbapauni being particularly controversial.[4] Similarly Kakabila lost any form of

---

1  See Central American and Caribbean Research Council (1998, 2006) for discussion.

2  See Gurdián et al. (2006: 173) for a map of these Bloques.

3  Usually called the Pearl Lagoon Bloque. I have used the Spanish "Laguna de Perlas" Bloque so to avoid confusion with Pearl Lagoon town.

4  I would like to thank Jane Freeland for drawing my attention to a very recent letter from "The Tasbapaunie Territorial Government" to CONADETI disputing the territorial claims made by the Laguna de Perlas Bloque. Central American and

legal recognition to the land north of Jackson Creek that they had previous, magnanimously in the view of some villagers, leased out on a permanent, rent-free basis to the people of Brown Bank and La Fe, who were now recognized as legitimate owners.

The incorporation of communities into Bloques also left unanswered the question of whether members of fellow Bloque towns might take advantage of their co-membership and exercise rights to lands in other communities within the same Bloque. Could, for example, people from Pearl Lagoon town, like Kakabila a member of the Laguna de Perlas Bloque, legitimately come to Kakabila, build houses and make swiddens and *potreros* without asking the people of Kakabila, simply because both the lands associated with both communities now belonged to the same Territorial Land group or Bloque? Could the inhabitants of co-Bloque communities come to Kakabila and cut down trees, either for their own use or even for commercial exploitation? On these questions Law 445 and CONADETI remain strangely silent. (See Central American and Caribbean Research Council [2006: 148-150] and URACCAN [2007].) One thing is clear, however. The ecology of informal arrangements between communities, layered over understandings of the validity of land titles dating back to the titling process initiated by Harrison-Altamirano (even if in many cases these were misunderstandings) has been somewhat destabilized.

One question for which answers may be found is that of why the communal leaders of Kakabila, who had more to lose, have been persuaded to join the Bloques, rather than holding out, like Tasbapauni and Marshall Point, for Communal titles organized around the well-defined principle that rights to land are the sole patrimony of villages.[1] Perhaps they were resigned to the fact that the lands north of Jackson Creek were already going to be recognized as Brown Bank and La Fe property and therefore part of the Garífuna Bloque. The idea that the communities would be stronger together certainly seems to have been one important factor, while peer pressure from leaders of other communities in the Cuenca seems to have been another. It has been harder for towns like Kakabila to stand outside the Bloque when

---

Caribbean Research Council (1998: 293-303) contains discussion of areas of potential dispute, internal and external, with regard to the Haulover and Garifuna Bloques during the earlier alignments.

1 Tasbapauni and Marshall Point, perhaps unified by their common suspicion of neighboring Orinoco. have since joined together to create a new Bloque called the Indigenous Territory of Tasbapawnie.

influential neighboring communities in the district have joined and wish their neighbors to join.

Another answer is, perhaps, more worrying. The community of Pearl Lagoon is also the Cuenca's municipal capital. According to Kakabila leaders, the Alcalde (mayor) of Pearl Lagoon, whose constituency includes all twelve communities, threatened cuts to the municipal services of those communities who refused to join. Given that the demarcation and titling process is supposed to be implemented by CONADETI independently without regard to municipal politics, threats of this kind represent in my view serious political interference in what is, essentially, a juridical matter. (See Central American and Caribbean Research Council [2006].) It is this failure by the local authorities in eastern Nicaragua to separate the legal and political which, this chapter argues below, threatens to destabilize civil society.

Taking the Law into Our Own Hands

An important aspect of land laws of whatever kind as they apply to many areas of eastern Nicaragua is that historically they have been exceptionally hard to enforce.[1] Even if the members of a particular community have a legitimate claim to an area of land that is occupied by "invading" campesinos, it is very difficult to persuade the members of an extremely under-resourced police force to come out and oversee the eviction of these invaders. As Kakabila people say, the police are only inclined to *burn gas* (waste petrol money in traveling to small villages by *panga* [motorized skiff]) when they hear drugs are involved, the implication being that individual police are likely to benefit from drug confiscations.

Because local police have been unable or unwilling to enforce land laws that very probably few of them properly understand, the people of the indigenous communities of eastern Nicaragua have in the past had to enforce the law themselves. This, however, has not always been easy. Riverstone (2004: 71-74) shows, for example, how Rama people in small scattered hamlets have been unable to defend their lands, because in many instances the invaders have been more numerous and better armed than they are. Meanwhile the memberships of more numerous and better organized communi-

---

1   This inability to enforce indigenous land rights informs much of Riverstone's (2004) perceptive analysis of the areas to Rama and Creole occupation south of Bluefields. See also Kaimowitz el al. (2003).

ties, because they too are unsure of how land laws might be interpreted by judiciaries biased towards mestizo and (in some instances) Creole elites in municipal and regional capitals, are loathe to risk being seen to act "illegally." It is only when they become aware of new legislation that apparently fortifies their rights to their lands that indigenous people are inclined to take matters into their own hands.[1]

The period immediately after the Sandinista revolution of 1979 provides an example of this for Kakabila. During the 1960s a mestizo from western Nicaragua with important connections to the Somoza administration had browbeaten the community into allowing him to rent lands close to the shore of the lagoon to the south of the town in order to make a *potrero* for grazing cattle. An annual rent had been agreed but this man, villagers told me, had only made the first payment and had ignored their agreement afterwards. In the months following the events of 1979, however, villagers, who had suffered this abuse of their lands for several years, now forcibly, without police help, took back their lands, these being given over to the community for the potential use of its members.[2]

The passing of Law 445 and the subsequent negotiation of the demarcation and titling processes in the Cuenca have produced a very similar effect, giving villagers new confidence in their legal rights to their lands. Thus in 2006, when Kakabila people encountered men from Pearl Lagoon entering community lands near the Tuba Creek to cut down trees for commercial gain, they brought these men to a community meeting, told them they must stop, and confiscated the lumber they had already cut. Community leaders in speaking to these men cited Law 445.

By 2010 confidence in recognition by CONADETI of Kakabila's rights to its lands was great enough to take even more decisive action. In previous years Spanish-speaking campesinos had crossed the Ñari River, the western boundary of community lands, and had established farms on the Kakabila side, near the head of Tuba Creek to the southwest of the village. Six mestizo families now lived there. The members of these families were docile and

---

1  The importance of the role of perceptions of the law and tenure security in Nicaragua is discussed in Broegaard (2005), for Honduras, in Coles-Coghi (1993) and Roquas (2002), and, for the Mosquitia in both countries, Hayes (2007). Broegaard (2005: 857-859) also discusses the influence of local elites in influencing the outcomes of disputes over land. Tyler's work (1990, 1994) has been instrumental in raising this and related issues.

2  This action was arguably sanctioned by Decree 3 of the Junta Government of National Reconstruction in 1979, which ordered confiscations of this kind.

all agreed, when first confronted with the fact that they were occupying Kakabila land, that they would respect this. The people of Kakabila, without the ratification of their rights to this land by CONADETI, had not felt empowered to act. However, other farmers following them were fast cutting down the Ñari Forest across the river just beyond their boundary and it was thought that these later arrivals might well also cross the river into Kakabila territory. Kakabila people were now in a quandary about what to do about these six families, as their presence became more foreboding. Some villagers had wanted to evict them as soon as possible, but many others pitied their poverty and proposed that they be allowed to stay on the understanding that they did not cut down the forest to make grazing lands, their permanent residence being conditional on this.[1] There was a great deal of debate about this, for while most villagers had nothing against these particular "Spaniards," many argued persuasively that they would be harder to get rid of once they began to raise children and multiply. Conceivably too these children, being born on village lands, might even have the right to remain in terms of village constitutional understanding, thereby posing for the future even greater dilemmas. Village meetings ensured that the latter proposal based on compassion had been adopted and the six families had been allowed to stay. One family even turned out to be an asset, in that it notified the village council of any movements in the upper River Ñari and Tuba Creek areas that might have augured further illegal settlement or exploitation of resources in Kakabila lands. Pity for these "Spaniards," coupled with reluctance to fall foul of Nicaraguan law, thus stayed the hand of villagers.

This tolerance, however, began to wear thin as in late 2009 news began to come to the village of the misdeeds of one of these settlers. This man had begun to stake out parcels of Kakabila land with a view to selling them to new arrivals. He was, in other words, trying to sell lands that were the inalienable property of the village as a whole to which he had no legal right. And just as villagers began to hear stories about this man's actions, a story come through about how one villager, who lived not in the village itself but on a farm near Insla Tingni and the upper Ñari River on Kakabila territory, had, without the permission of the village, given a mestizo farmer from far

---

1 Miskitu accommodation of mestizo migrants is more common that one might imagine. See, for example, Hayes (2007: 747).

away permission to graze cattle on an abandoned *potrero* formerly used by a deceased villager.

In early 2010 the Kakabila council decided to act against these squatters and called a meeting in which villagers agreed that enough was enough. Messages were sent down to Tuba Creek and the Ñari River to inform the six families that they would now have to leave Kakabila territory. They were given exactly one week in which to move. Towards the end of that week the village council met again and a date was fixed for a large group of village men to go down to Tuba Creek and the upper Ñari River to enforce the eviction should they find out that the villagers had not left their farms. These men were not to use violence, but were to burn the farm houses if the squatters resisted and many of the men were armed with machetes, with a few also carrying rifles. It was to be understood that should the squatters have evidently left, the farms were not to be burned.

Concerned about the possibility of violence, I asked Oscar, a friend of mine, if he felt that the younger and more hotheaded of these men could be restrained from acting improperly. He told me that the older men would be there to keep order and pointed out that village police would form part of this group. The Kakabila police, although originally a specifically local institution operating outside the remit of the Nicaraguan law, are now indeed recognized by the country's legislature and the police department have issued them with uniforms, though they are not paid. Watching the members of the eviction party set off that morning in groups of various sizes, perhaps thirty or forty men altogether, I saw Aguilar, one of the village policemen, heading off in his uniform, and felt more comfortable. Of course having a policeman, even a village policeman, accompany what might have been otherwise construed as a war party, lent this action by the villagers a legitimacy that some community members still felt it lacked. Indeed as the group of men set off, a young man called Sanu shouted after them "Malditos! Malditos!" ("Wrong doers! Wrong doers!").

That evening the men began to drift back to the village. They had indeed found the farms abandoned but some of the older men were angry that some of the boys had gone ahead of the main party and had burned all six. This was deemed to be sheer vandalism and risked placing the actions of the village outside the law. Worse still, although five of the families disappeared, presumably across the Ñari River to Arenitas, the nearest settlement west of Kakabila, one family did come into the village to ask for help. This was the same family that had played by the rules the villagers had originally set in allowing them to stay earlier on; the family that had given the community intelligence about violations of community territory in its otherwise poorly patrolled and most vulnerable southwestern corner. Unfortunately by then there was little that the community magistrate, or *wihta* (village arbitrator), could do for them.[1]

The re-awakening of a confidence among Kakabila people that they can take the law, specifically Law 445, into their own hands is hardly surprising. Indeed, given the apparent impotence of the Nicaraguan state to enforce much of its legislation in remote communities like Kakabila, we might even expect it. Nevertheless, it is also worrying, especially when accompanied by what might be described as vigilantism. Kakabila people do not feel that the Nicaraguan police and judicial systems — memberships of the former mainly mestizo, the latter Creole in local contexts - are there to work in the interests of law-abiding people within their community. They experience the police in particular as either uninterested, only taking a corrupt interest if drugs are involved, and frequently racist in their dealings with community members who they view, according to villagers, as "ignorant Indians," while their experience of the judiciary is that it generally represents the interests of a Pearl Lagoon Creole elite against those of the poor from the smaller communities like Kakabila.

Recently, for example, the Pearl Lagoon police confiscated beer legitimately bought by two young women from Kakabila. According to villagers, the police probably wanted the beer for themselves. Five village men who were present protested and all were taken to the police cells where they were kept for three nights without charge. During this time they were subjected to racist abuse, beatings and humiliations of various kinds. Only when a woman from Kakabila who represented a human rights organization in the village traveled to Bluefields to complain to the police headquarters there, was a message sent by the chief of police that these men should be released without charge. A pistol taken from one of these men (for which a legal permit was owned), has still to be returned, and many Kakabila people assume that this weapon has been illegally sold by the Pearl Lagoon police.

Indeed the possession of pistols by some Kakabila men (as opposed to rifles used exclusively for hunting) points to the failure of the local police and judiciary to protect ordinary people in a context where violence and

---

1 Another village meeting was arranged to consider this after I left Kakabila.

murder are becoming progressively more common.[1] As cocaine and arms flood the Cuenca the means of coercion and violence, as local people such as those in Kakabila experience these, are now encountered much more frequently in the hands of local gangsters, locally known as "mafia." These gangsters - some of whom are local to Pearl Lagoon, others who come from as far away as Colombia — are also moneyed, with the means to order and implement executions of those who get in their way, and to "buy" local police who often fear them.

Kakabila people are, generally speaking, grateful for Law 445, which they view as state recognition of lands they always knew were theirs by right. They are, however, rather sanguine about the ability of the state to enforce their protection. Managua is far away, CONADETI is under-resourced, and the local police and judiciary have neither the will nor the resources to offer them this protection. Many feel justified in taking the law into their own hands, believing that in doing so they are acting within the law.[2] And as the cocaine economy insinuates itself into that of the village, villagers acquire the means to purchase arms that allow them to do so, as evidenced in the recent events of Walpa Siksa, when villagers of that Miskitu community engaged in a fire fight with narco-traffickers against Nicaraguan police (Treminio 2009).

Apart from Law 445 the developments described here are reproducing for the people of Kakabila (and, no doubt the members of other, similar communities) an acute sense of marginalization. This sense of being marginalized is less a sense of detachment from the Nicaraguan state, an entity already centered far away in Managua to which professed loyalty is for many almost meaningless, than it is from the local representatives of that state. The police in particular are only able to demonstrate their impotence to carry out their prescribed duties, through acts of arbitrary, rather than universal, justice and in some cases violations of the constitutional rights of citizens for whom the sense of Nicaraguan citizenship is often already weak.

As far as Law 445 itself is concerned, it is for most Kakabila people, in theory at least, a welcome development. It has come at a time when the threat of invasion of community lands by campesino frontier families is

---

1  See Dennis (2003, 2004: 260-270) for discussion of similar developments in Awastara and Sandy Bay.
2  See Smith (2008) for comparative analysis study and of course Hobsbawn's (1969) influential study of banditry.

more salient than ever, and, with the completion of a road between Pearl Lagoon and Rama, an increase in speculative land purchases in the south-ernmost Cuenca communities and the Kukra Hill area. It gives people in the indigenous and Afro-descendant communities a sense that they specifically have rights, enshrined in Nicaraguan law, to defend their own territories. However, if local state institutions refuse to acknowledge the other rights of indigenous people supposedly enshrined in the autonomy law of 1987, specifically those to justice and equality before the law, people who have al-ready experienced the marginalization of a war many perceive to have been directed against them, it may have come with costs.[1]

There is a good case for stating that the predominantly Miskitu insur-gency during the 1980s in eastern Nicaragua was to a considerable extent ignited and sustained by the specific nature of local engagements with the representatives of the Nicaraguan state, rather than state policy directly. Interestingly too, some commentators on the Miskitu insurgency of the 1980s emphasize the significance of the refusal of the Nicaraguan state to recognize the extent of the Miskitu claim to territory, despite being invited to submit this claim.[2] It would be a shame if Law 445, on the whole a well conceived and certainly well intentioned piece of legislation, failed in its objectives because of (a) the inability of the state to enforce it, (b) the local marginalization of its beneficiaries, and (c) the combining influence of both to produce a worrying tendency amongst its beneficiaries to enforce the law themselves, as the people of Kakabila did along Tuba Creek and the Ñari River. On that particular day in January 2010 nobody offered the men of Kakabila resistance. This might not be the case next time.

## Acknowledgements

The Wenner-Gren Foundation, the Royal Anthropological Institute, the London School of Economics and Political Science, the University of Manchester, and the Centre for Research and Documentation of the Atlan-tic Coast (CIDCA) in Nicaragua have generously supported my research at different times. I am grateful to all these bodies and, of course, to the people of Kakabila and other communities in the region. This research is based pri-

---

1 Stepputat (2000, 2001) provides chilling analysis of the relationship between marginalization from the state and violence in Guatemala.
2 See chapter 4 of this volume.

marily on fieldwork conducted in Kakabila during 1992-3, 1997, 1998, 1999-2000, 2002 (twice), 2004, 2005-6, and 2009-10.

## References

Acosta, M.L. (2006a) 'Análisis Jurídico sobre la Compra-Venta de los Cayos Perlas' (first published in 2002) in Rivas, A. and Broegaard, R. (Eds) *Demarcacion Territorial de la Propiedad Comunal en la Costa Caribe de Nicaragua* (Managua, CIDCA-UCA), pp. 112-126.

Acosta, M.L. (2006b) 'Usurpación Estatal de Tierras Indígenas: El Caso de las comunidades de Monkey Point y Rama' (first published in 2000) in Rivas, A. and Broegaard, R. (Eds) *Demarcacion Territorial de la Propiedad Comunal en la Costa Caribe de Nicaragua* (Managua, CIDCA-UCA), pp. 127-144.

Brandon, K., Redford, H. and Sanderson S.E. (Eds) (1998) *Parks in Peril: People, Politics and Protected Areas.* (Washington DC, The Nature Conservatory, Island).

Broegaard, R. (2005) 'Land Tenure Insecurity and Inequality in Nicaragua' in *Development and Change*, Vol, 36, No. 5, pp. 845-864.

Central American and Caribbean Research Council (1998) *Diagnóstico General sobre la Tenencía de la Tierra en las Comunidades Indígenas de la Costa Atlántica: Resumen Ejecutivo* (Austin, CAARC).

Central American and Caribbean Research Council (2006) 'Diagnóstico General sobre la Tenencía de la Tierra en las Comunidades Indígenas de la Costa Atlántica' (first published in 2000) in Rivas, A. and Broegaard, R. (Eds) *Demarcacion Territorial de la Propiedad Comunal en la Costa Caribe de Nicaragua* (Managua, CIDCA-UCA), pp. 146-168.

Coles-Coghi, A. (1993) *Agricultural Land Rights and Title Security in Honduras* (PhD Thesis, University of Wisconsin, Madison).

Davidson, W. (1980) 'The Garífuna of Pearl Lagoon: Ethnohistory of an Afro-American Enclave in Nicaragua' in *Ethnohistory*, Vol. 27, pp. 31-47

Dennis, P. (2003) 'Cocaine in Miskitu Village' in *Ethnology*, Vol. 42, pp. 161-172.

Dennis, P. (2004) *The Miskitu of Awastara* (Austin, University of Texas Press).

Everingham, M. (2001) 'Agricultural Property Rights and Political Change in Nicaragua' in *Latin American Politics and Society*, Vol. 43, No. 3, pp. 61.93.

Gobierno de la República de Nicaragua (2005) Ley 445: *Del Regimen de Propiedad Comunal de los Pueblos Indígenas y Comunidades Etnicas* (La Gaceta No. 16, Diario Oficial 23-01-2003).

Goett, J. A. (2007) *Diasporic Identities, Autochthonous Rights: Race, Gender, and the Cultural Politics of Creole Land Rights in Nicaragua* (PhD dissertation, University of Texas).

Gordon, E., Gurdián, G. and Hale, C. R. (2003) 'Rights, Resources, and the Social Memory of Struggle: Relections on a Study of Indigenous and Black Community Land Rights on Nicaragua's Atlantic Coast' in *Human Organization*, Vol. 62, No.4, pp. 369-381.

Gould, J. (1998) *To Die in this Way: Nicaragua n Indians and the Myth of Mestizaje 1880-1965* (Durham N.C., Durke University Press).

Gurdián, G . (1987) 'Autonomy Rights, National Unity and National Liberation' in CIDCA (Eds.) *Ethnic groups and the National State: The Case of the Atlantic Coast in Nicaragua* (Managua, CIDCA/Study Development Unit), pp. 171-189.

Gurdián, G., Hale, C. R and Gordon, E. (2006) 'Derechos, Recursos y Memoria Social de la Lucha: Reflexiones sobre un Estudio acerca de los Derechos Territoriales de las Comunidades Indígenas y Negra en la Costa Caribe de Nicaragua' (first published in 2002) in Rivas, A. and Broegaard, R. (Eds) *Demarcacion Territorial de la Propiedad Comunal en la Costa Caribe de Nicaragua* (Managua, CIDCA-UCA), pp. 169-194.

Hale, C. R. (2006) 'Nociones Contenciosas de los Derechos sobre las Tierra en la Historia Miskita' (first published in 1992) in Rivas, A. and Broegaard, R. (Eds) *Demarcacion Territorial de la Propiedad Comunal en la Costa Caribe de Nicaragua* (Managua, CIDCA-UCA), pp. 14-37.

Hayes, T.M. (2007) 'Does Tenure Matter? A Comparitive Analysis of Agricultural Expansion in the Mosquitia Forest Corridor' in *Human Ecology*, Vol. 35, pp. 733-747.

Herlihy, P. (2001) 'Indigenous and Latino Peoples of the Río Plátano Reserve' in Stonich, S. (Eds) *Endangered Peoples of Latin America* (Westport, CT, Greenwood).

Hobsbawn, E. (1969) *Bandits* (London, Weidenfeld and Nicholson).

Howard, S. (2006a) 'Autonomía y Derechos Territoriales Indígenas: El Caso de la RAAN' (first published in 1993) in Rivas, A. and Broegaard, R. (Eds) *Demarcacion Territorial de la Propiedad Comunal en la Costa Caribe de Nicaragua* (Managua, CIDCA-UCA), pp. 38-61.

Howard, S. (2006b) 'Autonomía y Derechos Territoriales de los Sumos en Bosawas: El Caso de Sikilta' (first published in 1996) in Rivas, A. and Broegaard, R. (Eds) *Demarcacion Territorial de la Propiedad Comunal en la Costa Caribe de Nicaragua* (Managua, CIDCA-UCA), pp. 215-232.

Jamieson, M. (1998) 'Linguistic Innovation and Relationship Terminology in the Pearl Lagoon Basin of Nicaragua' in *Journal of the Royal Anthropological Institute*, Vol. 4. No. 4. pp. 713-730.

Jarquín L. (2006) 'El Nuevo Marco Jurídico de la Propiedad Communal en la Costa y los Ríos Bocay, Coco, Indio y Maíz' (first published in 2003) in Rivas, A. and Broegaard, R. (Eds) *Demarcacion Territorial de la Propiedad Comunal en la Costa Caribe de Nicaragua*. (Managua, CIDCA-UCA), pp. 63-80.

Jones, J. (1988) 'Colonization in Central America' in Manshard, W. and Morgan, W.B. (Eds) *Agricultural Expansion and Pioneer Settlements in the Humid Tropics* (Tokyo, United Nations University), pp. 241-265.

Kaimowitz, D., Faune, A. and Mendoza R. (2003) Your Biosphere in my Backyard: The Story of Bosawas in Nicaragua' in *Policy Matters*, Vol. 12, pp. 6-15.

Kasch, K., Kennedy, M., Nagel, A., Colon, M., Castillo, A., Anderson, R. and Somarriba, S. (1987) *Regional Study of Pearl Lagoon* (Pearl Lagoon, unpublished manuscript).

Naughton-Treves, L, Buck Holland, M. and Brandon, K. (2005) 'The Role of Protected Areas in Conserving Biodiversity and Sustaining Local Livelihoods' in *Annual Review of Environment and Resources*, Vol. 30, pp. 219-252.

Nietschmann, B. (1971) *Between Land and Water: The Subsistence of the Miskitu Indians, Eastern Nicaragua* (New York, Seminar Press).

Offen, K. (2003) 'Narrating Place and Identity, or Mapping Miskitu Land Claims in Northeastern Nicaragua' in *Human Organization*, Vol. 62, No. 4, pp. 382-392.

Riverstone, G. (2004) *Living in the Land of Our Ancestors: Rama Indian and Creole Territory in Caribbean Nicaragua* (Managua, ASDI).

Smith, D.J. (2008) 'The Bakassi Boys: Vigilantism, Vioence, and Political Imagination of Nigeria' in *Cultural Anthropology* Vol. 19, No. 3, pp. 429-455.

Roquas, E. (2003) *Stacked Law, Land, Property and Conflict in Honduras* (Amsterdam, Rosenberg Publishers).

Schlager, E. and Ostrom, E. (1992) 'Property-rights Regimes and Natural Resources: A Conceptual Analysis' in *Land Economics*, Vol. 68, No. 3, pp. 91-132.

Stansfield, J.D. (1995) 'Insecurity of Land Tenure in Nicaragua', LTC Research Paper 120 (Madison, WI, Land Tenure Center, University of Wisconsin-Madison).

Stepputat, F. (2000) 'At the Frontiers of the Modern State in Post-war Guatemala' in Arce, A. and Long, N. (Eds) *Anthropology, Development and Modernities* (London, Routledge), pp. 127-140.

Stepputat, F. (2001) 'Urbanizing the Countryside: Armed Conflict, State Formation, and the Politics of Place in Contemporary Guatemala' in Blom Hansen, T. and Stepputat, F. (Eds) *Ethnographic Explorations of the Postcolonial State* (London, Duke), pp. 284-312.

Stocks, A. (2003) 'Mapping Dreams in Nicaragua's Bosawas Reserve' in *Human Organization*, Vol. 62, No. 4, pp. 344-356.

Stocks, A., Jarquín, L. and Beauvais, J. (2006) 'El Activismo Ecológico Indígena en Nicaragua: Demarcación y Legalización de Tierras Indígenas en Bosawas' (first published in 2000) in Rivas, A. and Broegaard, R. (Eds) *Demarcacion Territorial de la Propiedad Comunal en la Costa Caribe de Nicaragua* (Managua, CIDCA-UCA), pp. 195-214.

Treminio, W. (2009) 'Droga, narcos y la comunidad de Walpa Siksa' in *Nuevo Diario*, 13 December, 2009.

Tyler, T. (1990) *Why People Obey the Law* (New Haven, CT, Yale University Press).

Tyler, T. (1994) 'Governing Amid Diversity: The Affect of Fair Decision-making Procedures on the Legitimacy of Government' in *Law and Society Review*, Vol. 28, No. 4, pp. 809-832.

URACCAN (2007) *Reglamento Interno de las Autoridades Territoriales de las Diez Comunidades Indígenas y Afrodescendientes de la Cuenca de Pearl Lagoon* (Pearl Lagoon, RAAS: Ford Foundation and URACCAN).

Vilas, C. (1989) *State, Class, and Ethnicity in Nicaragua: Capitalist Modernization and Revolutionary Change on the Atlantic Coast* (Boulder, Lynne Rienner Publishers).

Wiggins, A. (2006) 'El Caso de Awas Tingni: O el Futuro de los Derechos Territoriales de los Pueblos Indígenas del Caribe Nicaragüense' (first published in 2002) in Rivas, A. and Broegaard, R. (Eds) *Demarcacion Territorial de la Propiedad Comunal en la Costa Caribe de Nicaragua* (Managua, CIDCA-UCA), pp. 81-111.

Williamson Cuthbert, D. (2006) 'Tipología de Conflictos sobre la Propiedad Comunal en el Municipio de Puerto Cabezas' (first published in 2003) in Rivas, A. and Broegaard, R. (Eds) *Demarcacion Territorial de la Propiedad Comunal en la Costa Caribe de Nicaragua.* (Managua, CIDCA-UCA), pp. 247-249.

# CHAPTER 10. "WE ARE THE OWNERS": AUTONOMY AND NATURAL RESOURCES IN NORTHEASTERN NICARAGUA

*Mary Finley-Brook*

In Latin America, ethnic political parties and (semi-)autonomous regions promote self-governance for multicultural populations. Nonetheless, the legal recognition of these institutions in eastern Nicaragua does not eliminate attempts to undermine indigenous peoples" political power and resource access. Although there are opportunities for improved representation as a result of new institutional openings, a constantly shifting and highly contested regional political space increases the likelihood and frequency of polarizing or debilitating challenges. The pressures indigenous peoples and their organizations experience in Latin America are intense and often contradictory. Struggles for economic, political, and cultural rights play out among governance and market instability which is intensified by ecological degradation.

Regardless of the formal recognition of political autonomy in 1987, national and international institutions continue to strongly influence the delineation of land rights and natural resource access in the North Atlantic Autonomous Region (RAAN) of Nicaragua (Vilas 1990; Hale 1994; Finley-Brook 2007a; Dana 2008; Finley-Brook and Offen 2009). In 2003, Demarcation Law 445 created a legal framework for the recognition of indigenous territories. However, the exact roles of different decision-making authorities and the rules for them to employ are still under construction (Larson forthcoming). The autonomy statute and the Demarcation Law thus provide only partial legal victories because indigenous peoples' rights, including ownership of traditional lands, remain open to interpretation and challenge.

Boundary negotiations extend throughout the RAAN. In some cases, particularly in areas along the agrarian frontier, new land conflicts have developed as a result of Law 445 (Finley-Brook and Offen 2009). Meanwhile processes of decentralization, while breaking up some concentration of power, have created numerous sites of struggle (Larson forthcoming). With multiple land claims in most areas of the RAAN, demarcation activities are challenging and titling decisions are contested. Dana (2008) records significant social and spatial complexity in determining accurate and ethical boundaries in the RAAN and in Latin American indigenous territories more broadly.[1]

RAAN's regional government remains a weak and uneven platform from which to defend multi-ethnic territorial and resource rights. After the emergence of new regional political leaders in the 1970s and 1980s, a splintering of indigenous leadership at the end of the civil war continues to cause discord. Tensions in northeastern Nicaragua remain high due to ineffective networking across party and ethnic lines. Migration from the west and center of the country challenges RAAN political leaders to represent a growing number of mestizo inhabitants along with indigenous and Afro-Caribbean populations, in spite of competing demands from various groups.

Although focused predominately on Miskitu politics, this chapter identifies various constraints to multi-ethnic self-determination, while noting barriers exist even among aid programs targeting political empowerment and community development. Nevertheless, I also explore examples of progress toward decentralization at regional and local levels regardless of an overall national context of political containment and economic exploitation.

Events in northeastern Nicaragua influence the constant redefinition of indigenous and multi-ethnic rights across the Americas. Successful Inter-American Court of Human Rights (IACHR) cases involving RAAN indigenous groups, such as *Awas Tingni v. Nicaragua* and *YATAMA v. Nicaragua*, create international precedents (Carrión 2005; Campbell 2007). However, for

---

1 See also Sletto (2002, 2009).

the protagonists, these legal victories were only one step in a much larger process to defend indigenous rights.

The Miskitu political party YATAMA has led the RAAN government for fourteen of the years since it was established in 1990.[1] As a means to assess the potential for strengthening sub-national autonomy and ethnic self-determination, I analyze a series of case examples occurring during YATAMA's second round of administration from 2002 to the present.[2] In general, I focus my analysis at the level of the political party rather than discuss the actions of individual officials.

The first set of case studies covered in this chapter address foreign-sponsored community forestry projects in the Prinzapolka watershed. The stories are telling of the constraints regional institutions face as intermediaries between international donors and indigenous villages. Overall, decision-making at regional and local levels remained limited during the design of the aid programs. However, I refute a popular assumption of institutional inaction on the part of the regional government by demonstrating steps that were taken, although often down dead-end streets. The subsequent sections analyze demarcation processes and electoral politics at the scale of the regional government headquartered in Bilwi-Puerto Cabezas.[3] I demonstrate agency on the part regional officials and show their ability to change the trajectory of RAAN development in significant ways. Yet, events highlight how political fragmentation in regional institutions translates into missed opportunities for advancing the rights of multi-ethnic populations, whether through a regime of political autonomy or under the aegis of an indigenous political party.

Indigenous Institutions in Latin America

Experts suggest that regional autonomy can help protect indigenous governance and territorial or resource rights (Larson and Ribot 2004). Nevertheless, the mere legal existence of an autonomous region is not enough. Multi-scale governance is challenging in most contexts. It is important to

1 YATAMA's first round of regional leadership from 1990 to 1996 has been covered elsewhere (Butler 1997; González and Zapata 2003). See also chapter 5 of this volume.

2 Although there was a YATAMA governor during each term of this eight-year period, Sandinista allies shared top administrative roles, including the presidency of the regional council.

3 Bilwi, the indigenous place name, will be used throughout this chapter.

understand territorial "verticality" in addition to identifying horizontal spatial reach (Delaney 2005: 31-33). Within eastern Nicaragua there is a mosaic of levels and types of territories governed by conceptually distinct institutions with different power claims and access to resources. There can be cooperation between the various sectors and scales, but opportunities for conflict proliferate. Geographers have shown that in locations around the world people often develop identities nested at different scales (Herb and Kaplan 1999). Nevertheless, effective multi-scale governance generally requires clarity in the boundaries of each jurisdiction as well as communication and cooperation between layers of authority.

Within indigenous territories or states, the emergence of ethnic political parties is believed to reduce violent conflict, improve representation, and promote civic participation (Madrid 2005; Rice and Van Cott 2006). Rice and Van Cott (2006) define success of ethnic political parties as indigenous people being elected to state positions, although the events that follow must also be analyzed. Indigenous parties, it is often argued, are better able to represent historically marginalized groups and will be more responsive to the needs of ethnic populations than mainstream political parties (Madrid 2005). Ethnic parties can usually reach to the grassroots and encourage participation because they often emerge from existing social networks (Rice and Van Cott 2006). However, one may ask if the research findings of Madrid (2005) and Rice and Van Cott (2006), based on countries located in the Andes, are transferable to Nicaragua, where indigenous peoples make up a smaller percentage of the national population. The RAAN situation is complex because inhabitants are multi-ethnic and an ethnic hierarchy was created and reinforced across history (Hale 1994, 1998). Long-standing racism among the various RAAN ethnic groups weakens cooperation (Zapata Webb 2002). Cultural diversity in the RAAN, with Miskitu, Mayangna, and Afro-Caribbean populations, contrasts with other locations with strong indigenous autonomy, such as Nunavut in Canada or Kuna Yala in Panama (Howe 1998; Légaré 2001). According to YATAMA's statutes, the party supports "the integrity, harmony and unity of the pluriethnic and pluricultural diversity" of the Moskitia, which they define as the RAAN, the South Atlantic Autonomous Region (RAAS), and Jinotega (YATAMA 1999: 1). Once elected to the regional government, YATAMA had to represent mestizo populations, who make up a majority in large portions of the RAAN. YATAMA's base of support is weakest in the mestizo-dominated

Mining Triangle of Siuna, Rosita, and Bonanza, encouraging YATAMA's strategic alliance with the FSLN party in spite of historical conflicts. An anti-Sandinista faction of YATAMA continues to distance itself from the rest of party due to unwillingness to bury the hatchet with the FSLN.

The increase in the politicization of indigenous peoples across Latin America has often been linked to neoliberalism and globalization (Yashar 1999; Houghton and Bell 2004; Radcliffe 2007). However, YATAMA has a distinct history, since it formed as a result of indigenous military mobilization during Nicaragua's civil war (Solis 1989; Hale 1994). Whereas many indigenous populations in Latin America have criticized the exploitative nature of export trade, the Miskitu have been relatively receptive to commercial resource extraction. Indigenous elders remember affectionately the enclave economies of past decades, known colloquially as Company Time (Hale 1994). More recently, YATAMA has tied indigenous entrepreneurship to self-determination and party leaders remain open to participation in market-based initiatives of various types. Mercado et al. (2006) argue for additional YATAMA support for indigenous loan funds. Since 1990, the RAAN has had a positive experience with a micro-loan program called PANA-PANA, which YATAMA members helped start. PANA-PANA provides loans to indigenous populations who would not otherwise be eligible.

Community Forestry and Market Citizenship

Community forestry in Central America has often arisen as a market-based solution to the marginalization and exploitation of forest-based peoples that advanced following neoliberal reforms due to the promotion of export resource marketing and restricted state monitoring and oversight as a result of the streamlining of state agencies.[1] However, donors usually encourage indigenous communities to sell resources based on corporate structures that are vastly different from their traditional organizations (Brook 2005). Enhanced market integration is likely to influence cultural change as the fulfillment of demands becomes premised on economic criteria and incentives. Material or cultural change may be particularly strong for indigenous populations with collective or subsistence economies (Harvey 2001). Although many indigenous groups, including those in the RAAN, have been involved in external markets for decades or even centuries, the

---

1  See also McCarthy (2005).

expansion of trade linkages can still create social and cultural transitions and tensions. Furthermore, even in seemingly pluri-ethnic and inclusive national contexts, such as Canada, there is evidence of racial containment in forestry projects (Ross and Smith 2002; Baldwin 2009). Case studies of market-oriented development programs in indigenous territories of Mexico and Central America demonstrate the extension of deep and persistent inequalities in decision-making power and access to resources (Harvey 2001; Altamirano-Jiménez 2004; Bonta 2005; Brook 2005; Finley-Brook 2007a; Jordán 2008; Finley-Brook and Thomas forthcoming). Rapid and contained consultation processes and the pressure to quickly benchmark progress based on external guidelines can also lead to restrictions on local sovereignty. Examples of green imperialism, whereby agendas of industrialized nations are given precedence over local economies and value systems, are evident throughout many conservation and development initiatives of the Americas.[1]

In spite of the increased attention to Latin American indigenous economies in the past decade, many development programs do not adequately seek to understand the institutions they propose to change. Indigenous participation in neoliberal economic programs creates the potential for the "marketization of indigenous citizenship" (Altamirano-Jiménez 2004: 350). Citizenship becomes based on "an economic logic that identifies participation in regimes of capitalist accumulation as the ultimate sign of equality" (Rossiter and Wood 2005: 364). Nevertheless, in most instances, both economic development and the maintenance of cultural identity remain partial and uncertain for indigenous peoples. Hale (2005) argues that cultural rights are often granted in Central America in such a limited way within a broader neoliberal economic context that indigenous groups do not gain sufficient control over resources to actualize their rights, a process evident in the following RAAN case studies.

Forestry Case Studies

The Nicaraguan forestry sector decentralized significantly between 2000 and 2005. Approval of forest concessions transferred from the central office of the National Forestry Institute (INAFOR) in Managua to RAAN district offices. The regional government had very little oversight of forestry

---

1 See also Sletto (2002).

operations before 1998, but by 2003 drafted a regional sustainable forest management plan that incorporated multi-level state agencies, the private sector, and nongovernmental organizations (NGOs) (CRAAN 2003; Brook 2005). Many international consultants and NGOs advised policymakers during this transition: two particularly important groups were the World Wildlife Fund (WWF)[1] and the Tropical Agricultural Research and Higher Education Center (CATIE).[2] Meanwhile, a number of development banks and donors financed green projects in the RAAN. While there was attention to cultural rights (Gordon et al. 2003), a key focus was the search for business models that could reduce poverty, protect the environment, and assure profit.

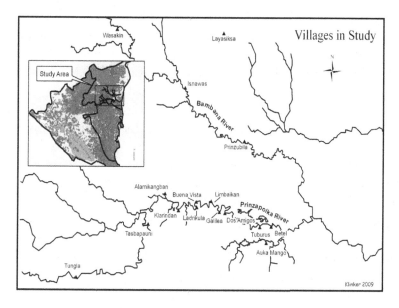

Map 1: Middle and Upper Prinzapolka Watershed (Cartographer: K. Klinker)

My fieldwork on three internationally-sponsored forestry projects, the Atlantic Biological Corridor, the Alamikangban Seed Bank, and Limi-Nawâh, occurred between 1998 and 2008 in Alamikangban and surround-

1  WWF's Central American branch set up an office in Bilwi in 2002. WWF representatives helped the regional government draft forestry policy and advised community forestry projects in Layasiksa and Sipba.
2  CATIE channeled money to and advised two RAAN sustainable forestry networks (Brook 2005).

ing villages (Map One), Rosita, Bilwi, and Managua. The Prinzapolka watershed is isolated in the east, but the upper river in the west lies along the agrarian frontier. This area is one of the most poverty-stricken and vulnerable portions of the RAAN, a region clearly marginalized within Nicaragua. With the three projects under analysis, foreign donors and the multi-scale Nicaraguan state aimed to address poverty and isolation as well as reduce the rate of deforestation.

The first case study addresses Nicaragua's large Atlantic Biological Corridor (ABC). The World Bank-financed ABC covers the majority of Nicaragua's two autonomous regions and connects to corridors extending the length of Central America (GEF 1997). The ABC project was set up around the idea of "selling nature to save it" (McAfee 1999: 133) and aimed to link indigenous peoples to outside markets for new products as the state and donors worked to encourage transition away from slash-and-burn agriculture and unregulated forest extraction (Brook 2005; Finley-Brook 2007). The second case study involves a Seed Bank in Alamikangban with World Bank funding. The goal was to harvest, process, and export pine seeds. Regional and village institutions could not meet the expectations of officials in Managua and foreign donors and, as a result, the project never got off the ground. The third case study describes an international project uniting Miskitu and Mayangna villages with Canadian indigenous partners. YATAMA members signed agreements with Cree and Dene First Nations. Bilateral donors later pushed YATAMA out of the initiative before a participatory forestry firm called Limi-Nawâh temporarily emerged. In each case, there were serious constraints to indigenous self-determination amid pressure to adapt to market-based conservation programs. Despite millions of dollars of investment, none of the case studies brought significant economic or social development to the target population.

Atlantic Biological Corridor

In 1998, an Atlantic Biological Corridor (ABC) project was started with assistance from the Global Environmental Facility, a financial mechanism of UN agencies, the World Bank, and other international finance institutions. The seven million dollar ABC initiative aimed to improve conservation in habitat corridors between protected areas in eastern Nicaragua (GEF 1997). Thousands of indigenous people, most living in poverty or extreme poverty, were identified as straining ecological limits in these corridors. Donors planned to support income production ventures they categorized as compatible with biodiversity protection (Brook 2005; Finley-Brook 2007).

The ABC project got off to a slow start due to political conflicts, institutional weaknesses, and Hurricane Mitch (Brook 2005). Decisions were made in Managua or abroad and donors seldom entered the Atlantic corridor zone. A regional NGO representative believed central government officials deterred visits: "they invent a million excuses — there are armed groups and it rains too much — and the donors return home with just the written report" (pers. comm., Bilwi, 2000).

An indigenous leader complained about the poor distribution of ABC resources to the RAAN, "Here there is no ABC truck or motorboat with the name painted on the side," noting that several such vehicles existed in Managua (pers. comm., Bilwi, 2000). The Atlantic Coast project appeared to have been co-opted by a central government eager for donor resources. A YATAMA representative criticized the ABC project in the following terms:

> People thought that the indigenous communities would be able to participate within the ABC, protect their resources, and look for new production options. But, after a period, it became obvious that the project had become politicized...All the funds are going to be gone and the people of the corridor project will never have visited Sandy Bay, the area around *Cayos Miskitos*, or Prinzapolka (pers. comm., Bilwi, 2000).

The project remained centralized until President Alemán (1997-2002) left office. The role of the regional officials in the ABC rapidly increased. Until 2002 there was only one ABC representative in Bilwi. By early 2003 nearly all representatives were located in Bilwi and Bluefields. Nevertheless, financial decisions were never decentralized. Communication with donors and the output of public information, such as the project website, also continued to be administered from Managua. Even after administrative transition to the regional offices, a RAAN ABC official asserted, "Decentralization is propaganda of the central government. In practice there has not been a lot of advance" (pers. comm., Bilwi, 2003).

With a year remaining in the project funding cycle, consultants quickly performed village assessments in fifty-three RAAN villages, including nine from the study area, and thirty-seven in the RAAS. Between two and fifteen subprojects were proposed per village. These development plans were put together by a team of multi-ethnic professionals originally from the RAAN and trained in Managua or abroad. The community development plans they created were sent in a draft form to Managua to be approved before public circulation.

In February of 2003, nine Prinzapolka villages were included in ABC diagnoses.[1] In spite of the fact that this was the fifth year of the ABC project, villagers were not informed about the corridors prior to their invitation to a rapid participatory appraisal. In Alamikangban, approximately twenty-five individuals attended the consultation: all were selected by one person associated with a local NGO, the Prinzapolka Project. When this person made the verbal invitations, community members assumed there was a connection between the ABC and this NGO. As his announcement went over the village loudspeaker inviting participants, an uninvited community member begrudgingly commented to me, "It's all politics." The announcement only stated the names of the people who were invited to the workshop without mentioning any specific objective, so people had no idea what they were invited to attend.

At the Alamikangban consultation, many participants strongly advocated for forest extraction. In spite of the fact that the consultant announced that the ABC wanted proposals for conservation and natural resource management, participants initially asked for a large outside logging firm to come harvest trees and bring employment. They complained about state forestry laws that limited local extraction through restrictive permitting processes. Later, some participants who had previously attended similar workshops or had greater knowledge of conservation rhetoric, suggested initiatives that would fit better with ABC objectives. In the end, the twelve proposed ABC sub-projects the consultant drafted for Alamikangban involved sustainable forestry, land demarcation, communal ecotourism, organic fertilizer with traditional agriculture, grain storage, livestock, transportation infrastructure, a high school, a sewing and craft school, potable water, electrification, and a communal bakery.

The consultation process shed light on the reproduction of development discourse. In an interview with the Alimakangban consultant, he admitted he was not a firm believer in international development projects after twen-

---

1  The villages of Alamikangban, Buena Vista, Dos Amigos, Galilea, Klarindan, Ladrikula, Limbaikan, and Tuburus border the Prinzapolka River (Map 1). La Palmera is located on the entrance road to Alamikangban.

ty years working in the field (pers. comm., Alamikangban, 2003). With the ABC, he was not convinced that participatory consultations were working, he stated: "People will turn into what they perceive that you want them to be...If you come talking about ranching, they are all ranchers."

Proposed ABC sub-projects from the ninety RAAN and RAAS villages were expected to provide a road map to orient future state programs and donor projects. These initiatives were biased toward market-based development, and somewhat ironically included activities that have been demonstrated to increase deforestation in Nicaragua and other Latin American locations. Intensification of cattle ranching was recommended in more than half of the village plans (Finley-Brook 2007). Thirty percent of projects focused on expanding economic production or infrastructure, such as bridges, roads, and docks. Agricultural modernization and intensification was a key element: in sixty percent of villages this involved improved seeds, likely imported from abroad, and production for export markets.

Upon completion of the consultations, regional ABC representatives began thirteen pilot projects in conjunction with regional and local NGOs (Brook 2005). The projects had varying success. No pilots began in any of the nine villages consulted in Prinzapolka. The ABC's National Technical Advisor suggested Prinzapolka watershed would face problems attracting additional funding because donors decided to avoid the area until the state resolved territorial conflicts (pers. comm., Managua, 2003).

As Global Environmental Facility funding ended, regional officials felt like the ABC was just getting started. One noted that they were able to achieve more in one year under regional institutions than central government project officials had been able to achieve since 1998 (Finley-Brook 2007). RAAN's ABC coordinator argued for an extension of financial support to the regional office, but it closed in 2004. Although a couple of foreign donors already working in the region financed a small number of proposed sub-projects, few ABC project recommendations were implemented.

RAAN habitat connectivity remains at risk. Rapid deforestation continues even within the Bosawas Reserve (Potosme 2010). Nicaraguan ABC efforts now focus on the Corazón Biosphere Reserve, which joins Nicaragua's large Bosawas Biosphere Reserve with several protected areas located in the Honduran Mosquitia. Even in this smaller transboundary conservation project, communication between international donor agencies, multi-level state offices, and villages remains inadequate.

Alamikangban Seed Bank

From 2001 to 2003 there were attempts to reopen a Seed Bank in Alamikangban formerly operated in the 1990s with support from the Danish International Development Agency (DANIDA). The high genetic quality of Alamikangban's Caribbean pine is known worldwide (Urbina 1994; Brook 2005). The regional government sought donor funding and attempted to create a community firm for the collection, processing, and sale of pine seeds. The proposal was to rehabilitate buildings and take advantage of existing infrastructure, but the project would have had a very different structure from when the central government managed it. Although pine has been extracted from the RAAN for centuries, most operations were managed by outsiders. The Seed Bank provided an opportunity to strengthen the resource management role of villagers in addition to the regional government and RAAN academic institutions.

A RAAN Regional Councilor initiated the idea for a new Seed Bank. The RAAN's new Secretary of Natural Resources, Production, and Territorial Demarcation (SERENA) wrote a proposal in 2001. Regional foresters from the Bilwi Campus of the Bluefields Indian Caribbean University (BICU) were recruited to provide administrative and technical support to the project. SERENA and BICU presented the project to a new Nicaraguan Forestry Promotion Project (PROFOR), financed by the World Bank from 1998 to 2003, and received approval. Then, with regional elections in March of 2002, and a chaotic transition of power from a Constitutionalist Liberal Party (PLC) governor to a YATAMA governor in May, the project was delayed for several months.

An initial community meeting with regional officials was poorly organized (Brook 2005). Officials from the regional institutions showed up in Alamikangban on a Sunday morning in October of 2002 without previous notice. Twenty minutes later, the meeting started. After a brief description of the project, a village representative was selected by a vote following a short discussion among the approximately two dozen community members in attendance. In spite of this haphazard process, a strong female candidate with experience working in the initial Seed Bank was elected.[1] She

---

1  This individual was affiliated with YATAMA, but decision-makers suggested other factors influenced their selection. Community members expressed a desire to limit corrupt behavior by promoting someone with a reputation for honesty and by not choosing prominent male leaders with a history of misusing funds.

helped organize community training about the project soon afterward. Participants identified a change among regional administrators, as one noted: "This regional government wants to be different from those in the past... When people think of a company, they think that it is going to come from outside, but they explained that this is our company. We are the owners" (pers. comm., Alamikangban, 2003).

However, as intermediaries between donors and village representatives, regional officials were challenged to define and establish a fiscally-accountable village-run firm in an area with a weak institutional base. A project administrator explained, "If a project wants to do community management well, then there are a thousand steps to initiate. Private companies can work much faster — within six months they are already harvesting" (pers. comm., Bilwi, 2003).

The Seed Bank's administrative board began to meet regularly in Bilwi along with members of a community forestry project in Layasiksa. Alamikangban's representative attended a percentage of meetings. One time, due to the poor condition of the roads, she arrived in Bilwi after the meeting had ended. On another occasion she was not issued an invitation because she would have traveled for days to attend what was expected to be a short meeting. Other times she missed meetings because she was not advanced travel funds and could not afford to get to the RAAN capital. At one point in 2003 she waited for two weeks in Bilwi for a transportation reimbursement needed to travel back to Alamikangban due to the slow dispersal of funds from Managua and lack of fiscal liquidity in RAAN offices. These delays were linked to donor requirements. A regional project administrator noted:

> The World Bank is so demanding in its technical specification that it has made things nearly impossible for a project learning as we go. They want us to define the size of the screw if we are asking for screws. They want us to define the thread that we will be using in making pants, when people here are only certain that they need pants (pers. comm., Bilwi, 2003).

PROFOR would not release project funds. Regional participants felt they did not comprehend the region: "They are being very rigid and they want everything by the book. People in the RAAN are trying to follow their requirements, but we need a little bit of flexibility here and there due to the situation in the region" (pers. comm., Bilwi, 2003). Product prices were high due to the abominable conditions of the roads, and many technical materials were difficult to purchase in the region, especially within a strict timeframe.

When regional officials explained this to PROFOR, they felt they were not treated seriously. A RAAN project representative said, "When people from here tell them the local reality and the costs of transportation, they think that we are lying and only trying to get more money out of them" (pers. comm., Bilwi, 2003).

There was increasing urgency to initiate the Seed Bank due to the pending termination of the five-year PROFOR program in 2003 and the retraction of any funds not distributed at that point. Unable to complete planning requirements before the deadline, regional representatives requested an extension. At the time, central government officials suggested that the project could transfer under another two-year program for indigenous forest management. Support for the project later disintegrated.

The Seed Bank project proposal demonstrated pressure to market communal resources (Taylor 2003). If it had moved forward, seed production may have become controversial due to multiple claims on the same forest and the unclear rights and responsibilities of different actors. The forest management plan, located within a state-recognized forest reserve but also within Alamikangban's communal claim (Dana et al. 1998), specifically targeted seed markets and not the fulfillment of other ecological and social roles. According to the draft management plan, all trees would be cut in a rotation of forty years so that seed production levels remained high (Taylor 2003). Approximately ninety-five percent of the trees would be harvested immediately, with the exception of four seed procurement areas of superior parent trees with the straight, thick trunk that makes Caribbean pine a valuable construction material. The project was clearly oriented toward seed markets designed to supply plantations for lumber production.

A major project justification was local employment, but lessons from the earlier functioning of the original Alamikangban Seed Bank (Malefant 1993; Urbina 1994) as well as the design of the project suggests there would have been trade-offs. Since 1991 the state has recognized this same forest as a protected area, but it was not demarcated at a local level and people extracted from it without knowledge of the state claim. With the Seed Bank project there could not have been the same public access to this pine area located adjacent to the village. The area was heavily utilized as a lumber reserve and hunting ground. To protect marketable seeds, there could not be unplanned logging or annual burns of savanna grasslands, a persistent village practice used to encourage the growth of palatable grass for livestock and wild game and to reduce pests such as ticks. State institutions have tried to discourage burning around Alamikangban for years with only partial success.[1]

There were numerous barriers to the Seed Bank project, but one of the largest challenges was the lack of a legal community oversight organization. Donors were looking for an institution that would be financially responsible for equipment. This type of mandate was completely unfamiliar to communal institutions in Alamikangban. Donors expected villagers to become project administrators nearly immediately. This is an important objective, but one that is unlikely to occur rapidly when previous management experience is limited. There was also an impractical expectation on the part of donors and regional officials that the community project could be supported long-distance from Bilwi, in spite of poor road networks, and without investing heavily in administrative training (e.g. leadership development, accounting, bookkeeping, seed production and processing) for participants in Alamikangban.

Limi-Nawâh

From 2002 to 2006, the Meadow Lake Tribal Council (MLTC) and the Canadian International Development Agency (CIDA) sponsored a three million dollar indigenous forestry corporation in sixteen villages in eastern Nicaragua (Map 1). This project grew out of YATAMA's efforts in the 1990s to promote inter-indigenous economic partnerships. *Limi-Nawâh* (meaning jaguar in the Miskitu and Mayangna languages) was legally instituted in July of 2003 as Nicaragua's first official indigenous corporation. With MLTC's tutelage, the firm was expected to advance economic development and self-governance, as occurred in Canadian First Nations (Newhouse 2000; Brook 2005).

Cooperation between Miskitu leaders and the MLTC solidified in 1995 in Canada at an international meeting organized around the theme of indigenous partnerships for trade and development. Participants from Nicaragua would later form a joint venture with MLTC called Makwa International (Anaya 1996). A Nicaraguan-Canadian of Miskitu origin was instrumental

---

1 Household surveys suggested that the majority of the village population understood state arguments against burning and a large number of community members had curtailed their burning practices (Brook 2005). It only takes a few individuals to set large fires, like the ones that continue to occur on Alamikangban's communal lands.

in bringing the partners together. He had previously co-founded the Indigenous Economic Development Corporation (CIDESA) with other Miskitu Nicaraguans active in YATAMA. At the 1995 Canadian meeting, a YATAMA delegate told participants:

> We are tired of companies coming in and using our resources and people...We fought a war to hang on to our communities and our way of life. Now we face another challenge — Economic Colonization. Now if we don't organize and train ourselves and create our own business structures we will be wiped out. We are looking for other indigenous partners to work with, so we can share our opportunities, capacities and resources (Apikan Indigenous Network 1995: 7).

Makwa International, the firm that developed between Canadian and Nicaraguan partners, was a joint venture. MLTC owned fifty-one percent and the rest belonged to the Prinzapolka Regional Development Corporation (CDRPSA), a reshuffling of CIDESA (Anaya 1996). Nicaraguan positions in Makwa's administrative structure were filled with YATAMA members. The firm proposed to work with twenty-one indigenous communities, many in the study area, on an 82,000 hectare pine concession.

Makwa's concession was not approved due to a national politics of exclusion that consistently limits indigenous peoples' benefit from natural resource extraction. President Chamorro (1990–1996) cited a ban on new concessions to justify rejecting Makwa's proposal (Contigo International 2002), even though other forest concessions advanced within the same time period. The subsequent Alemán Administration (1997–2002) also rejected the concession. Makwa's plan granted control of project resources directly to indigenous populations at a time when the state required all proceeds to pass through the central government, with the expectation that a significant portion of donor funds would stay in Managua. Makwa's plan was also not well received in Managua because officials in high government positions had personal investments in RAAN logging operations. Vast amounts of legal and illegal timber were extracted from the Prinzapolka area before Limi-Nawâh emerged during the Bolaños Administration (2002–2007).

Miskitu-MLTC discussions continued in spite of Makwa's problems. MLTC started Contigo International, a First Nation development NGO. After consultation with MLTC and Contigo, the Canadian government agreed to fund Contigo to oversee a community-based firm and train local partners in eastern Nicaragua for five years. Contigo promised CIDA that they would remain distant from regional political organizations (Contigo International 2002). This required a break in relations with YATAMA that left the project's status ambiguous for people aware of the political party's earlier involvement (Brook 2005).

Contigo International and Canadian advisors picked sixteen Miskitu and Mayangna member villages for Limi-Nawâh (Map 1) based on the location of pine and broadleaf forests. The majority of the territory was untitled: several areas had competing claimants, including private firms, ex-combatants, mestizo colonists, and foreigners (Brook 2005).

From the start, Limi-Nawâh struggled to get off the ground. The marketing of communal property created institutional and value shifts and contributed to inter- and intra-community tension over land and resources. Some problems emerged from the project's large-scale design. It attempted to "scale up" forest governance and extraction from the level of the village to a multi-village bloc with sixteen members. Since extraction in any one year would only occur in parts of the larger project area, there were concerns over how to distribute earnings. There was disagreement if income from extraction should mainly be given to the village from where the harvest occurred, or if it should be distributed to all members of Limi-Nawâh equally (Brook 2005). Other governance struggles pre-dated Limi-Nawâh. For example, at least initially, tensions emerged between Mayangna and Miskitu villages about the election of firm leaders due to the disproportionately high number of Miskitu participants.

When extraction began, other challenges became apparent. Poor transportation infrastructure drove production costs up in comparison to lumber originating from more accessible areas. The nascent firm fought for buyers on national lumber markets, where prices for wood from legitimate businesses are undermined by competition with illegal timber. Illegal lumber is less expensive to produce because it does not require the preparation of long-term management plans and operators avoid taxes and state fees.

Limi-Nawâh was carrying out small-scale intermittent timber extraction, but donor funds were rapidly becoming depleted. Project leaders felt a sense of urgency to generate income and find additional sponsors. In 2004 the Inter-American Development Bank (IADB) promised aid that would be channeled to the project through Nicaragua's Institute of Rural Development (Brook 2005). The bank later withheld the funds when a former Limi-Nawâh employee denounced unsustainable logging practices, and regional and municipal officials, including a Miskitu governor and mayor, distanced themselves from the firm. Limi-Nawâh disputed these charges, but public support waned. A Canadian project manager had provided a personal loan for Limi-Nawâh to buy equipment after IADB funds were promised, but this loan remained unpaid when the IADB later withheld support.

A major constraint for Limi-Nawâh emerged in 2005 in the form of a national environmental policy. After decades of overextraction, the central government suddenly imposed a forestry moratorium on select lumber species, including a few of central importance to Limi-Nawâh. The state's ban impeded extraction by indigenous entrepreneurs with legal logging permits. Ninety villagers with Limi-Nawâh placed a court indictment against the state claiming that the moratorium violated their economic and cultural rights. They argued that foreign companies exploited their forests for more than a century and so it was particularly unfair to restrict harvest for local benefit. The moratorium stood.

The company underwent "privatization," as local people referred to it, at the end of 2006. The firm's board members signed their rights over to the Canadian to whom they owed the debt: indigenous decision-making authority was dissolved. At the time, the Canadian argued that he intended to pass administration back to local villagers when financial solvency was achieved. With limited production in the subsequent period as a result of the moratorium, land tenure disputes, and funding limitations, the Canadian investor sold Limi-Nawâh's project machinery and materials to a Costa Rican businessman in 2008. The Costa Rican investor financed legal forest management plans in Prinzapolka, but the downturn of the global economy caused contraction in his other international construction businesses and he was forced to exit Nicaragua before harvesting. Today, former Limi-Nawâh board members seek partners with access to financial capital with the hope to activate these management plans and reinitiate logging.

The three case studies supported neoliberal development models that did not significantly improve the economic conditions of participants. Local power remained difficult to actualize in spite of the autonomy regime and the involvement of communal authorities. The institutional structures and tenure claims in the Prinzapolka watershed continue to be highly dynamic.

While these community forestry cases demonstrate constraints to regional and local power, they also show windows of opportunity for decentered decision-making. Significant political control was transferred to RAAN leaders with the passage of the Demarcation Law. As discussed below, the law encouraged positive gains in self-determination, but also created opportunities for the misuse of power. If regional officials are able to actualize Law 445 they can achieve one of the most important privileges and responsibilities of a state - the power to form land boundaries and determine ownership. Nonetheless, this role also creates the ability to enfranchise or disenfranchise particular groups.

### The RAAN Government and the National Demarcation Committee

Boundary making is important to the formation of regional and local identities as well as to define and protect access to natural resources (Sletto 2002, 2009). With the creation of CONADETI in 2003, Nicaragua's General Assembly decentralized titling responsibilities for eastern indigenous territories to the regional government, although the central government continues to determine CONADETI's annual budget. CONADETI also includes representatives of relevant state agencies, such as environmental and economic ministries. CONADETI's mandate was immediately complicated by conflict among political parties and between the autonomous regions and with areas located outside the RAAN and RAAS (Finley-Brook and Offen 2009). Article 41 of the Demarcation Law, annotated in Figure 1, shows the commission's multi-scale, multi-sector structure.

In spite of a seemingly elaborate scheme for representation, CONADETI's president and a small number of regional officials have been central to demarcation decisions. Oversight of CONADETI rotates between the RAAN and RAAS. The two regions have different proportions of ethnic groups and unique histories. Opposing political parties often lead the two regions.[1]

There have been examples of CONADETI acting impartially, yet, more commonly, the unequal power wielded in the regional government influences demarcation processes. The majority of elected leaders are Miskitu.[2] Historical tension between the Miskitu and Sumu-Mayangna came to a head after the ruling of the Inter-American Court of Human Rights (IACHR). The 2001 IACHR sentence in support of Awas Tingni, the Mayangna village that charged the Nicaraguan state with violating their land rights by granting a foreign logging concession in their territory, was interpreted internationally as a major advance for indigenous rights (Hale 2006; Campbell 2007). Years after the IACHR's recommendation to formally demarcate boundaries, the RAAN territory remained undefined and untitled (Acosta 2007). Two blocs of Miskitu communities known as Tasba Raya and Diez Comu-

---

1 Although a handful of different regional and national parties run candidates, the PLC and FSLN are the main power blocks in the RAAS and these same parties and YATAMA vie to govern the RAAN.

2 The 2005 national census registered the RAAN's population as 57 percent Miskitu and 4 percent Mayangna.

nidades contested Awas Tingni's land claim. Tasba Raya's land claims were marginal to the initial IACHR case and treated in a series of addendums after the initial court hearings (Finley-Brook and Offen 2009). In spite of long standing territorial overlaps and shared land use, the IACHR ruling and Law 445 sought a singular owner for each land unit. Conflict-ridden negotiations dragged over two years contributing to an increase in tension between ethnic groups. Mayangna leaders criticized YATAMA officials for their slow action and bias during demarcation decisions as well as for their promotion of or involvement in unsustainable timber extraction from indigenous territories (pers. comm., Bilwi, 2007; Potosme 2010).

FIGURE 1: KEY ARTICLES OF DEMARCATION LAW 445

| Article | Purpose | Implications |
| --- | --- | --- |
| 3 | Creates a formal legal definition for traditional communal authority, territorial authority, communal property, and indigenous peoples | Freezes and universalizes fluid and locally differentiated institutions |
| 35–38 | Eliminates land claims of third parties without legal titles or that arrived after 1987; they must leave or pay rent. Invalid claimants must be indemnified to leave | Requires indemnification and sales of homesteads and farms to indigenous communities, but does not provide funding Violates the Autonomy Statute (i.e., communal land cannot be rented or transferred) |
| 41 | CONADETI members include: Presidents of the RAAN and RAAS Council The Director of the Rural Titling Office A Ministry of Agriculture, Livestock and Forestry delegate The Nicaraguan Institute of Territorial Studies director A representative of each regional ethnic group Two representatives of the Bocay watershed A Commission on Ethnic Affairs and Atlantic Coast Communities representative The mayors of municipalities in areas of demarcation | Creates the potential for scale conflict between national, regional, municipal and local representatives Creates the potential for regional conflict because the RAAN and RAAS share leadership and the Bocay watershed barely overlaps the Autonomous Region It is expensive to get all actors together and thus it happens infrequently |

| 45 | Defines *saneamiento* (the removal of third parties), a process that can be interpreted as ethnic cleansing | Threat of removal feeds conflict Territories must contain a single ethnic group |
|---|---|---|

Conflict was magnified by the lack of indigenous land titles, now nearly a century overdue.[1] Tenure conflicts weaken cooperation toward multi-ethnic autonomy. In some instances RAAN demarcation has intensi-fied long-standing racial and economic disputes (Finley-Brook and Offen 2009). There is a spectrum of justifications for ownership with differing legal validity and cultural authenticity based on evidence and interpreta-tion. Multiple groups, including indigenous peoples, colonists, and resource concessionaires, declare ownership of overlapping areas creating a remark-able diversity of multifaceted territorial and resource claims (Gordon et al. 2003; Dana 2008).

Collective land ownership is a cultural foundation in eastern Nicara-gua. Land demarcation is essential to strengthening autonomy and local self-governance. The lack of tenure security also represents a significant obstacle to sustainable and participatory forestry in the RAAN.[2] With titles recognizing land ownership, RAAN populations would have greater power to decide when and on what terms they chose to participate in external markets. This is particularly important because market-based conservation continues to be integrated into many internationally-financed RAAN for-estry and tourism projects.

### YATAMA and RAAN Political Representation

RAAN electoral politics are divisive, contentious, and messy. Politiciza-tion and polarization obscure YATAMA's indigenous rights and economic development platform. Conflict spills over from national contests and a main source of tension is the political pact between ex-President Arnoldo Alemán and FSLN leader Daniel Ortega.[3] Aimed at concentrating political power, the pact created an "80-percent rule." Subsequently, RAAN parties had to present candidates in 4/5 of RAAN municipalities. The seven munic-ipalities in the RAAN, each with a different ethnic make-up, are large ter-

1  A Moskitia land titling commission was first created in 1915.
2  See Roper (2003) and Finley-Brook (2007b).
3  YATAMA's electoral bedfellows over the years include members of the UNO (National Opposition Union; *Unión Nacional Opositora*) coalition, the PLC, and the FSLN.

ritories with a principle town or small city surrounded by dozens of smaller villages. Small and ethnic parties seldom have the spatial reach required in the pact and, as a result, they can be left off ballots.[1]

YATAMA was predicted to win several seats in the 2000 municipal elections, but was excluded from running candidates when it could not meet the pact's stipulations. YATAMA appealed and got its ballot position restored (Mercado et al. 2006). After reversal of this decision in the Supreme Court, violence erupted in Bilwi as YATAMA members staged boisterous demonstrations and even exchanged gunshots with riot police. People on both sides were wounded and an affiliate of YATAMA later died as a result of his wounds. When YATAMA supporters boycotted the 2000 municipal election, RAAN abstention rates reached sixty percent.

Following the election, YATAMA took the Nicaraguan government to the IACHR to defend its right to run candidates. YATAMA won the case in 2005 (Campbell 2006). Nonetheless, the Alemán-Ortega pact continues to place pressure on small, local, and regional parties.

Regional politicians learned to use different messages with various audiences. Miskitu leaders would lose support if they used the same words with villagers on the Wangki River as with FSLN allies in regional government offices. Horton (2010) notes a similar practice in Kuna *comarcas* (semi-autonomous indigenous territories) of Panama of framing arguments for different audiences. Experienced politicians understand the value of this type of strategic "double speak," but it can alienate base supporters.

Central government institutions and national leaders clearly influence the RAAN through the political party structure. YATAMA signed a pact in 2006 with President Ortega prior to his reelection. The FSLN leader agreed to strengthen regional autonomy. Critics now suggest Ortega has not delivered, even though a significant number of autonomous region politicians did received high posts in the central government. By signing the pact, YATAMA alienated some formerly supportive constituents and antagonized Ortega's opponents.

The Miskitu Council of Elders, a group of older leaders selected at region-wide assemblies to represent the self-designated Communitarian Miskitu Nation, views political parties as non-indigenous forms of organization. They criticize YATAMA leaders for conformation with state rules that warp indigenous interactions and relationships. An elder explains:

---

1  See also chapter 5 of this volume.

"The traditional institutions of the Miskitu are the family and the community. At a larger scale, we work with assemblies and conventions. Political parties are not part of our history" (pers. comm., Bilwi, 2002). The Council of Elders does not recognize the authority of the Nicaraguan central government in the RAAN. They contend that the state created the regional government as its accomplice and define cooperation with state institutions as condoning illegitimate control over an indigenous nation.

YATAMA's (1999) statutes promote community-based democracy (*democracia comunitaria*) in the context of a unified Nicaraguan nation-state. Various assemblies and grassroots structures are built into the internal structure of YATAMA (YATAMA 1999; Mercado et al. 2006), yet these receive little media attention. More frequently, critics highlight how party officials make important decisions with little or no consultation, demonstrating a fundamental change from customary Miskitu political practices. So, while there may be national and regional political gains as a result of indigenous politicians gaining entry into positions of power, there are also costs, including the potential loss of base support. One indication of this are the abstention rates in the RAAN which have been greater than fifty percent in regional and municipal elections over the past decade.

There has been multi-ethnic and multi-party representation within the RAAN government since its creation. Yet, simultaneously, there has been disproportionate control by Miskitu officials and national political parties (e.g., FSLN and PLC). To support more equitable and participatory multi-ethnic governance, RAAN leaders need to better defend the rights of Mayangna, Rama, and Afro-Caribbean populations. However, mestizos are, or shortly will become, the majority population in the RAAN. What this means for YATAMA, or even for the future of the autonomous region, remains unclear.

Conclusions

While autonomy has the potential to help reverse Nicaragua's uneven east-west development, contemporary inequality is rooted in a long history of marginalization. Throughout this chapter I have documented structural constraints to RAAN autonomy, but I have also showed decision-making agency, although often without broad participation or equal representation. Positive shifts can be overshadowed by political, social, and economic tensions. The tendency in the region for sporadic eruptions of politically and racially-charged violence suggests conflict resolution efforts deserve prioritization.

RAAN officials from all parties and ethnic groups must continue to prioritize land titling as a means to achieve long-term political stability in the region, while recognizing the potential for conflict may increase during boundary negotiation processes. CONADETI has defined fifteen territories impacting over two hundred Miskitu, Mayangna, Creole and Garífuna village claims, but much of this progress did not occur until the end of 2009. In 2010 CONADETI initiated steps to define boundaries in a number of highly conflictive areas, including the Prinzapolka watershed.

Although defining large, highly-contested territories is a daunting task, it is an urgent one that is long overdue. Setbacks and flare ups are likely as demarcation and titling processes move forward. The economic costs to conduct boundary negotiations in a truly participatory, inclusive manner are higher. Financial support for titling efforts must remain a priority for state agencies, non-governmental organizations, and donors as a means to address numerous inter-ethnic and inter-village conflicts.

## References

Acosta, M. L. (2007) 'Awas Tingni versus Nicaragua, y el proceso de demarcación de tierras indígenas en la Costa Caribe Nicaragüense' in *Wani* No. 48, pp. 6-15.

Altamirano-Jiménez, I. (2004) 'North American First Peoples: Slipping up into Market Citizenship?' in *Citizenship Studies* Vol. 8, No. 4, pp. 349-365.

Anaya, S. J. (1996) 'Native Nations Sign Historic Pact: North-South Indigenous Partnership Holds Economic Promise' in *Native Americas* Vol. XIII, No. 2, pp. 46-49.

Apikan Indigenous Network (1995) 'Indigenous Partnership in Action. International Workshop on Indigenous Partnerships for Trade and Development' (September 23, Winnipeg, MB).

Baldwin, A. (2009) 'Carbon nullius and racial rule: Race, nature and the cultural politics of forest carbon in Canada' in *Antipode* Vol. 41, No. 2, pp. 231-255.

Bonta, M. (2004) 'Death toll one: An ethnography of hydro power and human rights violations in Honduras' in *GeoJournal* Vol. 60, No. 1, pp. 19-30.

Brook, M. M. (2005) *Re-scaling the Commons: Miskitu Indians, Forest Commodities, and Transnational Development Networks* (Ph.D. dissertation, University of Texas at Austin).

Butler, J. 'The Peoples of the Atlantic Coast' in Walker, T. W. (1997) (Eds) *Nicaragua Without Illusions* (Wilmington, Scholarly Resources), pp. 219-234.

Campbell, M. S. (2007) 'The Right of Indigenous Peoples to Political Participation and the Case of YATAMA v. Nicaragua' *Arizona Journal of International and Comparative Law* Vol. 24, No. 2, pp. 499-540.

Carrión, F. (2005) 'Inter-American System: YATAMA v. Nicaragua' in *Human Rights Brief* Vol. 13, pp. 28-29.

Contigo International (2002) *Prinzapolka-Bambana Community Development Project, Project Implementation Plan* (Managua, Nicaragua: Canadian International Development Agency).

Consejo Regional Autónomo Atlántico Norte (2003) Estrategia de Desarrollo Forestal: Región Autónoma del Atlántico Norte, Nicaragua.

Dana, P. 'Surveys of People and Place' in Wilson, J. P. and Fotheringham, A. S. (2008) (Eds) *The Handbook of Geographic Information Science* (Malden, MA: Blackwell), pp. 494-503.

Dana, P., Gordon, E. T., Gurdián, G., and Hale, C. (1998) *Diagnóstico general sobre la*

*tenencia de la tierra en las comunidades indígenas de la Costa Atlántica* (Bluefields and Puerto Cabezas, Nicaragua: Central American and Caribbean Research Council).

Delaney, D. (2005) *Territory: A Short Introduction* (Malden: Blackwell).

Finley-Brook, M. (2007a) 'Green Neoliberal Space: The Case of the Mesoamerican Biological Corridor' in *Journal of Latin American Geography* Vol. 5, No. 2, pp. 101-124.

Finley-Brook, M. (2007b) 'Indigenous land tenure insecurity fosters illegal logging in Nicaragua' in *International Forestry Review* Vol. 9, No. 4, pp. 850-864.

Finley-Brook, M and Offen, K. (2009) 'Bounding the Commons: Land Demarcation in Northeastern Nicaragua' in *Bulletin of Latin American Research* Vol. 28, No. 3, pp. 1-21.

Finley-Brook, M and Thomas, C. (forthcoming) 'From malignant neglect to extreme intervention: treatment of displaced indigenous populations in two large hydro projects' in *Water Alternatives*.

Global Environmental Facility (1997) *Nicaragua: Atlantic Biological Corridor Project* (Washington, DC: GEF/World Bank).

González, M. and Y. Zapata. 2003. 'YATAMA en los Noventa: Fragmentación y Pragmatismo Político' in *Wani* No. 33, pp. 6-20.

Gordon, E. T., Gurdián, G. C., and Hales, C. R. (2003) 'Rights, Resources, and the Social Memory of Struggle: Reflections on a Study of Indigenous and Black Community Land Rights on Nicaragua's Atlantic Coast' in *Human Organization* Vol. 62, No. 4, pp. 369-381.

Hale, C. R. (1994) *Resistance and Contradiction: Miskitu Indians and the Nicaraguan State, 1894-1987* (Stanford, CA: Stanford University Press).

Hale, C. R. (1998) 'Inter-Ethnic Relations and Class Structure in Nicaragua's Atlantic Coast: A Historical Overview' in Whiteford, M. B. and Whiteford, S. (Eds) *Crossing Currents: Continuity and Change in Latin America* (Upper Saddle River: Prentice Hall), pp. 98-112.

Hale, C. R. (2005) 'Neoliberal Multiculturalism: The Remaking of Cultural Rights and Racial Dominance in Central America' in *PoLAR: Political and Legal Anthropology Review* Vol. 28, No.1, pp. 10-28.

Harvey, N. (2001) 'Globalisation and resistance in post-cold war Mexico: difference, citizenship and biodiversity conflicts in Chiapas' in *Third World Quarterly* Vol. 22, No. 6, pp. 1045-1061.

Herb, G. H. and Kaplan, D. H. (1999) *Nested Identities: Nationalism, Territory, and Scale* (Lanham, MD: Littlefield Publishers).

Houghton, J. and Bell, B. (2004) *Latin American Indigenous Movements in the Context of Globalization* (Silver City, NM: Interhemispheric Resource Center).

Howe, J. (1998) *A People Who Would Not Kneel: Panama, the United States, and the San Blas Kuna* (Washington, DC: Smithsonian).

Jordán, O. (2008) '"I entered during the day, and came out during the night": Power, Environment, and Indigenous Peoples in a Globalizing Panama' in *Tennessee Journal of Law and Policy* Vol. 4, No. 2, pp. 467-505.

Larson, A. M. (forthcoming) 'Making the "rules of the game": Constituting territory and authority in Nicaragua's indigenous communities' *Land Use Policy* doi:10.1016/j.landusepol.2010.03.004

Larson, A. M. and Ribot, J. (2004) 'Democratic Decentralization through a Natural Resource Lens: An Introduction' in *The European Journal of Development Research* Vol. 16, No. 1, pp. 1-25.

Larson, A.M., Cronkleton, P., Barry, D. and Pacheco, P. (2008) *Tenure Rights and Beyond: Community access to forest resources in Latin America* (Bogor, Indonesia: Center for International Forestry Research).

Légaré, A. (2001) 'The spatial and symbolic construction of Nunavut: Towards the emergence of a regional collective identity' in *Inuit Studies* Vol. 25, No. 1-2, pp. 141-168.

McAfee, K. (1999) 'Selling nature to save it? Biodiversity and the rise of green developmentalism' in *Environment and Planning D: Society and Space* Vol. 17, No. 2, pp. 133-154.

McCarthy, J. (2005) 'Devolution in the woods: community forestry as hybrid neoliberalism' in *Environment and Planning A* Vol. 37, pp. 995-1014.

Madrid, R. (2005) 'Indigenous parties and democracy in Latin America' in *Latin American Politics and Society* Vol. 47, No. 4, pp. 161-179.

Malefant, D. (1993) *Estudio de la zona de Alamikamba. Perspectivas para el desarrollo del Proyecto CMG & BSF* (Managua, DANIDA).

Mendoza, R. and Kuhnekath, K. (2005) 'Conflictos en La Costa: expresión de la transnacionalización de conflictos societales en Centroamérica' in *Wani* No. 41, pp. 10-26.

Mercado, E., Wilson, L. y González, M. (2006) *YATAMA: La Lucha por Una Verdadera Autonomía en la Moskitia Nicaragüense* (Bilwi, Puerto Cabezas, RAAN).

Newhouse, D. (2000) 'Modern Aboriginal Economies: Capitalism with a Red Face' in *Journal of Aboriginal Economic Development* Vol. 1, No. 2, pp. 55-61.

Potosme, R. H. (2010) 'YATAMA quiere colonizer a los Mayangna.' *El Nuevo Diario* (20 de marzo). Available: http://www.elnuevodiario.com.ni/politica/70655.

Radcliffe, S. A. (2007) 'Latin American Indigenous Geographies of Fear: Living the Shadow of Racism, Lack of Development, and Antiterror Measures' in *Annals of the Association of American Geographers* Vol. 97, pp. 385-397.

Rice, R. and Van Cott, D. L. (2006) 'The Emergence and Performance of Indigenous Peoples' Parties in South America: A Subnational Statistical Analysis' in *Comparative Political Studies* Vol. 39, No. 6, pp. 709-732.

Roper, J. M. (2003) *An assessment of indigenous participation in commercial forestry markets: The case of Nicaragua's Northern Atlantic Region* (Washington, DC: Forest Trends).

Ross, M. M. and Smith, P. (2002) *Accommodation of Aboriginal Rights: The Need for an Aboriginal Forest Tenure* (Edmonton, AB: Sustainable Forest Management Network, University of Alberta).

Rossiter, D. and Wood, P. K. (2005) 'Fantastic topographies: neo-liberal responses to Aboriginal land claims in British Columbia.' in *The Canadian Geographer* Vol. 49, No. 4, pp. 352-366.

Sletto, B. (2002) 'Boundary Making and Regional Identities in a Globalized Environment: Rebordering the Nariva Swamp, Trinidad' in *Environment and Planning D: Society and Space* No. 20, pp. 183-208.

Sletto, B. (2009) ' "Indigenous People Don't Have Boundaries:" Reborderings, Fire Management, and Productions of Authenticities in Indigenous Landscapes' in *Cultural Geographies* No. 16, pp. 253-277.

Taylor, T. (2003) 'Plan General de Manejo Forestal, "La Pista."' Alamikangban, RAAN (borredor).

Urbina, M. (1994) 'El Centro de Mejoramiento Genético y Banco de Semillas Forestales' *Pinos de Nicaragua* (MARENA-DANIDA, Managua), pp. 42-44.

Vilas, C. M. (1990) *Del Colonialismo a la Autonomía: Modernización Capitalista y Revolución Social en la Costa Atlántica* (Managua, Nueva Nicaragua).

Yashar, J. D. (1999) 'Democracy, Indigenous Movements, and the Postliberal Challenge in Latin America' in *World Politics* Vol. 52, No. 1, pp. 76-104.

YATAMA (1999) 'Estatutos y estructura organizativa de YATAMA' Aprobados por la Asamblea General de las Comunidades.

Zapata Webb, Y. (2002) *Factors and Expressions of Ethnicity, Race and Racism: Social Relations in Bilwi, Nicaragua* (Managua: Universidad de las Regiones Autónomas de la Costa Caribe Nicaragüense).

# INDEX